Jiu Jiu

Vol. 3

Story & Art by
Touya Tobina

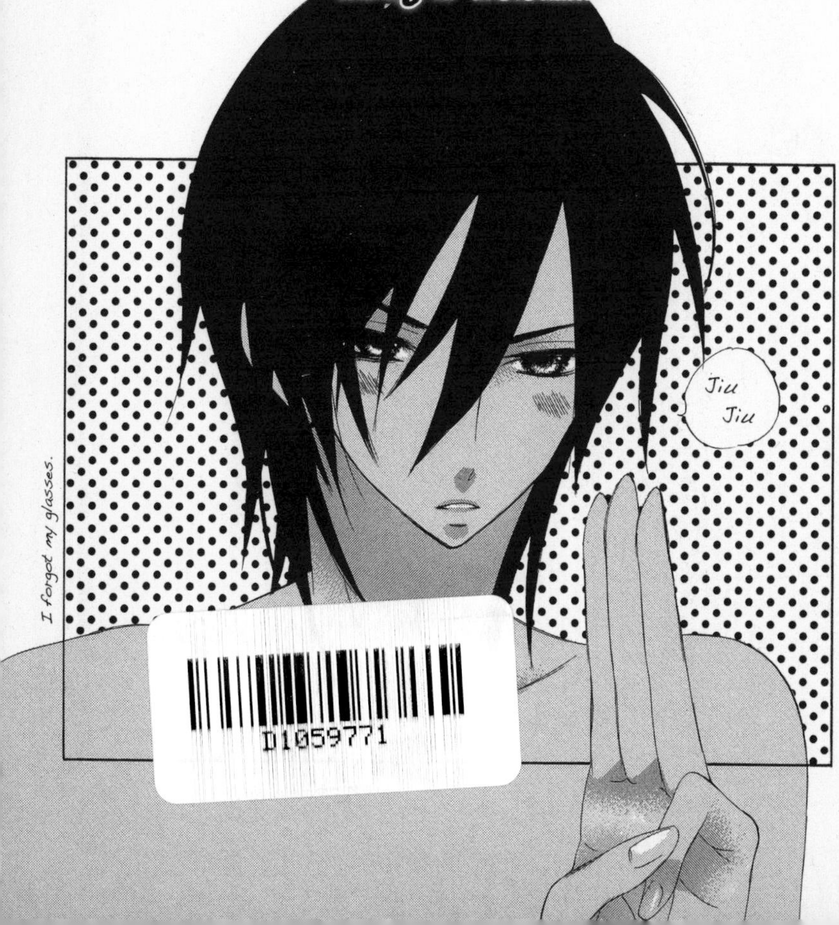
Jiu Jiu
I forgot my glasses.

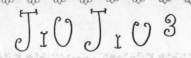
JOJO 3

It's Night.

Contents.

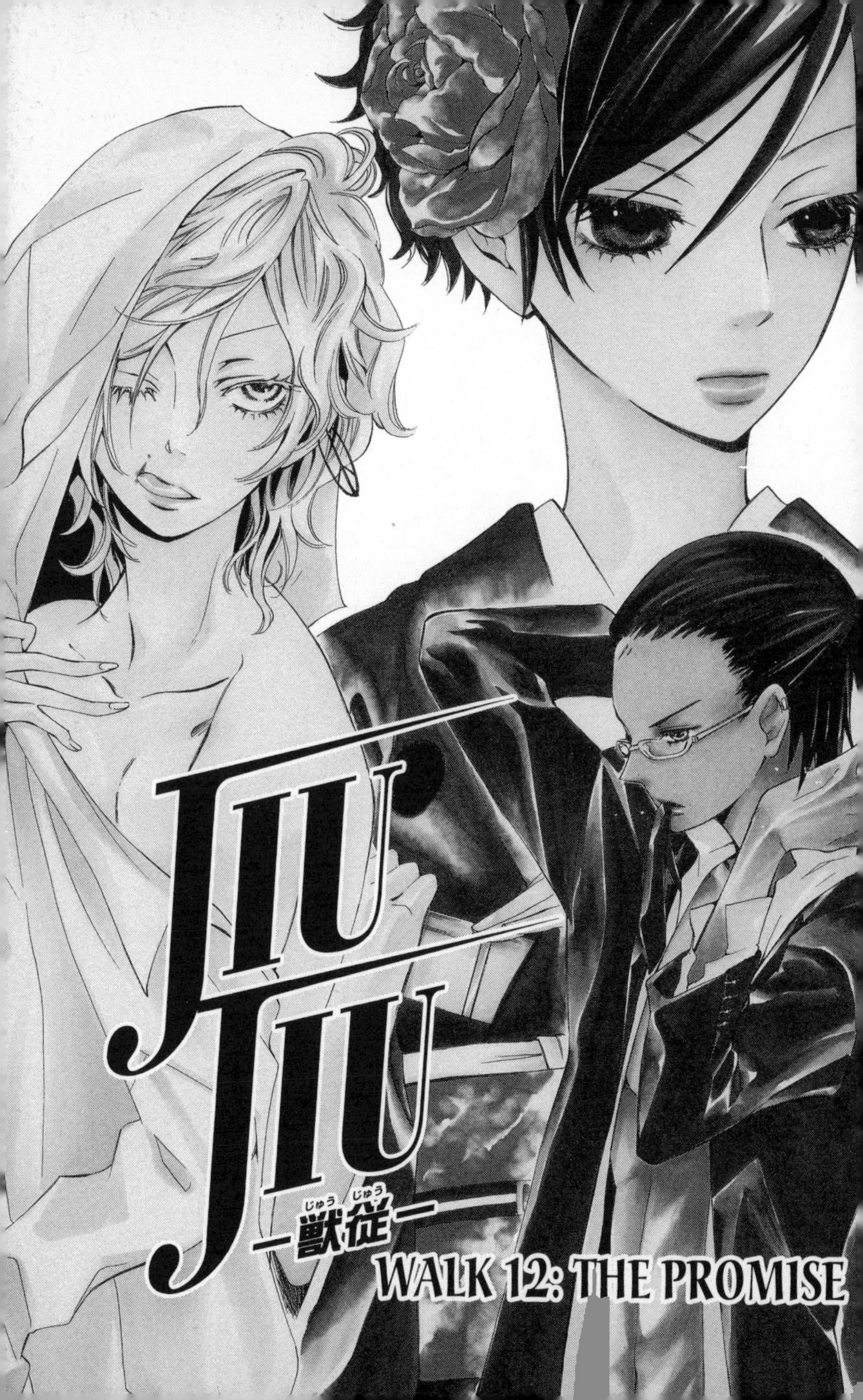
JIU JIU
じゅう じゅう
—獣従—
WALK 12: THE PROMISE

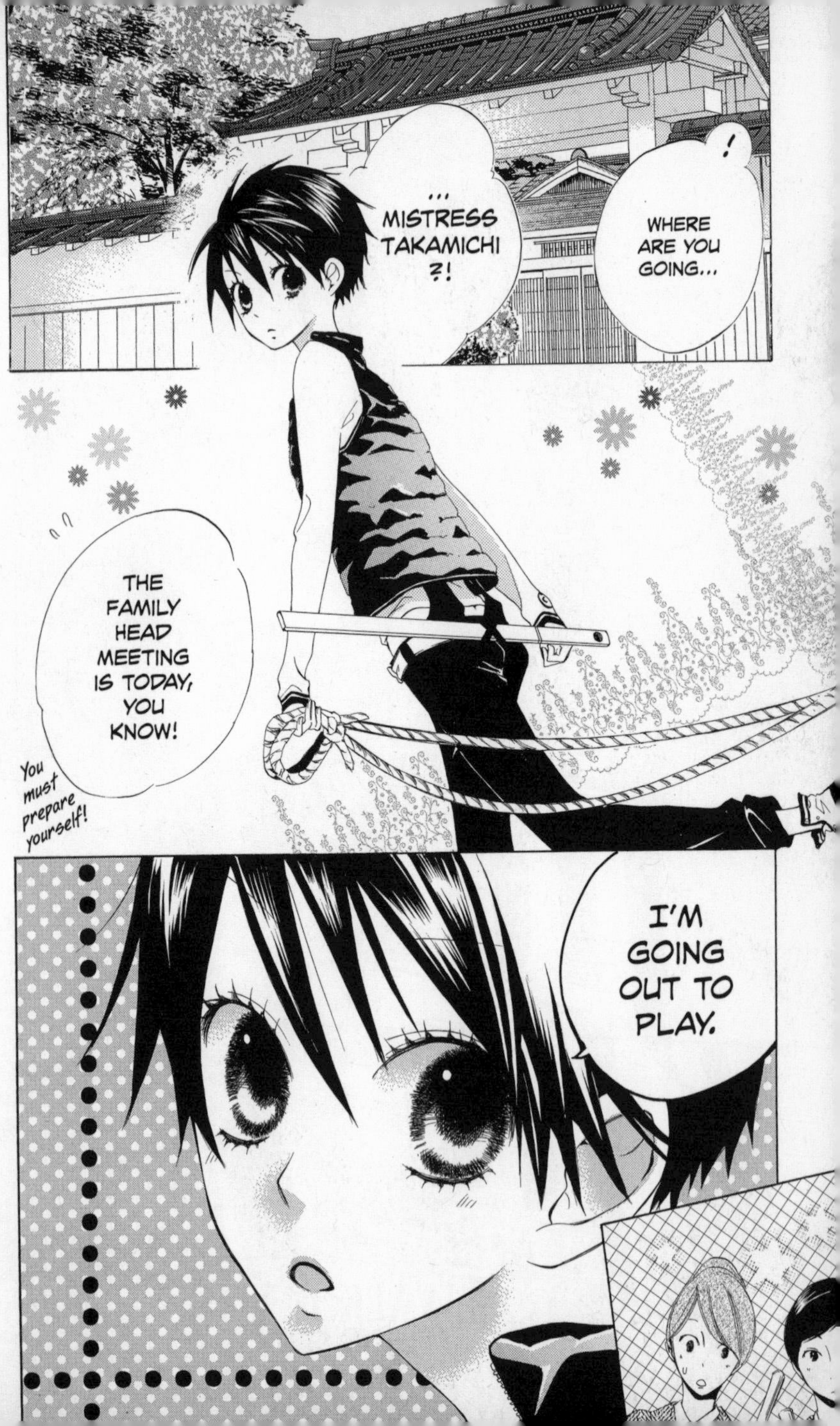
!
WHERE ARE YOU GOING...
...MISTRESS TAKAMICHI?!
THE FAMILY HEAD MEETING IS TODAY, YOU KNOW!
You must prepare yourself!
I'M GOING OUT TO PLAY.

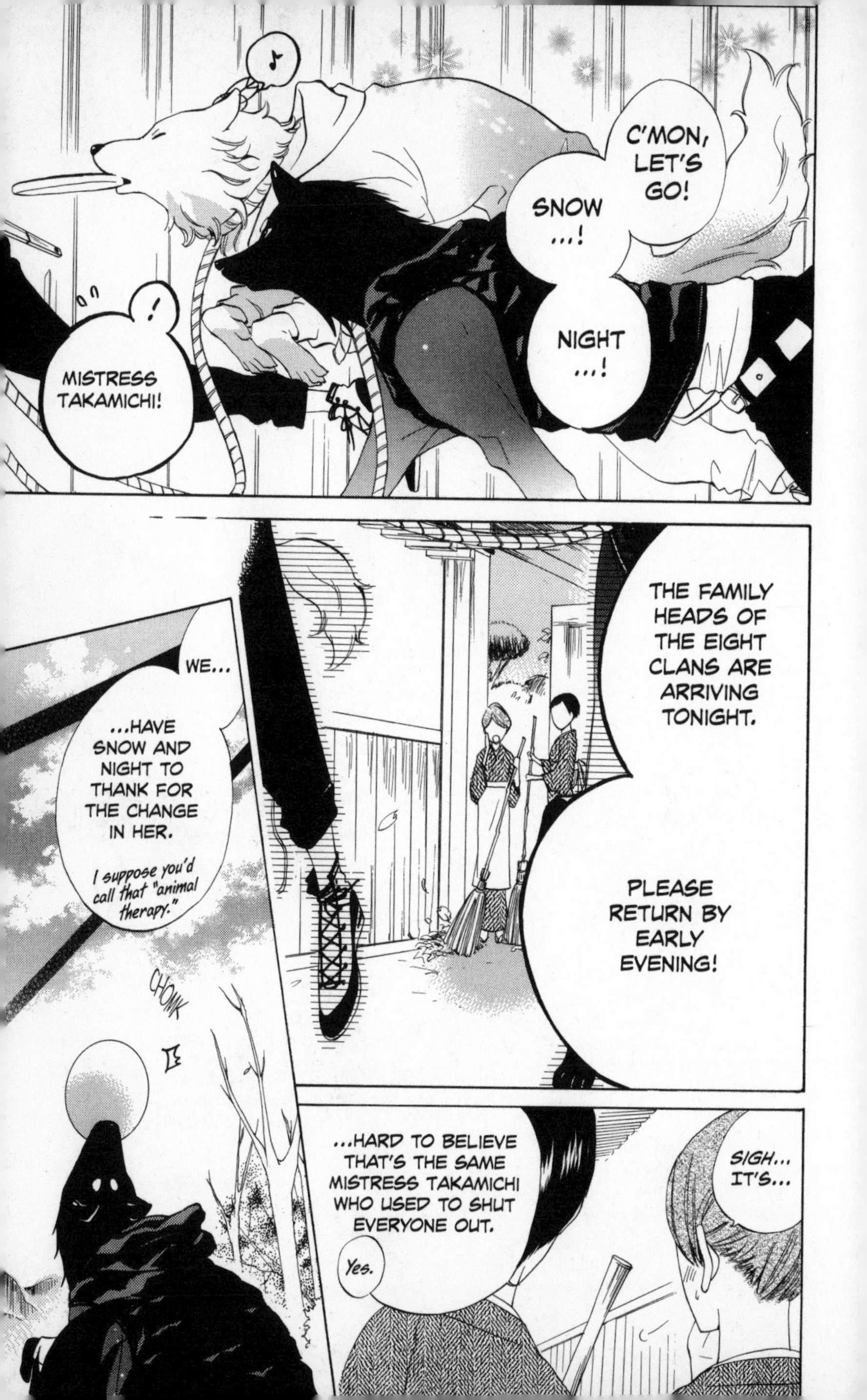
C'MON, LET'S GO!
SNOW ...!
NIGHT ...!
MISTRESS TAKAMICHI!
THE FAMILY HEADS OF THE EIGHT CLANS ARE ARRIVING TONIGHT.
PLEASE RETURN BY EARLY EVENING!
SIGH... IT'S...
...HARD TO BELIEVE THAT'S THE SAME MISTRESS TAKAMICHI WHO USED TO SHUT EVERYONE OUT.
Yes.
WE...
...HAVE SNOW AND NIGHT TO THANK FOR THE CHANGE IN HER.
I suppose you'd call that "animal therapy."
CHOMK

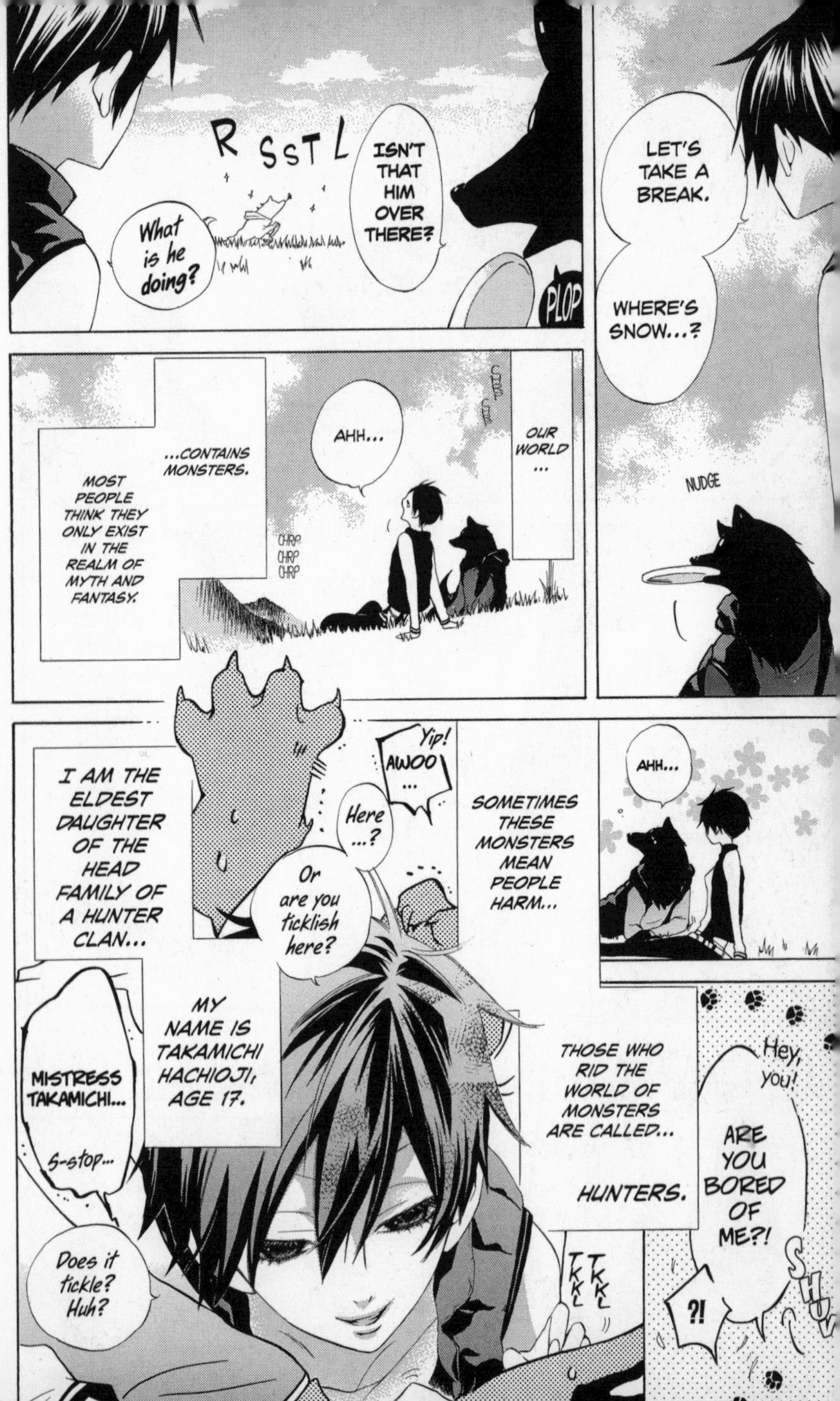

LET'S TAKE A BREAK.
WHERE'S SNOW...?
NUDGE
PLOP
ISN'T THAT HIM OVER THERE?
R SSTL
What is he doing?
OUR WORLD ...
AHH...
...CONTAINS MONSTERS.
MOST PEOPLE THINK THEY ONLY EXIST IN THE REALM OF MYTH AND FANTASY.
CHRP CHRP CHRP
AHH...
SOMETIMES THESE MONSTERS MEAN PEOPLE HARM...
Yip! AWOO ...
Here ...?
Or are you ticklish here?
I AM THE ELDEST DAUGHTER OF THE HEAD FAMILY OF A HUNTER CLAN...
Hey, you!
ARE YOU BORED OF ME?!
SHUV
?!
THOSE WHO RID THE WORLD OF MONSTERS ARE CALLED...
HUNTERS.
TKKL TKKL
MY NAME IS TAKAMICHI HACHIOJI, AGE 17.
MISTRESS TAKAMICHI...
S-stop...
Does it tickle? Huh?

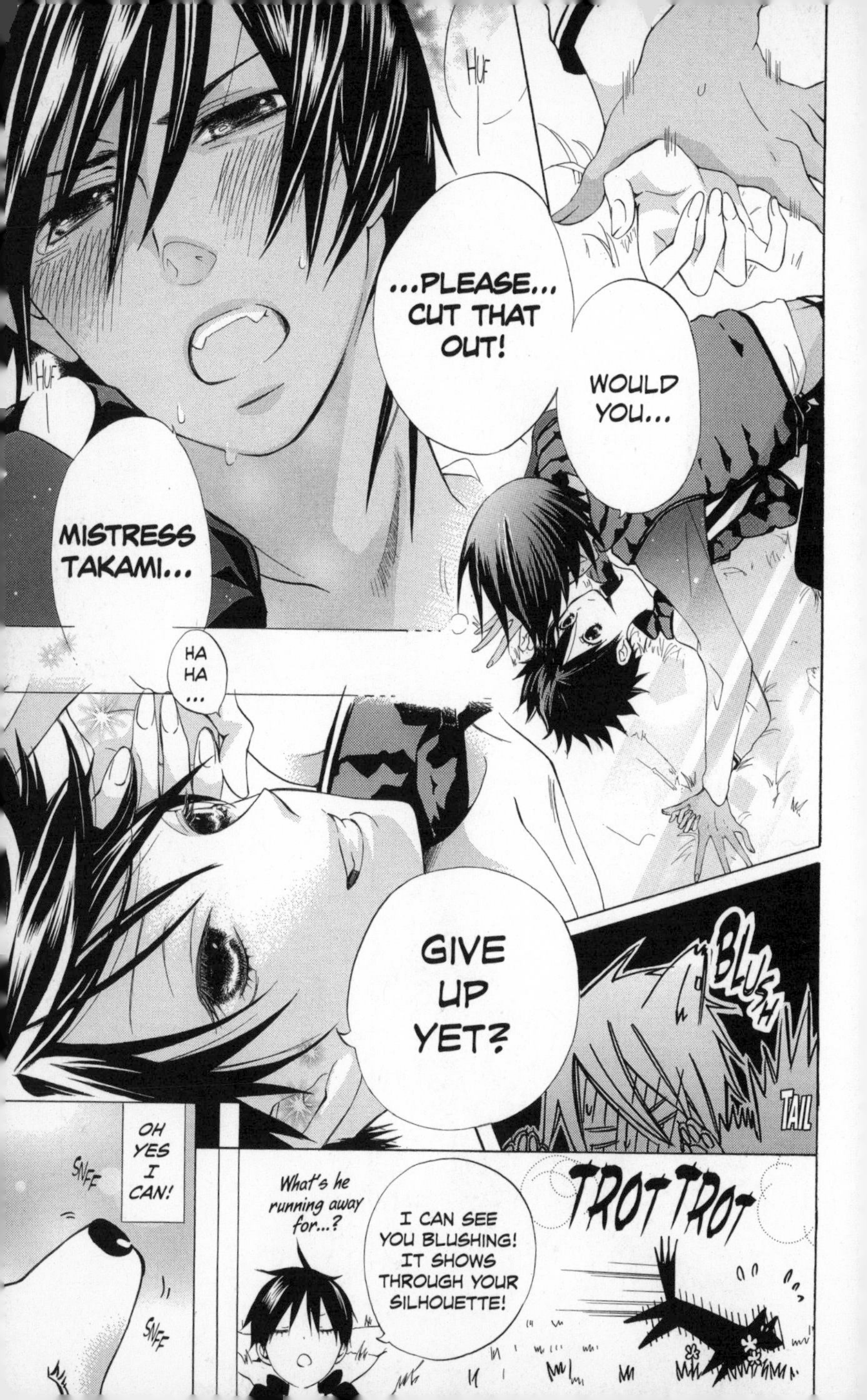
HUF
WOULD YOU...
...PLEASE... CUT THAT OUT!
HUF
MISTRESS TAKAMI...
HA HA...
GIVE UP YET?
BLUSH
TAIL
TROT TROT
I CAN SEE YOU BLUSHING! IT SHOWS THROUGH YOUR SILHOUETTE!
What's he running away for...?
OH YES I CAN!
SNFF
SNFF

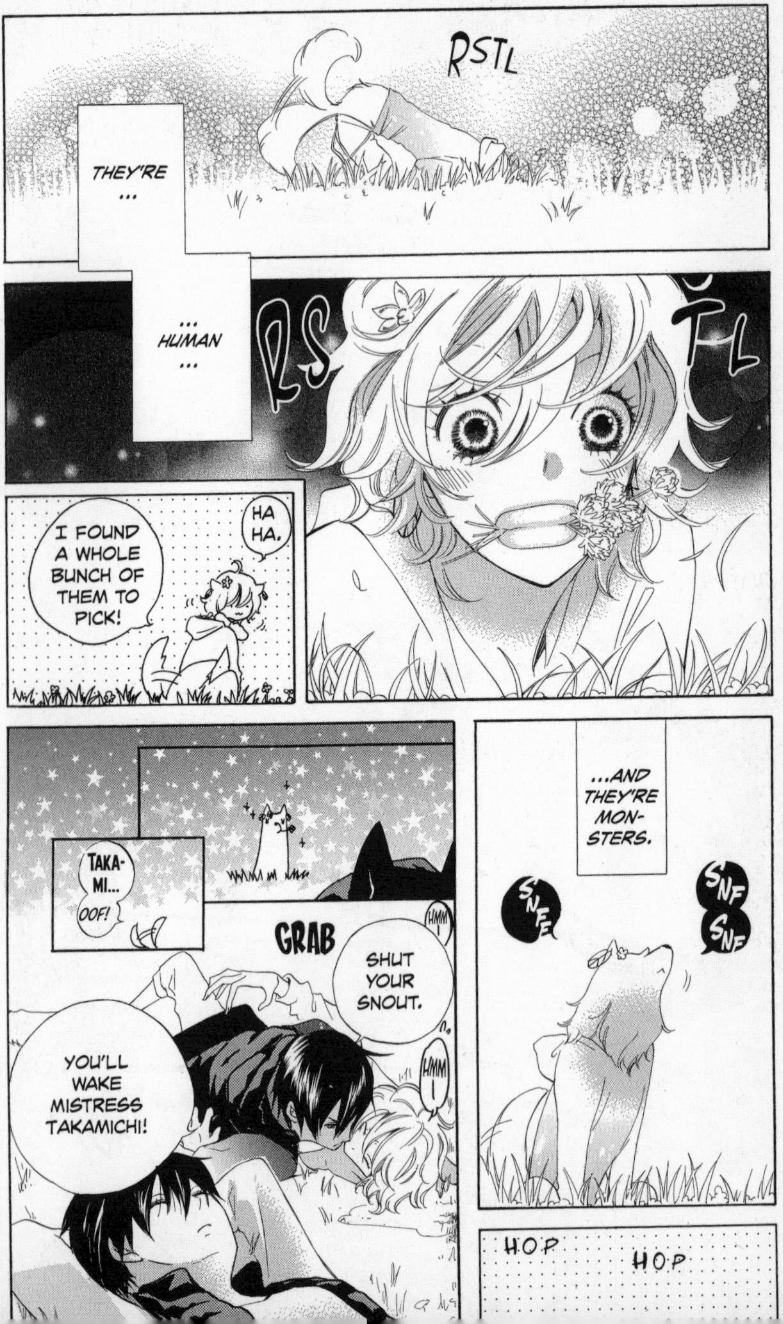
RSTL
THEY'RE ...
... HUMAN ...
RS TL
HA HA.
I FOUND A WHOLE BUNCH OF THEM TO PICK!
...AND THEY'RE MON-STERS.
SNF
SNF SNF
HOP HOP
TAKA-MI...
OOF!
GRAB
HMM
SHUT YOUR SNOUT.
HMM
YOU'LL WAKE MISTRESS TAKAMICHI!

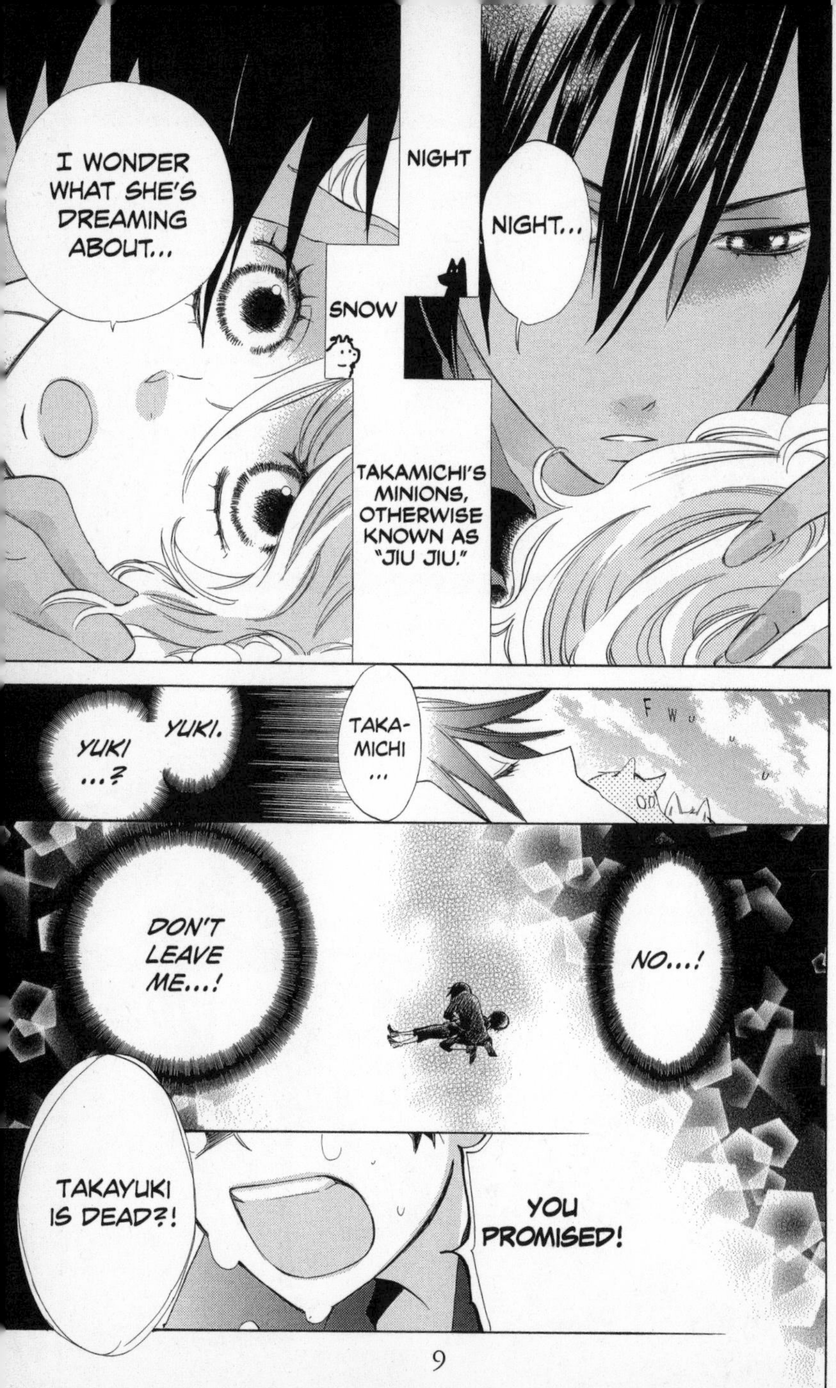
NIGHT...
NIGHT
SNOW
TAKAMICHI'S MINIONS, OTHERWISE KNOWN AS "JIU JIU."
I WONDER WHAT SHE'S DREAMING ABOUT...
FWuuu
TAKA-MICHI...
YUKI.
YUKI...?
NO...!
DON'T LEAVE ME...!
YOU PROMISED!
TAKAYUKI IS DEAD?!

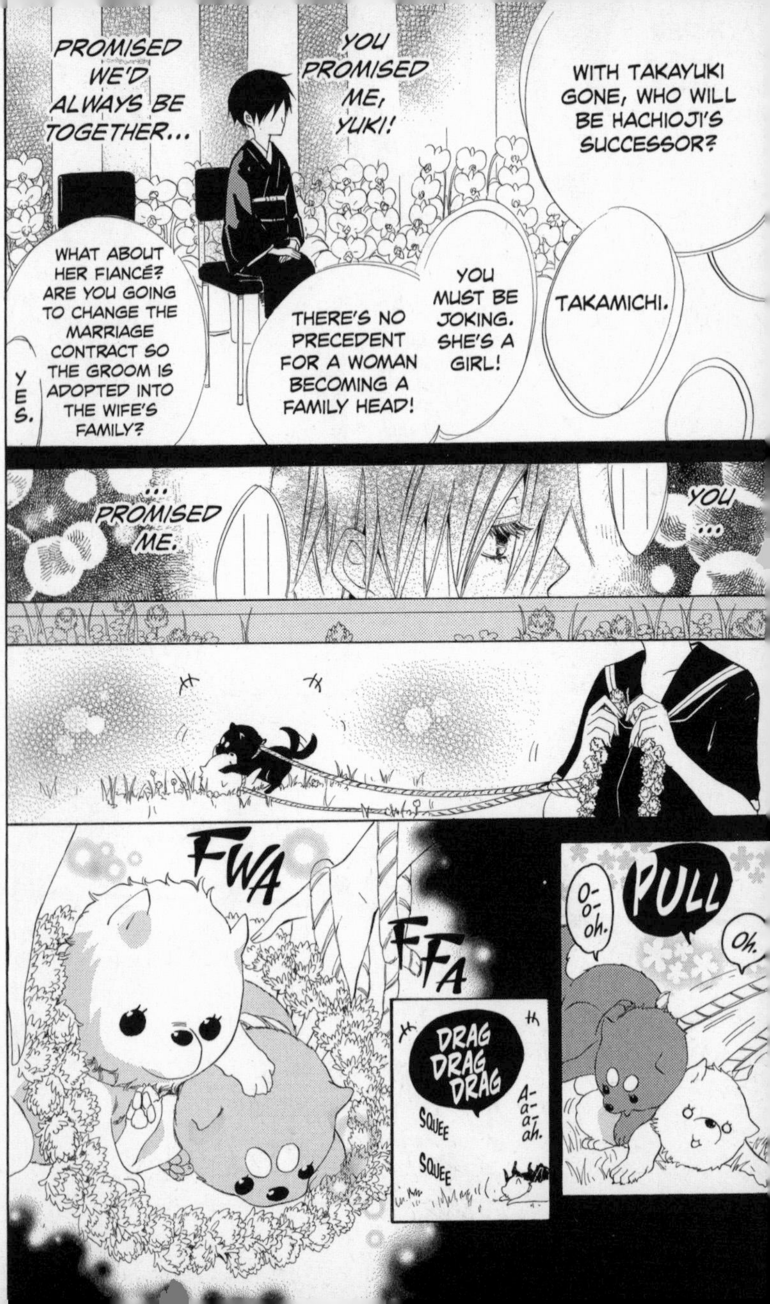
WITH TAKAYUKI GONE, WHO WILL BE HACHIOJI'S SUCCESSOR?
YOU PROMISED ME, YUKI!
PROMISED WE'D ALWAYS BE TOGETHER...
TAKAMICHI.
YOU MUST BE JOKING. SHE'S A GIRL!
THERE'S NO PRECEDENT FOR A WOMAN BECOMING A FAMILY HEAD!
WHAT ABOUT HER FIANCÉ? ARE YOU GOING TO CHANGE THE MARRIAGE CONTRACT SO THE GROOM IS ADOPTED INTO THE WIFE'S FAMILY?
YES.
YOU...
...PROMISED ME.
Oh.
PULL
O-o-oh.
DRAG DRAG DRAG
A-a-a-ah.
SQUEE
SQUEE
FFA
FWA

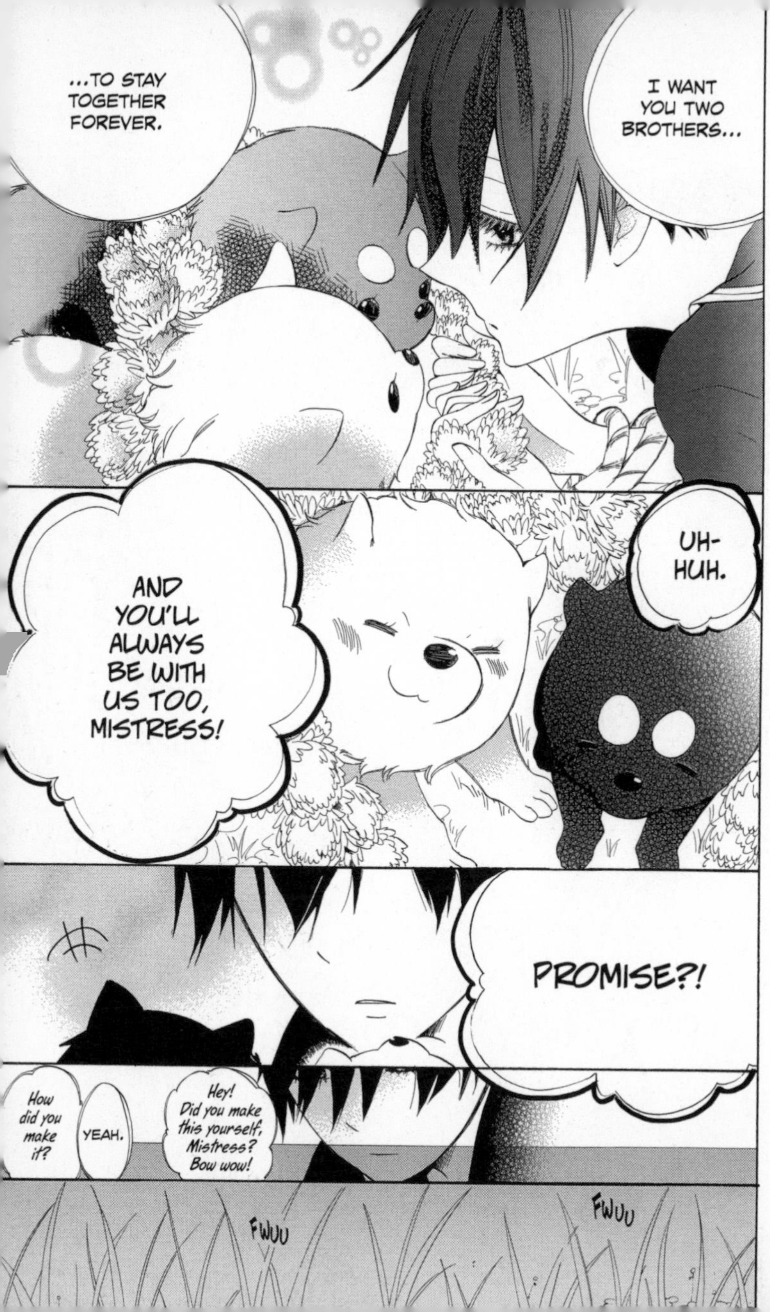
I WANT YOU TWO BROTHERS...
...TO STAY TOGETHER FOREVER.
UH-HUH.
AND YOU'LL ALWAYS BE WITH US TOO, MISTRESS!
PROMISE?!
Hey! Did you make this yourself, Mistress? Bow wow!
YEAH.
How did you make it?
FWUU
FWUU

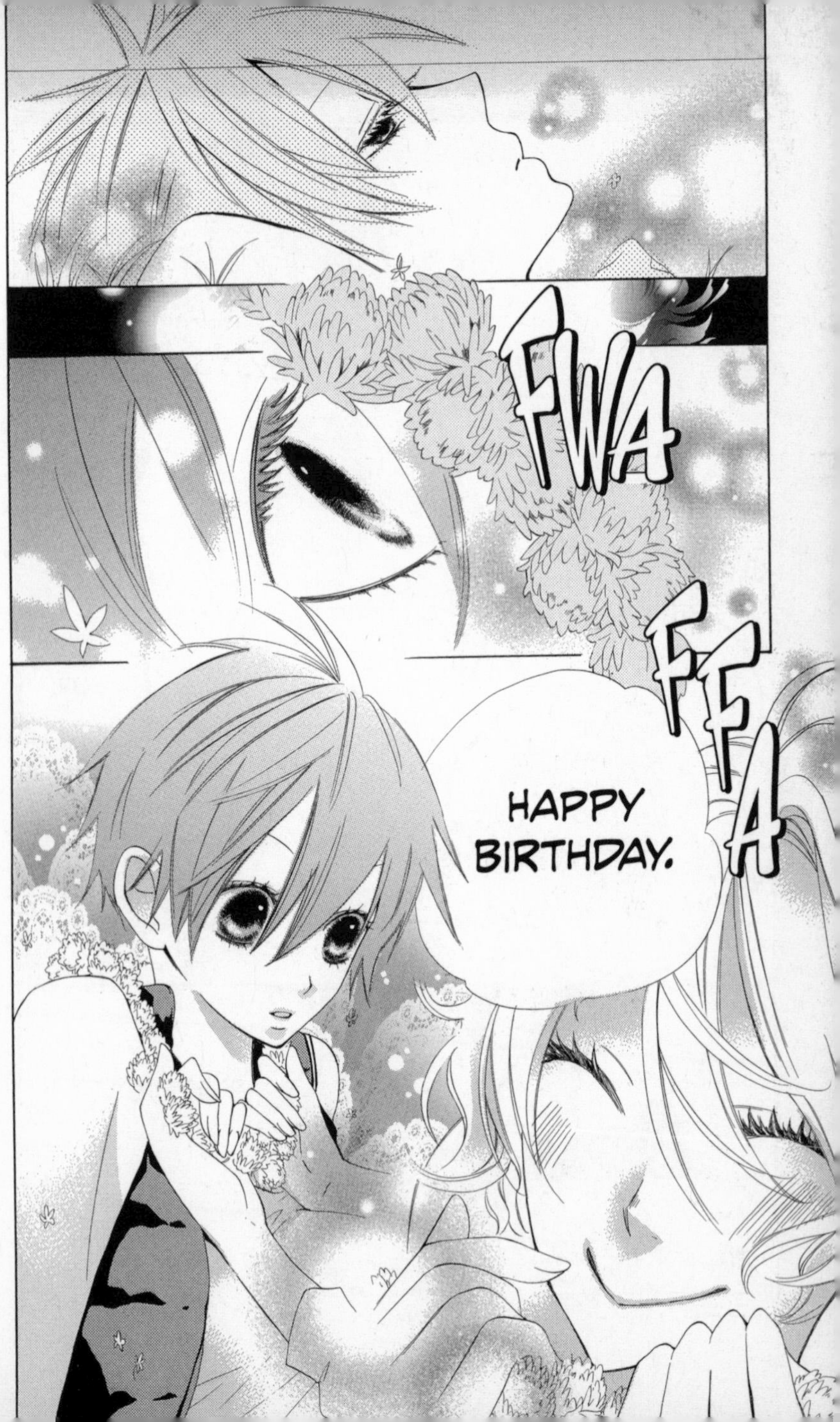
FWA
FFA
HAPPY BIRTHDAY.

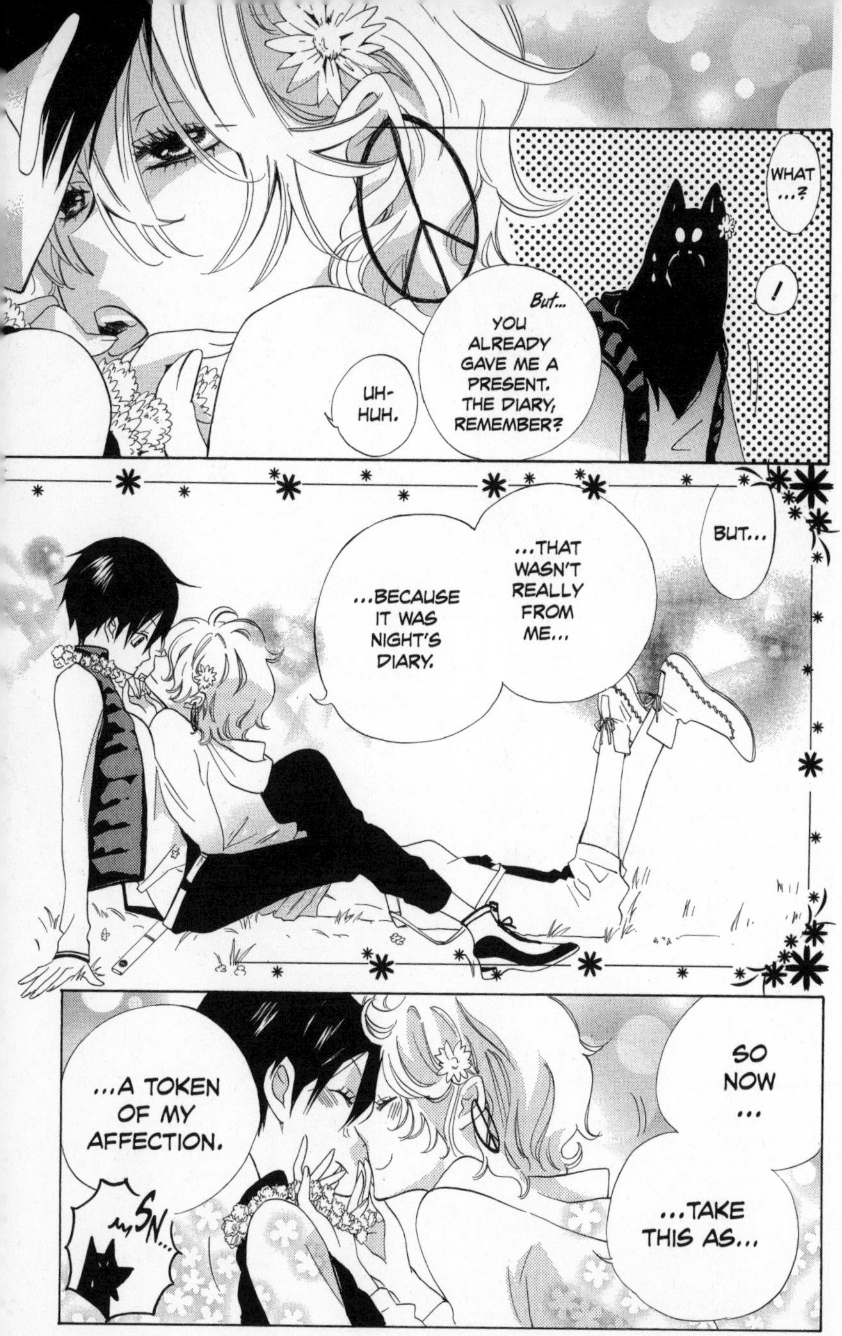
WHAT ...?
!
But... YOU ALREADY GAVE ME A PRESENT. THE DIARY, REMEMBER?
UH-HUH.
BUT...
...THAT WASN'T REALLY FROM ME...
...BECAUSE IT WAS NIGHT'S DIARY.
SO NOW ...
...TAKE THIS AS...
...A TOKEN OF MY AFFECTION.
SN...

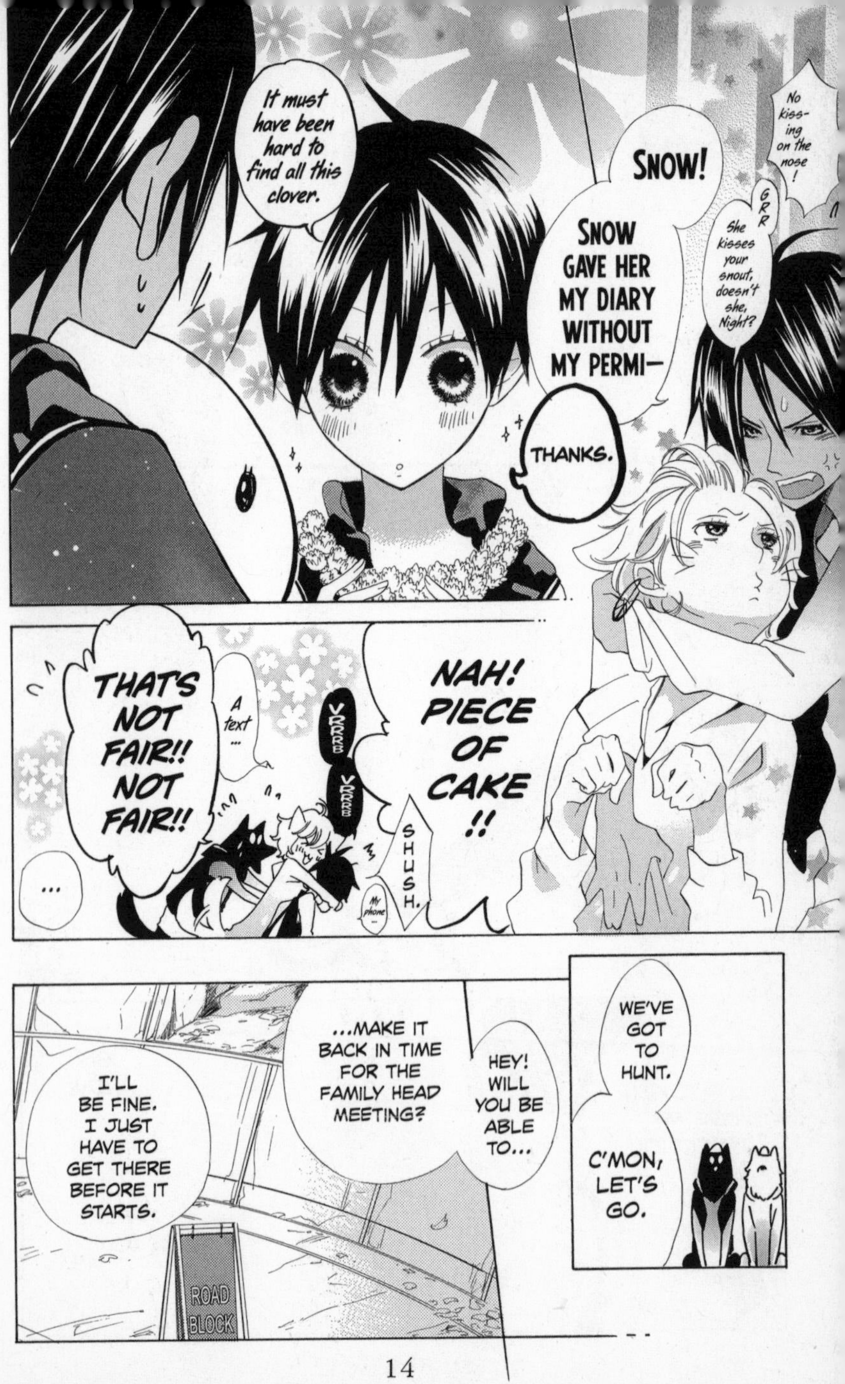
No kissing on the nose!
GRR
She kisses your snout, doesn't she, Night?
SNOW!
SNOW GAVE HER MY DIARY WITHOUT MY PERMI—
It must have been hard to find all this clover.
THANKS.
NAH! PIECE OF CAKE!!
VRRRB
VRRRB
SHUSH.
My phone...
A text...
THAT'S NOT FAIR!! NOT FAIR!!
...
WE'VE GOT TO HUNT.
C'MON, LET'S GO.
HEY! WILL YOU BE ABLE TO...
...MAKE IT BACK IN TIME FOR THE FAMILY HEAD MEETING?
I'LL BE FINE. I JUST HAVE TO GET THERE BEFORE IT STARTS.
ROAD BLOCK

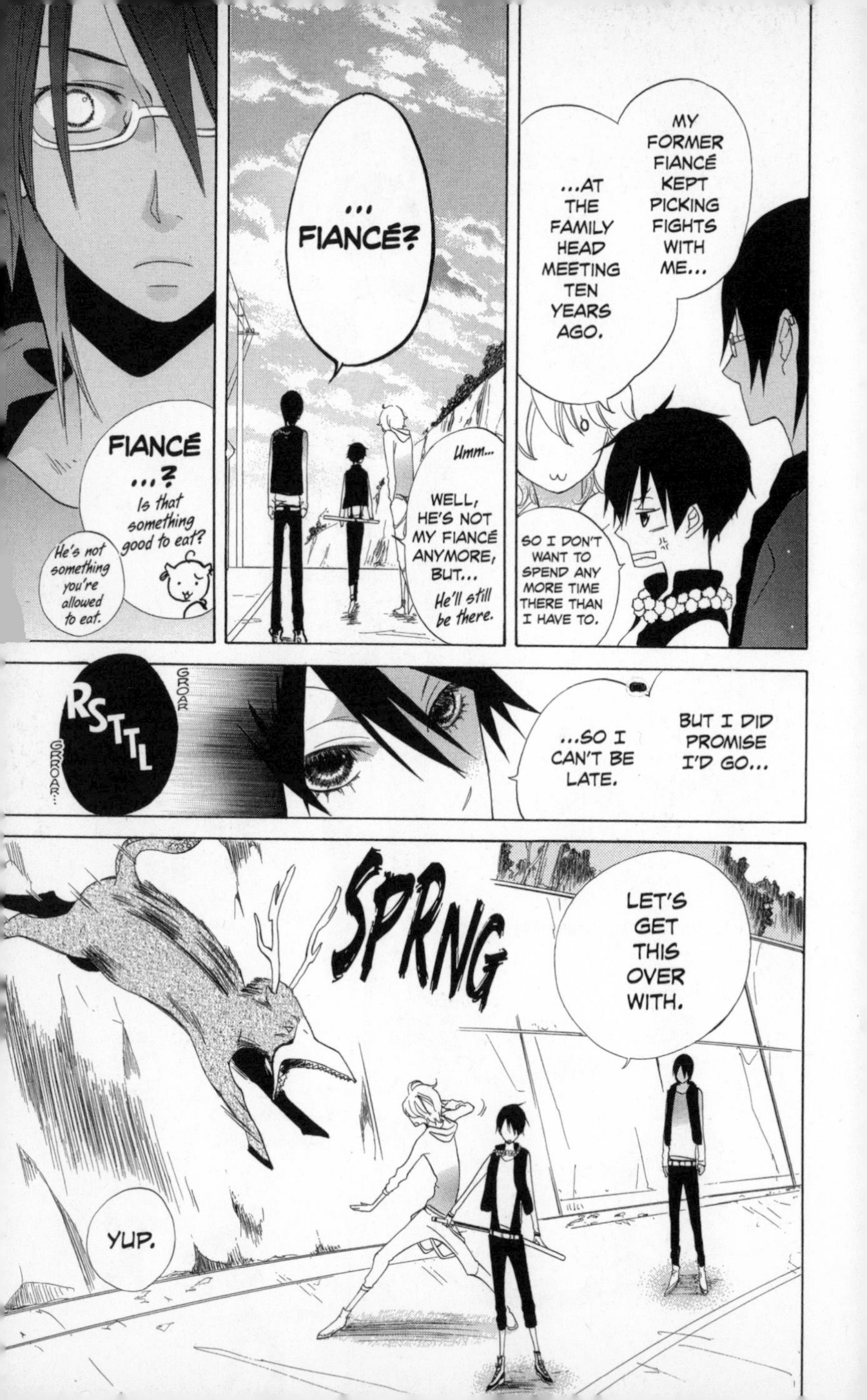
MY FORMER FIANCÉ KEPT PICKING FIGHTS WITH ME...
...AT THE FAMILY HEAD MEETING TEN YEARS AGO.
SO I DON'T WANT TO SPEND ANY MORE TIME THERE THAN I HAVE TO.
...FIANCÉ?
Umm...
WELL, HE'S NOT MY FIANCÉ ANYMORE, BUT...
He'll still be there.
FIANCÉ...? Is that something good to eat?
He's not something you're allowed to eat.
BUT I DID PROMISE I'D GO...
...SO I CAN'T BE LATE.
RSTTL
GROAR GROAR...
SPRNG
LET'S GET THIS OVER WITH.
YUP.

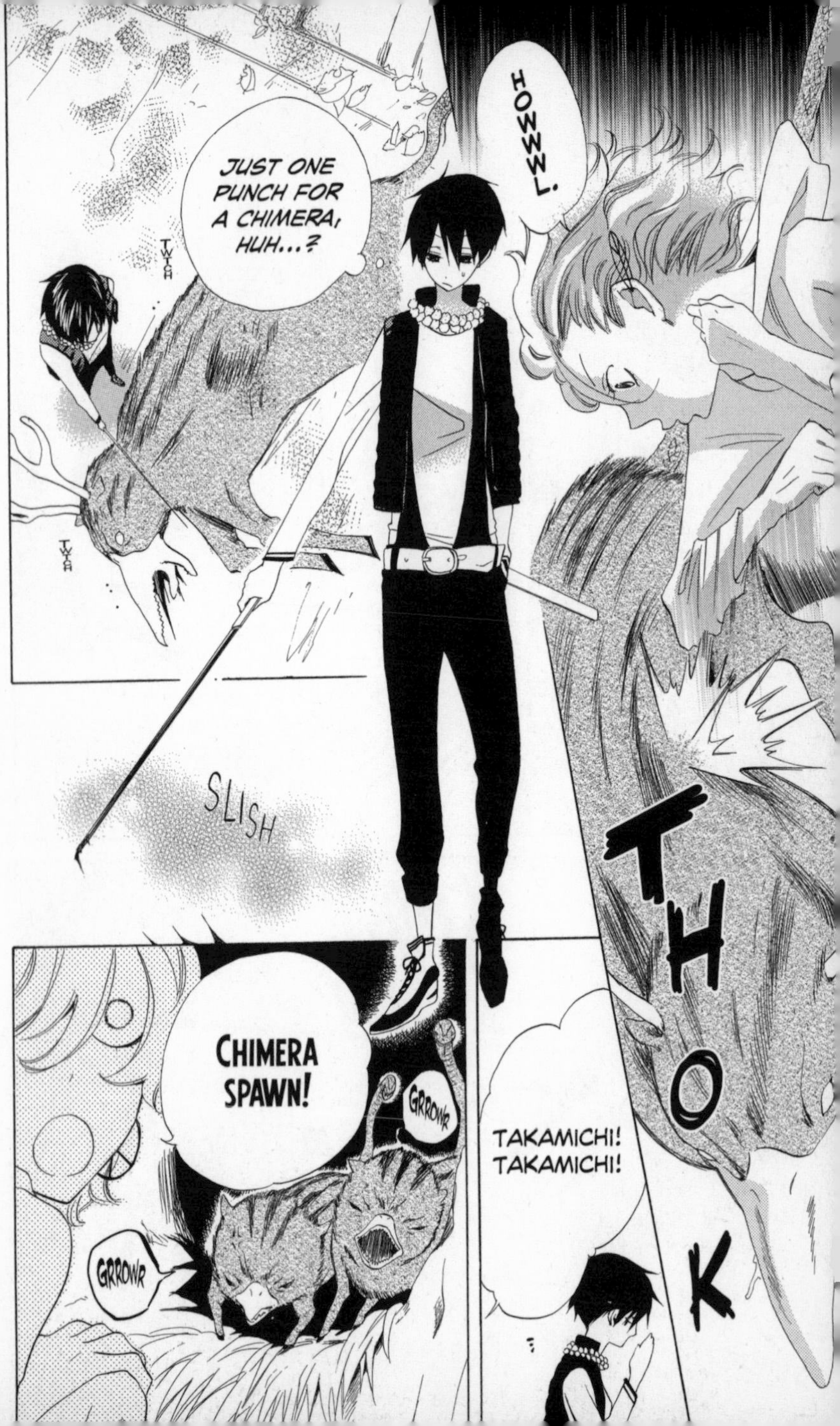
HOWWWL.
THOK
JUST ONE PUNCH FOR A CHIMERA, HUH...?
TWITCH
TWITCH
SLISH
TAKAMICHI! TAKAMICHI!
CHIMERA SPAWN!
GRROWR
GRROWR

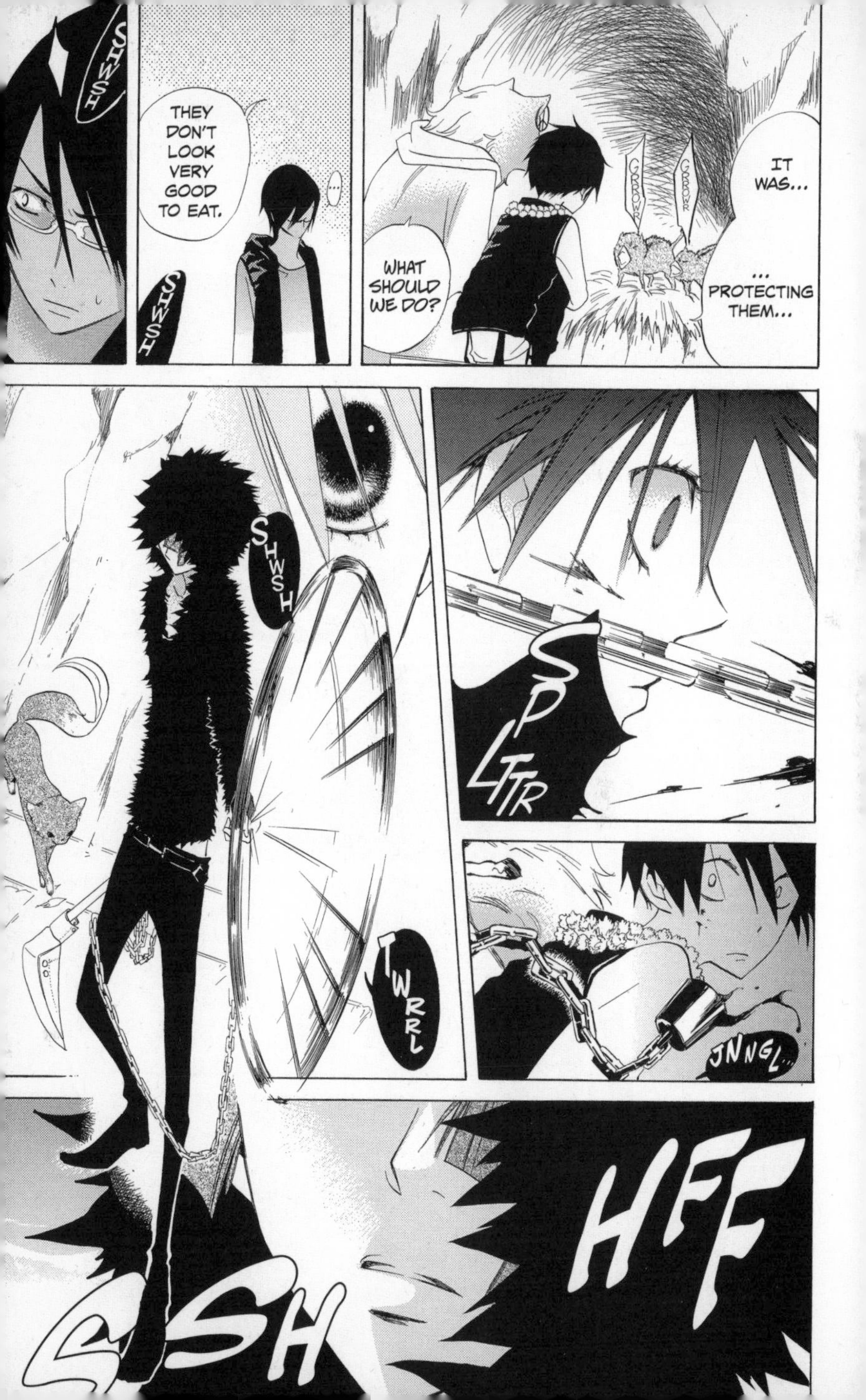
IT WAS...
... PROTECTING THEM...
GRROWR
GRROWR
WHAT SHOULD WE DO?
THEY DON'T LOOK VERY GOOD TO EAT.
...
SHWSH
SHWSH
SPLTTR
JNNGL...
SHWSH
TWRRL
HFF
SSH

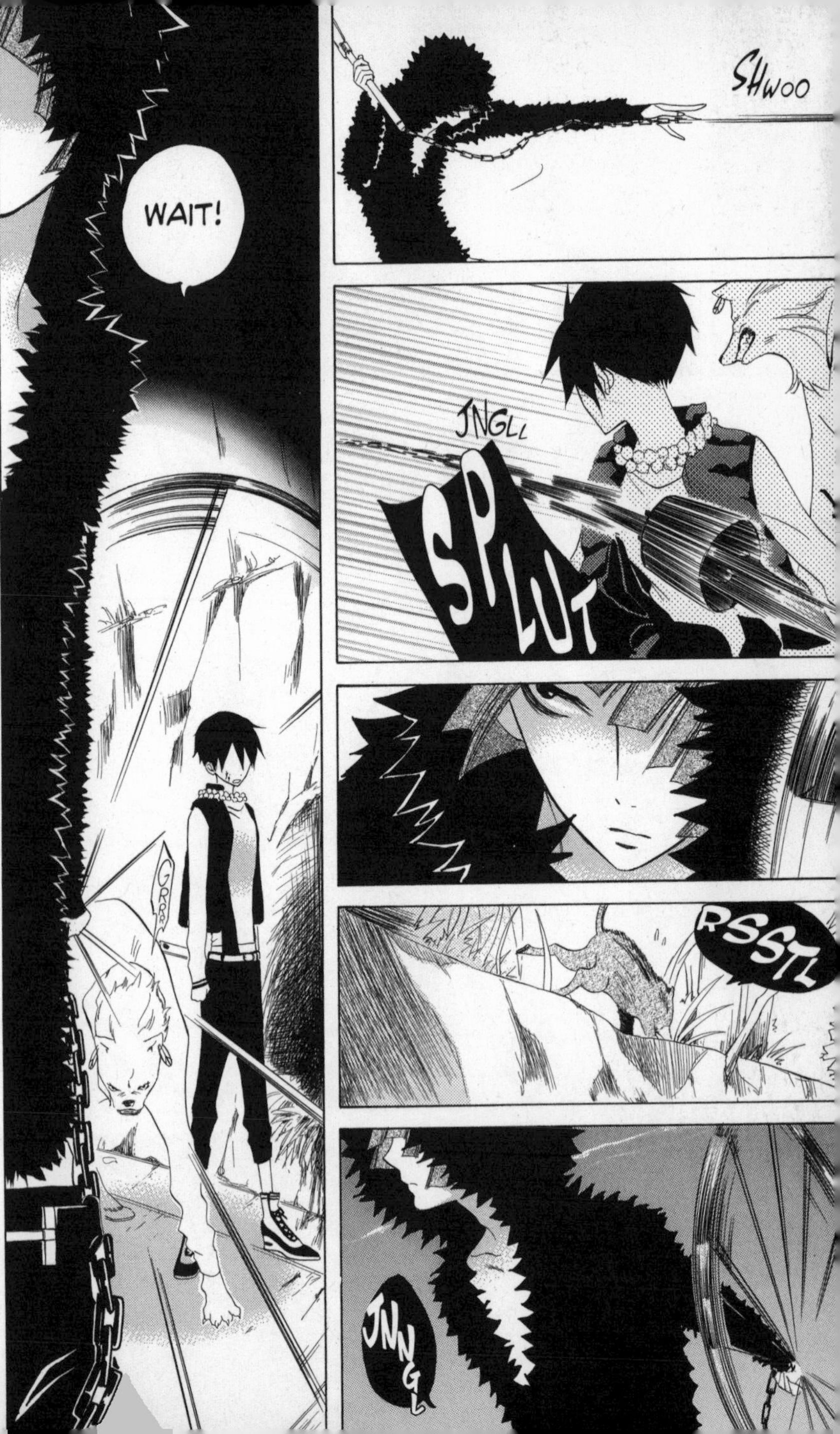
SHWOO
JNGLL
SPLUT
RSSTL
JNNGL
WAIT!
GRRR

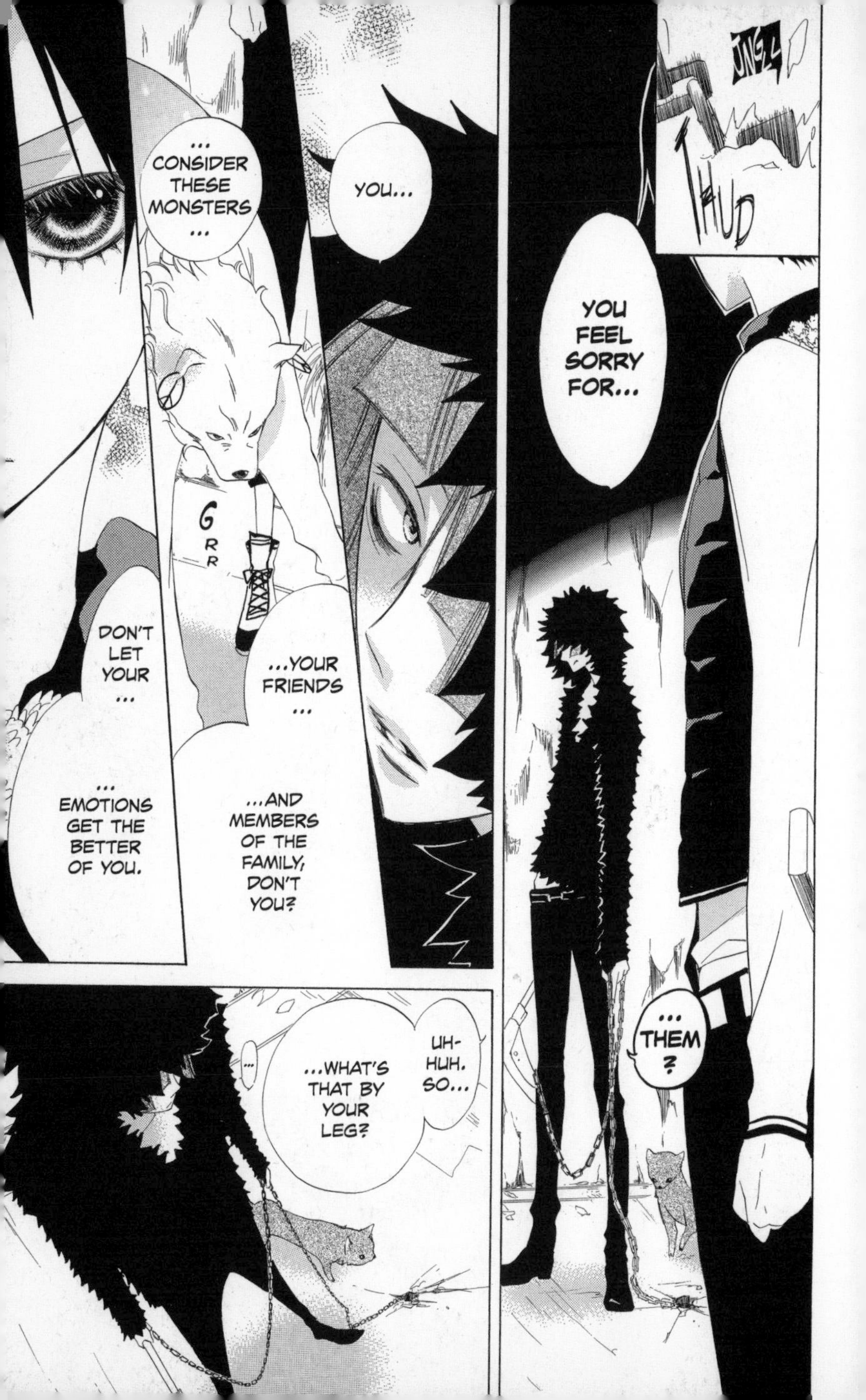
JINGLE
THUD
YOU FEEL SORRY FOR...
...THEM?
YOU...
...CONSIDER THESE MONSTERS...
...YOUR FRIENDS...
...AND MEMBERS OF THE FAMILY, DON'T YOU?
GRR
DON'T LET YOUR...
...EMOTIONS GET THE BETTER OF YOU.
UH-HUH. SO...
...WHAT'S THAT BY YOUR LEG?
...

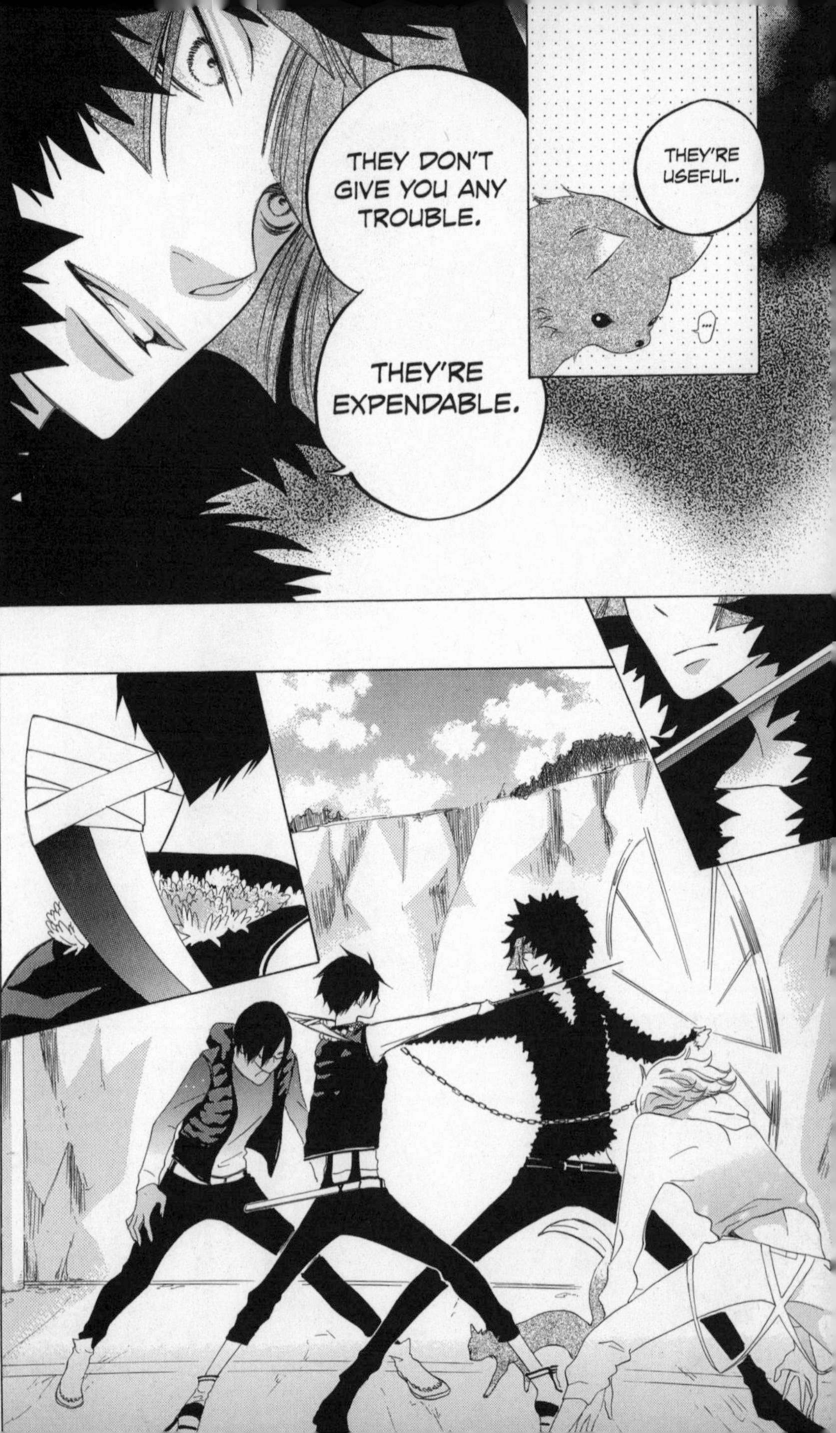
THEY'RE USEFUL.
...
THEY DON'T GIVE YOU ANY TROUBLE.
THEY'RE EXPENDABLE.

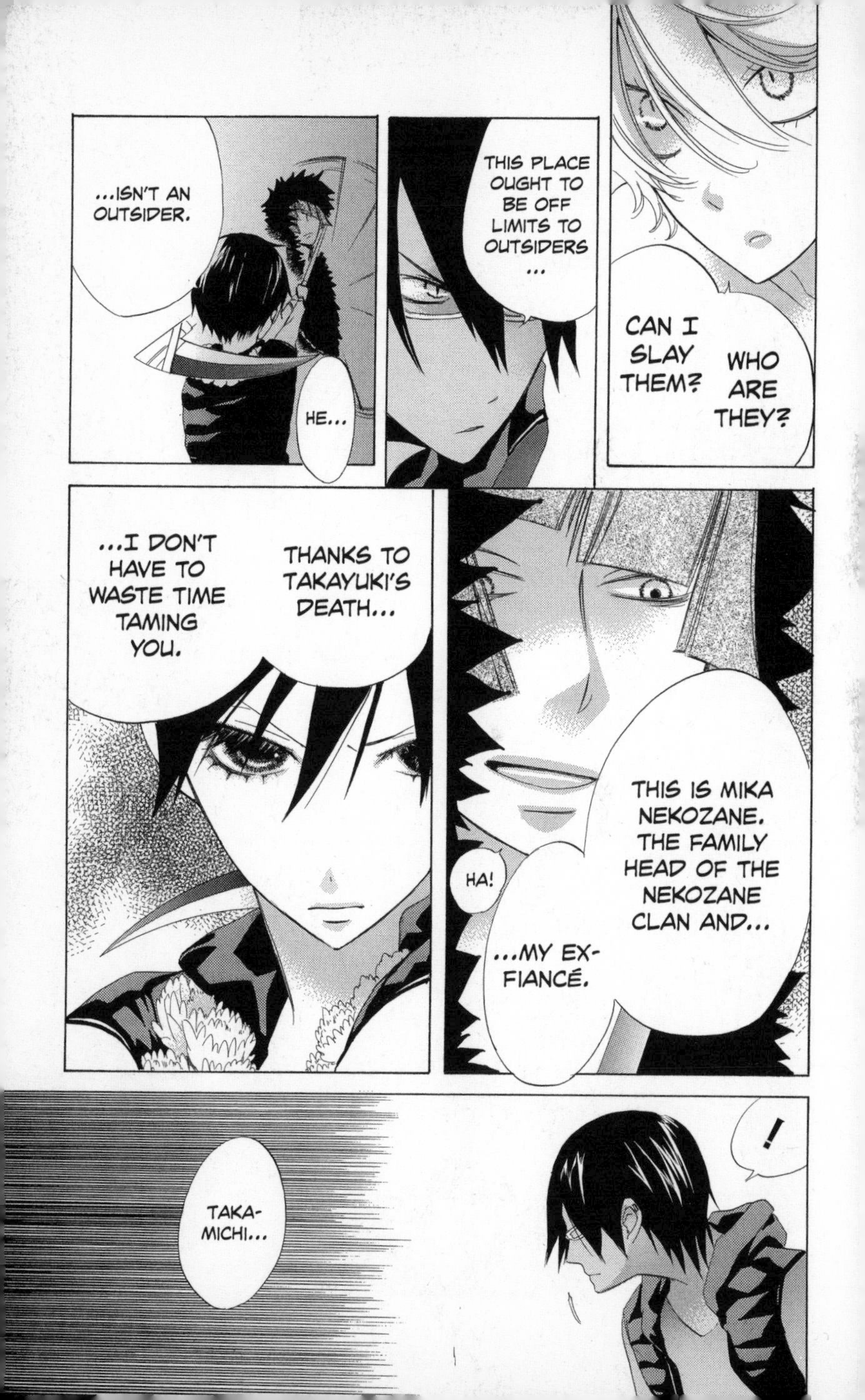
WHO ARE THEY?
CAN I SLAY THEM?
THIS PLACE OUGHT TO BE OFF LIMITS TO OUTSIDERS ...
HE...
...ISN'T AN OUTSIDER.
THIS IS MIKA NEKOZANE. THE FAMILY HEAD OF THE NEKOZANE CLAN AND...
HA!
...MY EX-FIANCÉ.
THANKS TO TAKAYUKI'S DEATH...
...I DON'T HAVE TO WASTE TIME TAMING YOU.
!
TAKA-MICHI...

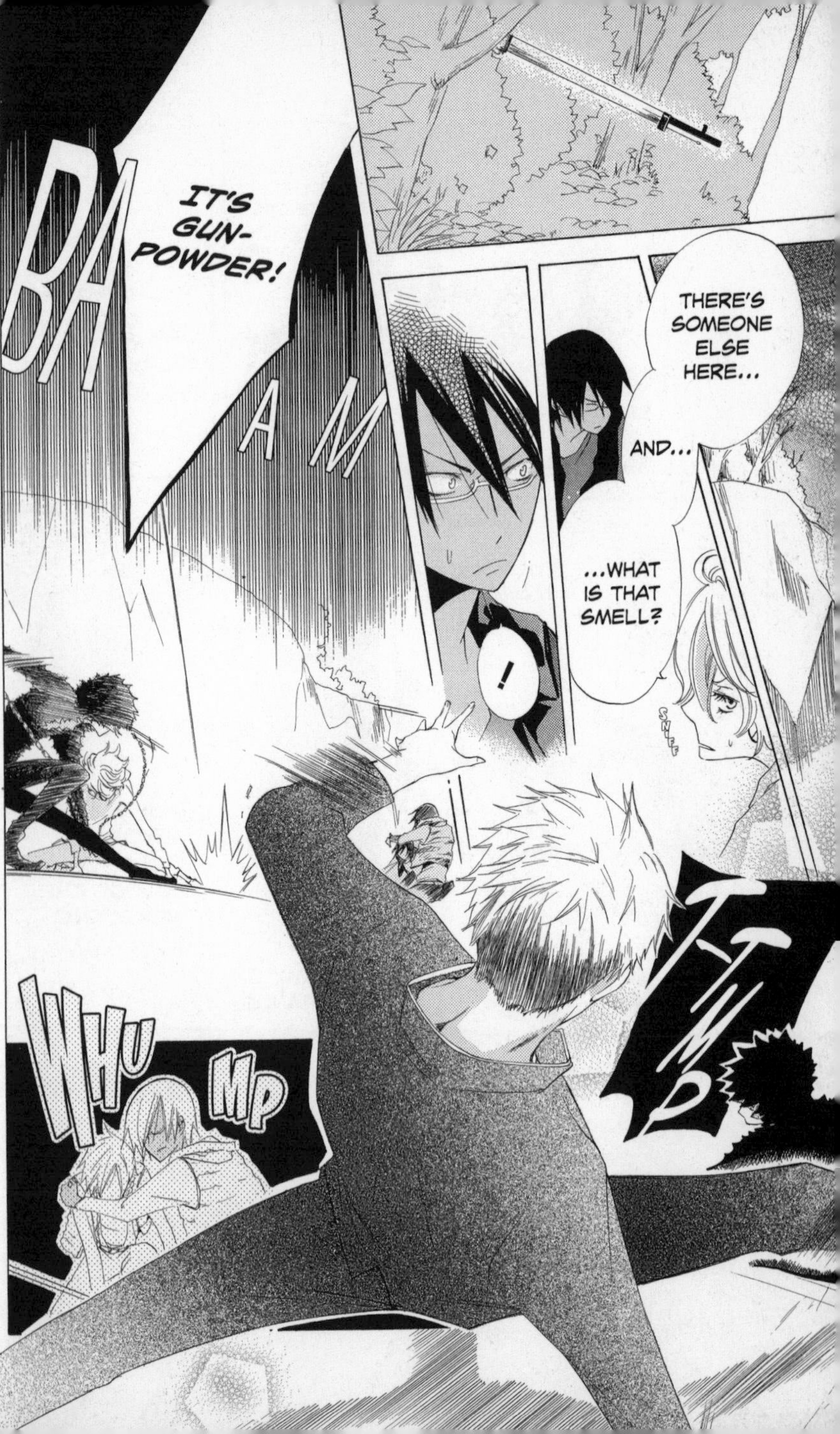
THERE'S SOMEONE ELSE HERE...
AND...
...WHAT IS THAT SMELL?
SNIFF
!
IT'S GUN-POWDER!
BAAM
THMP
WHUMP

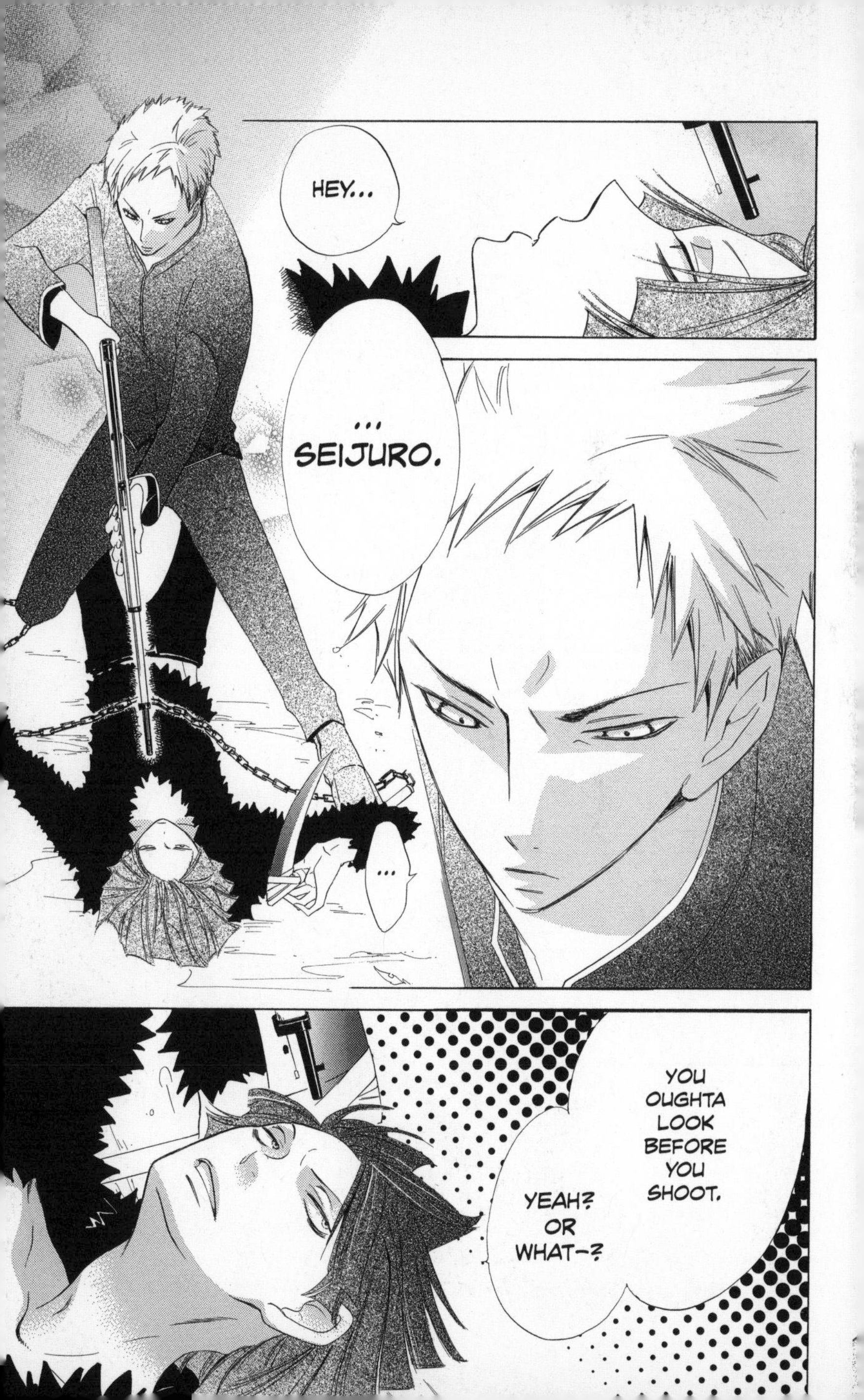
HEY...
... SEIJURO.
...
YOU OUGHTA LOOK BEFORE YOU SHOOT.
YEAH? OR WHAT-?

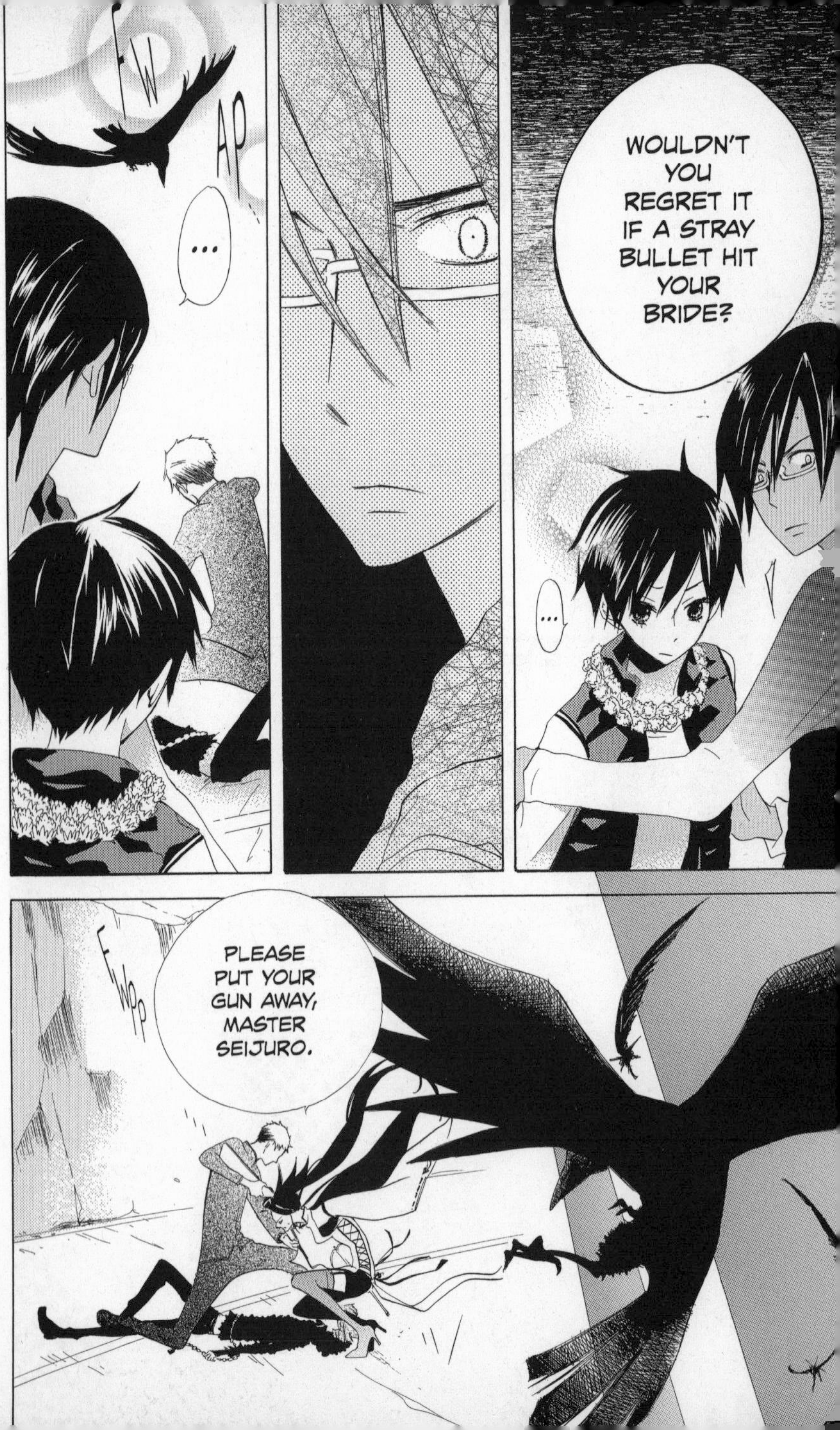
WOULDN'T YOU REGRET IT IF A STRAY BULLET HIT YOUR BRIDE?
...
FWAP
...
PLEASE PUT YOUR GUN AWAY, MASTER SEIJURO.
FWOPP

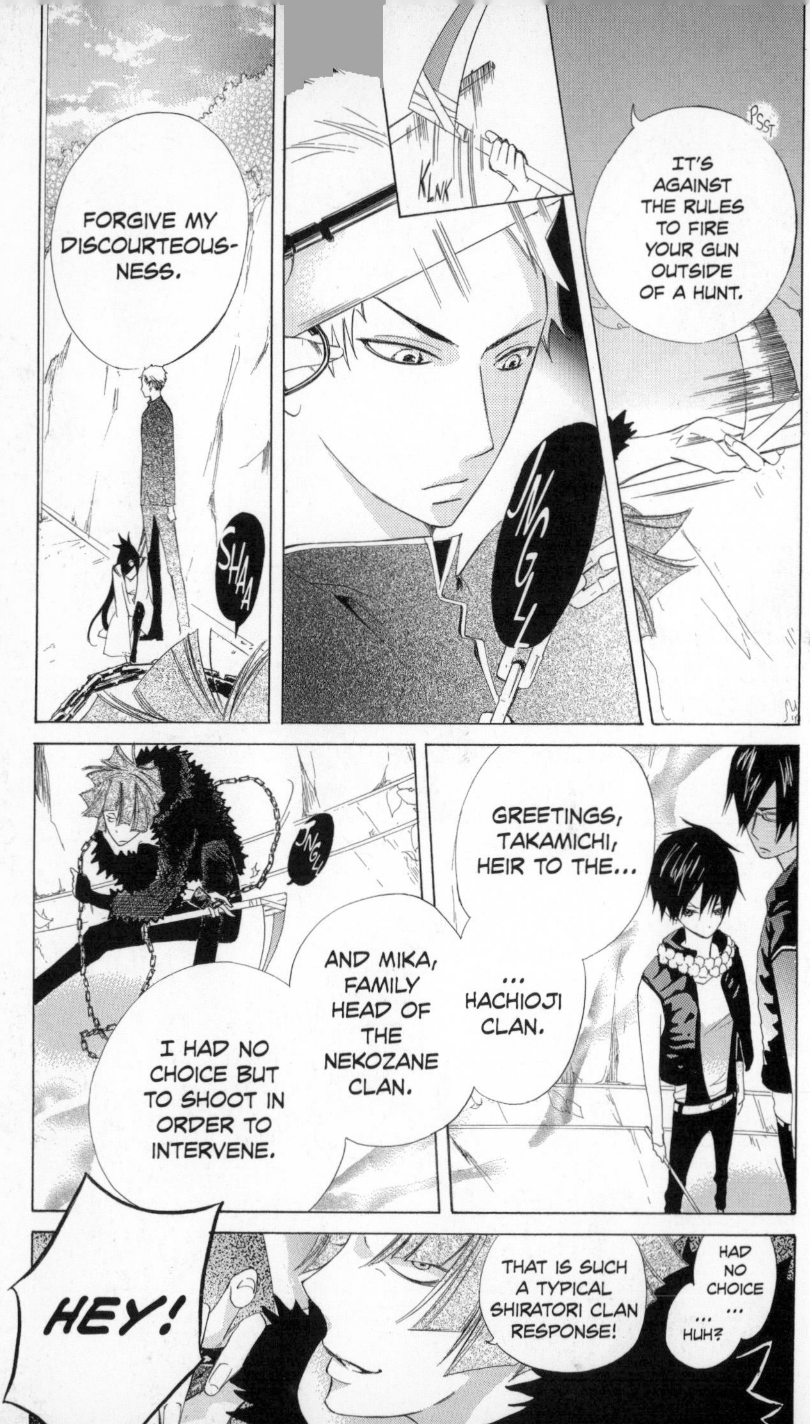
PSST
IT'S AGAINST THE RULES TO FIRE YOUR GUN OUTSIDE OF A HUNT.
KLNK
JNGLL
FORGIVE MY DISCOURTEOUSNESS.
SHAA
GREETINGS, TAKAMICHI, HEIR TO THE...
...HACHIOJI CLAN.
AND MIKA, FAMILY HEAD OF THE NEKOZANE CLAN.
JNGL
I HAD NO CHOICE BUT TO SHOOT IN ORDER TO INTERVENE.
HAD NO CHOICE... ...HUH?
THAT IS SUCH A TYPICAL SHIRATORI CLAN RESPONSE!
HEY!

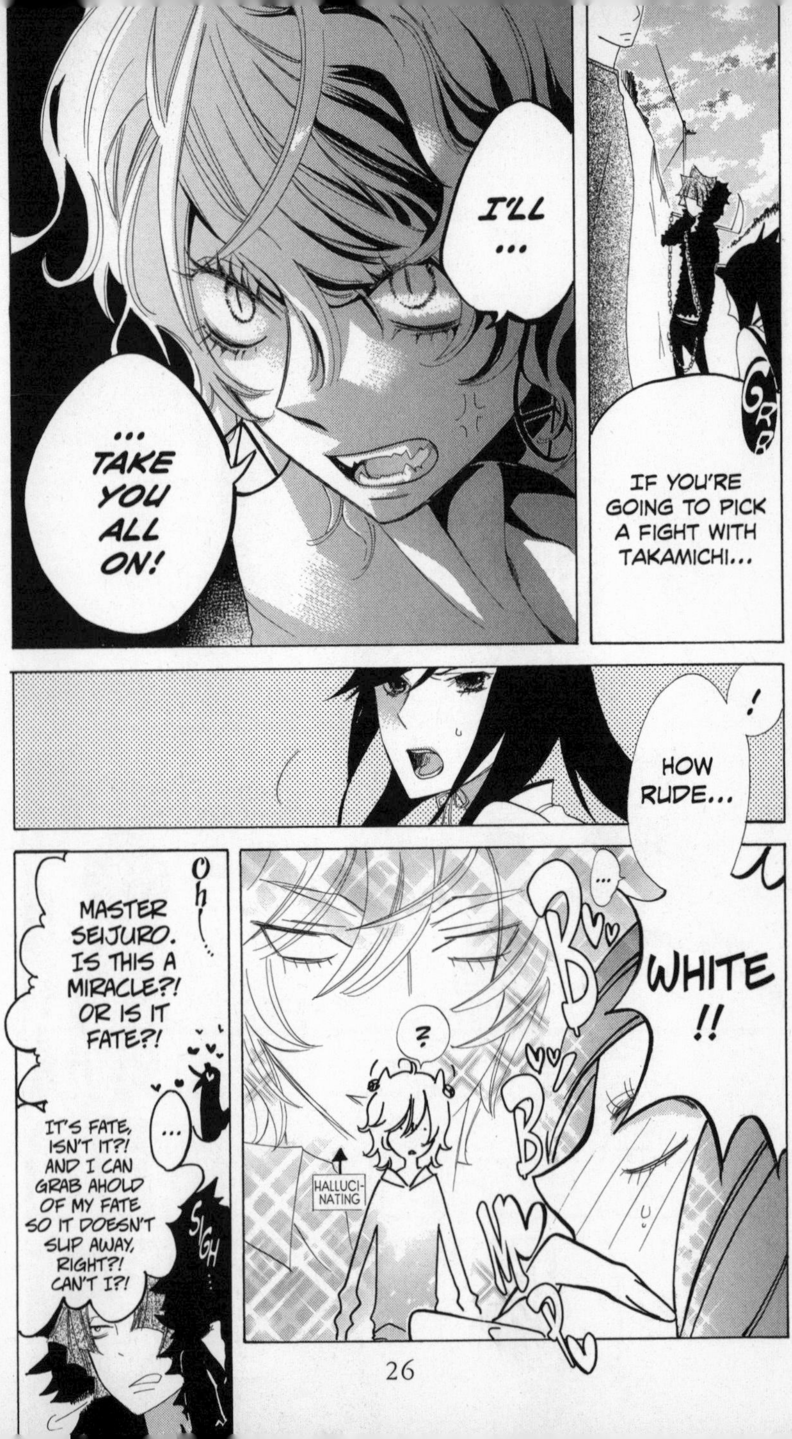
GRR
IF YOU'RE GOING TO PICK A FIGHT WITH TAKAMICHI...
I'LL ...
... TAKE YOU ALL ON!
!
HOW RUDE...
...
WHITE !!
?
HALLUCI-NATING
Oh...
MASTER SEIJURO. IS THIS A MIRACLE?! OR IS IT FATE?!
...
IT'S FATE, ISN'T IT?! AND I CAN GRAB AHOLD OF MY FATE SO IT DOESN'T SLIP AWAY, RIGHT?! CAN'T I?!
SIGH...

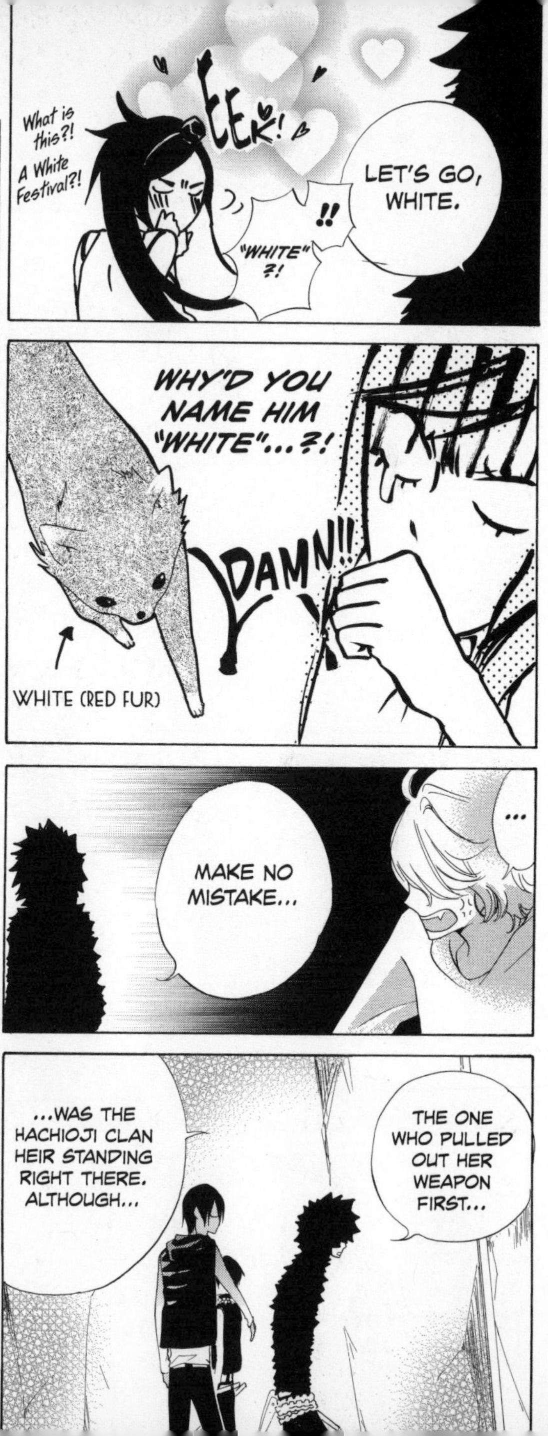
LET'S GO, WHITE.
!!
EEK!
"WHITE" ?!
What is this?! A White Festival?!
WHY'D YOU NAME HIM "WHITE"...?!
DAMN!!
WHITE (RED FUR)
...
MAKE NO MISTAKE...
THE ONE WHO PULLED OUT HER WEAPON FIRST...
...WAS THE HACHIOJI CLAN HEIR STANDING RIGHT THERE. ALTHOUGH...

For starters...

Hey there! Tobina here!

I've learned how to ink dark areas!!

I don't know if I'm doing a good job of it though.

I tried to start this note off all casual, but now I'm totally embarrassed.

Anyway, Jiu Jiu vol. 3 is full of all kinds of new characters, but unlike the joke illustration in the table of contents, the story itself is pretty serious.

Although in some ways, the male family heads all look comical...

They should joke around more.

Anyway, here begins a very long day...

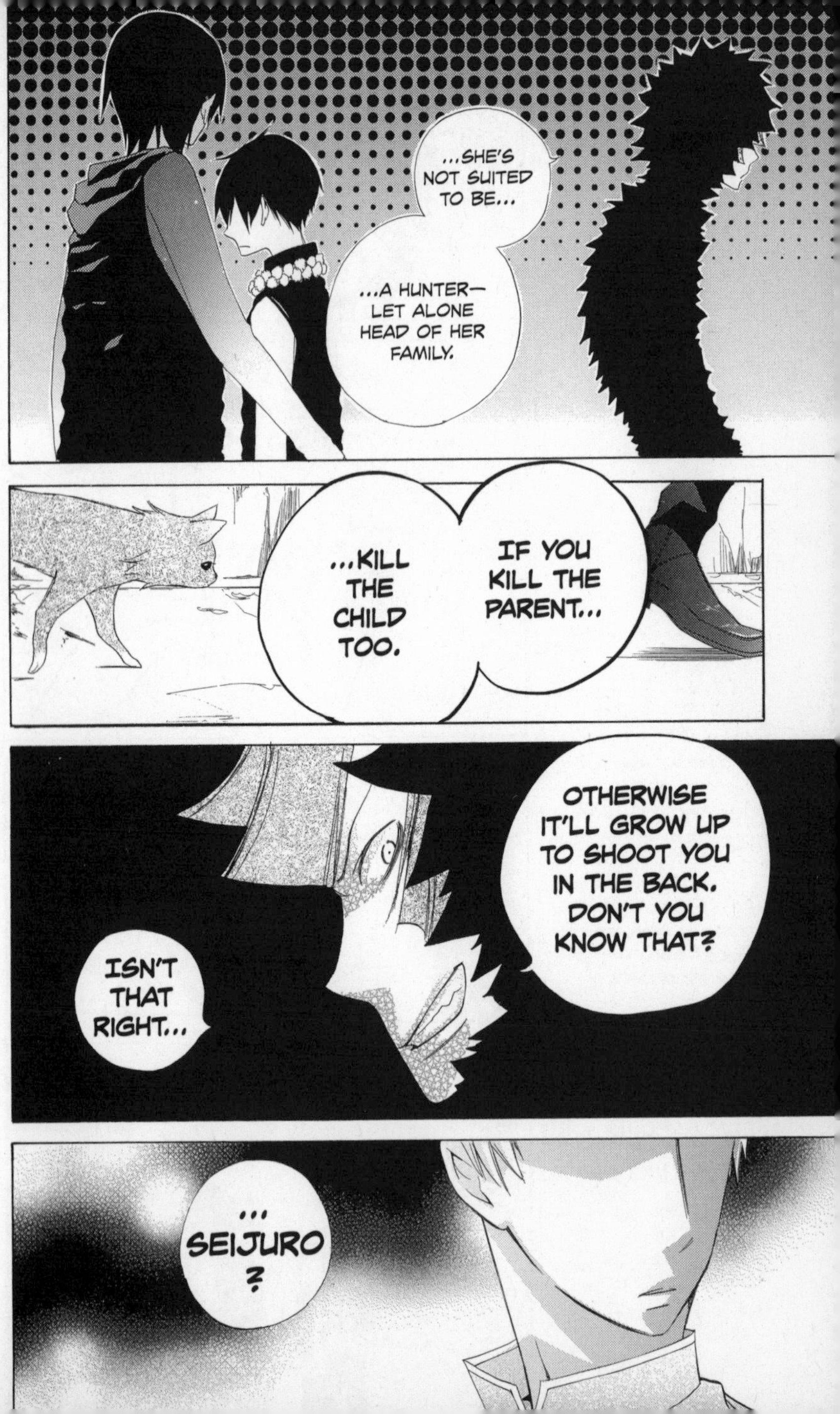
...SHE'S NOT SUITED TO BE...
...A HUNTER—LET ALONE HEAD OF HER FAMILY.
IF YOU KILL THE PARENT...
...KILL THE CHILD TOO.
OTHERWISE IT'LL GROW UP TO SHOOT YOU IN THE BACK. DON'T YOU KNOW THAT?
ISN'T THAT RIGHT...
... SEIJURO ?

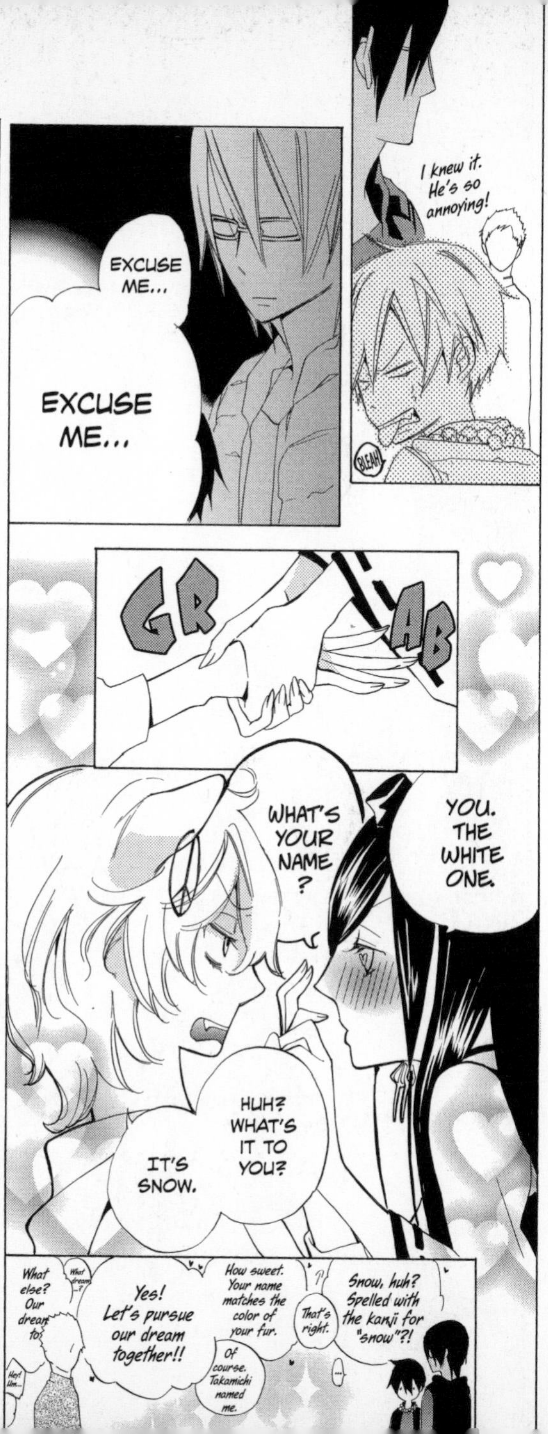
I knew it. He's so annoying!
BLEAH
EXCUSE ME...
EXCUSE ME...
GR
AB
YOU. THE WHITE ONE.
WHAT'S YOUR NAME?
HUH? WHAT'S IT TO YOU?
IT'S SNOW.
Snow, huh? Spelled with the kanji for "snow"?!
...
That's right.
How sweet. Your name matches the color of your fur.
Of course. Takamichi named me.
Yes! Let's pursue our dream together!!
What dream...?
What else? Our dream to...
Hey! Um...

2010, June 29.
A dog came to my house.

Back in vol. 2 I wrote that I only received two letters. Two!! Two?!

Sorry! To tell the truth, I've been getting tons of love letters!! Thank you, everybody!!

And after vol. 2 came out, I got even more love letters—and questions too. Thank you, thank you.

But!

I need permission to repeat your questions here, so I'm only going to answer the ones I get permission for.

Yes, as always, I forgot to do my homework...

There were lots of interesting questions, so it's too bad. But I'll try to answer some in vol. 4 if I get the chance!

I'll write more later, but if you don't mind having your questions printed here, please write a little note in your letter telling me, "Sure, I don't mind!"

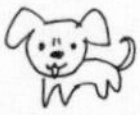 ← My dog.

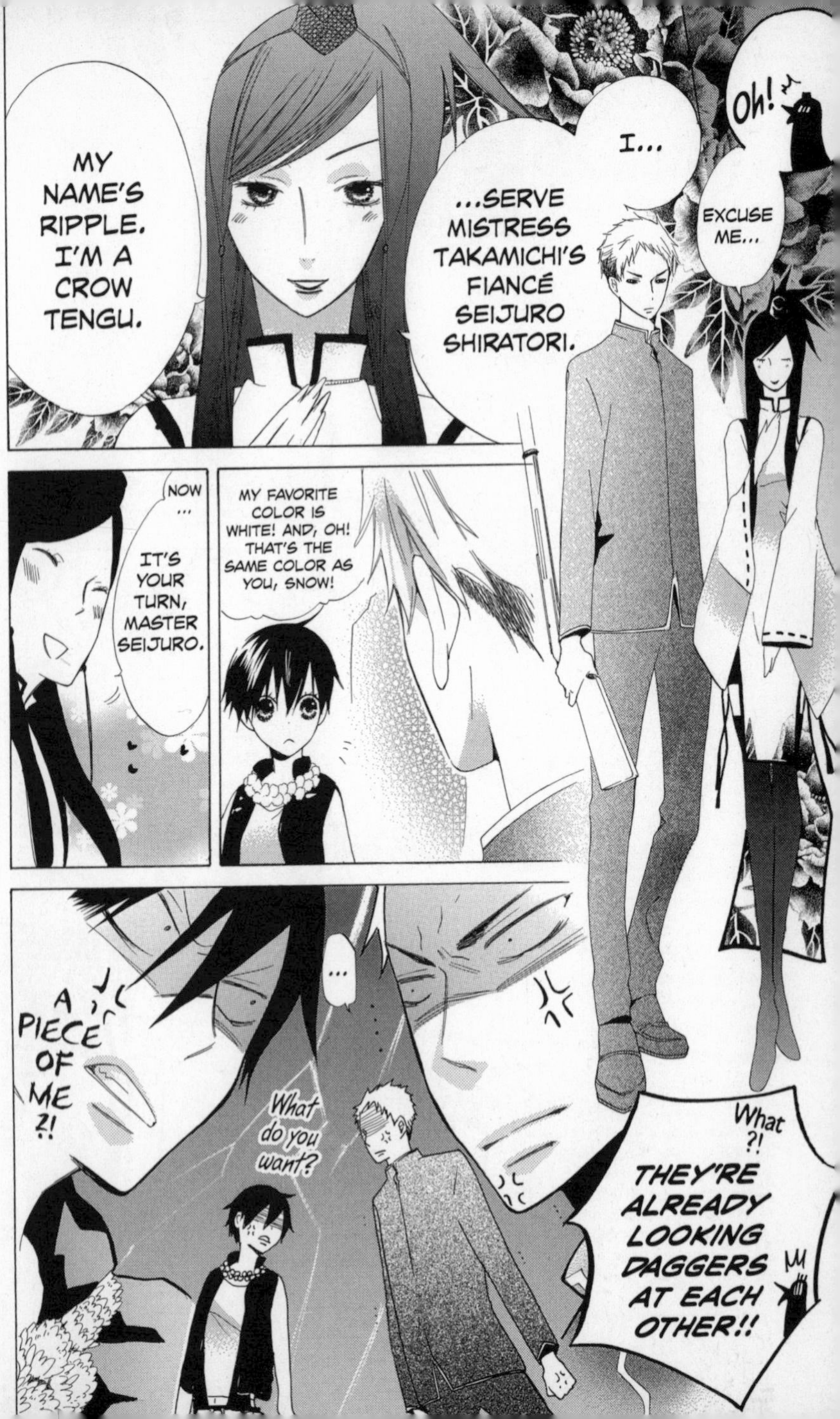
Oh!
EXCUSE ME...
I...
...SERVE MISTRESS TAKAMICHI'S FIANCÉ SEIJURO SHIRATORI.
MY NAME'S RIPPLE. I'M A CROW TENGU.
MY FAVORITE COLOR IS WHITE! AND, OH! THAT'S THE SAME COLOR AS YOU, SNOW!
NOW ...
IT'S YOUR TURN, MASTER SEIJURO.
What ?!
THEY'RE ALREADY LOOKING DAGGERS AT EACH OTHER!!
...
What do you want?
A PIECE OF ME ?!

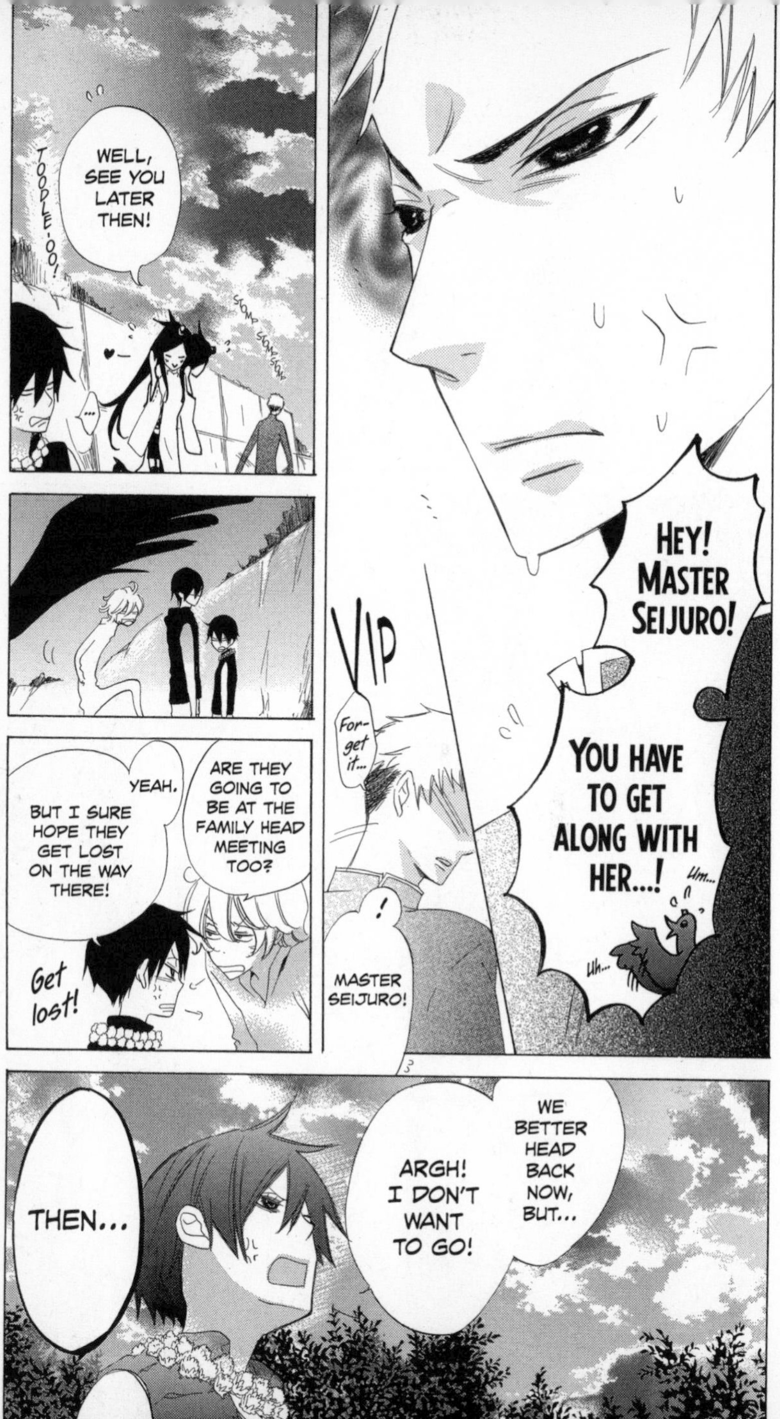
HEY! MASTER SEIJURO!
YOU HAVE TO GET ALONG WITH HER...!
Um...
Uh...
VIP
Forget it...
!
MASTER SEIJURO!
WELL, SEE YOU LATER THEN!
TOODLE-OO!
STOMP STOMP STOMP
...
ARE THEY GOING TO BE AT THE FAMILY HEAD MEETING TOO?
YEAH.
BUT I SURE HOPE THEY GET LOST ON THE WAY THERE!
Get lost!
WE BETTER HEAD BACK NOW, BUT...
ARGH! I DON'T WANT TO GO!
THEN...

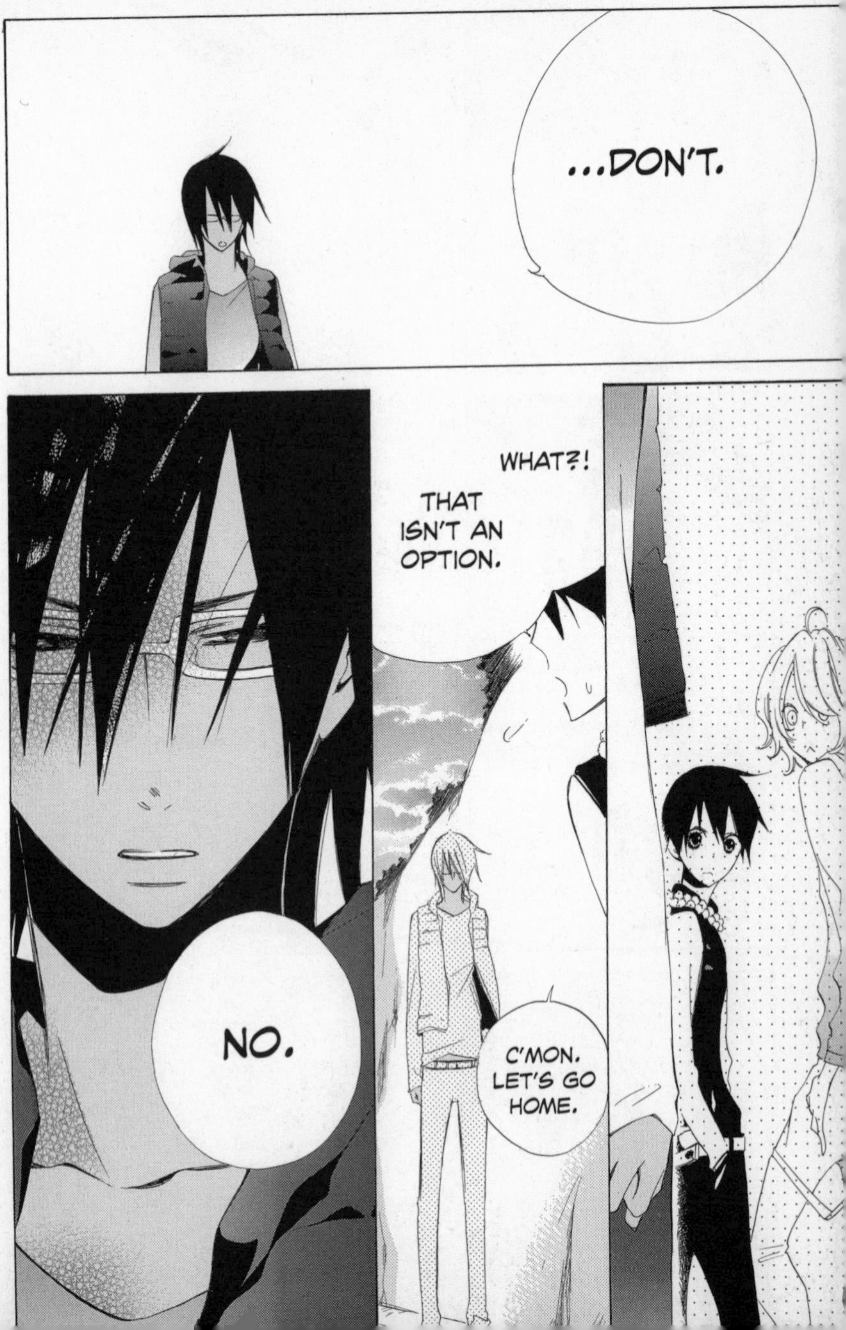
...DON'T.
WHAT?!
THAT ISN'T AN OPTION.
C'MON. LET'S GO HOME.
NO.

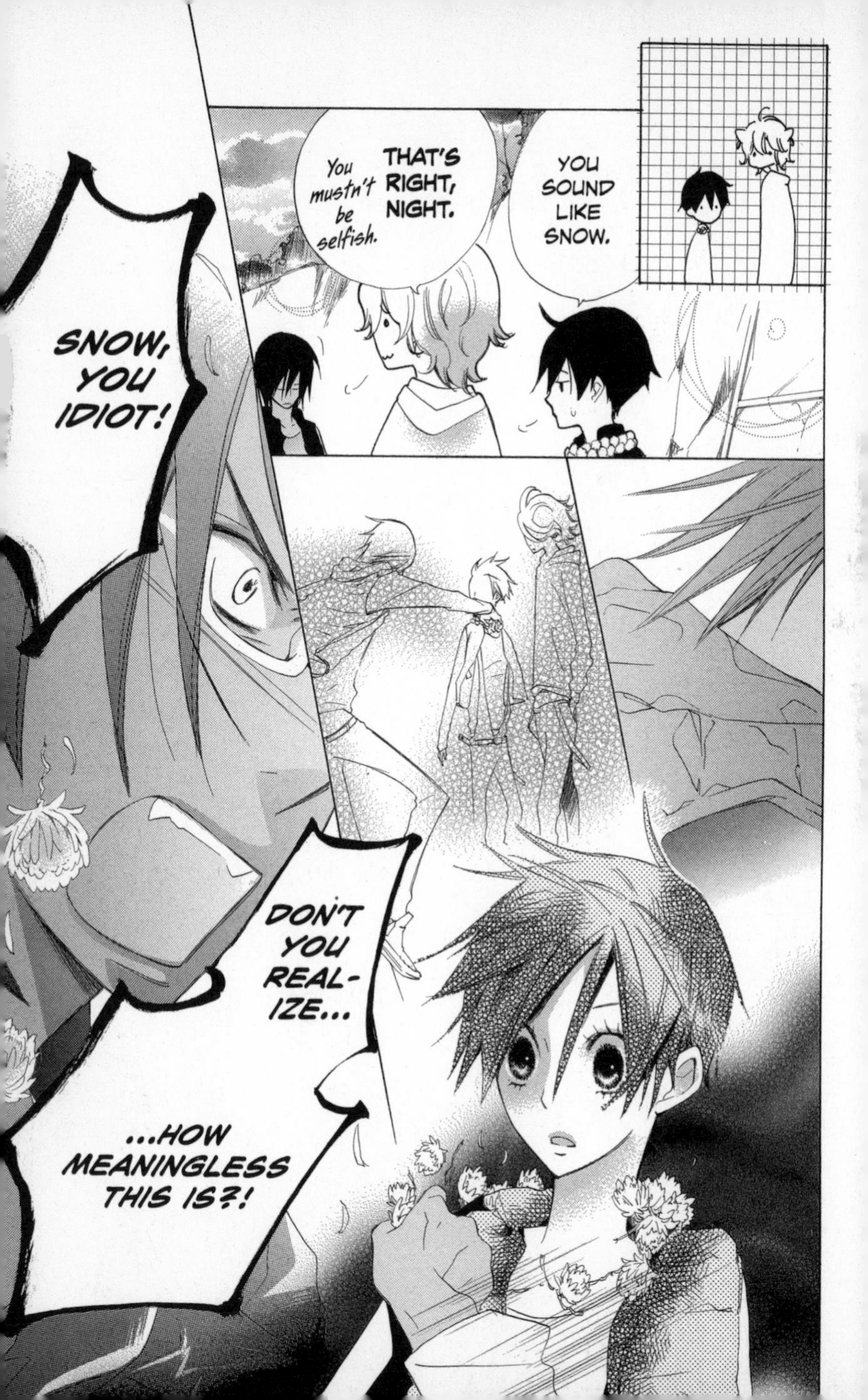

YOU SOUND LIKE SNOW.
THAT'S RIGHT, NIGHT.
You mustn't be selfish.
SNOW, YOU IDIOT!
DON'T YOU REAL-IZE...
...HOW MEANINGLESS THIS IS?!

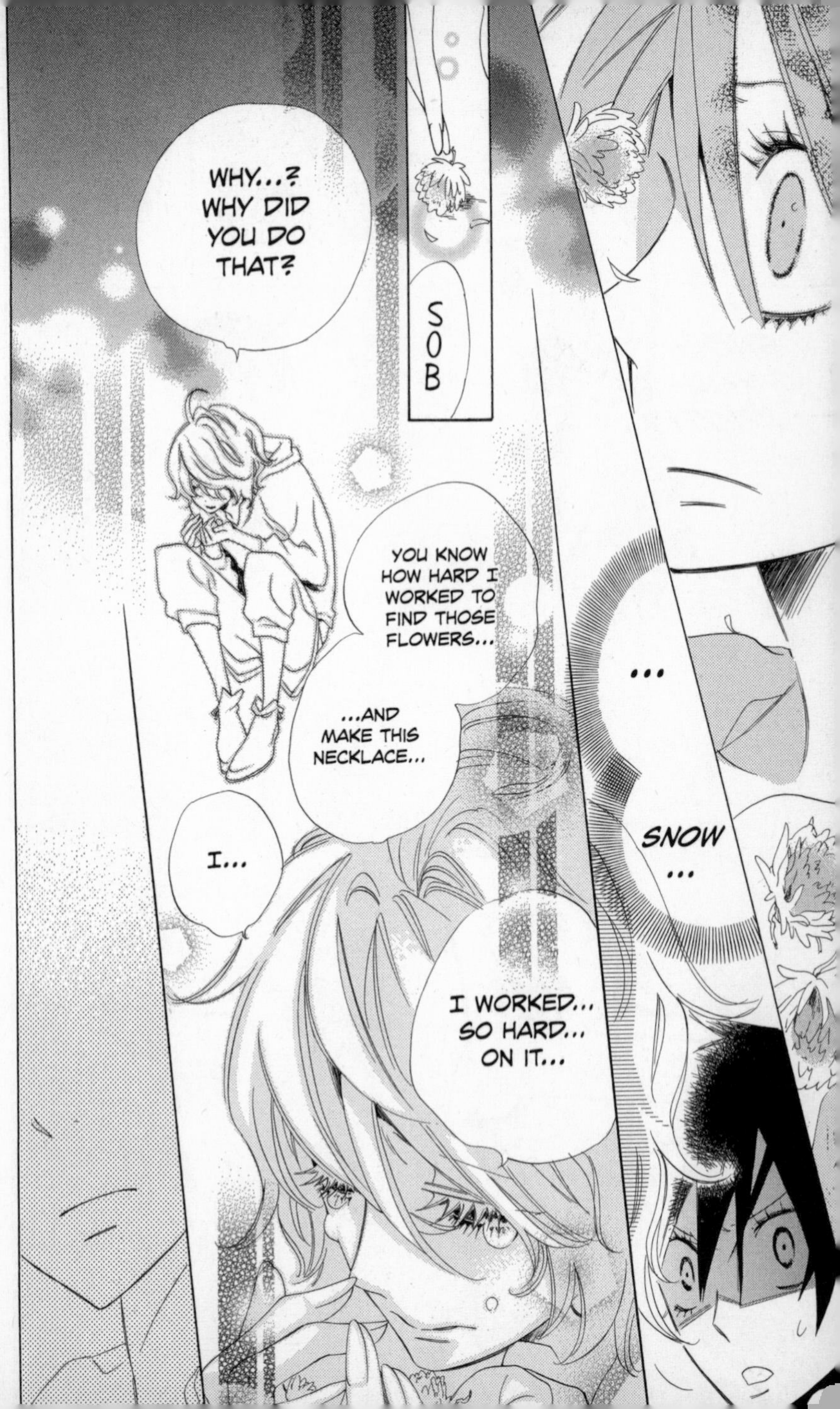
...
SNOW...
SOB
WHY...? WHY DID YOU DO THAT?
YOU KNOW HOW HARD I WORKED TO FIND THOSE FLOWERS...
...AND MAKE THIS NECKLACE...
I...
I WORKED... SO HARD... ON IT...

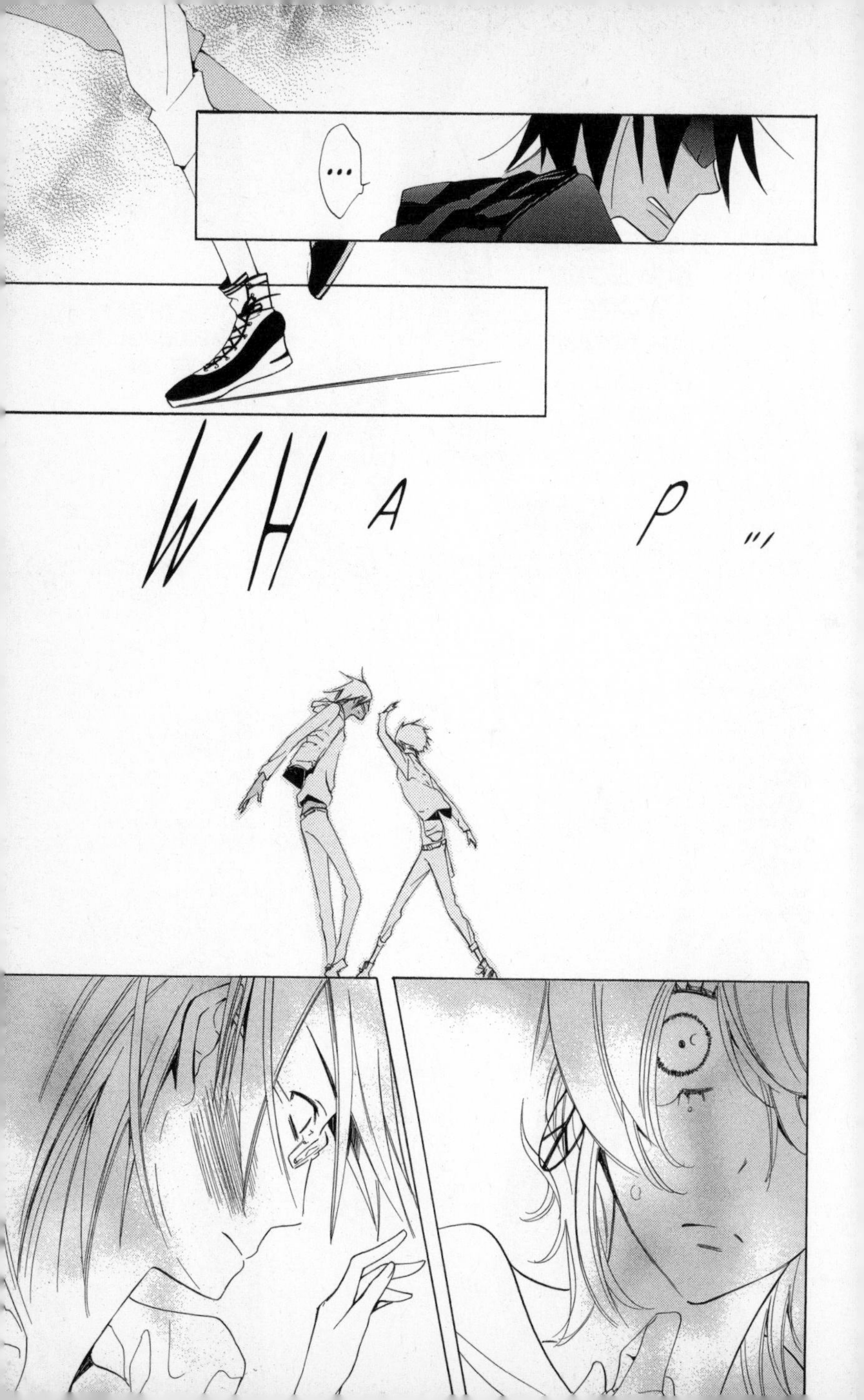
...
WHAP!!

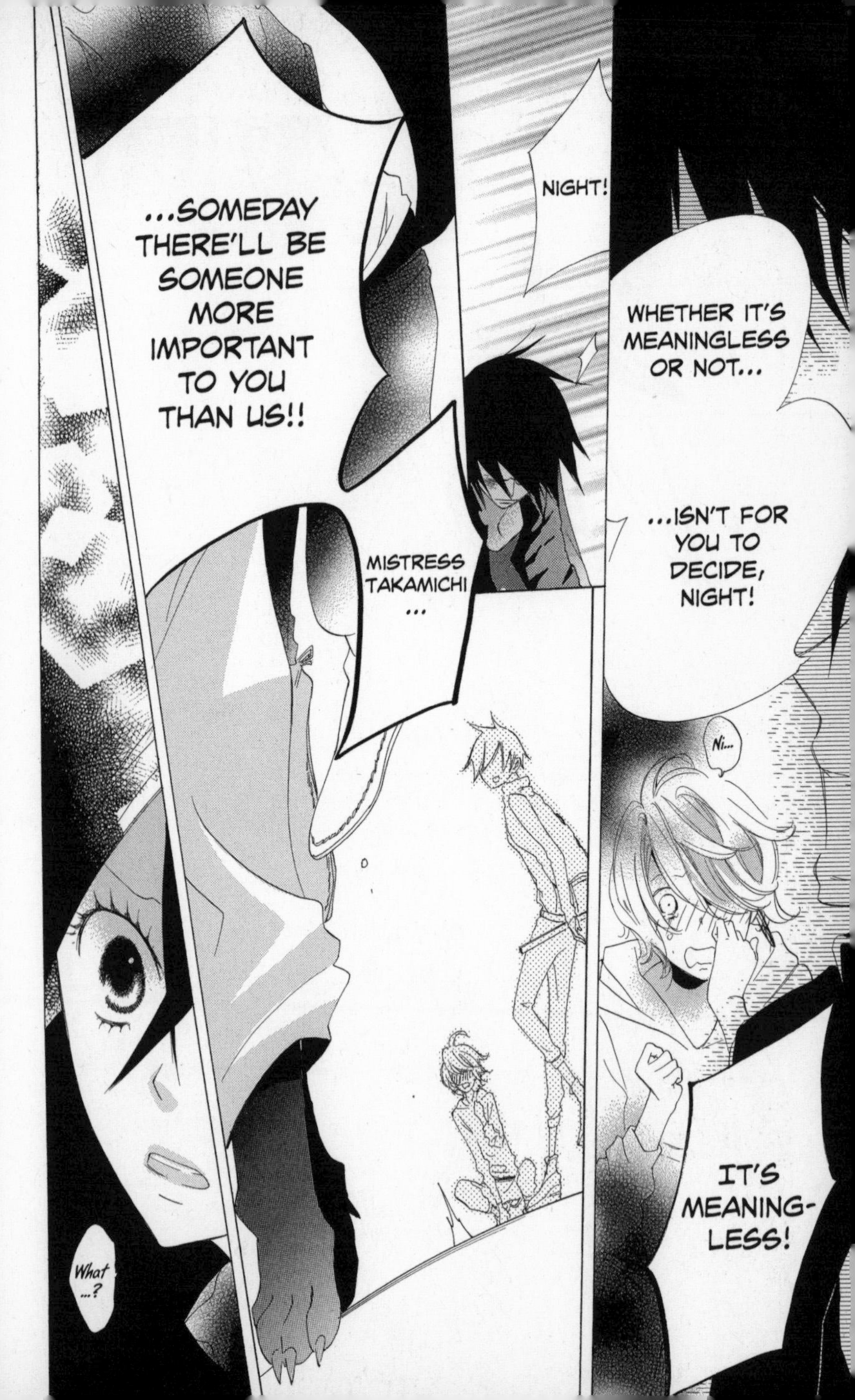
WHETHER IT'S MEANINGLESS OR NOT...
...ISN'T FOR YOU TO DECIDE, NIGHT!
Ni...
IT'S MEANING-LESS!
NIGHT!
MISTRESS TAKAMICHI ...
...SOMEDAY THERE'LL BE SOMEONE MORE IMPORTANT TO YOU THAN US!!
What ...?

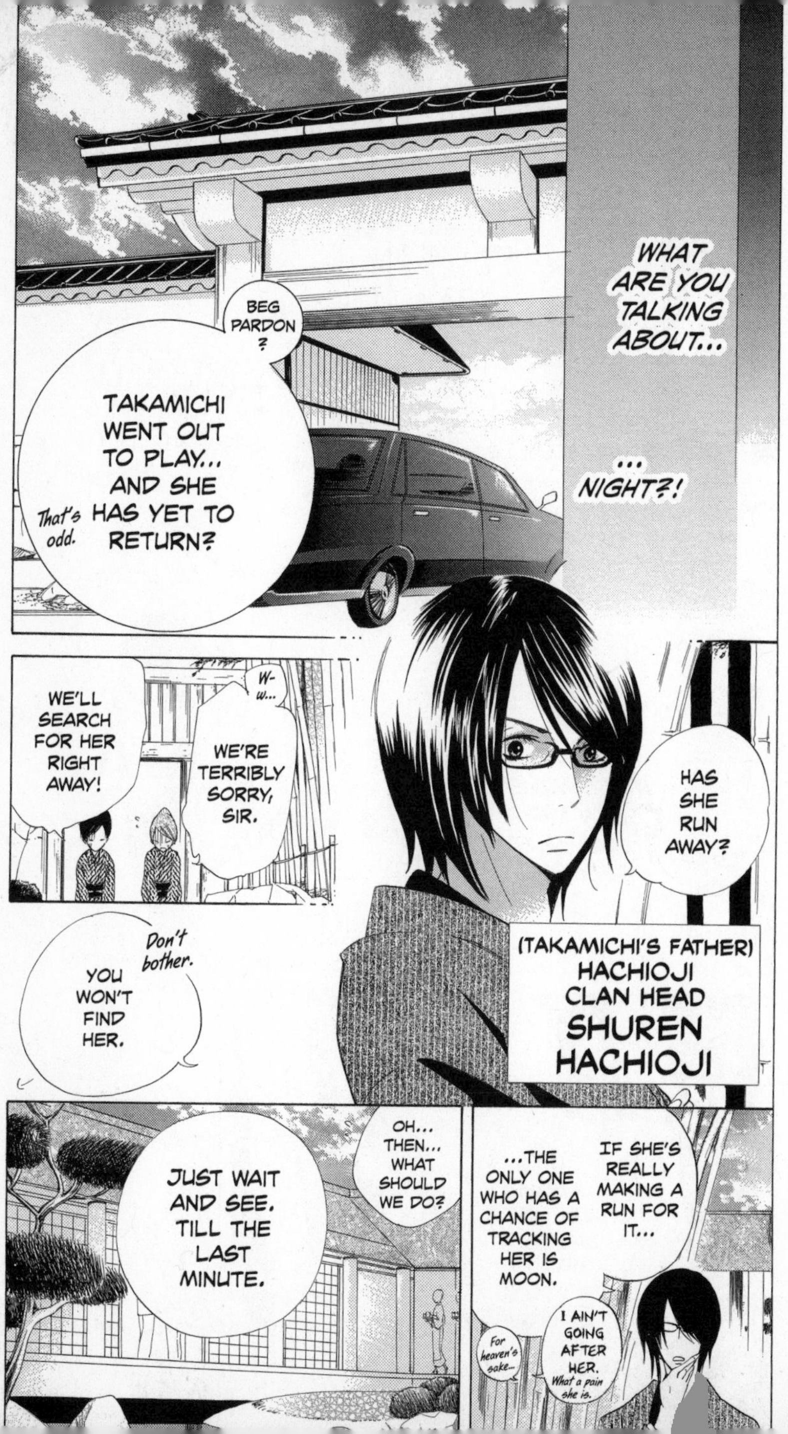

WHAT ARE YOU TALKING ABOUT...
BEG PARDON?
...NIGHT?!
TAKAMICHI WENT OUT TO PLAY... AND SHE HAS YET TO RETURN?
That's odd.
HAS SHE RUN AWAY?
(TAKAMICHI'S FATHER) HACHIOJI CLAN HEAD SHUREN HACHIOJI
W-w...
WE'RE TERRIBLY SORRY, SIR.
WE'LL SEARCH FOR HER RIGHT AWAY!
Don't bother.
YOU WON'T FIND HER.
IF SHE'S REALLY MAKING A RUN FOR IT...
...THE ONLY ONE WHO HAS A CHANCE OF TRACKING HER IS MOON.
I AIN'T GOING AFTER HER.
What a pain she is.
For heaven's sake...
OH... THEN... WHAT SHOULD WE DO?
JUST WAIT AND SEE. TILL THE LAST MINUTE.

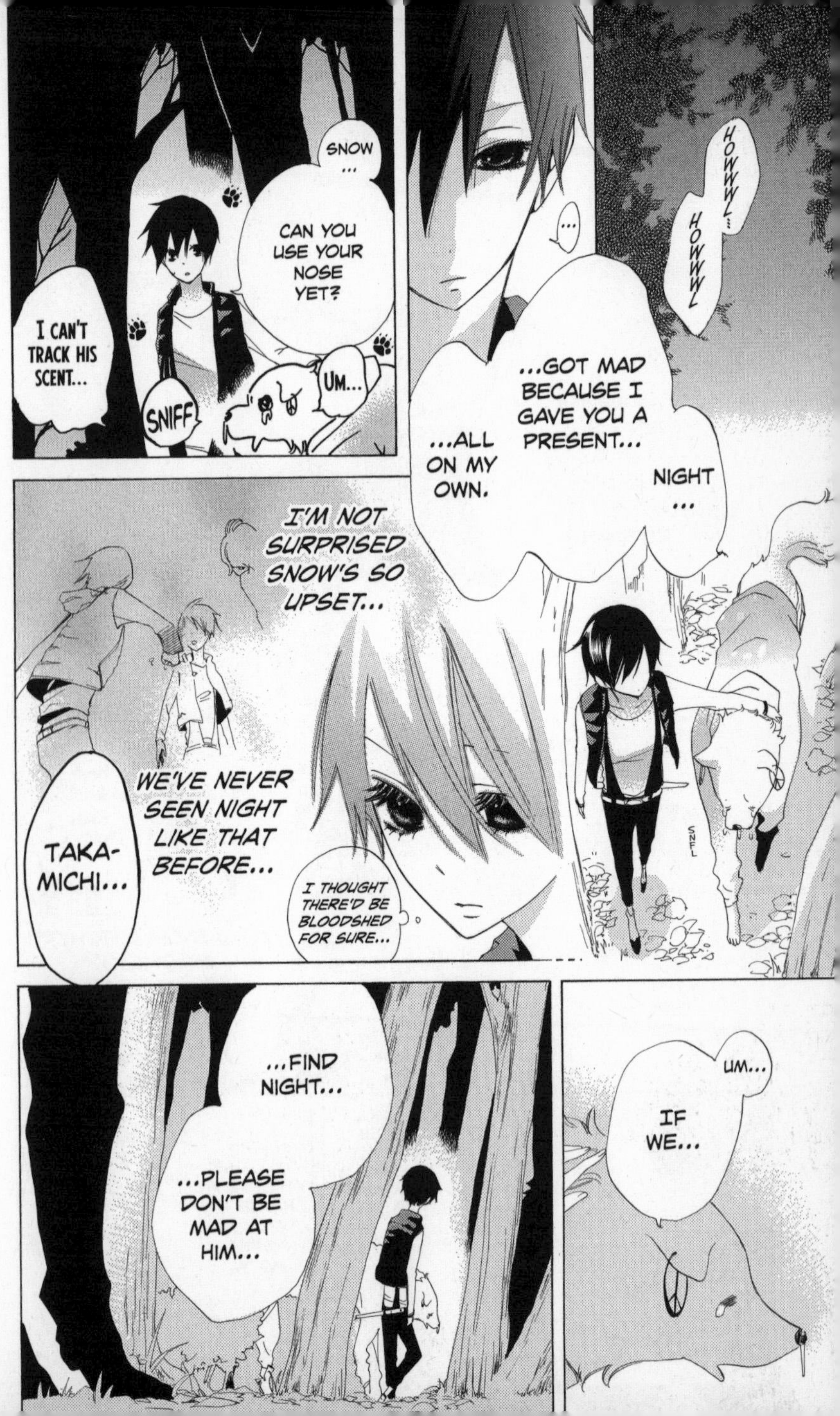
HOWWWL... HOWWWL
...
NIGHT ...
...GOT MAD BECAUSE I GAVE YOU A PRESENT...
...ALL ON MY OWN.
SNOW ...
CAN YOU USE YOUR NOSE YET?
UM...
SNIFF
I CAN'T TRACK HIS SCENT...
I'M NOT SURPRISED SNOW'S SO UPSET...
SNFL
I THOUGHT THERE'D BE BLOODSHED FOR SURE...
WE'VE NEVER SEEN NIGHT LIKE THAT BEFORE...
TAKA-MICHI...
UM...
IF WE...
...FIND NIGHT...
...PLEASE DON'T BE MAD AT HIM...

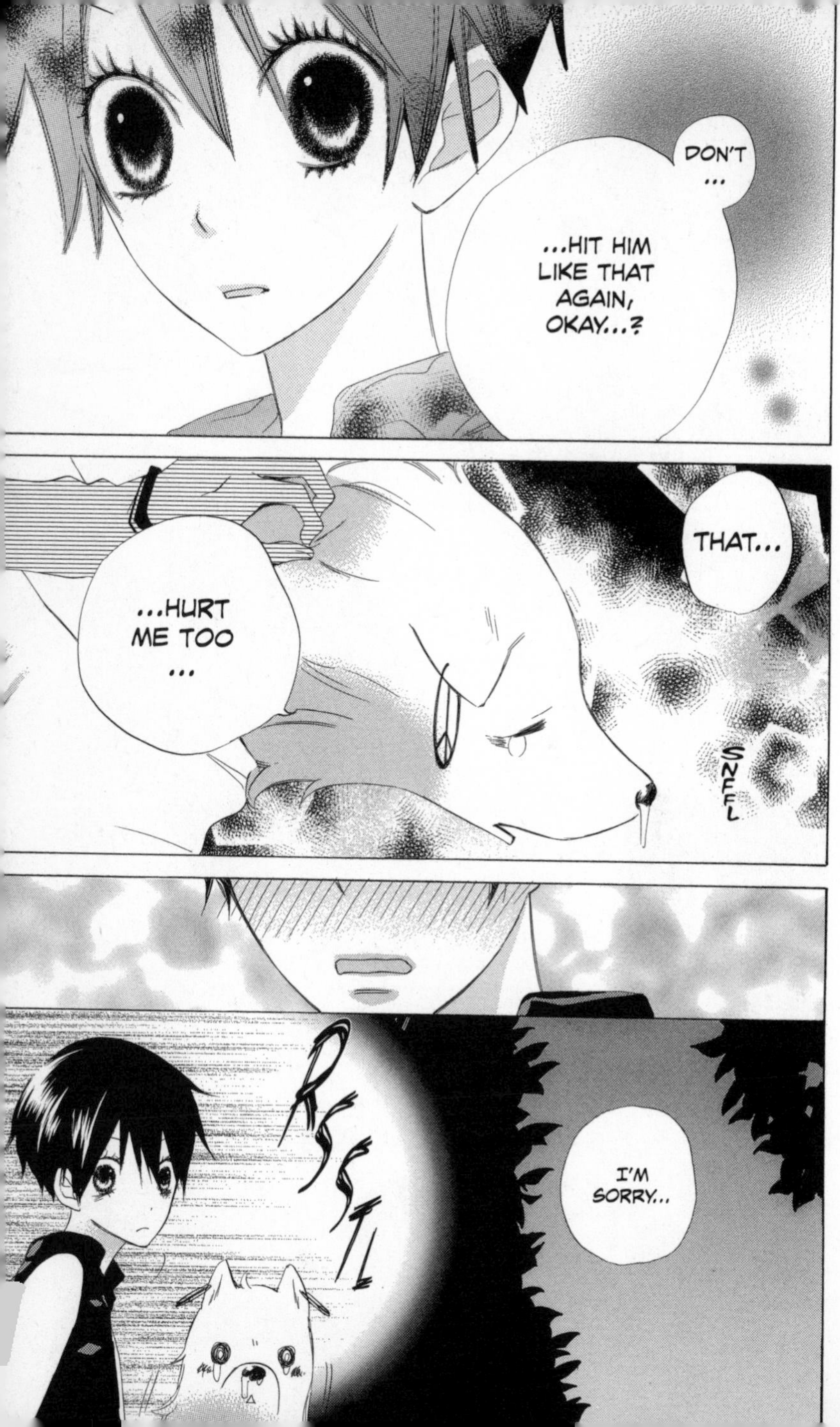
DON'T ...
...HIT HIM LIKE THAT AGAIN, OKAY...?
THAT...
SNFFL
...HURT ME TOO ...
I'M SORRY...
RSTL

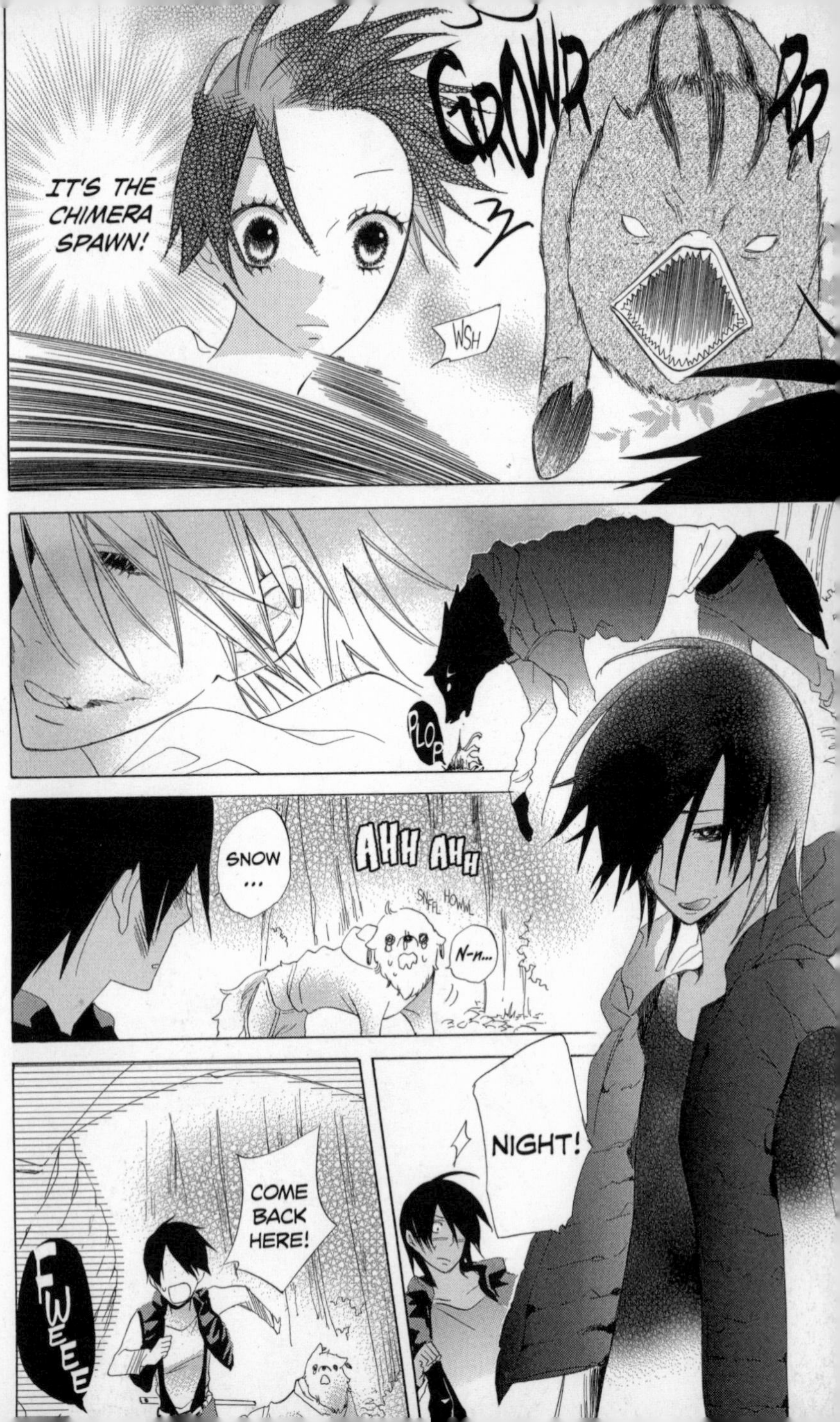
GROWR RR
IT'S THE CHIMERA SPAWN!
WSH
PLOP
AHH AHH
N-n...
HOWWL
SNFFL
SNOW ...
NIGHT!
COME BACK HERE!
FWEEE

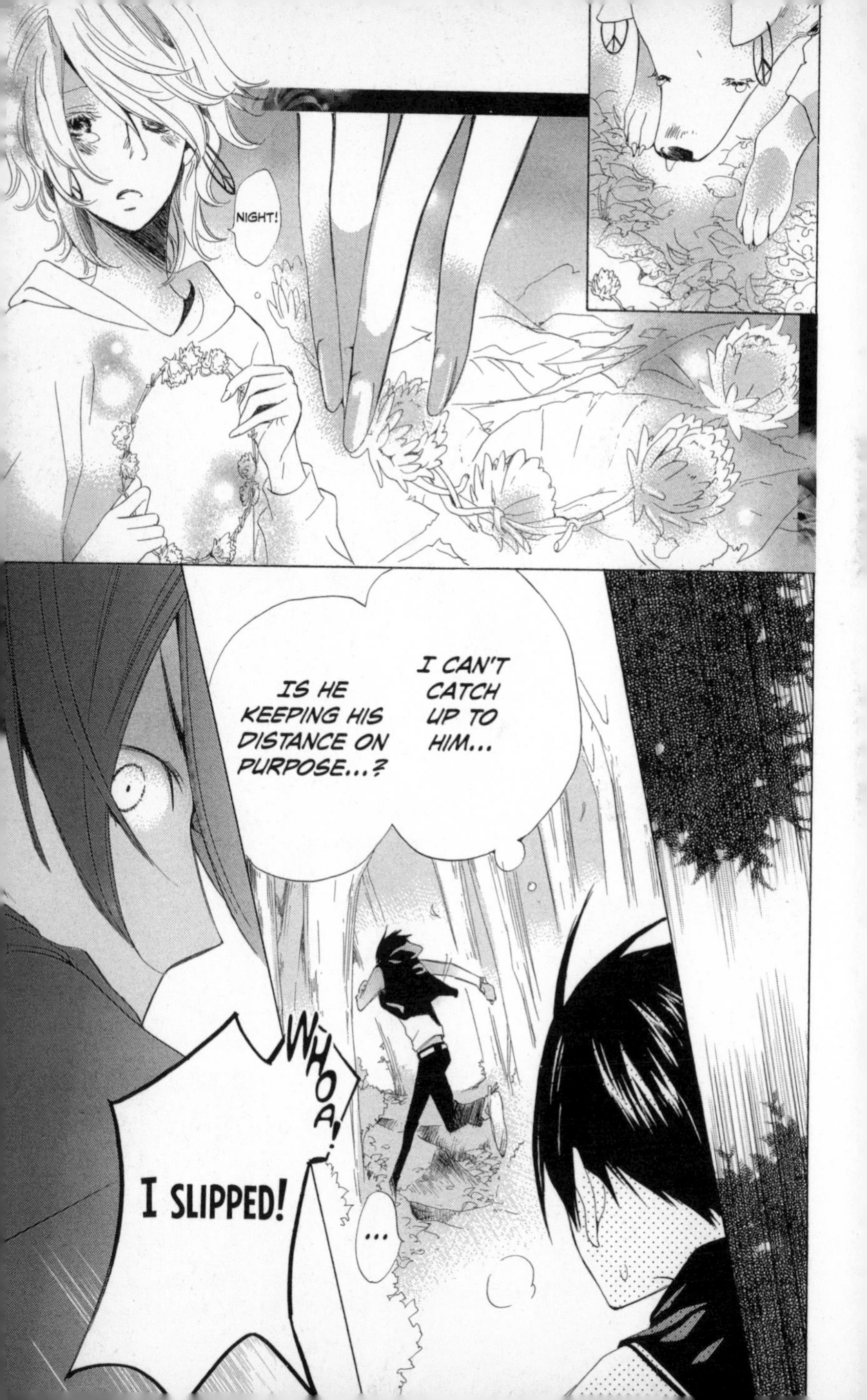
NIGHT!
I CAN'T CATCH UP TO HIM...
IS HE KEEPING HIS DISTANCE ON PURPOSE...?
WHOA!
I SLIPPED!
...

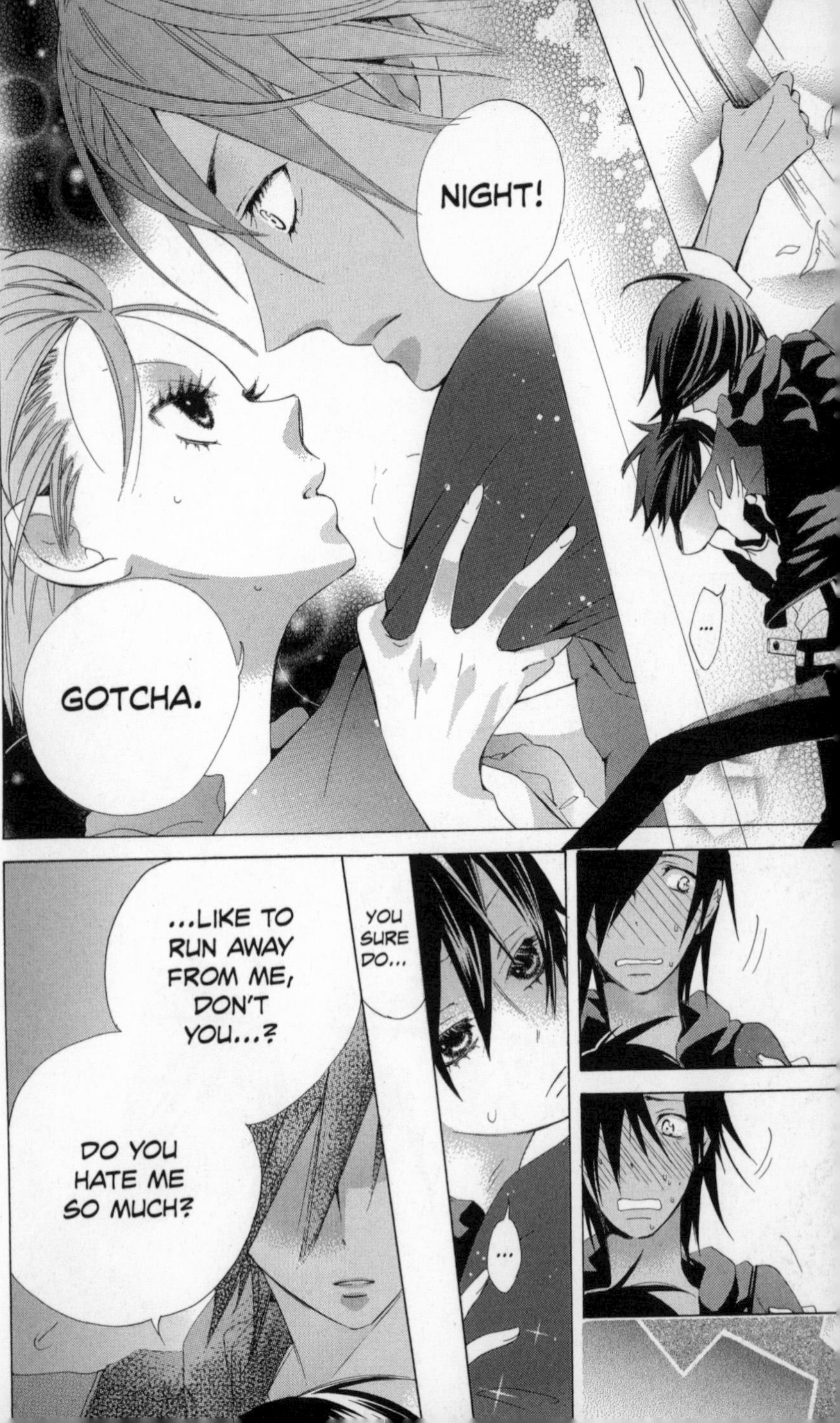
NIGHT!
...
GOTCHA.
YOU SURE DO...
...LIKE TO RUN AWAY FROM ME, DON'T YOU...?
DO YOU HATE ME SO MUCH?
...

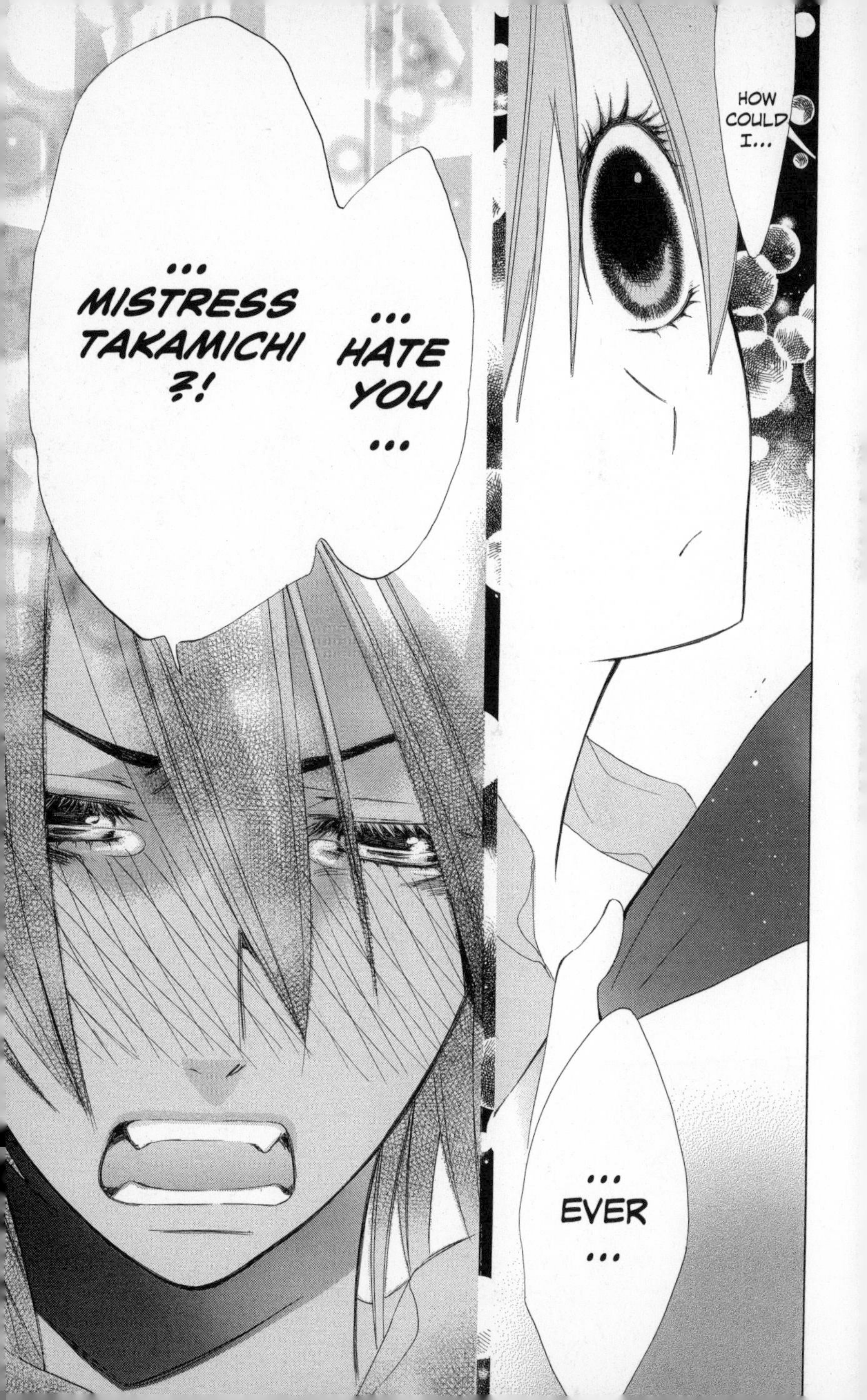
HOW COULD I...
...EVER...
...HATE YOU...
...MISTRESS TAKAMICHI?!

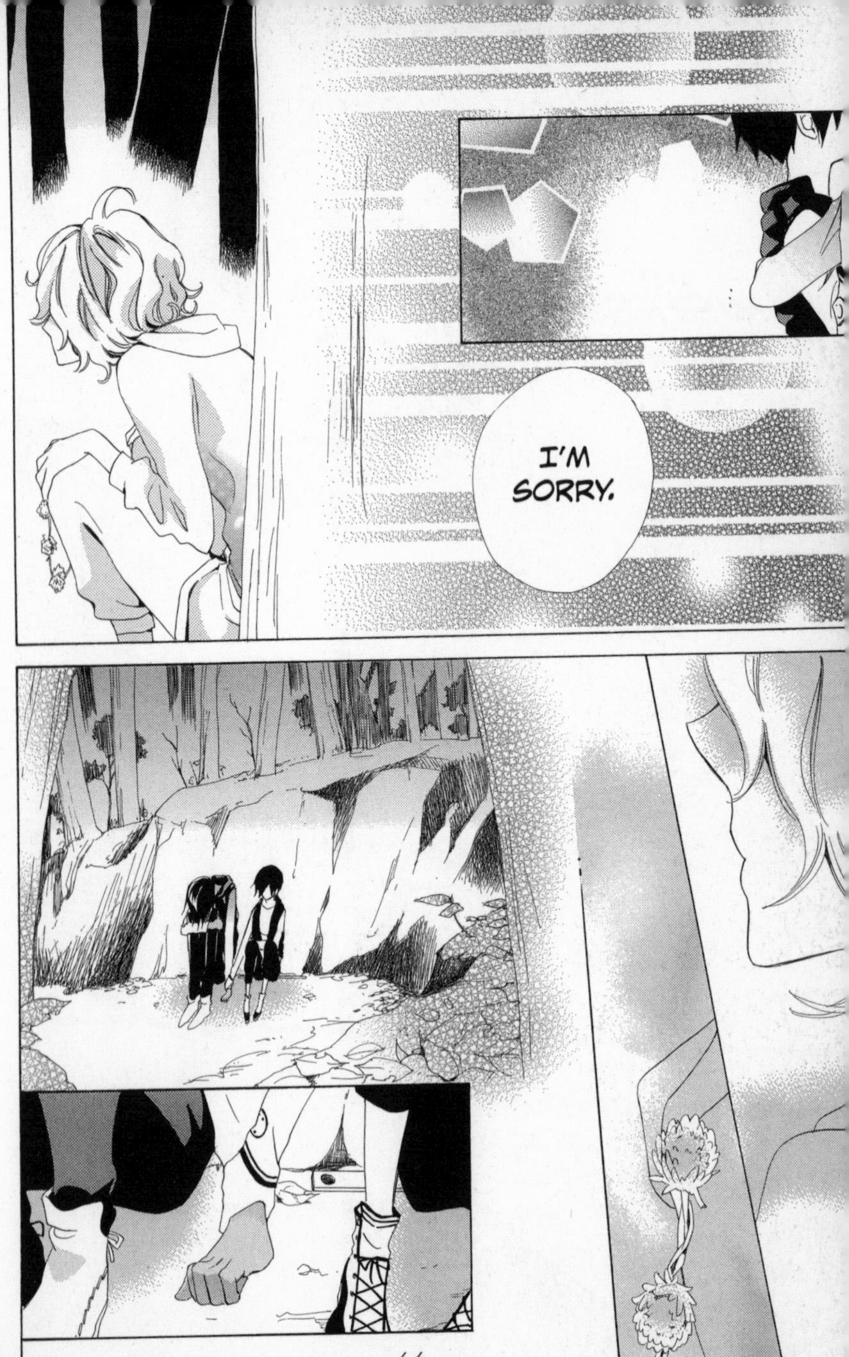
I'M SORRY.

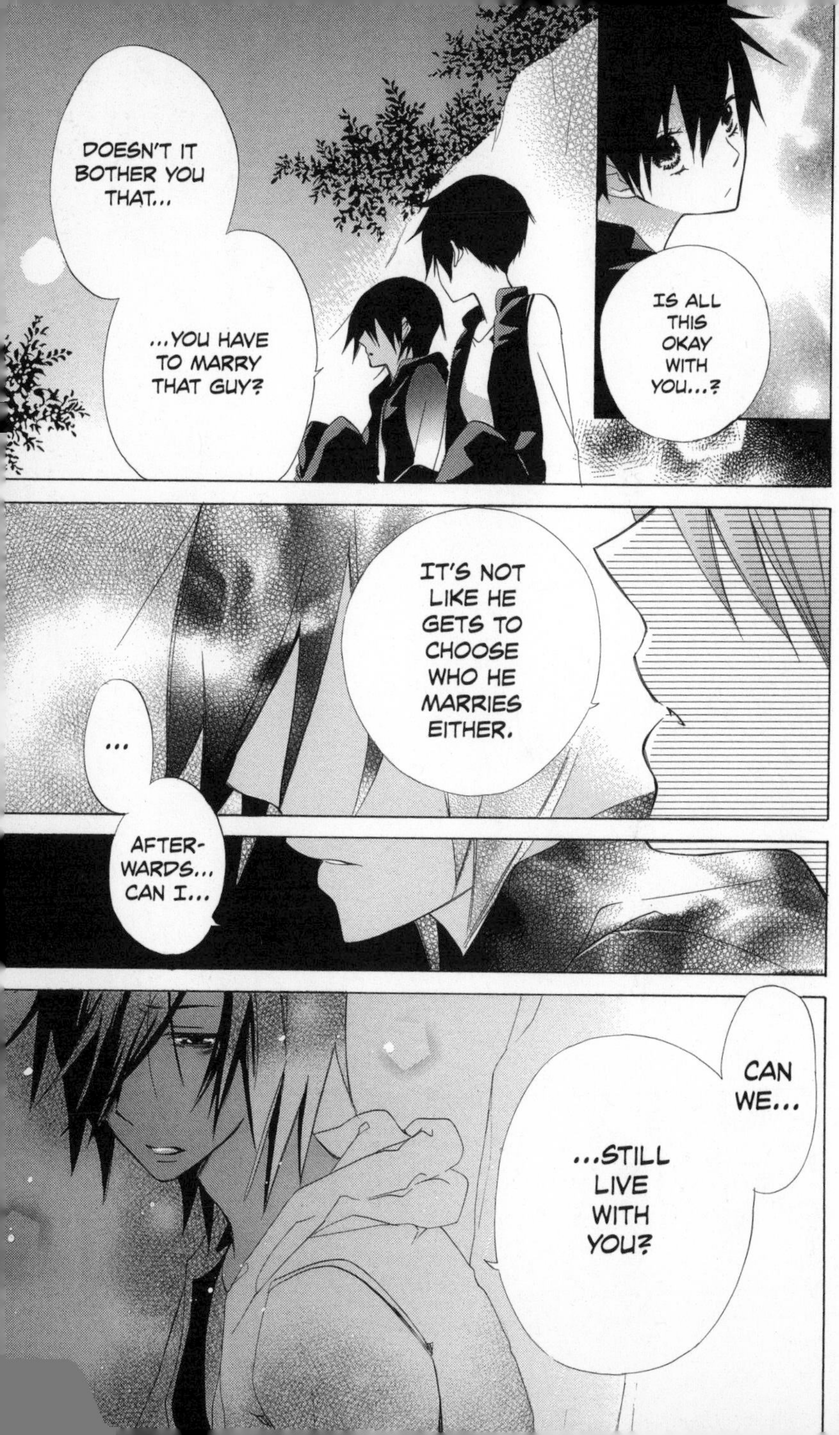
IS ALL THIS OKAY WITH YOU...?
DOESN'T IT BOTHER YOU THAT...
...YOU HAVE TO MARRY THAT GUY?
IT'S NOT LIKE HE GETS TO CHOOSE WHO HE MARRIES EITHER.
...
AFTER-WARDS... CAN I...
CAN WE...
...STILL LIVE WITH YOU?

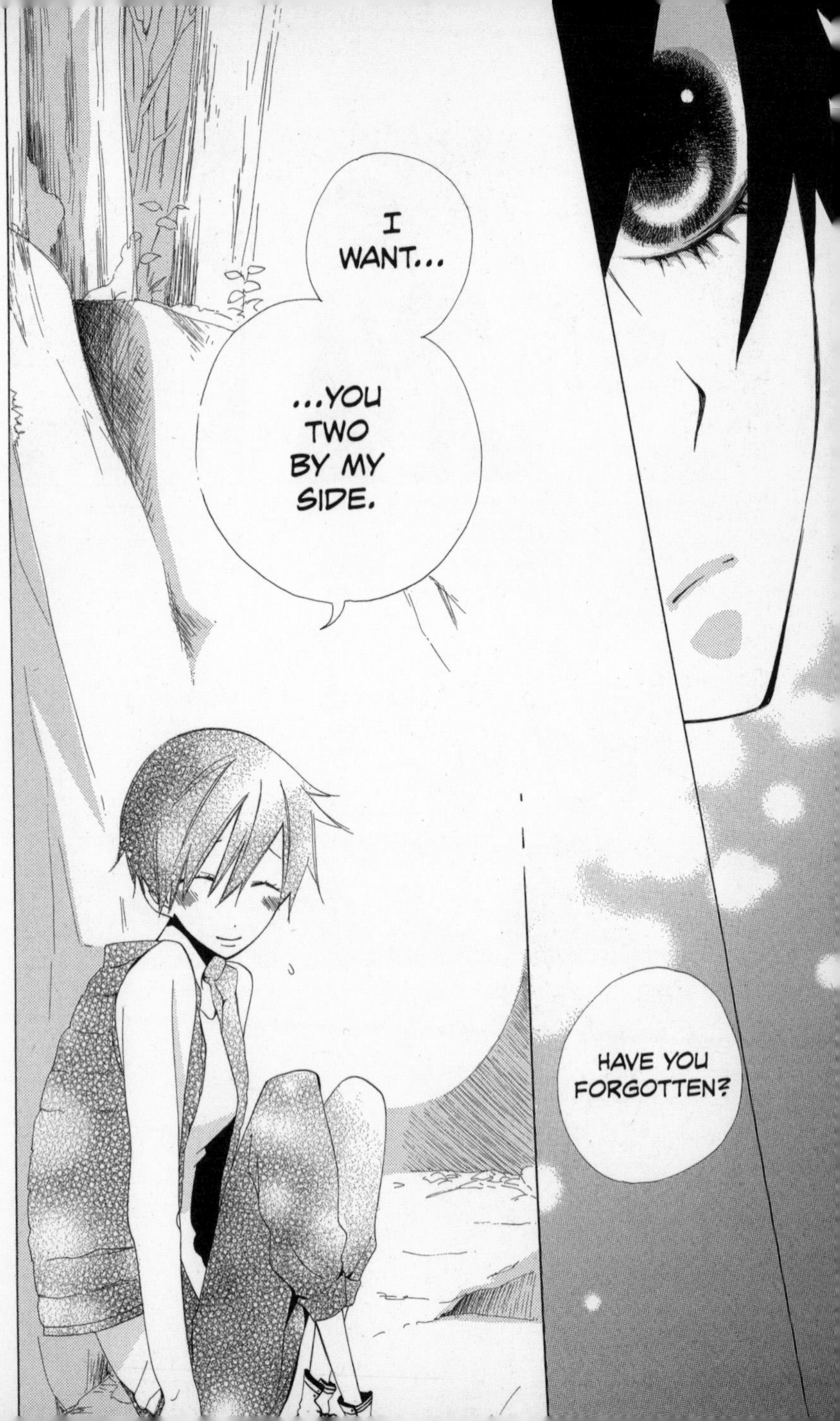
I WANT...
...YOU TWO BY MY SIDE.
HAVE YOU FORGOTTEN?

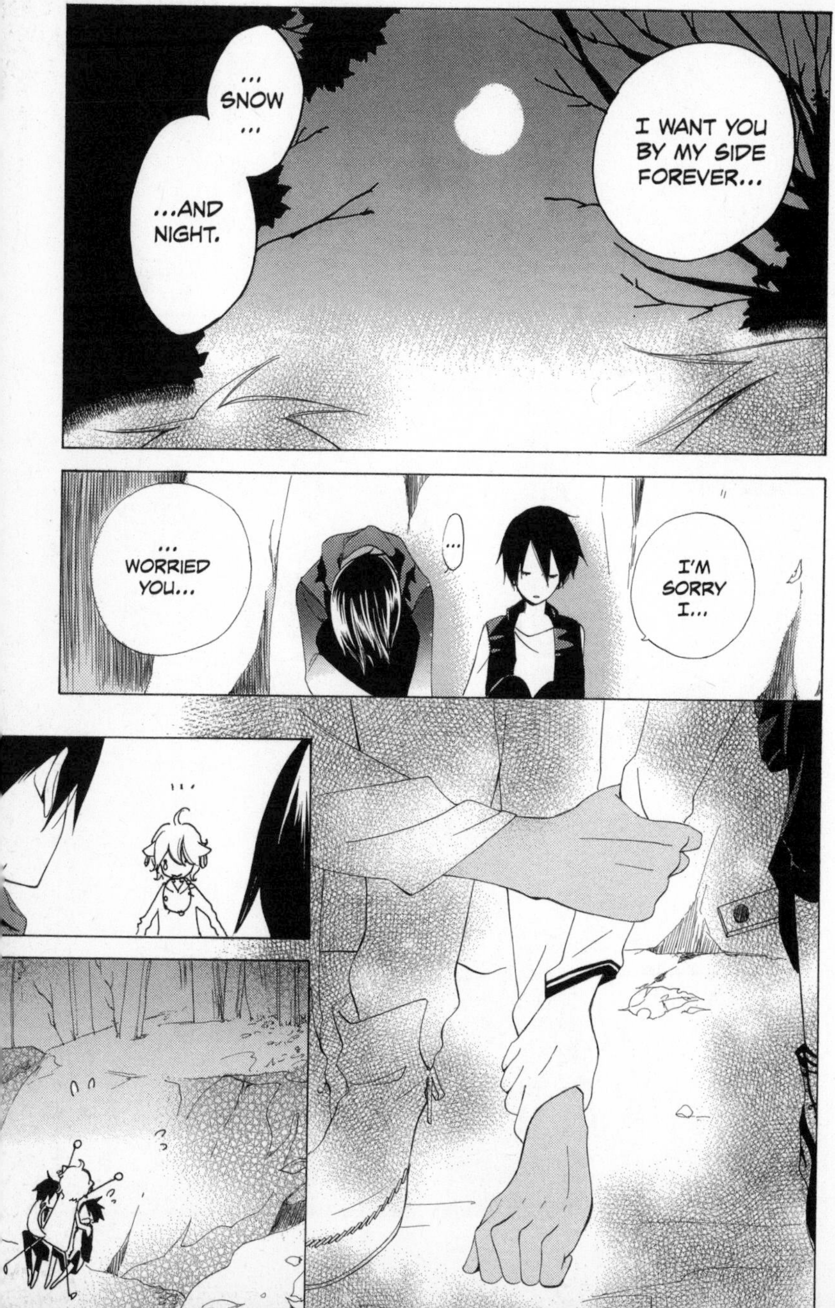
I WANT YOU BY MY SIDE FOREVER...
... SNOW ...
...AND NIGHT.
I'M SORRY I...
...
... WORRIED YOU...

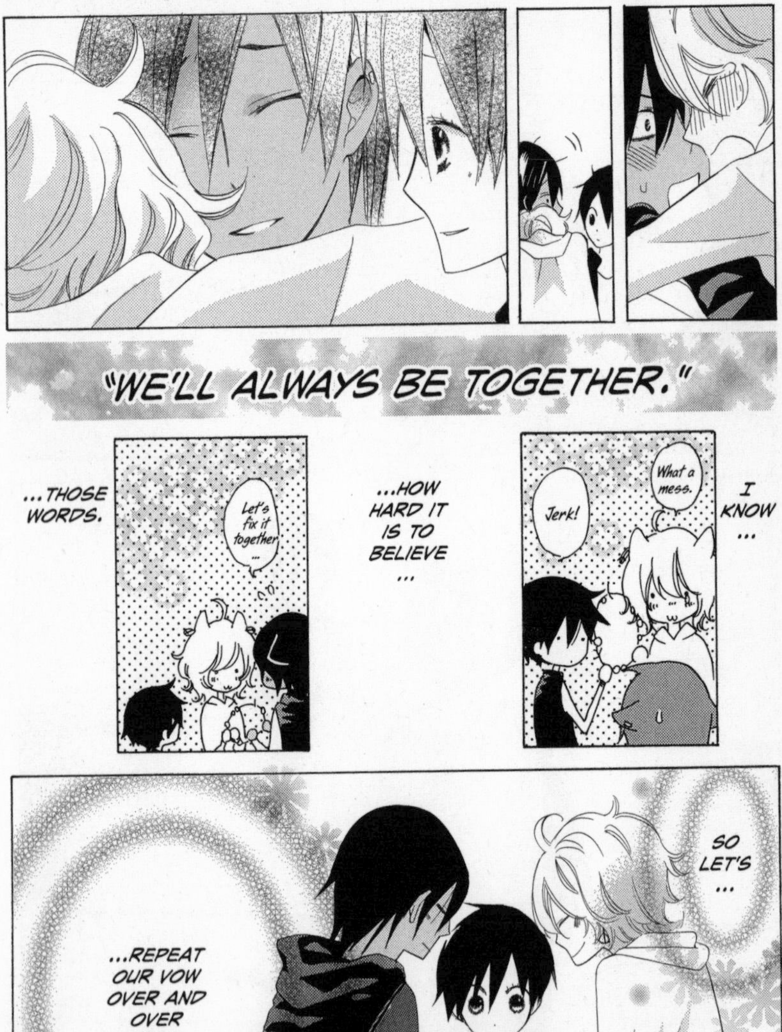
"WE'LL ALWAYS BE TOGETHER."
I KNOW...
What a mess.
Jerk!
...HOW HARD IT IS TO BELIEVE...
Let's fix it together...
...THOSE WORDS.
SO LET'S...
...REPEAT OUR VOW OVER AND OVER AGAIN.

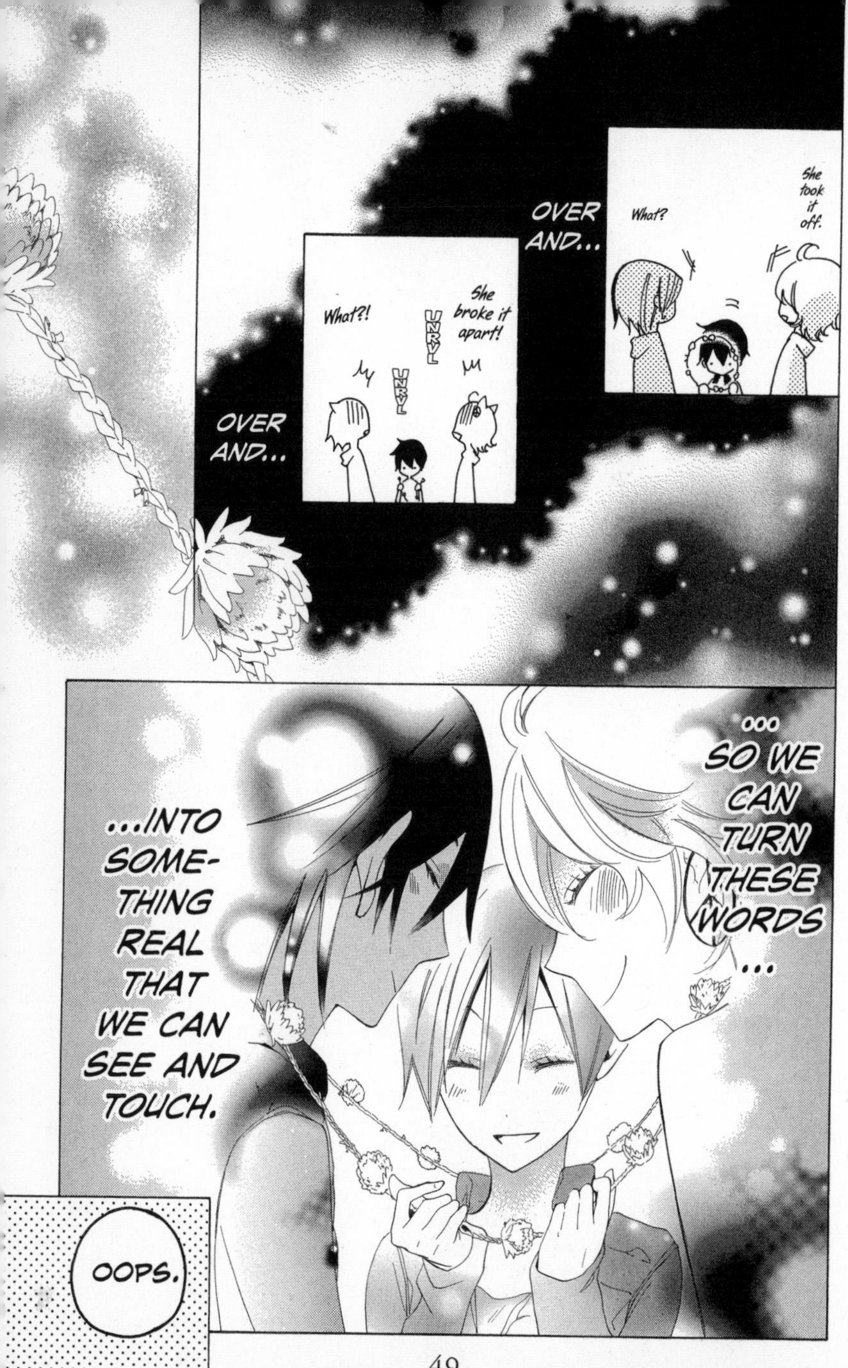
She took it off.
What?
OVER AND...
She broke it apart!
UNRVL
UNRVL
What?!
OVER AND...
...SO WE CAN TURN THESE WORDS...
...INTO SOME-THING REAL THAT WE CAN SEE AND TOUCH.
OOPS.

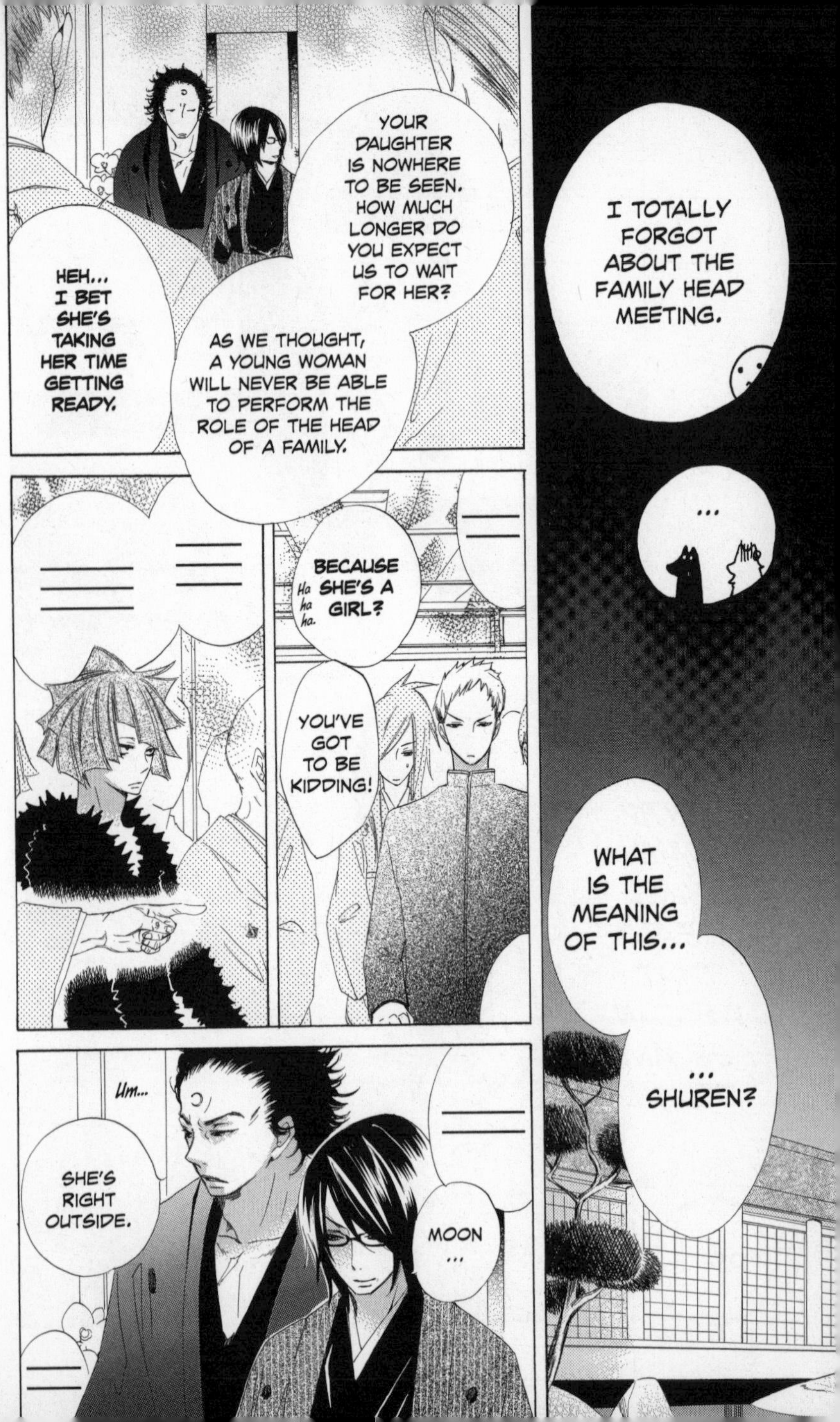

I TOTALLY FORGOT ABOUT THE FAMILY HEAD MEETING.
...
WHAT IS THE MEANING OF THIS...
... SHUREN?
YOUR DAUGHTER IS NOWHERE TO BE SEEN. HOW MUCH LONGER DO YOU EXPECT US TO WAIT FOR HER?
HEH... I BET SHE'S TAKING HER TIME GETTING READY.
AS WE THOUGHT, A YOUNG WOMAN WILL NEVER BE ABLE TO PERFORM THE ROLE OF THE HEAD OF A FAMILY.
BECAUSE SHE'S A GIRL?
Ha ha ha.
YOU'VE GOT TO BE KIDDING!
MOON ...
Um...
SHE'S RIGHT OUTSIDE.

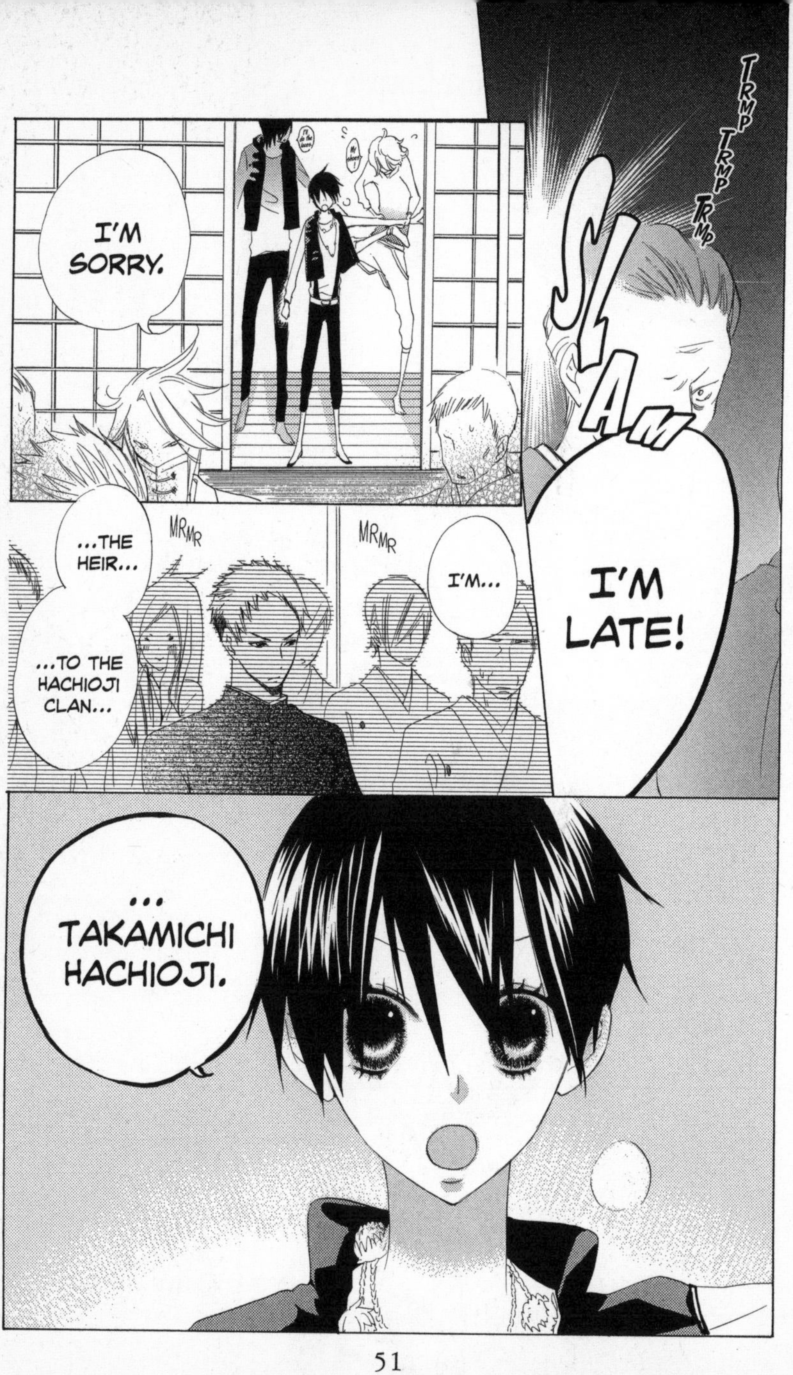
TRMP TRMP TRMP
SLAM
I'M LATE!
My shoes!
I'll do the laces.
I'M SORRY.
I'M...
MRMR
MRMR
...THE HEIR...
...TO THE HACHIOJI CLAN...
... TAKAMICHI HACHIOJI.

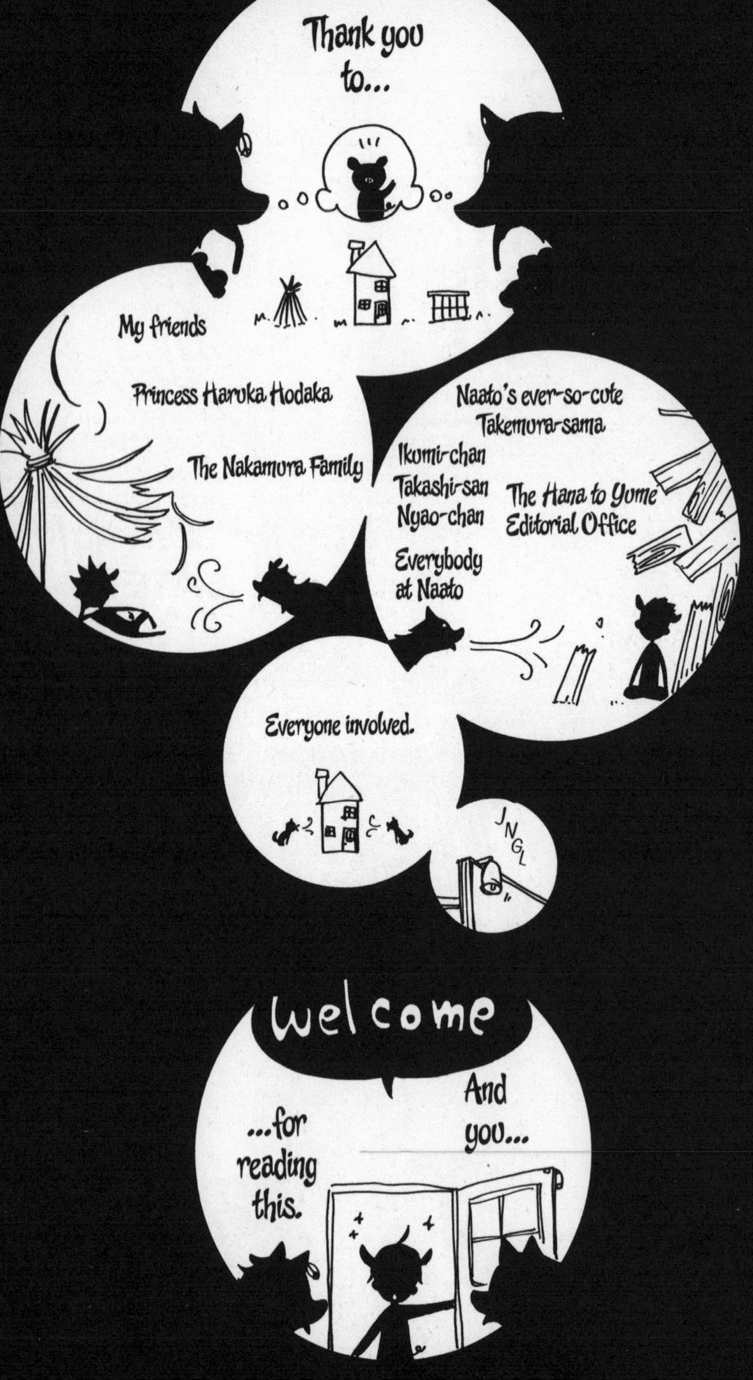

Thank you to...
Naato's ever-so-cute Takemura-sama
Ikumi-chan
Takashi-san
Nyao-chan
The Hana to Yume Editorial Office
Everybody at Naato
My friends
Princess Haruka Hodaka
The Nakamura Family
Everyone involved.
JNGL
welcome
And you...
...for reading this.

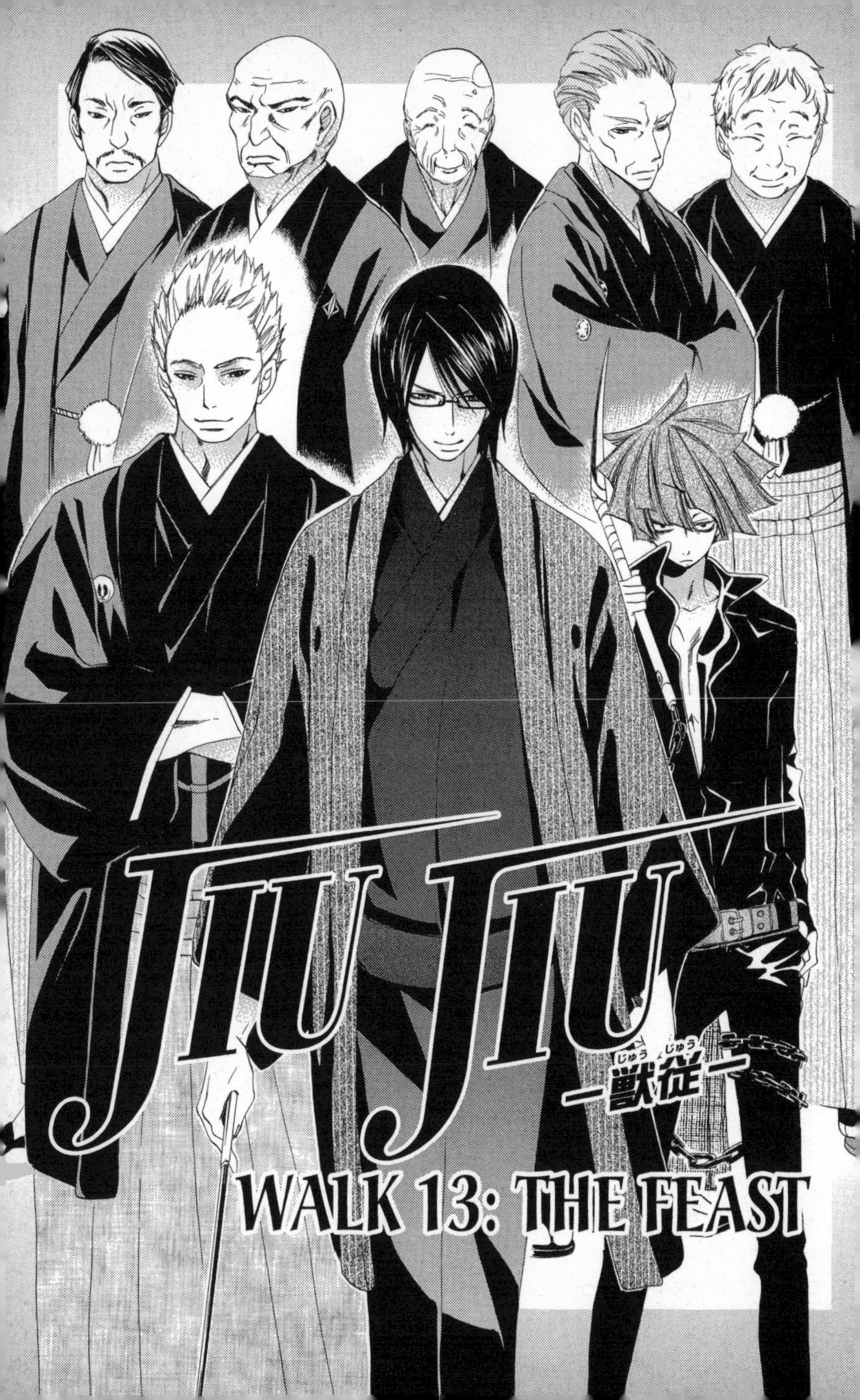
JIU JIU
じゅう じゅう
—獣従—
WALK 13: THE FEAST

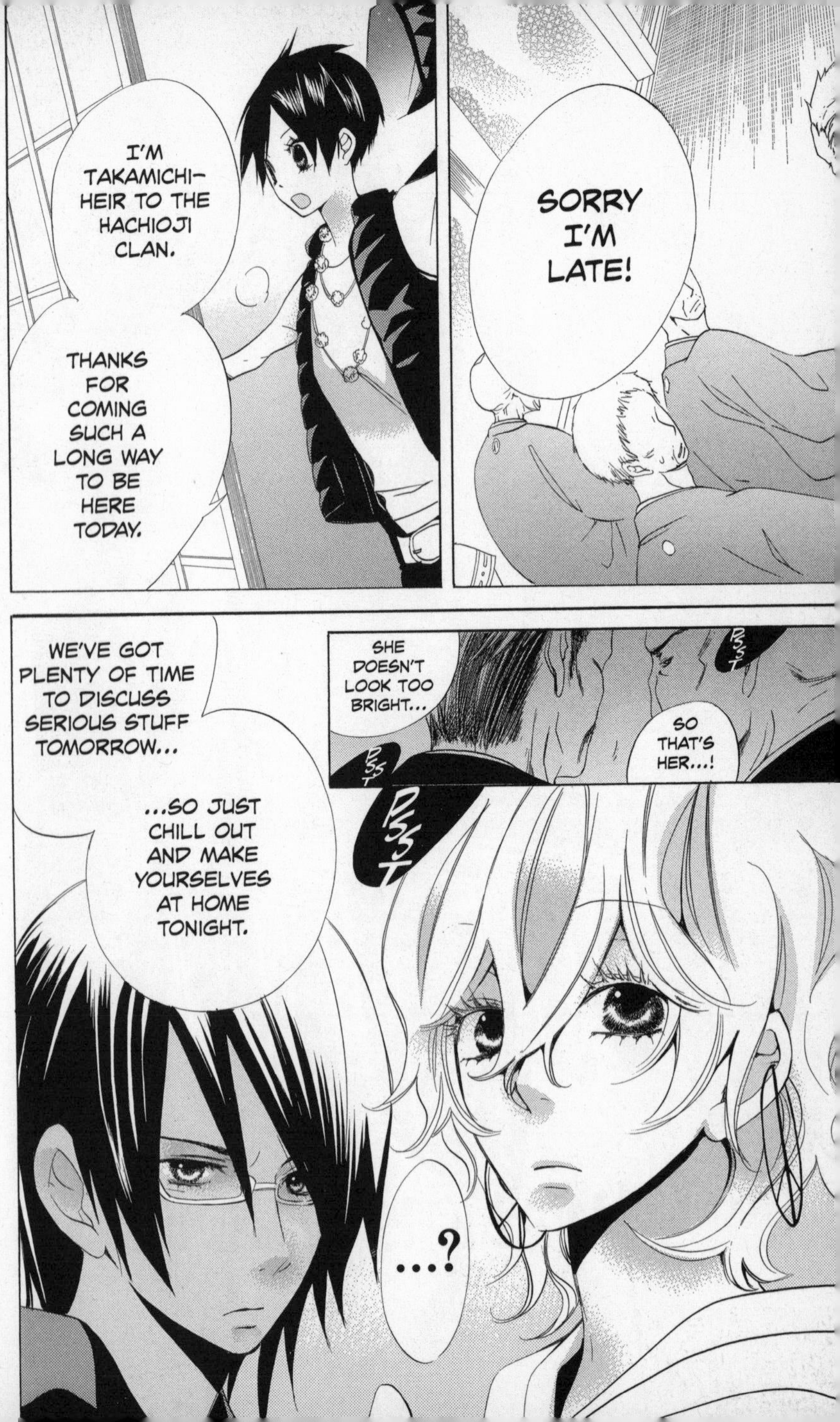
SORRY I'M LATE!
I'M TAKAMICHI—HEIR TO THE HACHIOJI CLAN.
THANKS FOR COMING SUCH A LONG WAY TO BE HERE TODAY.
PSST
SHE DOESN'T LOOK TOO BRIGHT...
SO THAT'S HER...!
PSST
PSST
WE'VE GOT PLENTY OF TIME TO DISCUSS SERIOUS STUFF TOMORROW...
...SO JUST CHILL OUT AND MAKE YOURSELVES AT HOME TONIGHT.
...?

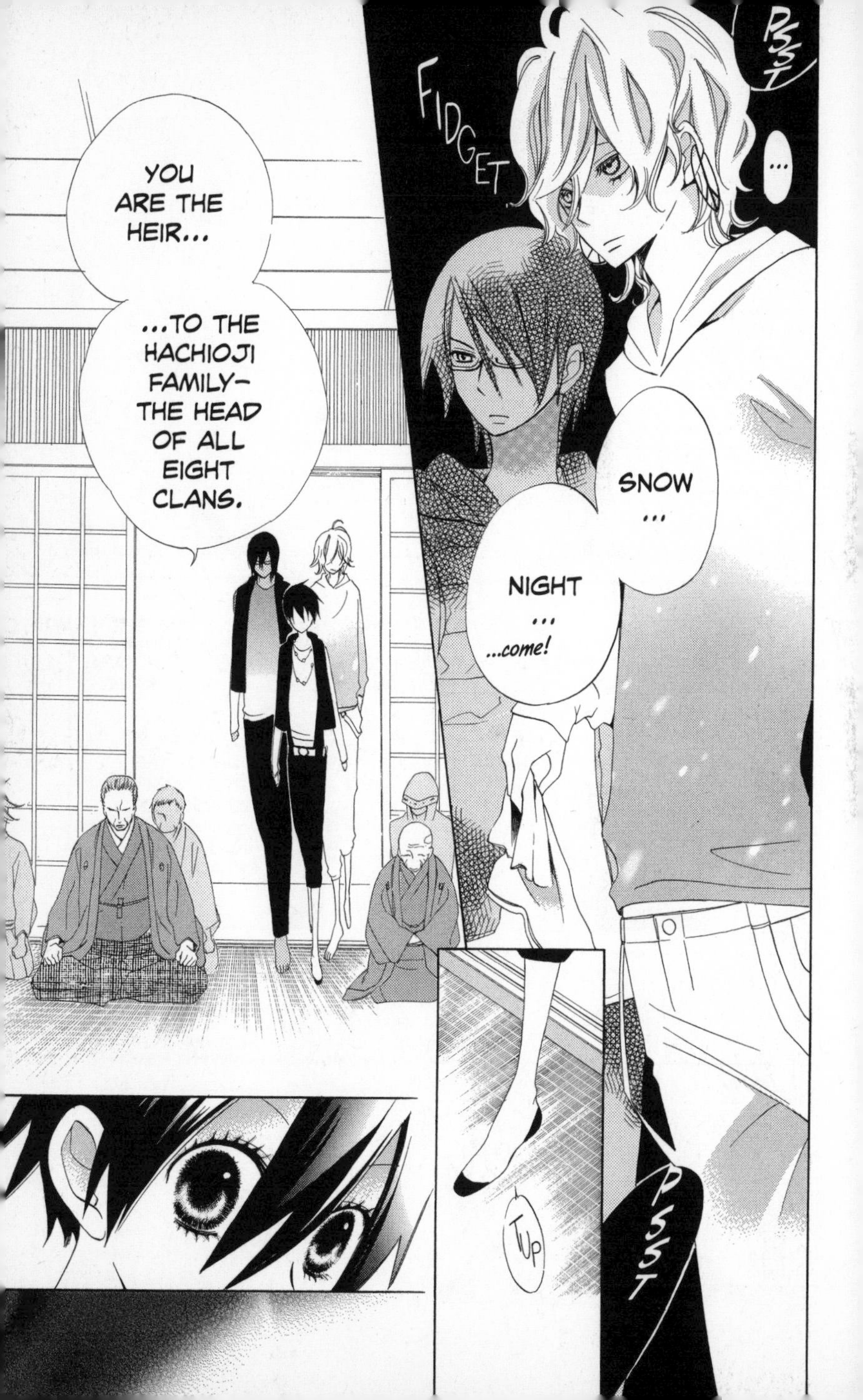
PSST
...
FIDGET.
SNOW ...
NIGHT ... ...come!
TUP
PSST
YOU ARE THE HEIR...
...TO THE HACHIOJI FAMILY—THE HEAD OF ALL EIGHT CLANS.

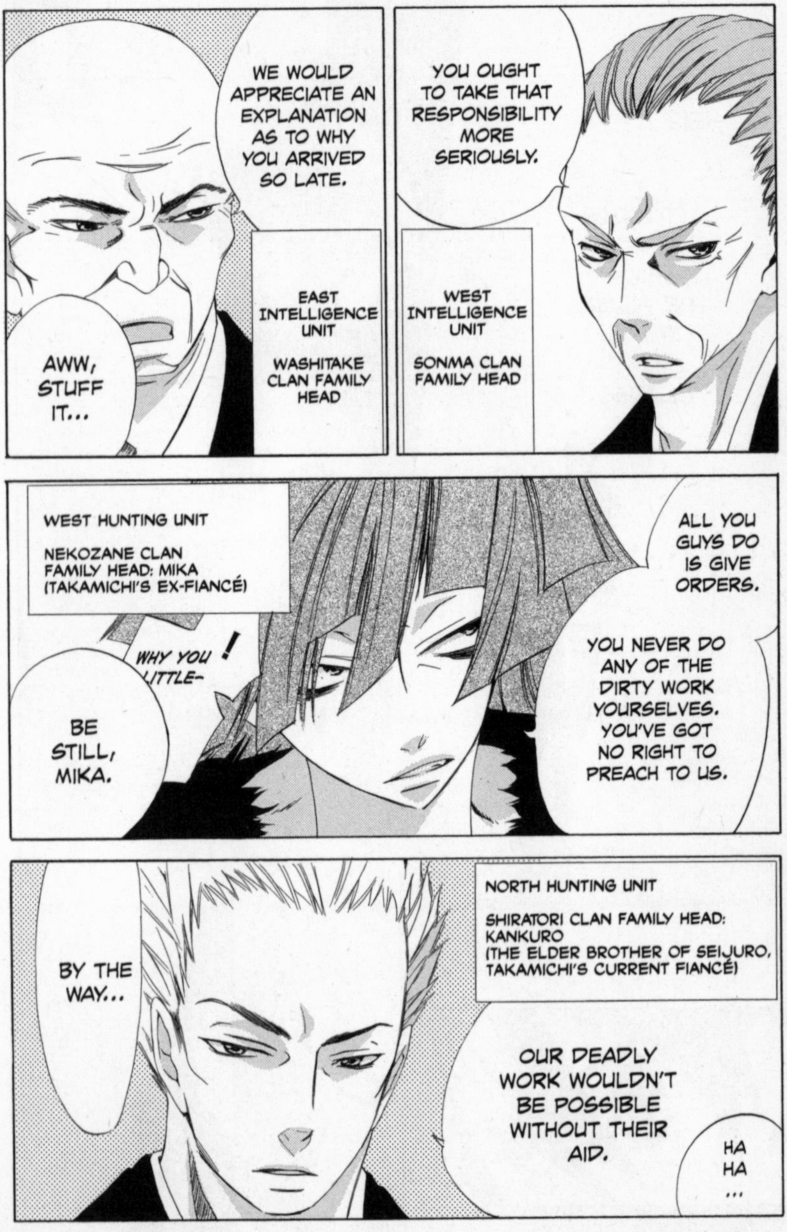
YOU OUGHT TO TAKE THAT RESPONSIBILITY MORE SERIOUSLY.
WEST INTELLIGENCE UNIT
SONMA CLAN FAMILY HEAD
WE WOULD APPRECIATE AN EXPLANATION AS TO WHY YOU ARRIVED SO LATE.
EAST INTELLIGENCE UNIT
WASHITAKE CLAN FAMILY HEAD
AWW, STUFF IT...
ALL YOU GUYS DO IS GIVE ORDERS.
WEST HUNTING UNIT
NEKOZANE CLAN FAMILY HEAD: MIKA (TAKAMICHI'S EX-FIANCÉ)
YOU NEVER DO ANY OF THE DIRTY WORK YOURSELVES. YOU'VE GOT NO RIGHT TO PREACH TO US.
WHY YOU LITTLE- !
BE STILL, MIKA.
NORTH HUNTING UNIT
SHIRATORI CLAN FAMILY HEAD: KANKURO (THE ELDER BROTHER OF SEIJURO, TAKAMICHI'S CURRENT FIANCÉ)
BY THE WAY...
OUR DEADLY WORK WOULDN'T BE POSSIBLE WITHOUT THEIR AID.
HA HA ...

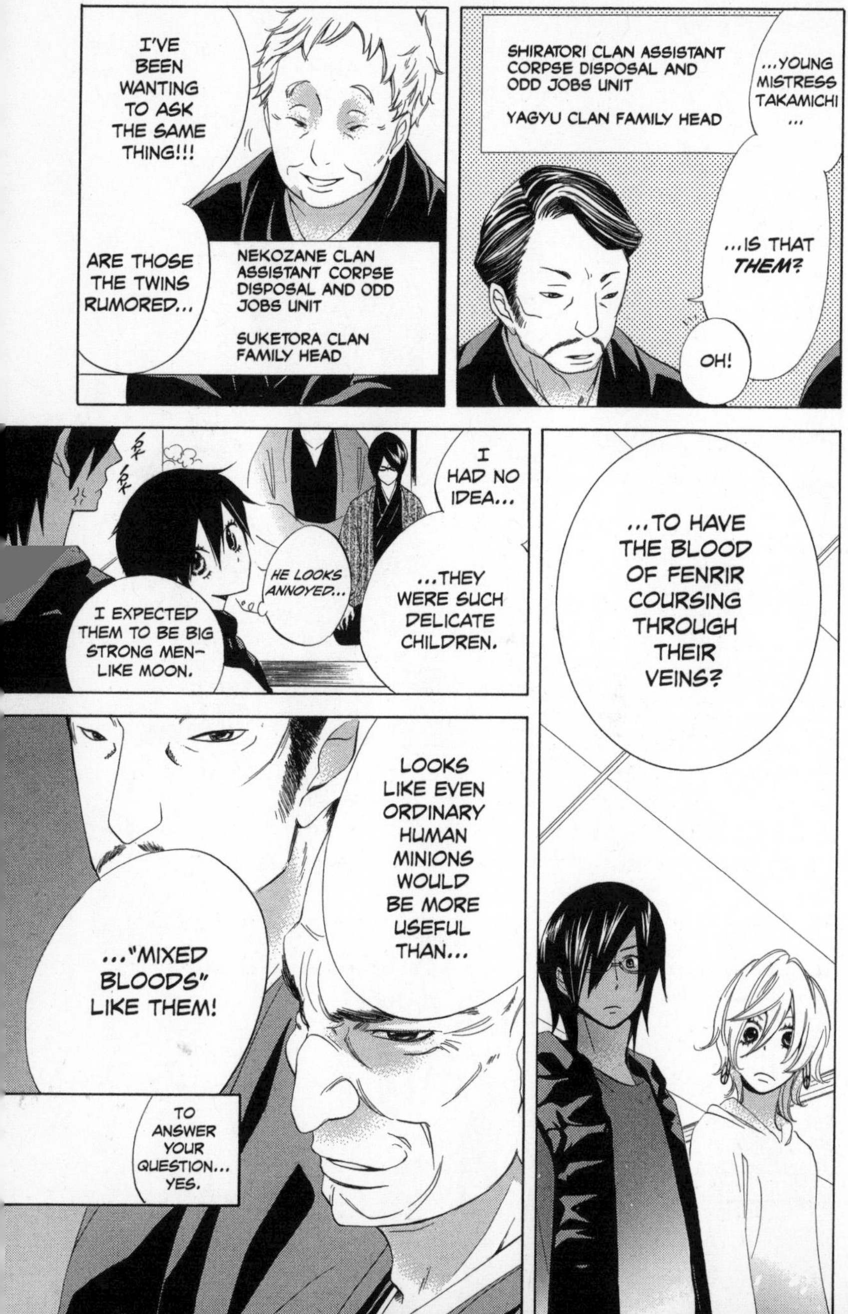
...YOUNG MISTRESS TAKAMICHI ...
SHIRATORI CLAN ASSISTANT CORPSE DISPOSAL AND ODD JOBS UNIT
YAGYU CLAN FAMILY HEAD
...IS THAT *THEM?*
OH!
I'VE BEEN WANTING TO ASK THE SAME THING!!!
NEKOZANE CLAN ASSISTANT CORPSE DISPOSAL AND ODD JOBS UNIT
SUKETORA CLAN FAMILY HEAD
ARE THOSE THE TWINS RUMORED...
...TO HAVE THE BLOOD OF FENRIR COURSING THROUGH THEIR VEINS?
I HAD NO IDEA...
...THEY WERE SUCH DELICATE CHILDREN.
HE LOOKS ANNOYED...
I EXPECTED THEM TO BE BIG STRONG MEN—LIKE MOON.
LOOKS LIKE EVEN ORDINARY HUMAN MINIONS WOULD BE MORE USEFUL THAN...
..."MIXED BLOODS" LIKE THEM!
TO ANSWER YOUR QUESTION... YES.

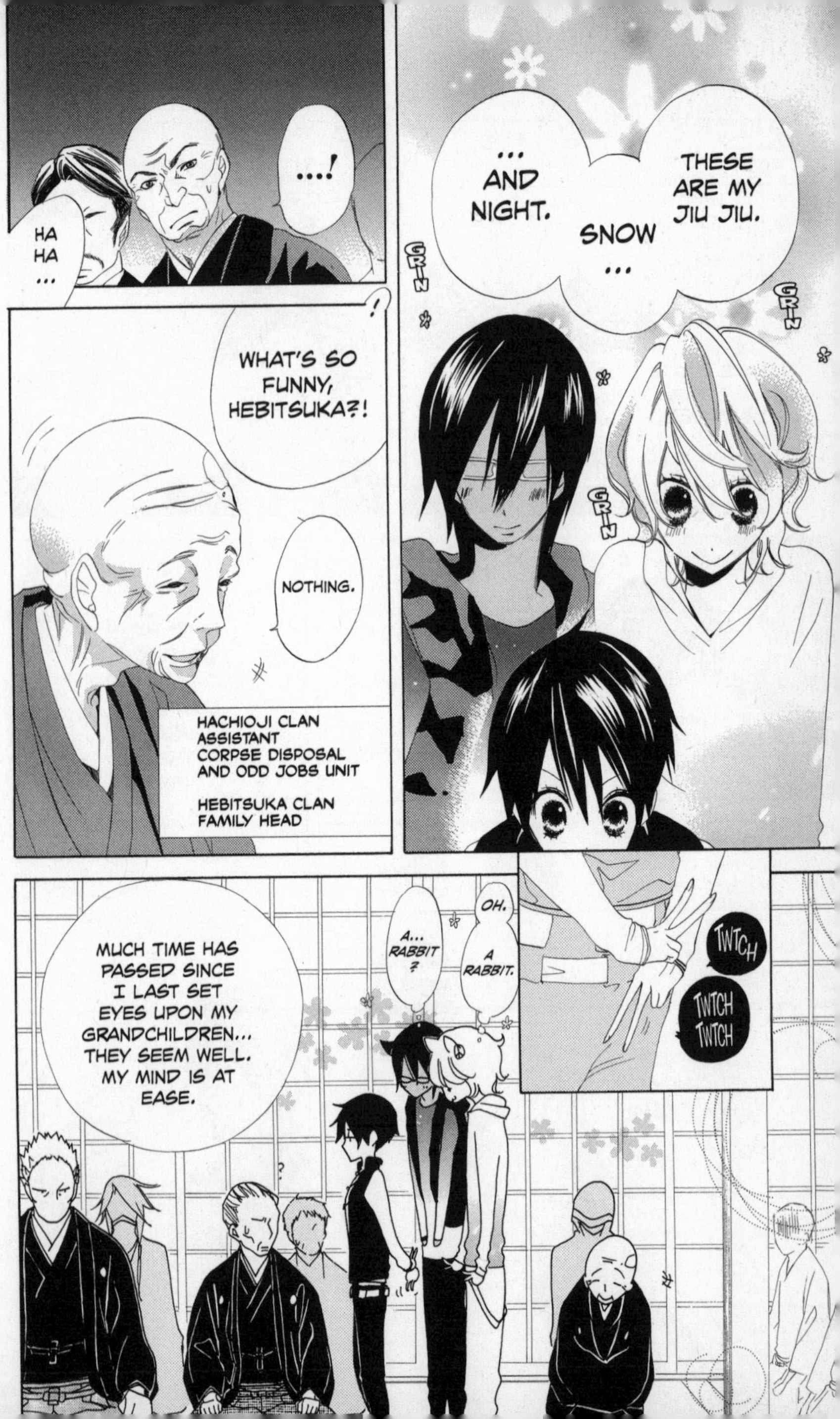
THESE ARE MY JIU JIU.
SNOW ...
... AND NIGHT.
GRIN
GRIN
GRIN
...!
HA HA ...
!
WHAT'S SO FUNNY, HEBITSUKA?!
NOTHING.
HACHIOJI CLAN ASSISTANT CORPSE DISPOSAL AND ODD JOBS UNIT
HEBITSUKA CLAN FAMILY HEAD
TWTCH
TWTCH TWTCH
OH.
A RABBIT.
A... RABBIT?
MUCH TIME HAS PASSED SINCE I LAST SET EYES UPON MY GRANDCHILDREN... THEY SEEM WELL. MY MIND IS AT EASE.

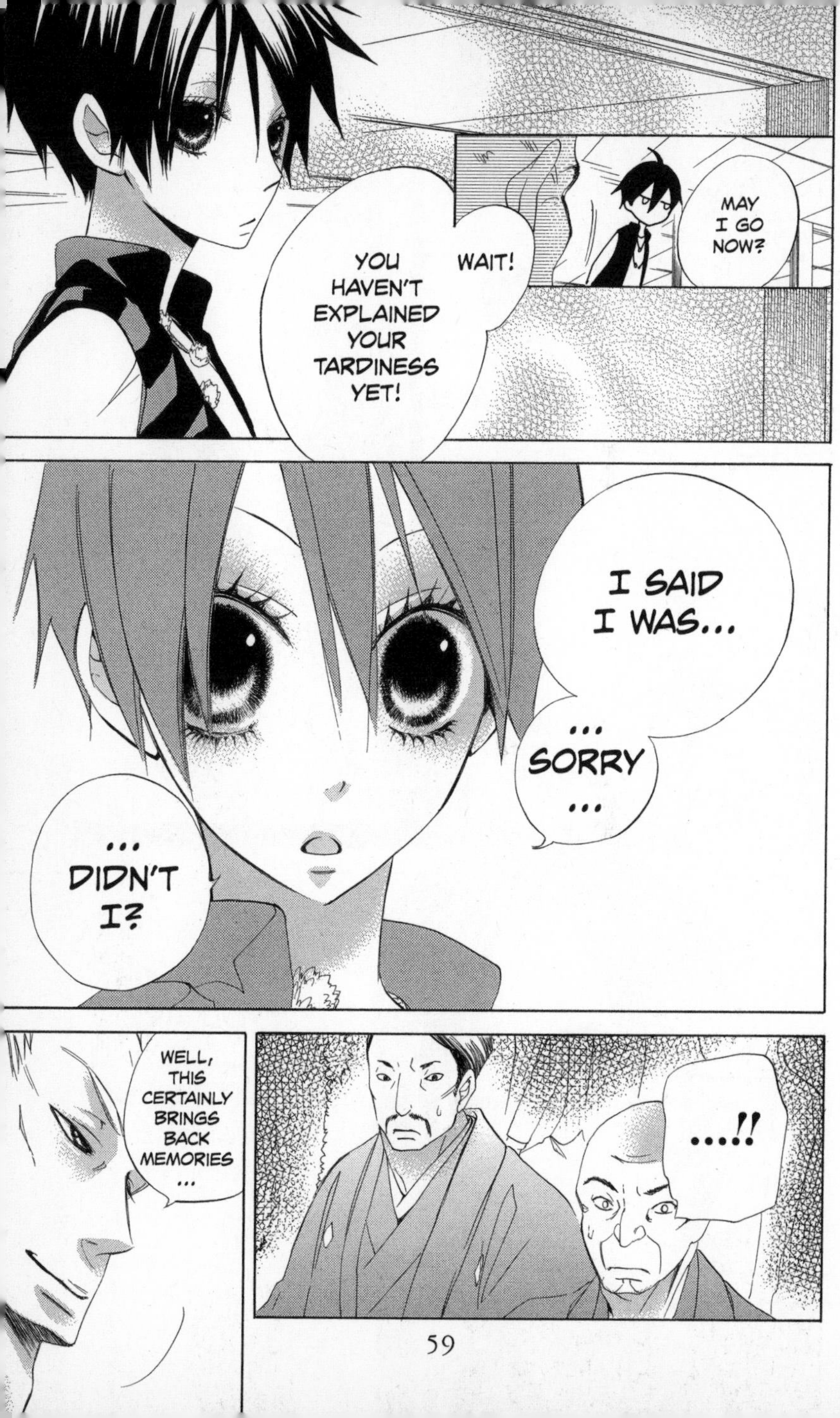
MAY I GO NOW?
WAIT!
YOU HAVEN'T EXPLAINED YOUR TARDINESS YET!
I SAID I WAS...
...SORRY...
...DIDN'T I?
...!!
WELL, THIS CERTAINLY BRINGS BACK MEMORIES...

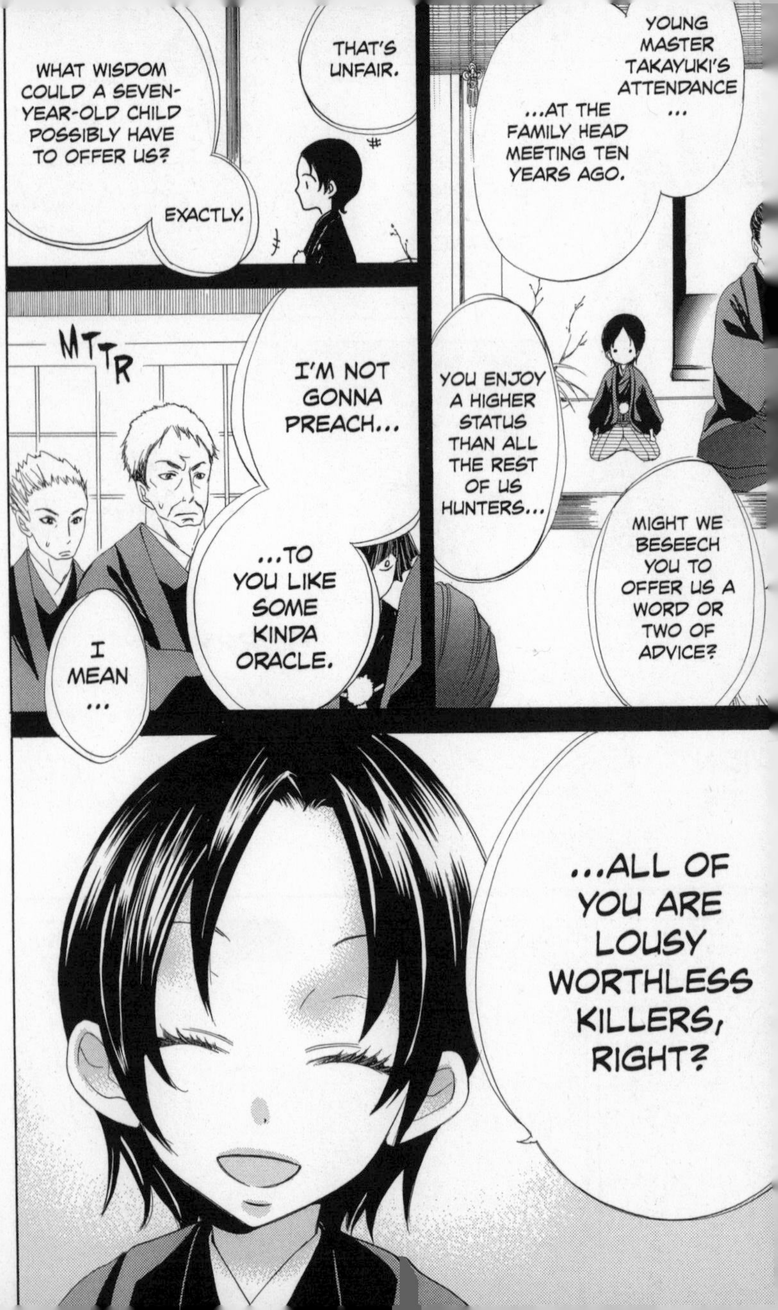
YOUNG MASTER TAKAYUKI'S ATTENDANCE ...
...AT THE FAMILY HEAD MEETING TEN YEARS AGO.
YOU ENJOY A HIGHER STATUS THAN ALL THE REST OF US HUNTERS...
MIGHT WE BESEECH YOU TO OFFER US A WORD OR TWO OF ADVICE?
THAT'S UNFAIR.
WHAT WISDOM COULD A SEVEN-YEAR-OLD CHILD POSSIBLY HAVE TO OFFER US?
EXACTLY.
MTTR
I'M NOT GONNA PREACH...
...TO YOU LIKE SOME KINDA ORACLE.
I MEAN ...
...ALL OF YOU ARE LOUSY WORTHLESS KILLERS, RIGHT?

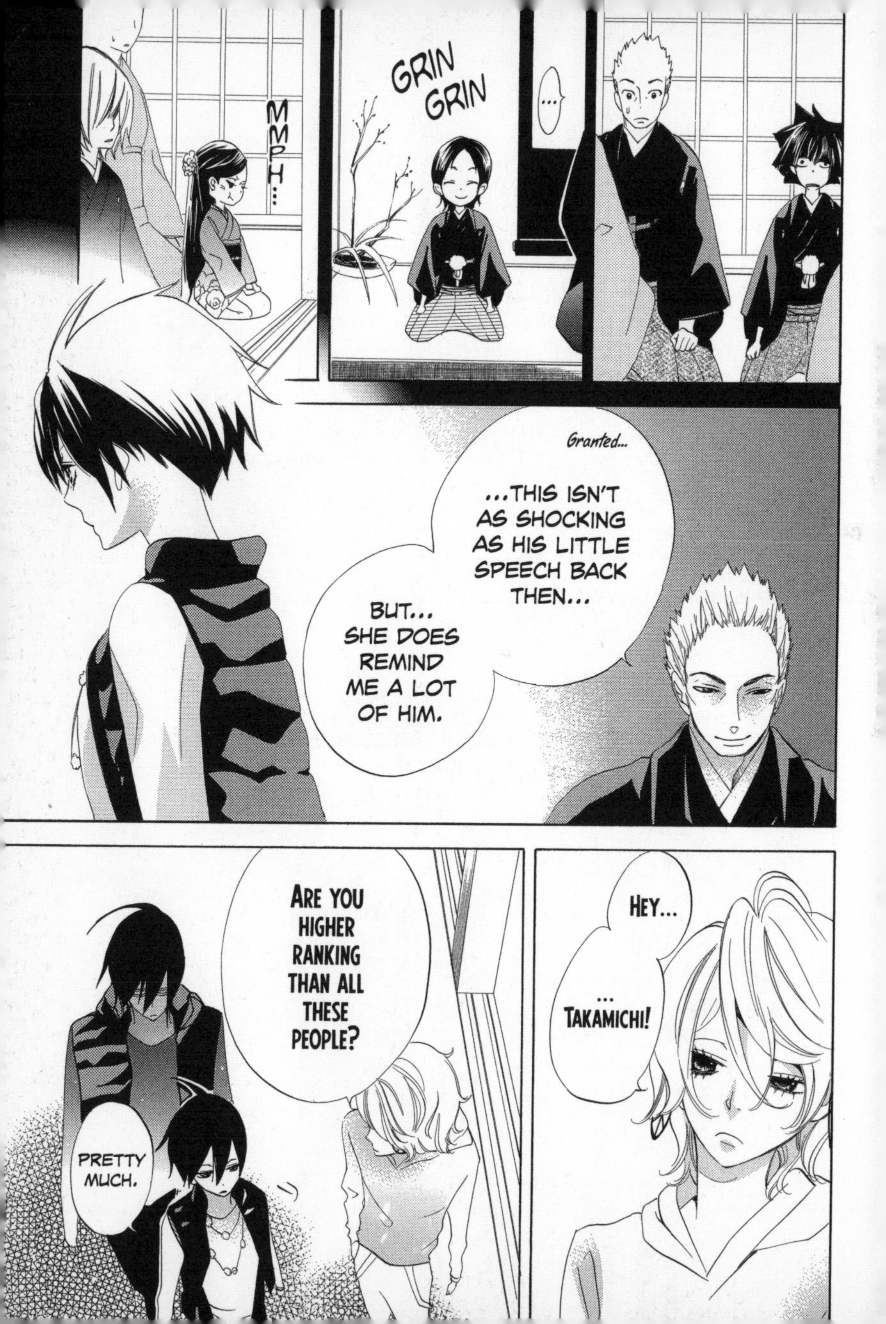
...
GRIN GRIN
MMPH...
Granted...
...THIS ISN'T AS SHOCKING AS HIS LITTLE SPEECH BACK THEN...
BUT... SHE DOES REMIND ME A LOT OF HIM.
HEY...
... TAKAMICHI!
ARE YOU HIGHER RANKING THAN ALL THESE PEOPLE?
PRETTY MUCH.

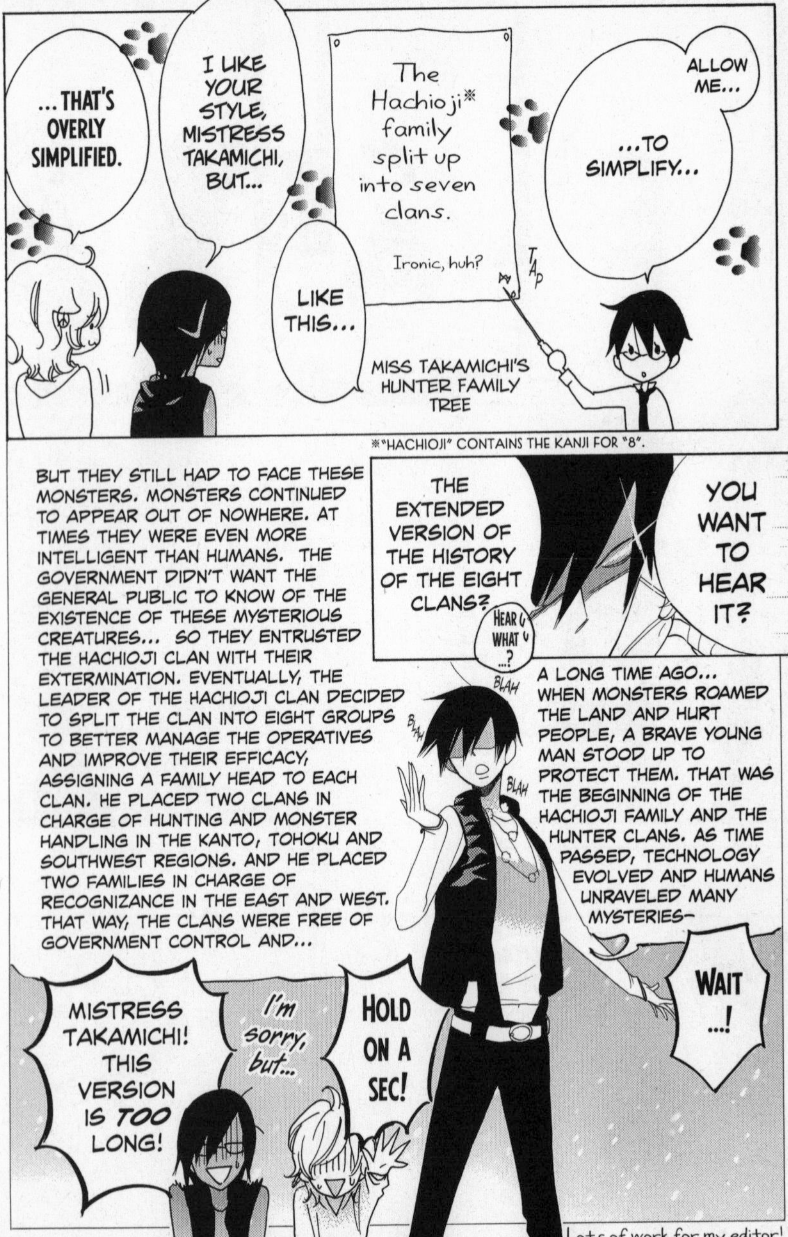
ALLOW ME...
...TO SIMPLIFY...
The Hachioji※ family split up into seven clans.
Ironic, huh?
TAP
LIKE THIS...
MISS TAKAMICHI'S HUNTER FAMILY TREE
I LIKE YOUR STYLE, MISTRESS TAKAMICHI, BUT...
...THAT'S OVERLY SIMPLIFIED.
※"HACHIOJI" CONTAINS THE KANJI FOR "8".
YOU WANT TO HEAR IT?
THE EXTENDED VERSION OF THE HISTORY OF THE EIGHT CLANS?
HEAR WHAT ...?
BLAH
BLAH
BLAH
A LONG TIME AGO... WHEN MONSTERS ROAMED THE LAND AND HURT PEOPLE, A BRAVE YOUNG MAN STOOD UP TO PROTECT THEM. THAT WAS THE BEGINNING OF THE HACHIOJI FAMILY AND THE HUNTER CLANS. AS TIME PASSED, TECHNOLOGY EVOLVED AND HUMANS UNRAVELED MANY MYSTERIES–
BUT THEY STILL HAD TO FACE THESE MONSTERS. MONSTERS CONTINUED TO APPEAR OUT OF NOWHERE. AT TIMES THEY WERE EVEN MORE INTELLIGENT THAN HUMANS. THE GOVERNMENT DIDN'T WANT THE GENERAL PUBLIC TO KNOW OF THE EXISTENCE OF THESE MYSTERIOUS CREATURES... SO THEY ENTRUSTED THE HACHIOJI CLAN WITH THEIR EXTERMINATION. EVENTUALLY, THE LEADER OF THE HACHIOJI CLAN DECIDED TO SPLIT THE CLAN INTO EIGHT GROUPS TO BETTER MANAGE THE OPERATIVES AND IMPROVE THEIR EFFICACY, ASSIGNING A FAMILY HEAD TO EACH CLAN. HE PLACED TWO CLANS IN CHARGE OF HUNTING AND MONSTER HANDLING IN THE KANTO, TOHOKU AND SOUTHWEST REGIONS. AND HE PLACED TWO FAMILIES IN CHARGE OF RECOGNIZANCE IN THE EAST AND WEST. THAT WAY, THE CLANS WERE FREE OF GOVERNMENT CONTROL AND...
WAIT ...!
HOLD ON A SEC!
I'm sorry, but...
MISTRESS TAKAMICHI! THIS VERSION IS TOO LONG!

Lots of work for my editor!

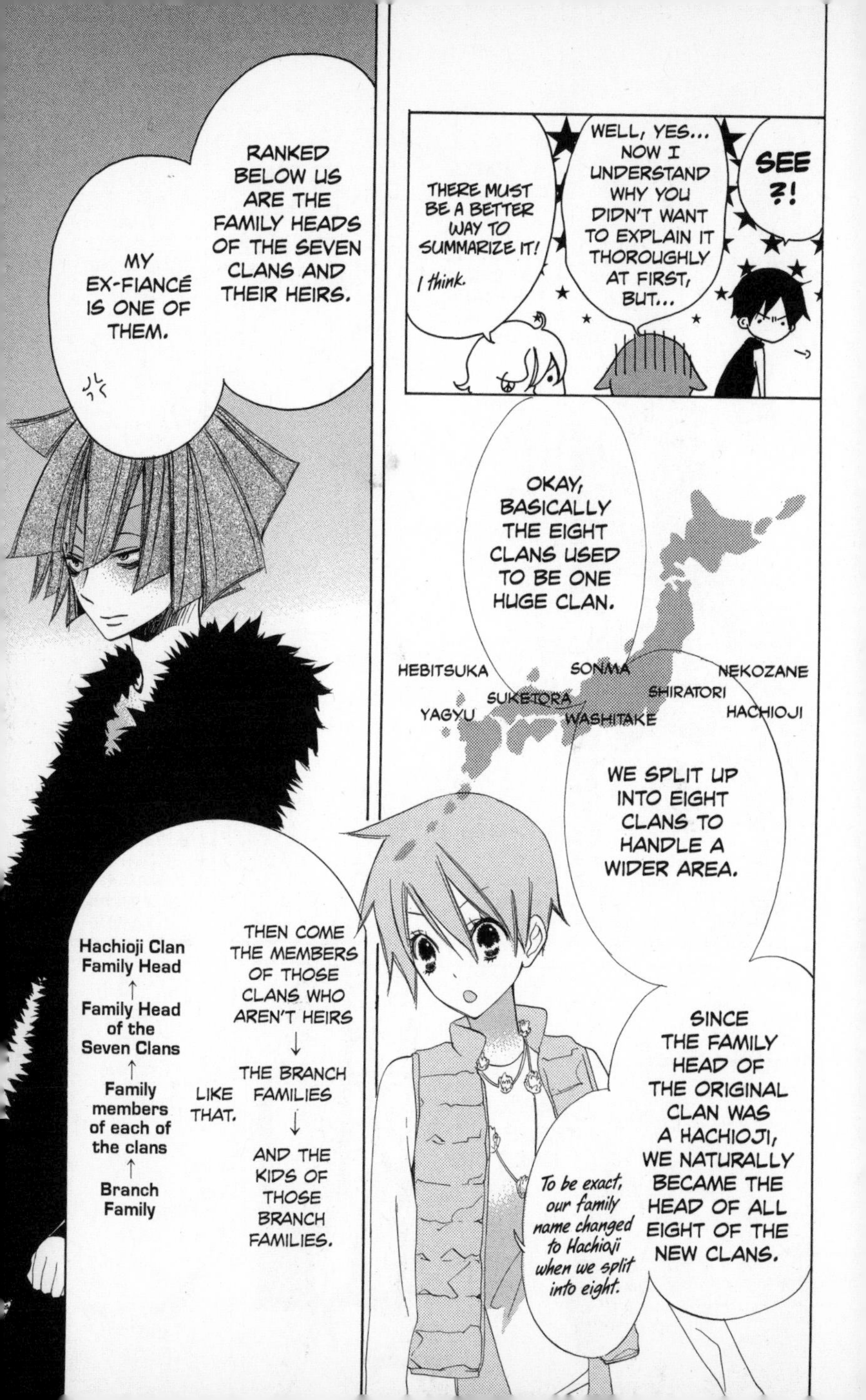
SEE?!
WELL, YES... NOW I UNDERSTAND WHY YOU DIDN'T WANT TO EXPLAIN IT THOROUGHLY AT FIRST, BUT...
THERE MUST BE A BETTER WAY TO SUMMARIZE IT! I think.
OKAY, BASICALLY THE EIGHT CLANS USED TO BE ONE HUGE CLAN.
HEBITSUKA
SONMA
NEKOZANE
SUKETORA
SHIRATORI
YAGYU
WASHITAKE
HACHIOJI
WE SPLIT UP INTO EIGHT CLANS TO HANDLE A WIDER AREA.
SINCE THE FAMILY HEAD OF THE ORIGINAL CLAN WAS A HACHIOJI, WE NATURALLY BECAME THE HEAD OF ALL EIGHT OF THE NEW CLANS.
To be exact, our family name changed to Hachioji when we split into eight.
RANKED BELOW US ARE THE FAMILY HEADS OF THE SEVEN CLANS AND THEIR HEIRS.
MY EX-FIANCÉ IS ONE OF THEM.
THEN COME THE MEMBERS OF THOSE CLANS WHO AREN'T HEIRS ↓ THE BRANCH FAMILIES ↓ AND THE KIDS OF THOSE BRANCH FAMILIES.
LIKE THAT.
Hachioji Clan Family Head ↑ Family Head of the Seven Clans ↑ Family members of each of the clans ↑ Branch Family

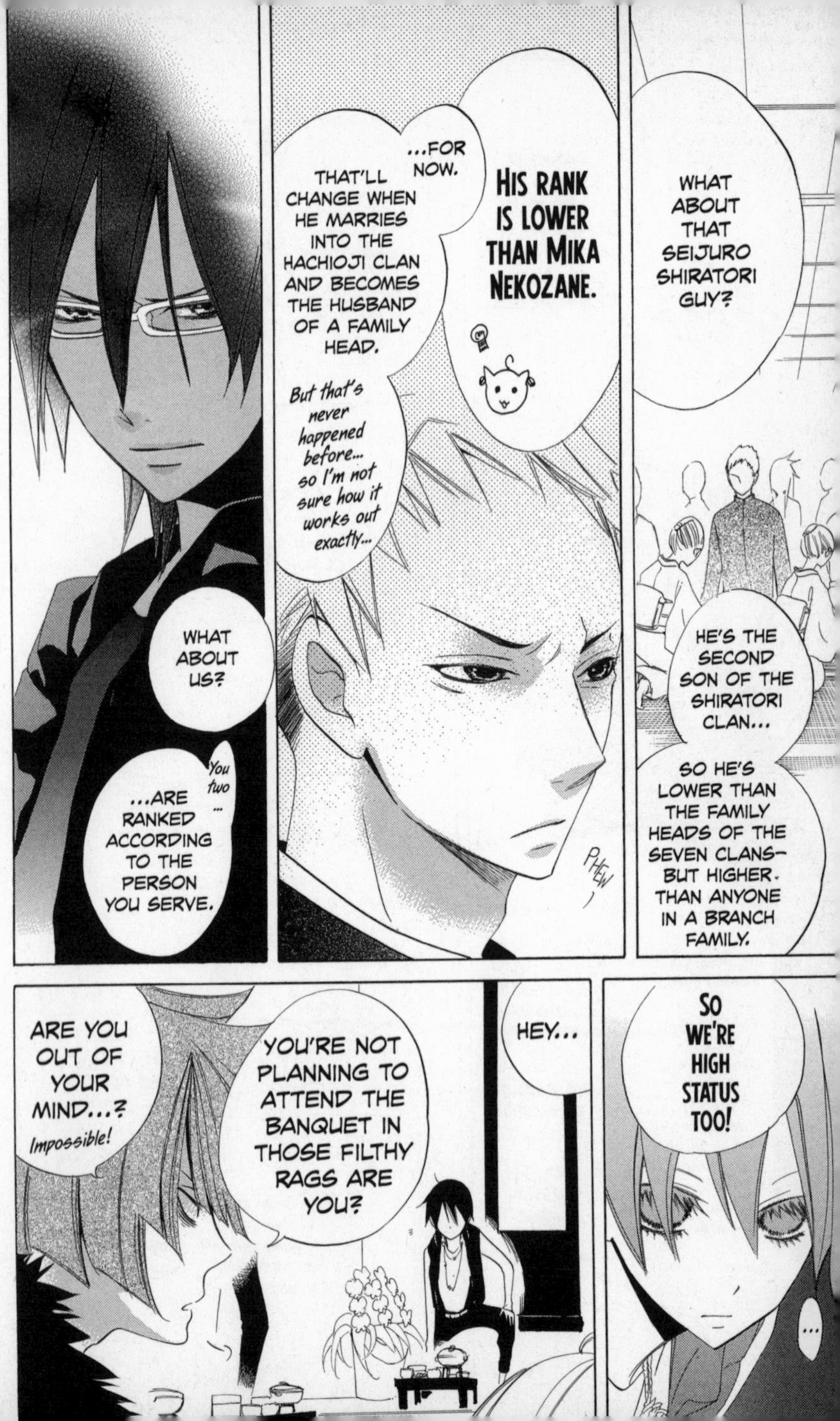

WHAT ABOUT THAT SEIJURO SHIRATORI GUY?
HE'S THE SECOND SON OF THE SHIRATORI CLAN...
SO HE'S LOWER THAN THE FAMILY HEADS OF THE SEVEN CLANS—BUT HIGHER THAN ANYONE IN A BRANCH FAMILY.
HIS RANK IS LOWER THAN MIKA NEKOZANE.
...FOR NOW.
THAT'LL CHANGE WHEN HE MARRIES INTO THE HACHIOJI CLAN AND BECOMES THE HUSBAND OF A FAMILY HEAD.
But that's never happened before... so I'm not sure how it works out exactly...
PHEW
WHAT ABOUT US?
You two...
...ARE RANKED ACCORDING TO THE PERSON YOU SERVE.
SO WE'RE HIGH STATUS TOO!
...
HEY...
YOU'RE NOT PLANNING TO ATTEND THE BANQUET IN THOSE FILTHY RAGS ARE YOU?
ARE YOU OUT OF YOUR MIND...?
Impossible!

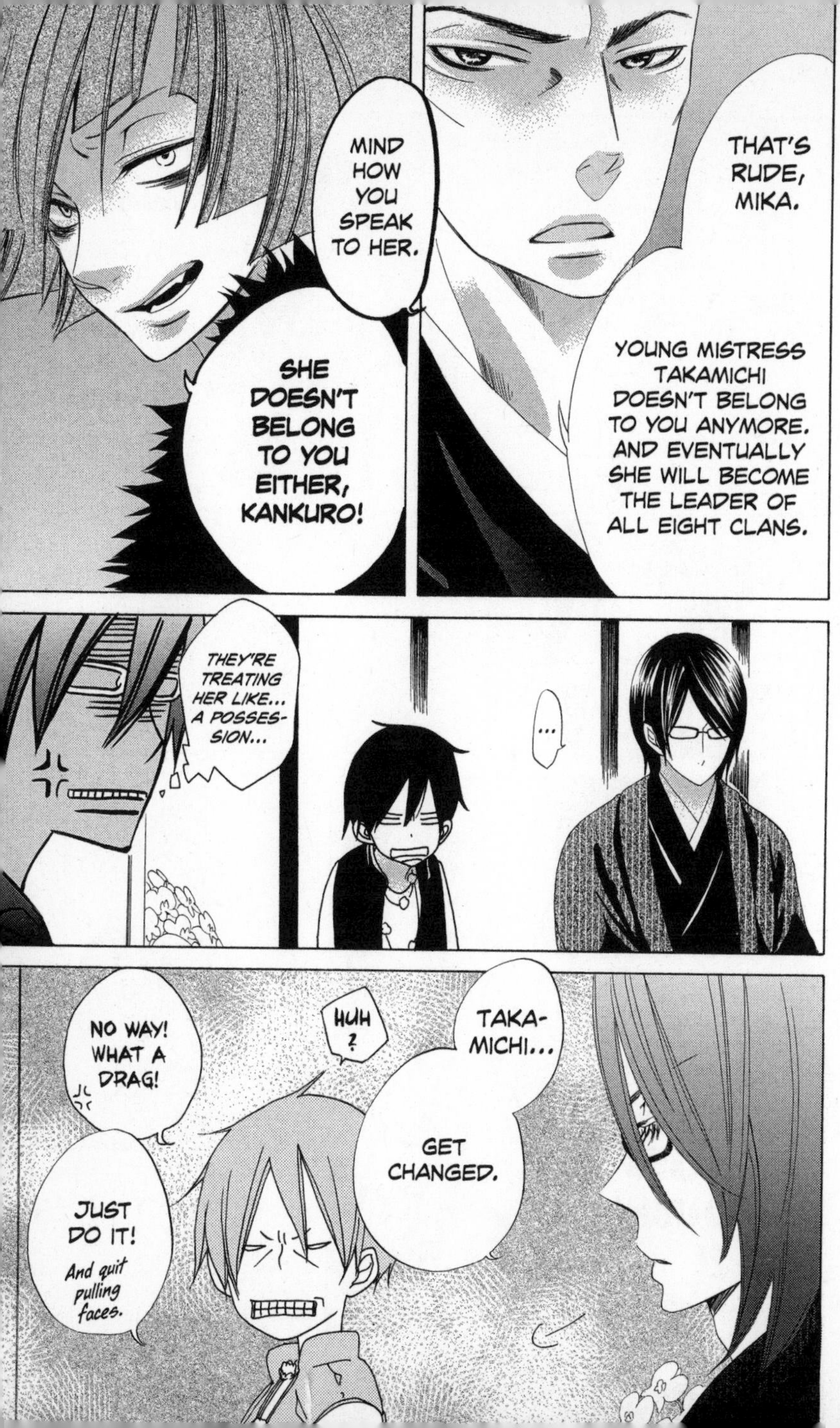
THAT'S RUDE, MIKA.
YOUNG MISTRESS TAKAMICHI DOESN'T BELONG TO YOU ANYMORE. AND EVENTUALLY SHE WILL BECOME THE LEADER OF ALL EIGHT CLANS.
MIND HOW YOU SPEAK TO HER.
SHE DOESN'T BELONG TO YOU EITHER, KANKURO!
...
THEY'RE TREATING HER LIKE... A POSSESSION...
TAKAMICHI...
GET CHANGED.
HUH?
NO WAY! WHAT A DRAG!
JUST DO IT!
And quit pulling faces.

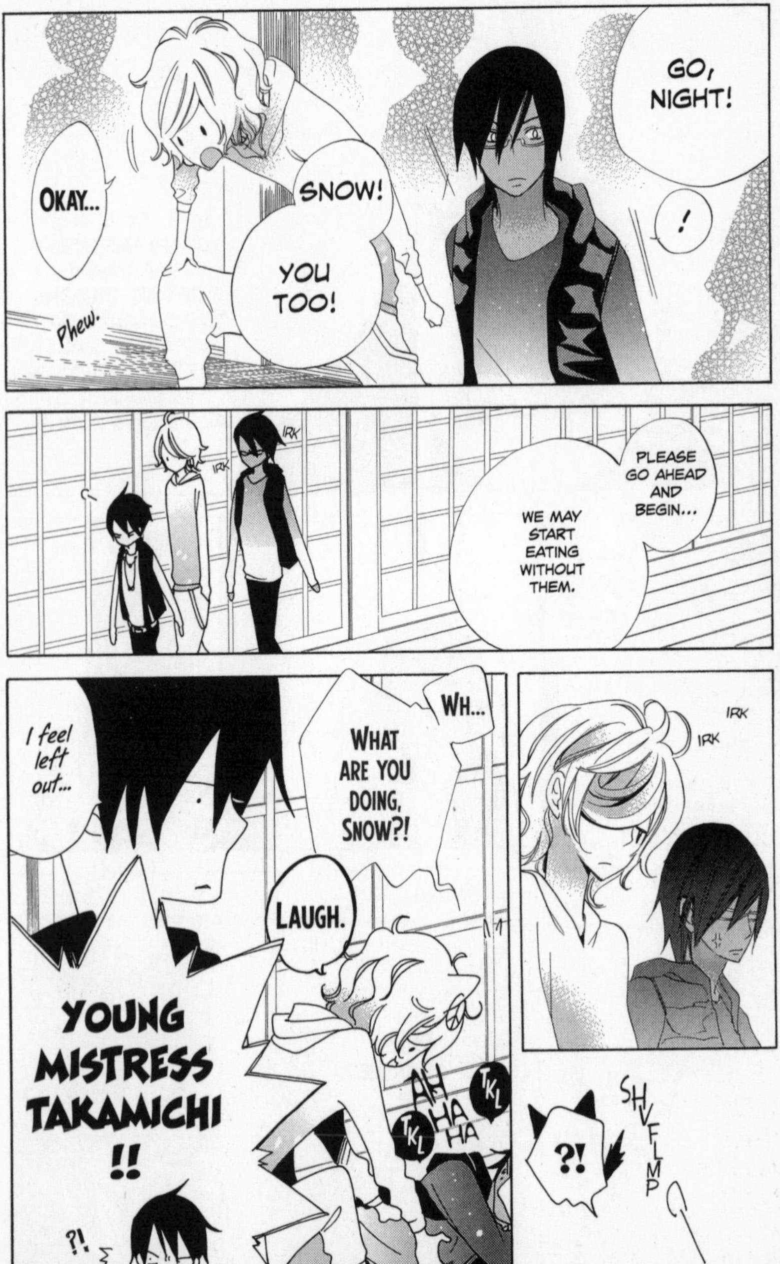
GO, NIGHT!
!
SNOW!
YOU TOO!
OKAY...
Phew.
PLEASE GO AHEAD AND BEGIN...
WE MAY START EATING WITHOUT THEM.
IRK
IRK
IRK
IRK
?!
SHVFLMP
WH...
WHAT ARE YOU DOING, SNOW?!
I feel left out...
LAUGH.
TKL
AH HA HA
TKL
YOUNG MISTRESS TAKAMICHI !!
?!

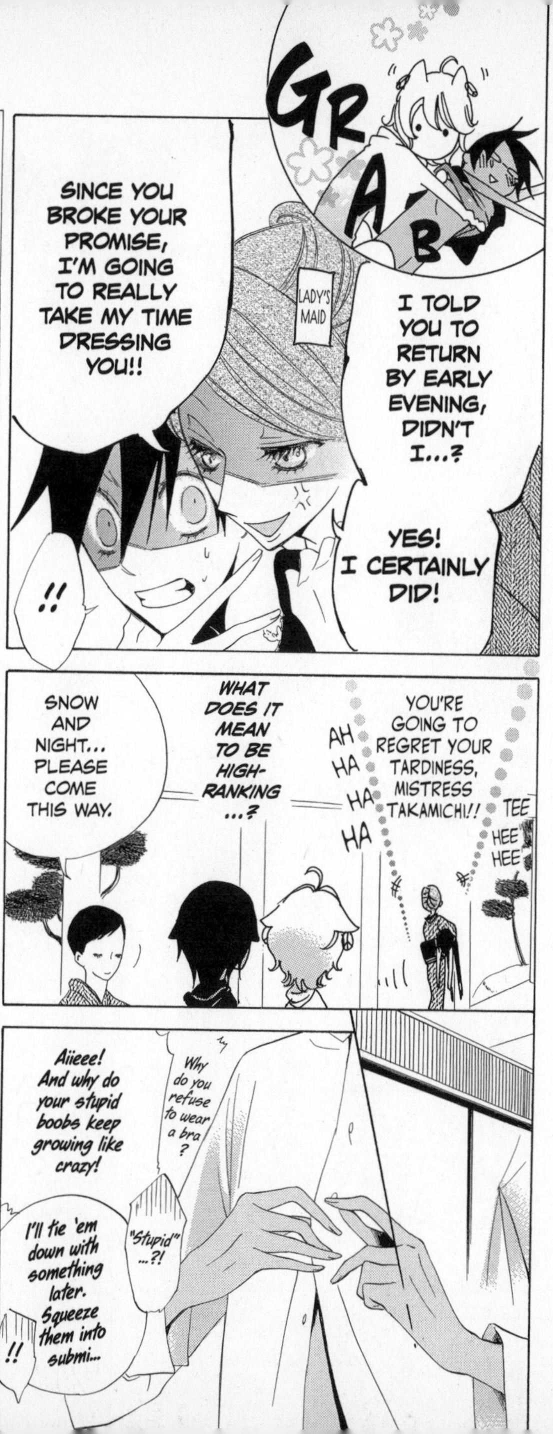
GRAB
I TOLD YOU TO RETURN BY EARLY EVENING, DIDN'T I...?
LADY'S MAID
SINCE YOU BROKE YOUR PROMISE, I'M GOING TO REALLY TAKE MY TIME DRESSING YOU!!
YES! I CERTAINLY DID!
!!
TEE HEE HEE
YOU'RE GOING TO REGRET YOUR TARDINESS, MISTRESS TAKAMICHI!!
AH HA HA HA
WHAT DOES IT MEAN TO BE HIGH-RANKING ...?
SNOW AND NIGHT... PLEASE COME THIS WAY.
Why do you refuse to wear a bra?
Aiiee! And why do your stupid boobs keep growing like crazy!
"Stupid" ...?!
I'll tie 'em down with something later. Squeeze them into submi...
!!

Questions.

Okay, here are some of the questions I've received.~

How old is Takamichi's father?

Hyogo Prefecture: Asami

Takamichi's father (AKA Shuren Hachioji) appears every now and then in this volume, but he remains rather mysterious, doesn't he? As for his age, umm, let's say...40.

① Meru's earring looks like a cross. Is it okay for a vampire to wear a cross?

② All the classmates in *Jiu Jiu* have an animal in their names, don't they?

Nagasaki Prefecture: Kuro

(Forgive me for my rudeness in misreading your name before...!! I'm terribly sorry!! I suspect I do that a lot!! Apologies to everyone whose name I've gotten wrong!!

① → The cross? Well, that's... part of his training.

(I just made that up.)

② → That's right. Everybody except the Hachiojis have an animal in their last name.

I was being a bit playful. Asami and Kuro, thank you very much!

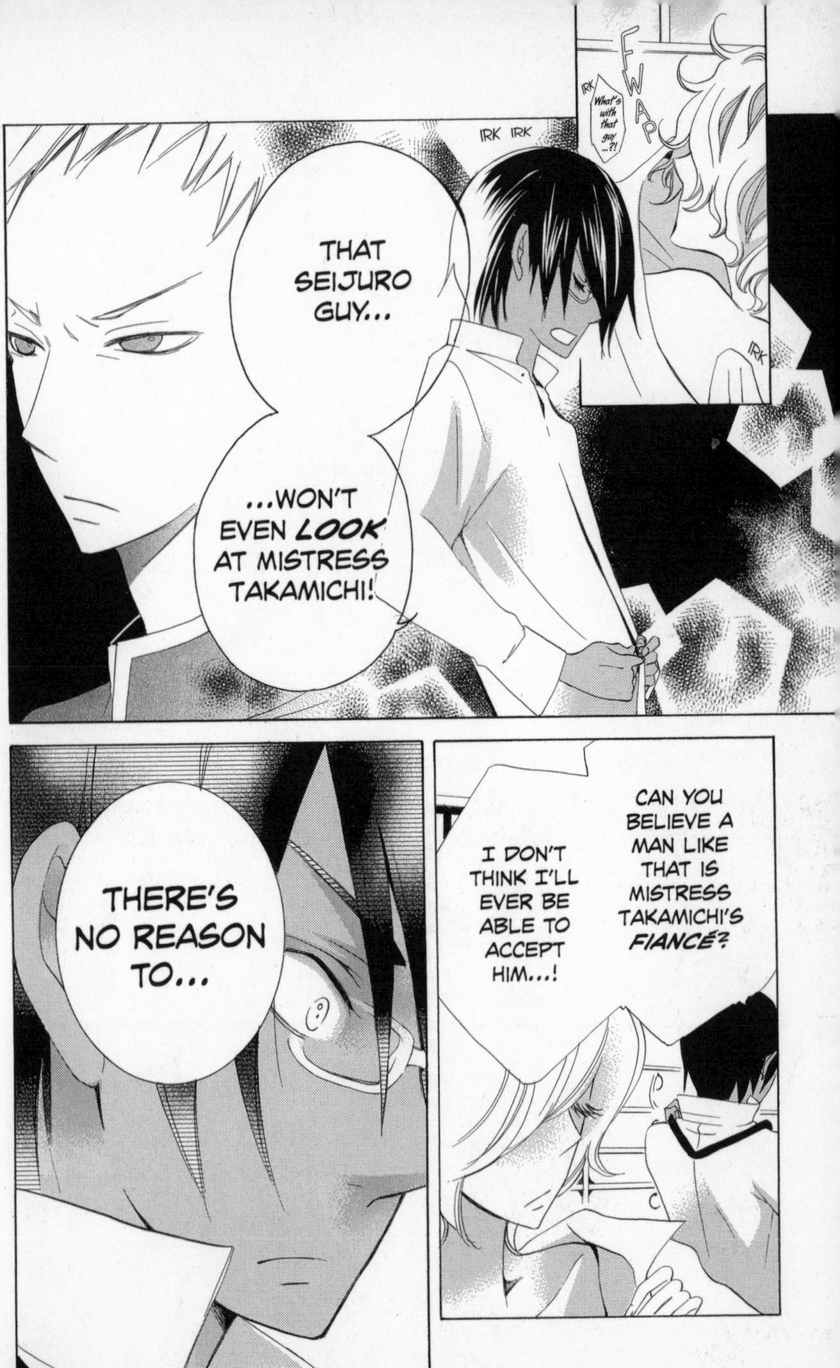
FWAP
IRK
What's with that guy ...?!
IRK
IRK IRK
THAT SEIJURO GUY...
...WON'T EVEN *LOOK* AT MISTRESS TAKAMICHI!
CAN YOU BELIEVE A MAN LIKE THAT IS MISTRESS TAKAMICHI'S *FIANCÉ*?
I DON'T THINK I'LL EVER BE ABLE TO ACCEPT HIM...!
THERE'S NO REASON TO...

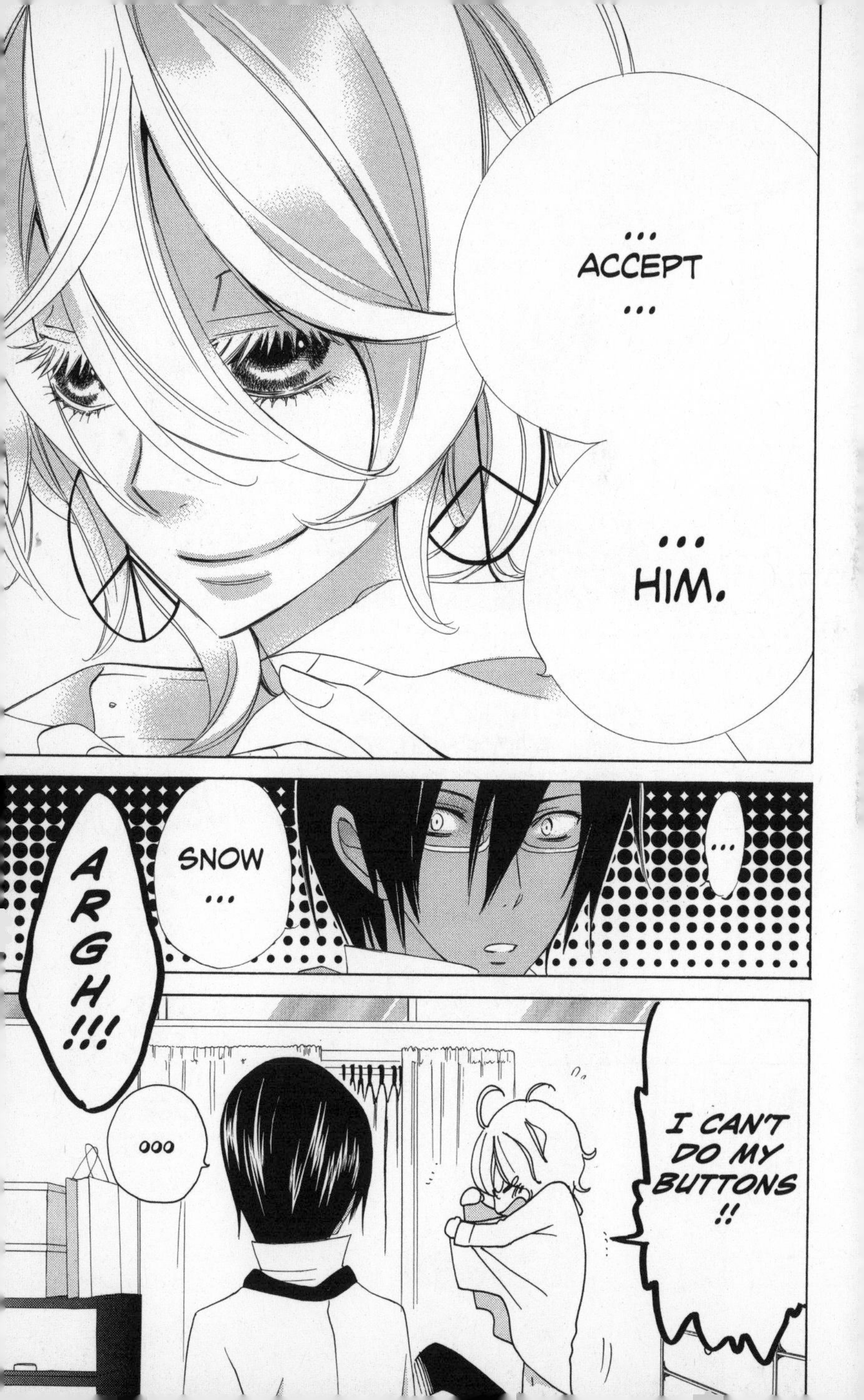
... ACCEPT ...
... HIM.
...
SNOW ...
ARGH!!!
I CAN'T DO MY BUTTONS !!
ooo

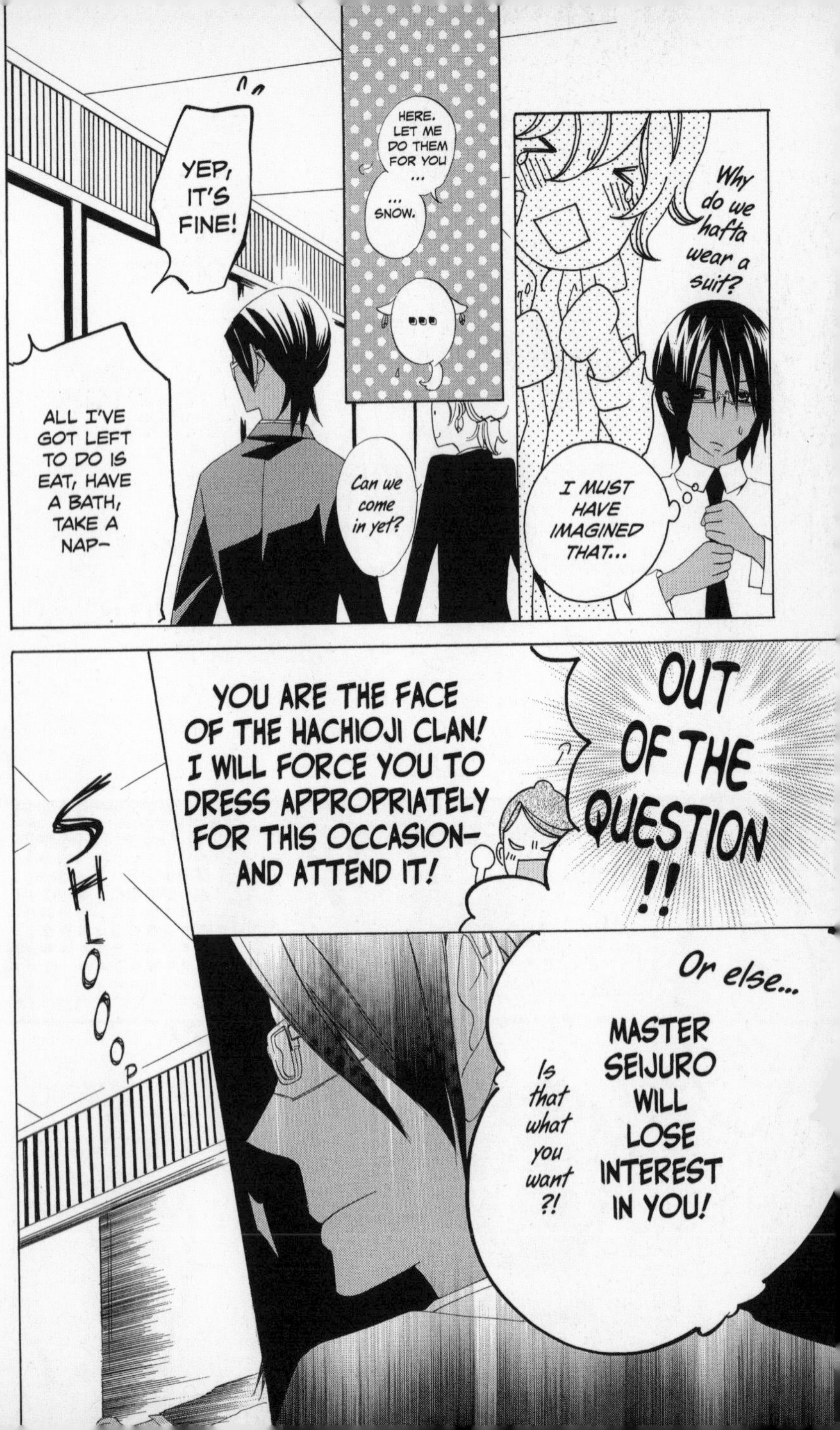
Why do we hafta wear a suit?
I MUST HAVE IMAGINED THAT...
HERE. LET ME DO THEM FOR YOU...
...SNOW.
...
Can we come in yet?
YEP, IT'S FINE!
ALL I'VE GOT LEFT TO DO IS EAT, HAVE A BATH, TAKE A NAP—
OUT OF THE QUESTION!!
YOU ARE THE FACE OF THE HACHIOJI CLAN! I WILL FORCE YOU TO DRESS APPROPRIATELY FOR THIS OCCASION—AND ATTEND IT!
SHLOOOOP
Or else...
MASTER SEIJURO WILL LOSE INTEREST IN YOU!
Is that what you want?!

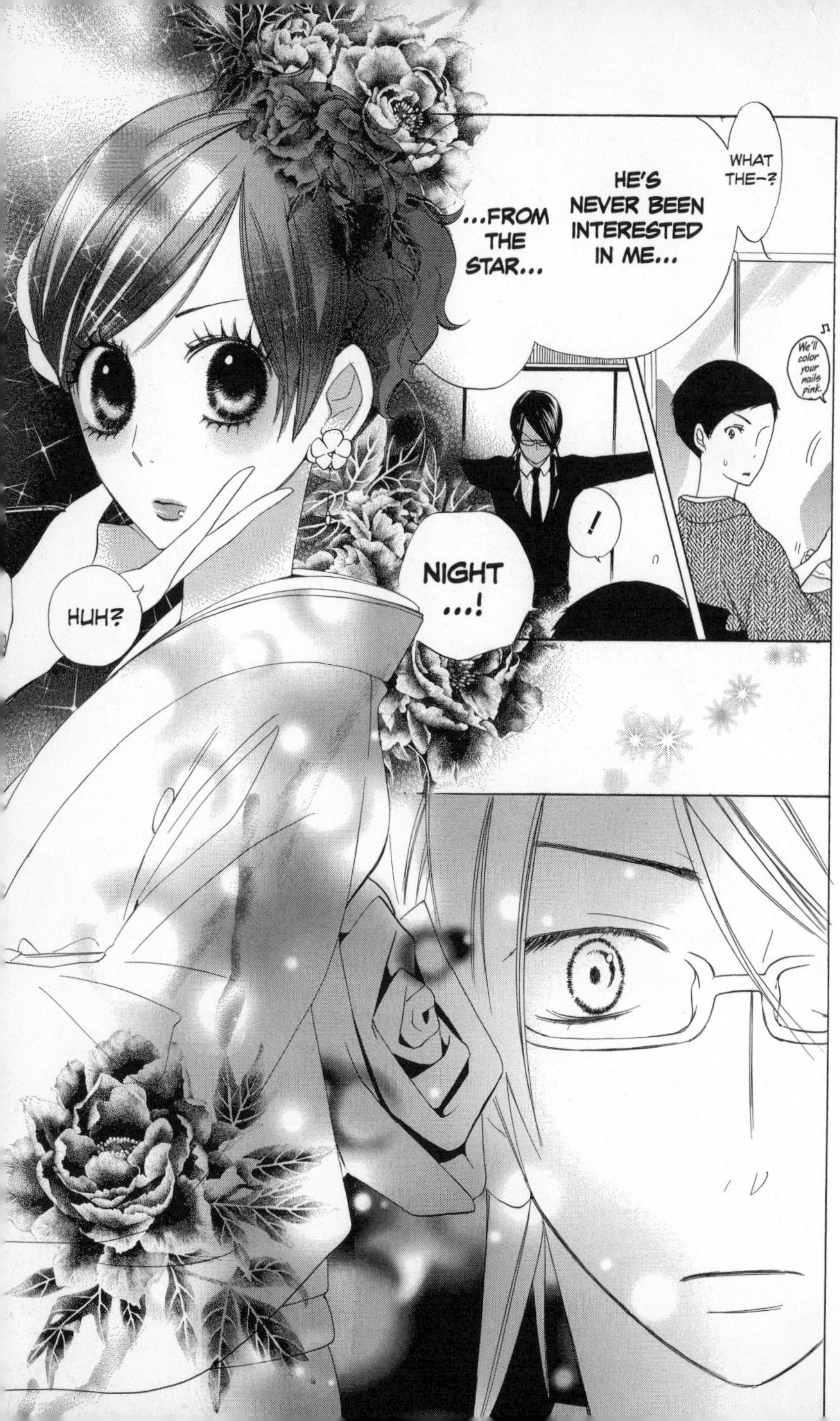
WHAT THE-?
HE'S NEVER BEEN INTERESTED IN ME...
...FROM THE STAR...
We'll color your nails pink.
!
NIGHT ...!
HUH?

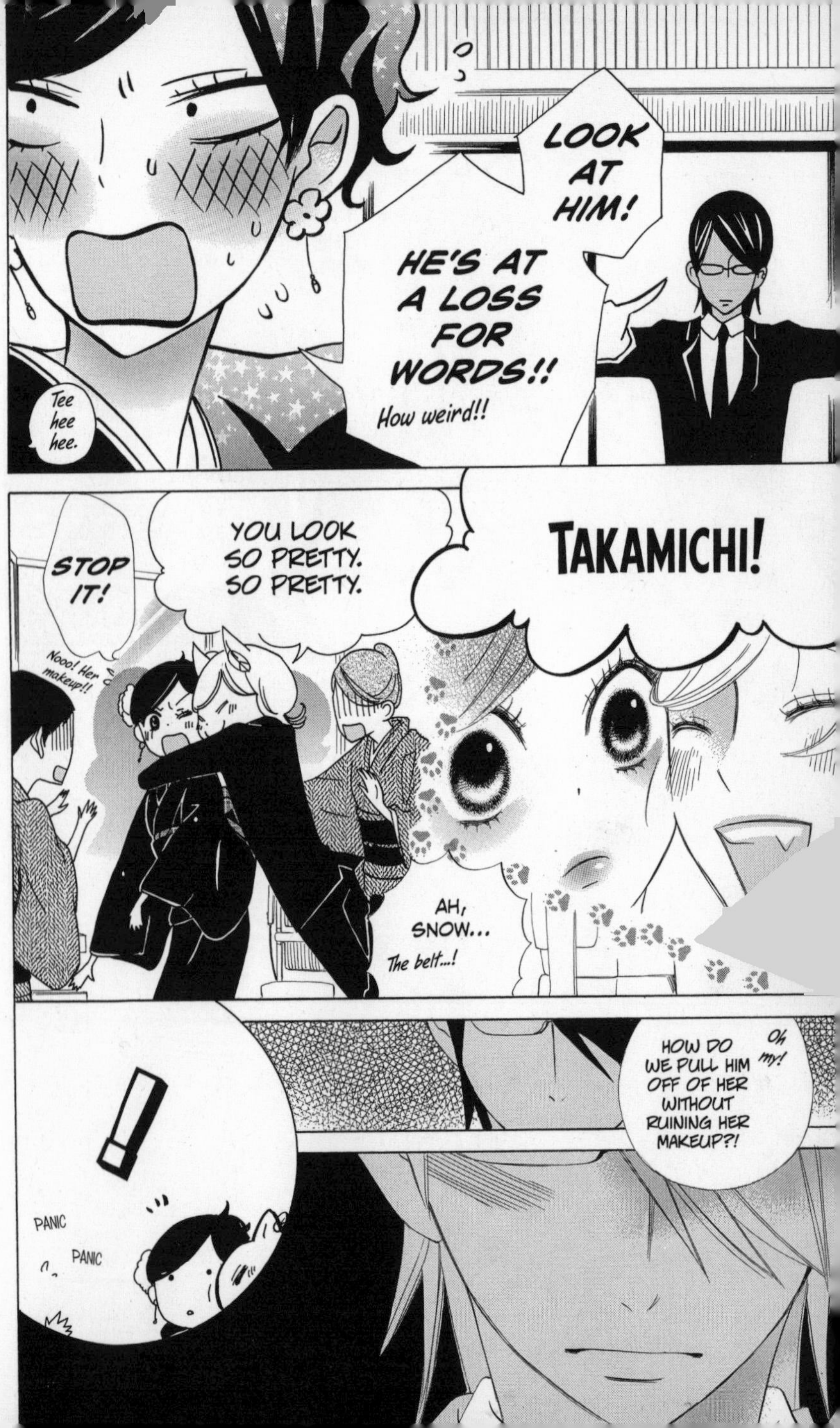
LOOK AT HIM!
HE'S AT A LOSS FOR WORDS!!
How weird!!
Tee hee hee.
TAKAMICHI!
YOU LOOK SO PRETTY. SO PRETTY.
STOP IT!
Nooo! Her makeup!!
AH, SNOW...
The belt...!
Oh my!
HOW DO WE PULL HIM OFF OF HER WITHOUT RUINING HER MAKEUP?!
!
PANIC
PANIC

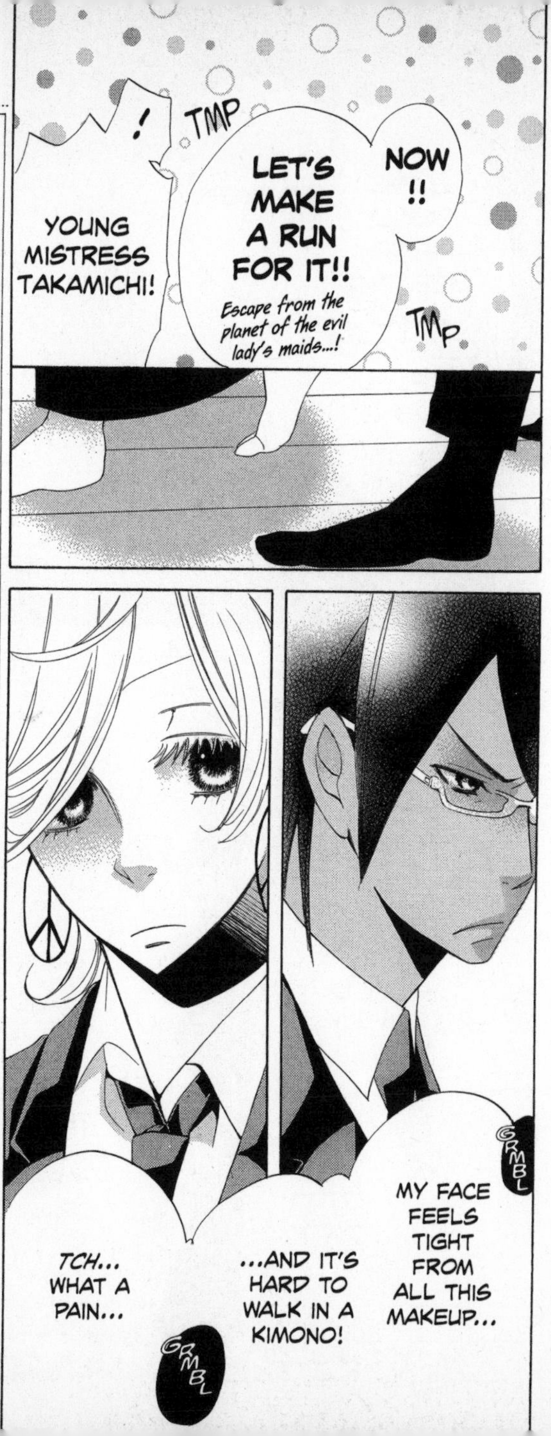
NOW!!
TMP
LET'S MAKE A RUN FOR IT!!
Escape from the planet of the evil lady's maids...!
TMP
!
YOUNG MISTRESS TAKAMICHI!
GRMBL
MY FACE FEELS TIGHT FROM ALL THIS MAKEUP...
...AND IT'S HARD TO WALK IN A KIMONO!
TCH... WHAT A PAIN...
GRMBL

The Family Head Meeting...

...has basically turned into a big feast.

In the beginning, I was going to fit all of volume 3 inside the 50 pages of Chapter 12.

Um... I don't think that's possible.

A nice guy. Mr. Editor

Me: No? You think not?

And so I got to relax and take my time with the story.

Most of all I was happy to get to draw Takayuki over and over in Chapter 14.

And then I was going to write all kinds of stuff about the Family Head Meeting. But I forgot what I was going to say. So I'll skip that part.

Oh, and I've very briefly hinted at Snow and Night's true identities. Will I reveal more in the future? Keep your eyes peeled!

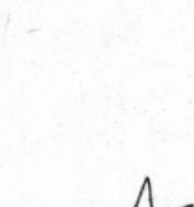

←My dog.

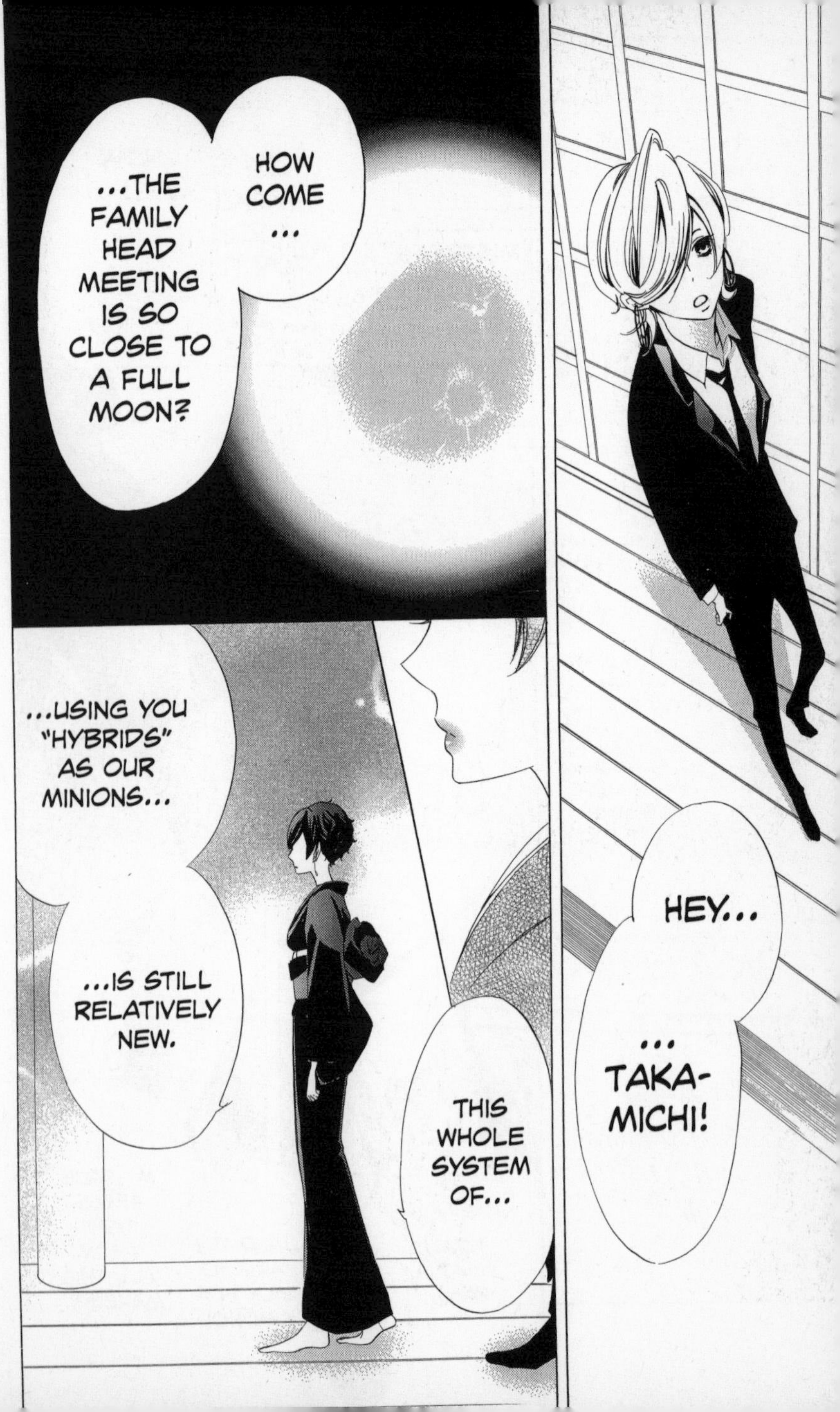
HEY...
...TAKA-MICHI!
HOW COME...
...THE FAMILY HEAD MEETING IS SO CLOSE TO A FULL MOON?
THIS WHOLE SYSTEM OF...
...USING YOU "HYBRIDS" AS OUR MINIONS...
...IS STILL RELATIVELY NEW.

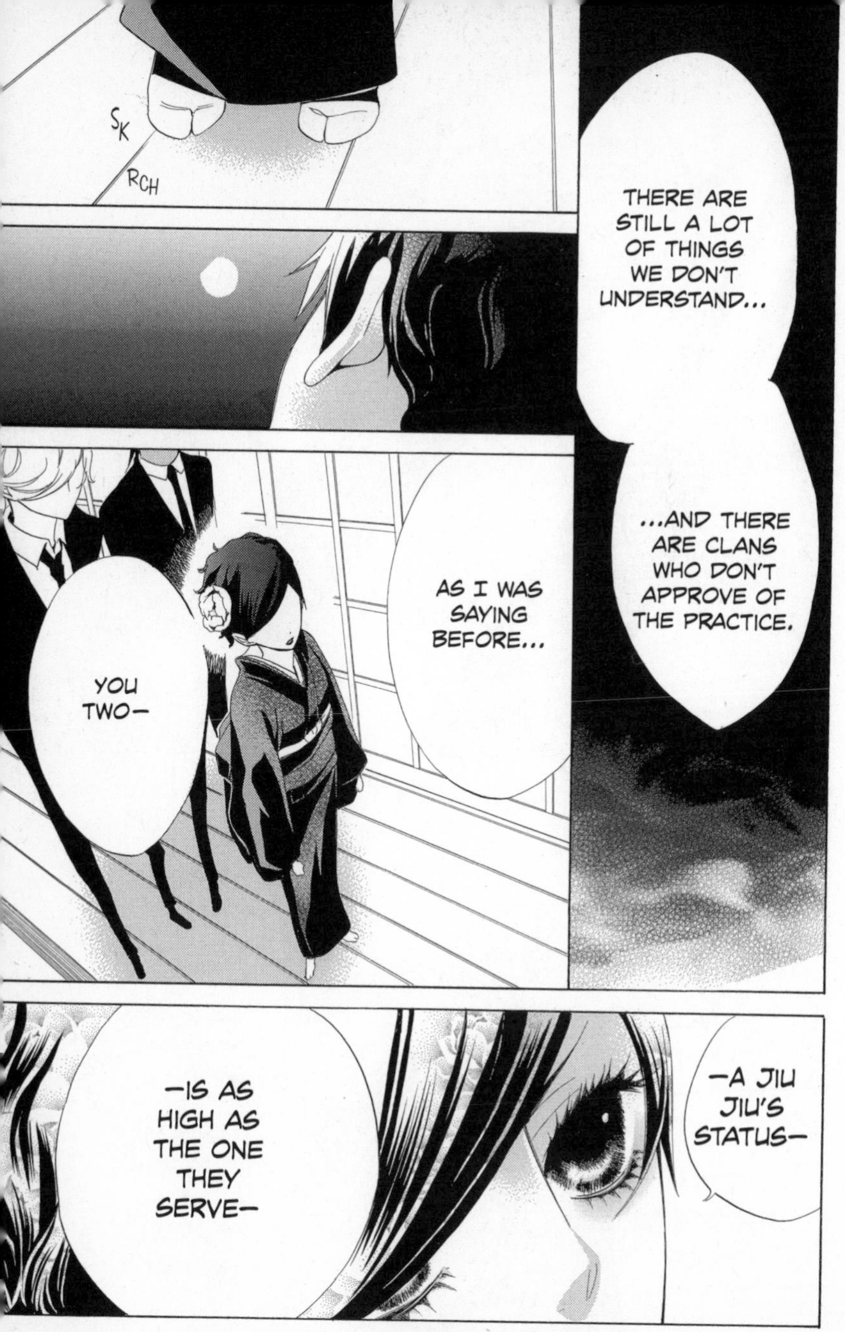
THERE ARE STILL A LOT OF THINGS WE DON'T UNDERSTAND...
...AND THERE ARE CLANS WHO DON'T APPROVE OF THE PRACTICE.
SK
RCH
AS I WAS SAYING BEFORE...
YOU TWO—
—A JIU JIU'S STATUS—
—IS AS HIGH AS THE ONE THEY SERVE—

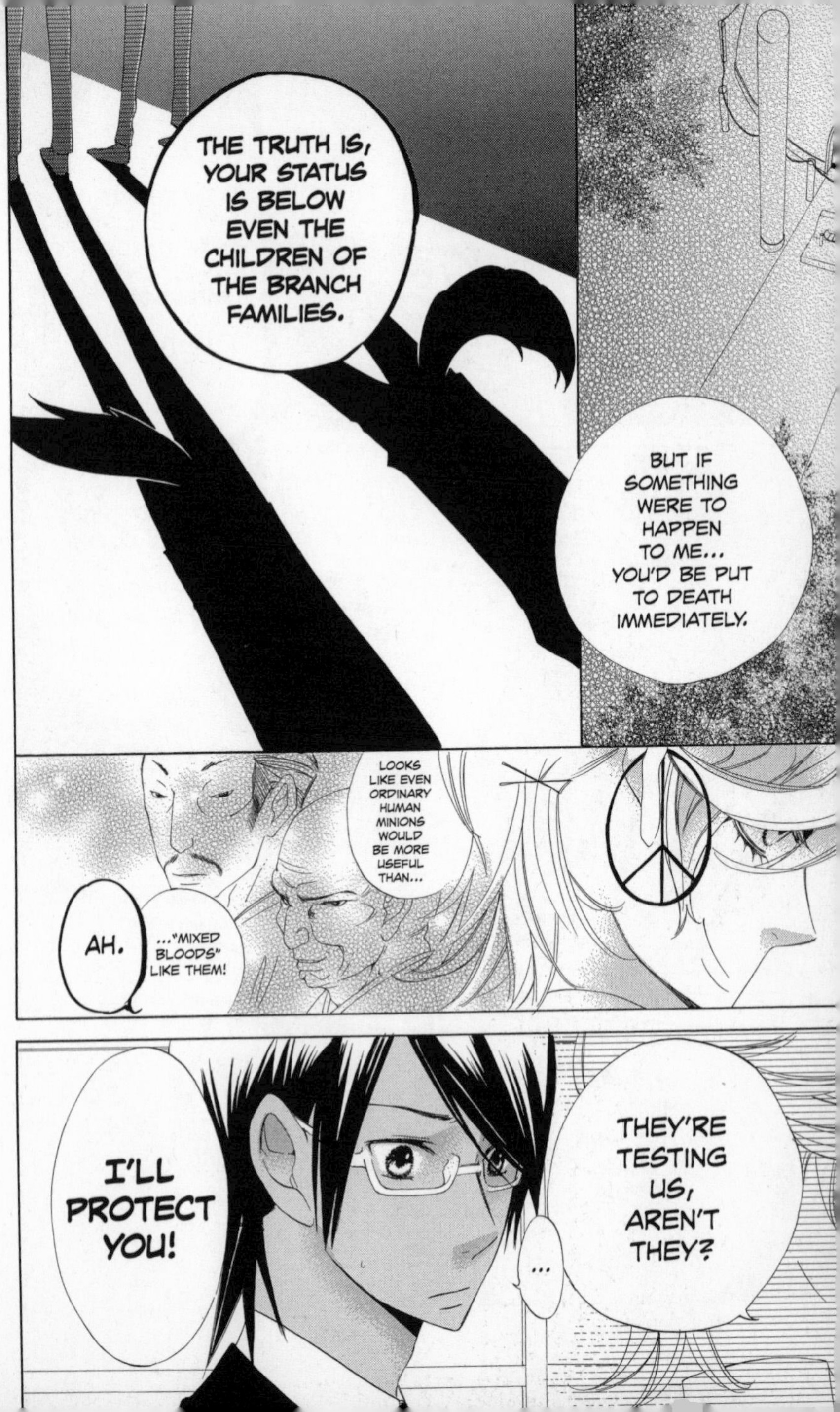
BUT IF SOMETHING WERE TO HAPPEN TO ME... YOU'D BE PUT TO DEATH IMMEDIATELY.
THE TRUTH IS, YOUR STATUS IS BELOW EVEN THE CHILDREN OF THE BRANCH FAMILIES.
LOOKS LIKE EVEN ORDINARY HUMAN MINIONS WOULD BE MORE USEFUL THAN...
..."MIXED BLOODS" LIKE THEM!
AH.
THEY'RE TESTING US, AREN'T THEY?
...
I'LL PROTECT YOU!

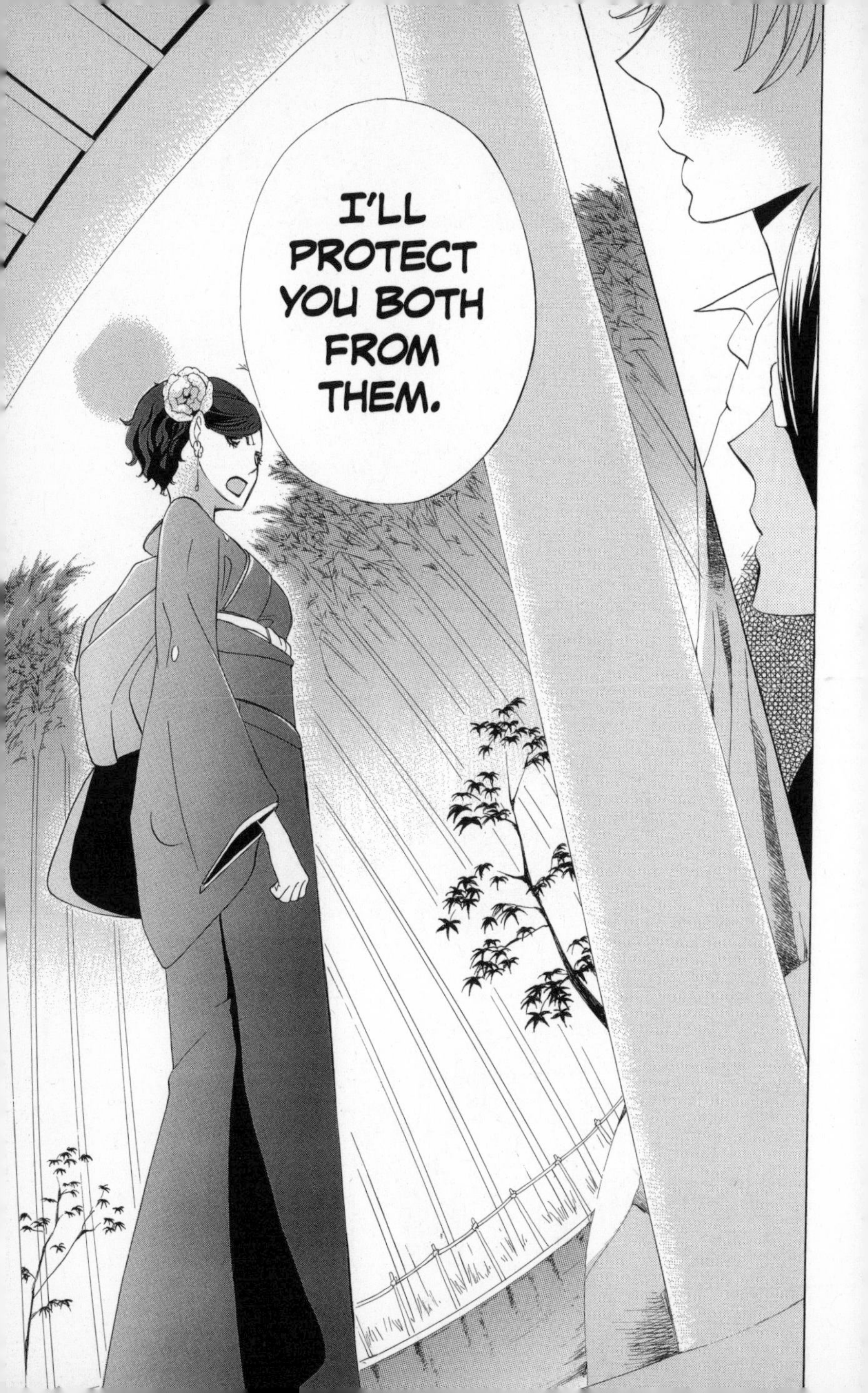
I'LL PROTECT YOU BOTH FROM THEM.

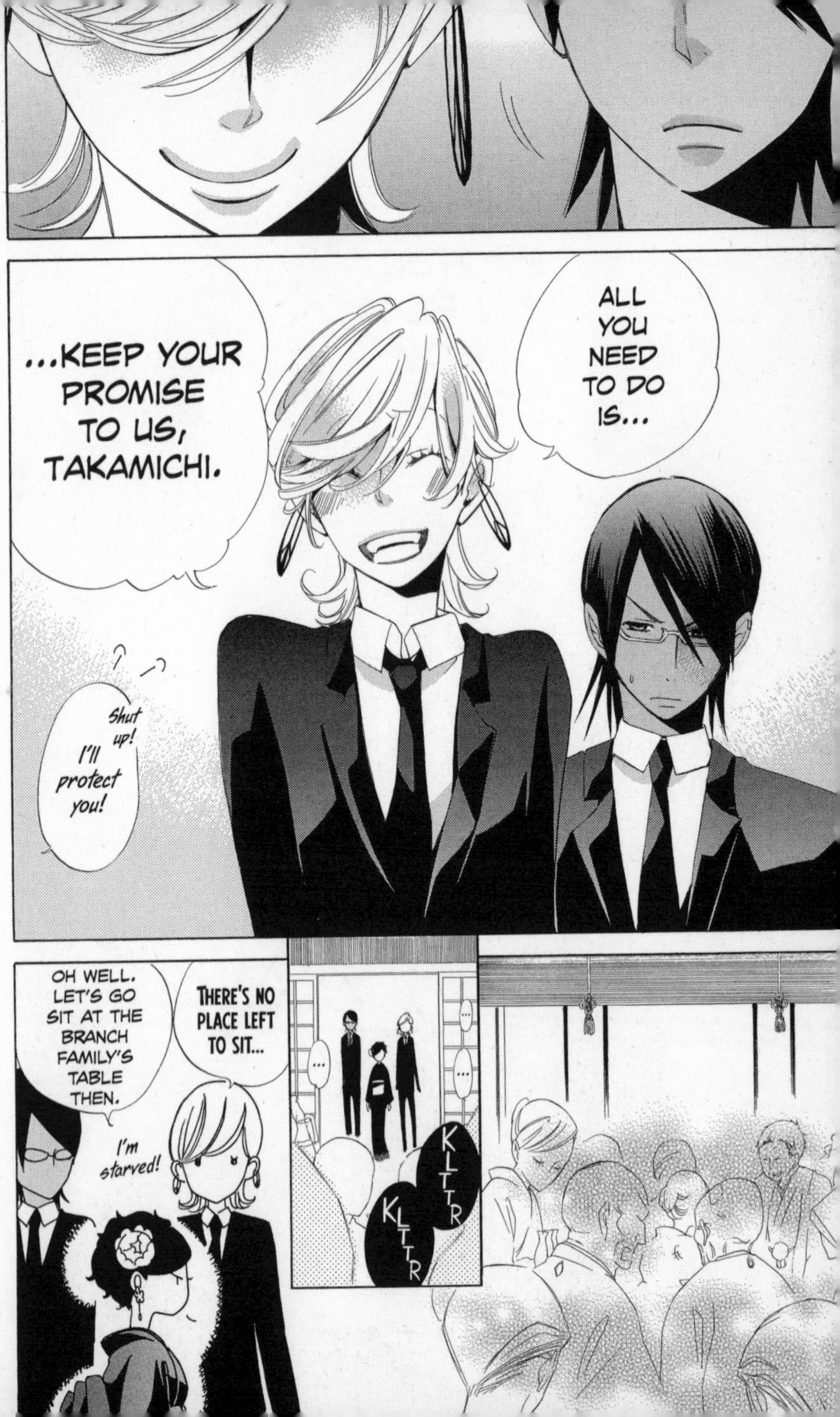
ALL YOU NEED TO DO IS...
...KEEP YOUR PROMISE TO US, TAKAMICHI.
Shut up! I'll protect you!
...
...
...
KLTTR
KLTTR
THERE'S NO PLACE LEFT TO SIT...
OH WELL. LET'S GO SIT AT THE BRANCH FAMILY'S TABLE THEN.
I'm starved!

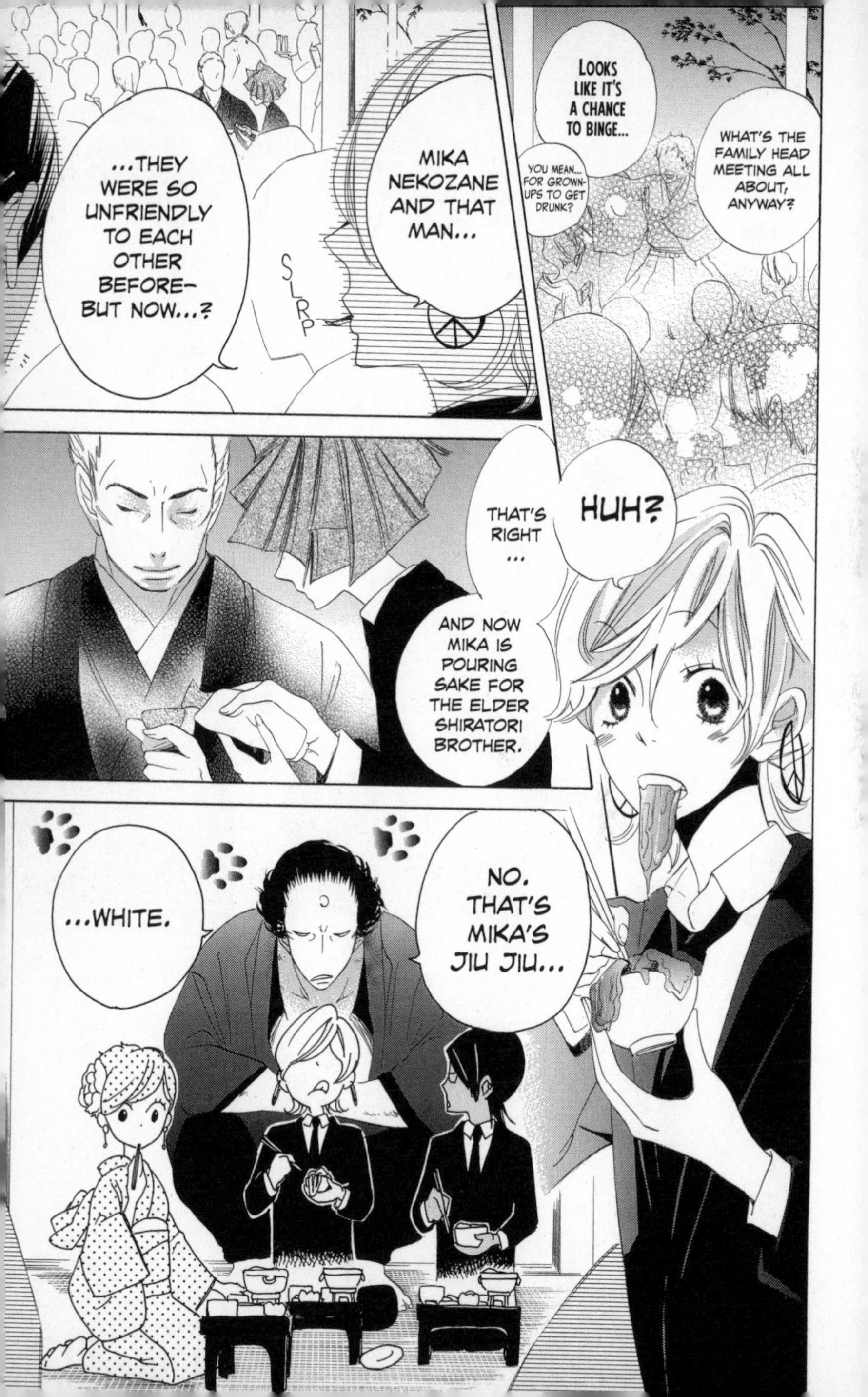
WHAT'S THE FAMILY HEAD MEETING ALL ABOUT, ANYWAY?
LOOKS LIKE IT'S A CHANCE TO BINGE...
YOU MEAN... FOR GROWN-UPS TO GET DRUNK?
MIKA NEKOZANE AND THAT MAN...
SLRP
...THEY WERE SO UNFRIENDLY TO EACH OTHER BEFORE-BUT NOW...?
HUH?
THAT'S RIGHT...
AND NOW MIKA IS POURING SAKE FOR THE ELDER SHIRATORI BROTHER.
NO. THAT'S MIKA'S JIU JIU...
...WHITE.

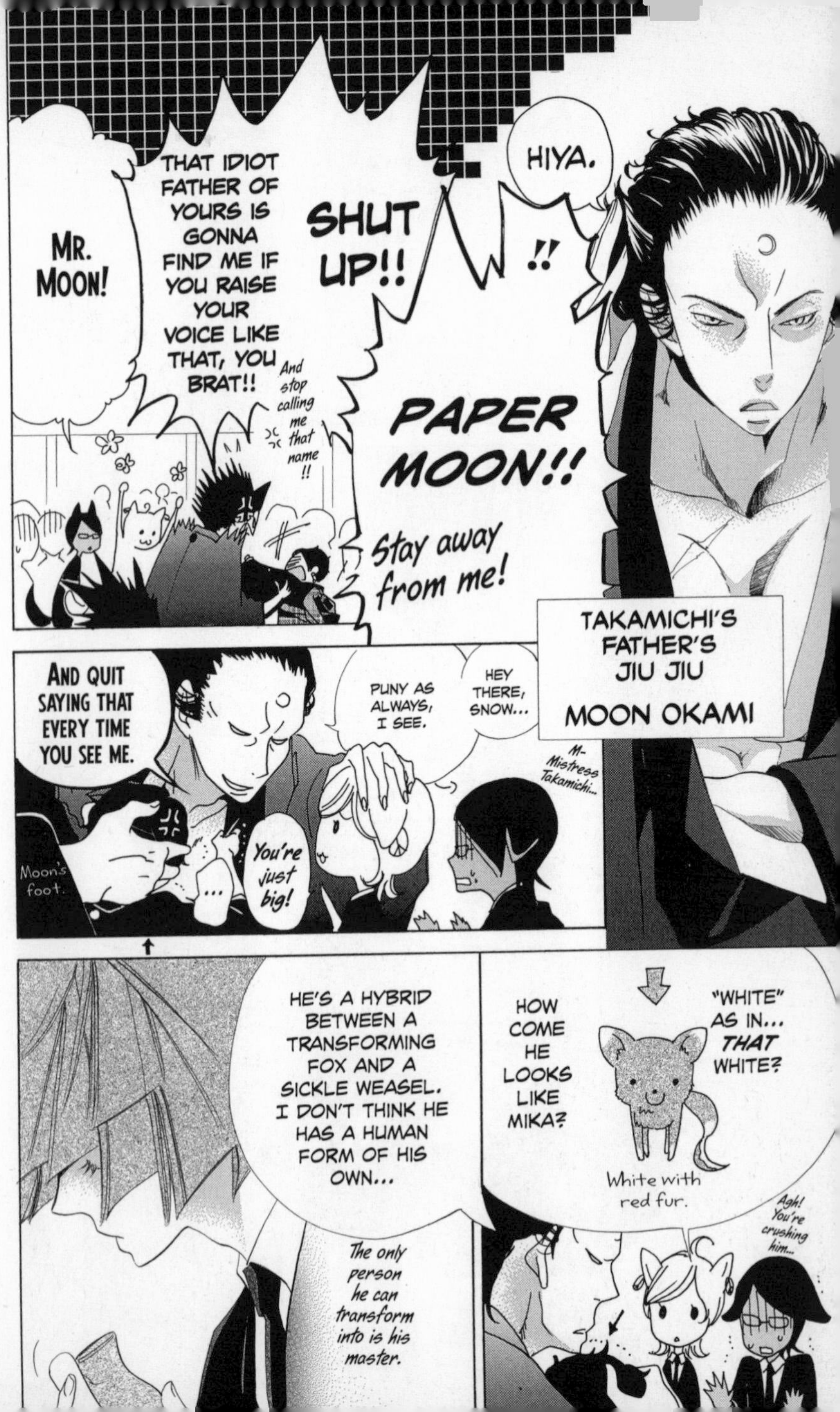
HIYA.
!!
TAKAMICHI'S FATHER'S JIU JIU
MOON OKAMI
SHUT UP!!
MR. MOON!
THAT IDIOT FATHER OF YOURS IS GONNA FIND ME IF YOU RAISE YOUR VOICE LIKE THAT, YOU BRAT!!
And stop calling me that name!!
PAPER MOON!!
Stay away from me!
HEY THERE, SNOW...
PUNY AS ALWAYS, I SEE.
M-Mistress Takamichi...
AND QUIT SAYING THAT EVERY TIME YOU SEE ME.
You're just big!
...
Moon's foot.
"WHITE" AS IN... THAT WHITE?
HOW COME HE LOOKS LIKE MIKA?
White with red fur.
Agh! You're crushing him...
...
HE'S A HYBRID BETWEEN A TRANSFORMING FOX AND A SICKLE WEASEL. I DON'T THINK HE HAS A HUMAN FORM OF HIS OWN...
The only person he can transform into is his master.

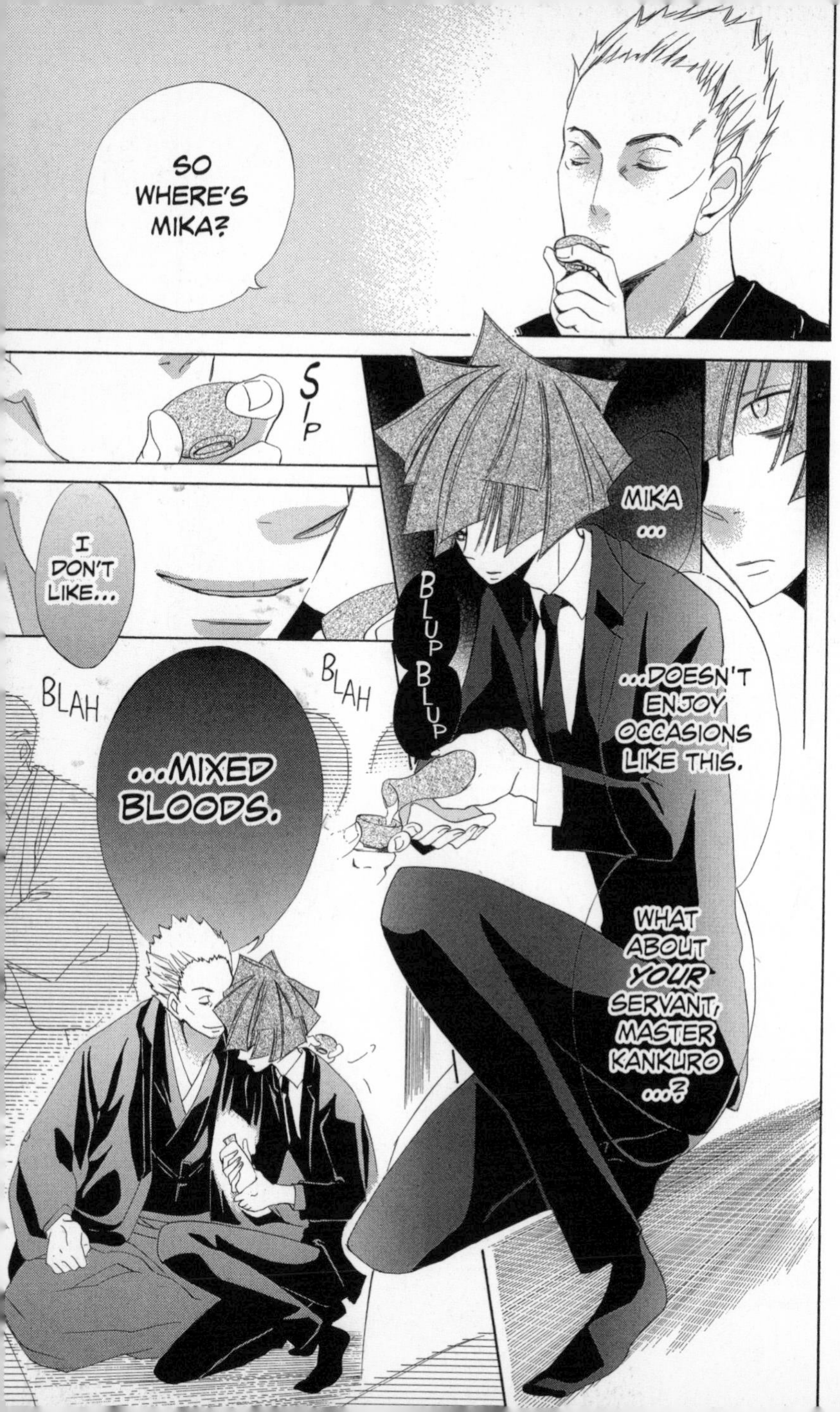
SO WHERE'S MIKA?
MIKA...
BLUP BLUP
...DOESN'T ENJOY OCCASIONS LIKE THIS.
WHAT ABOUT *YOUR* SERVANT, MASTER KANKURO...?
SIP
I DON'T LIKE...
BLAH
BLAH
...MIXED BLOODS.

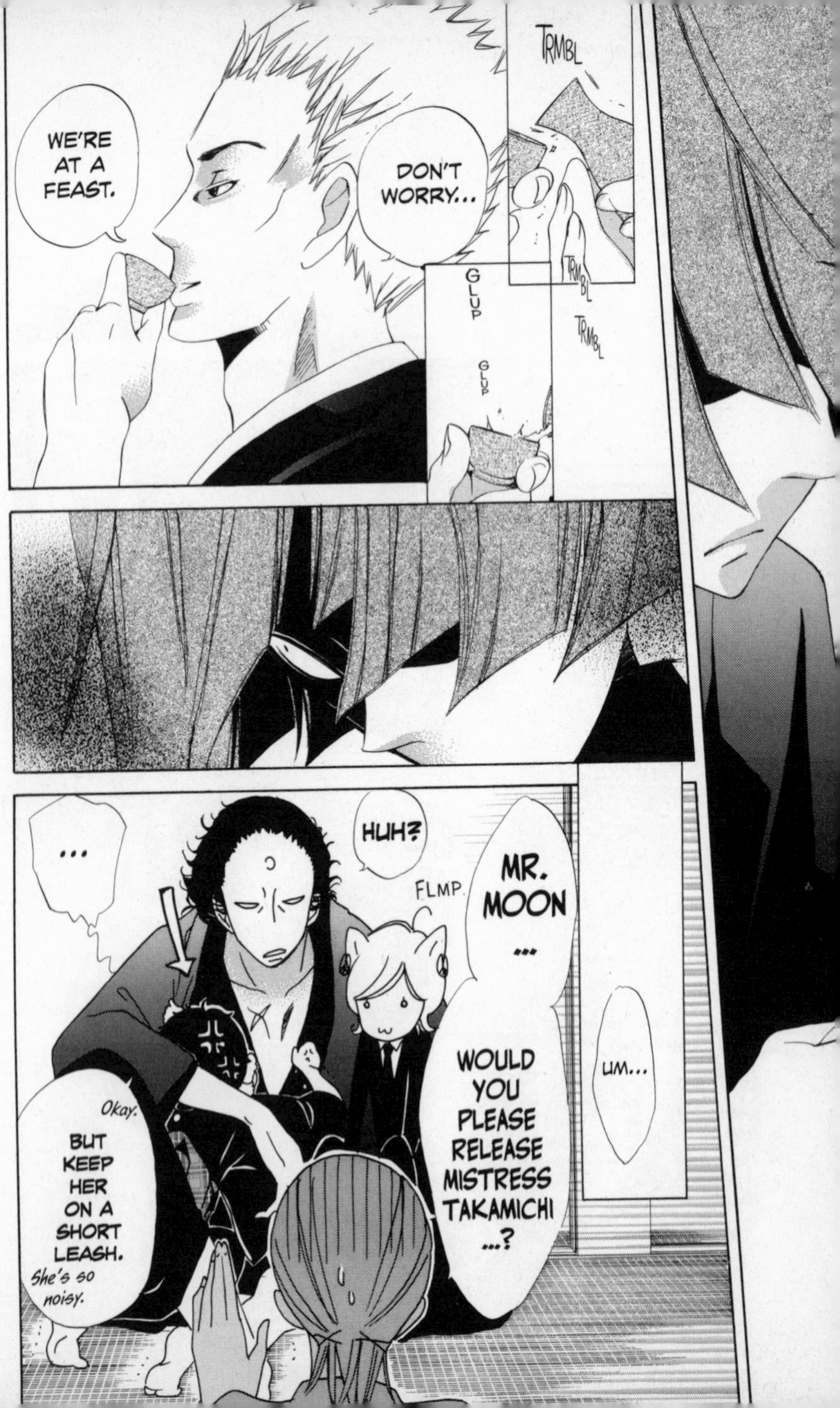
TRMBL
TRMBL
TRMBL
GLUP
GLUP
DON'T WORRY...
WE'RE AT A FEAST.
UM...
MR. MOON ...
WOULD YOU PLEASE RELEASE MISTRESS TAKAMICHI ...?
HUH?
FLMP.
...
Okay.
BUT KEEP HER ON A SHORT LEASH.
She's so noisy.

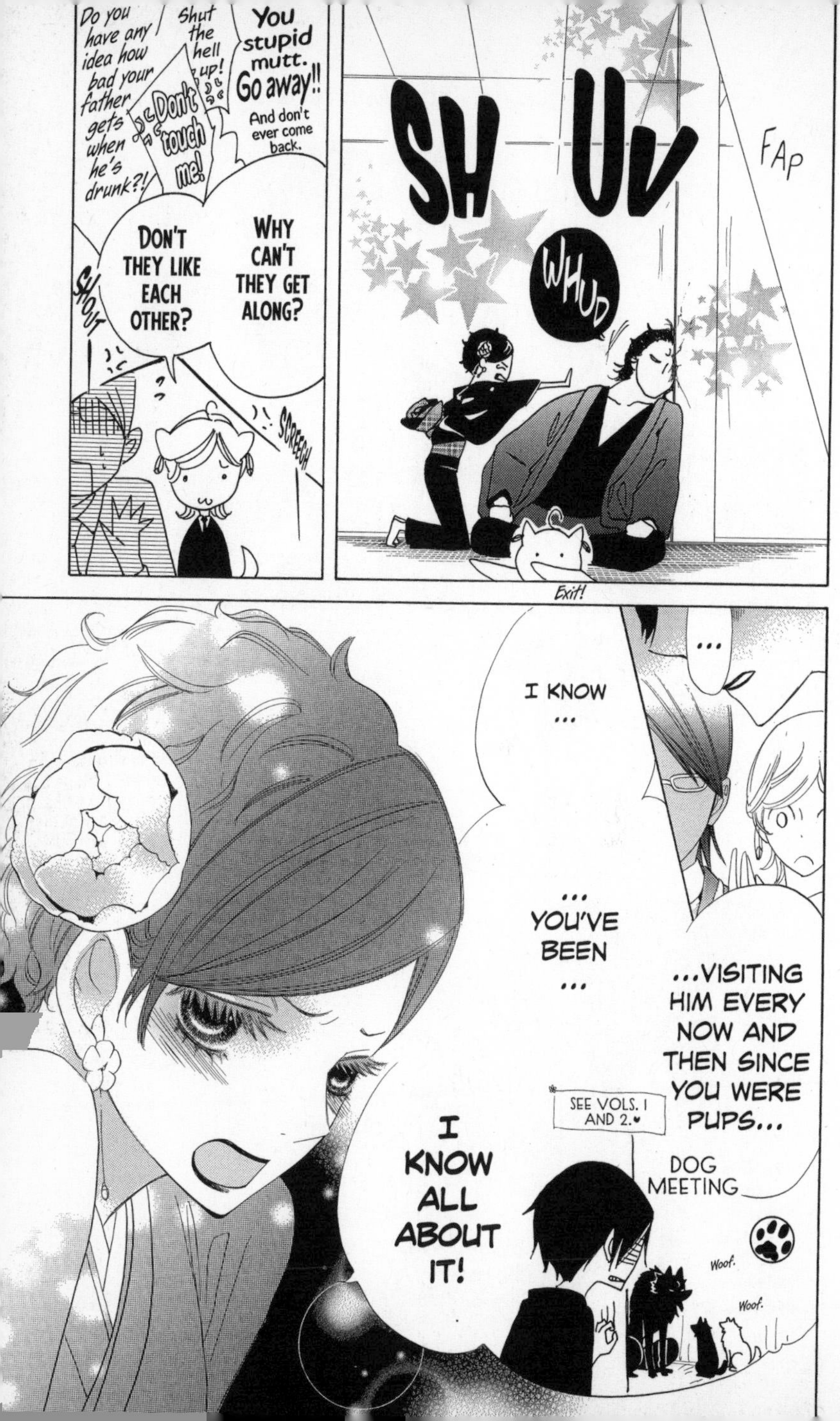
SHUV
WHUD
FAP
Exit!
You stupid mutt. Go away!!
And don't ever come back.
Shut the hell up!
Don't touch me!
Do you have any idea how bad your father gets when he's drunk?!
SHOUT
WHY CAN'T THEY GET ALONG?
DON'T THEY LIKE EACH OTHER?
SCREECH
...
I KNOW ...
... YOU'VE BEEN ...
...VISITING HIM EVERY NOW AND THEN SINCE YOU WERE PUPS...
SEE VOLS. 1 AND 2.
DOG MEETING
Woof.
Woof.
I KNOW ALL ABOUT IT!

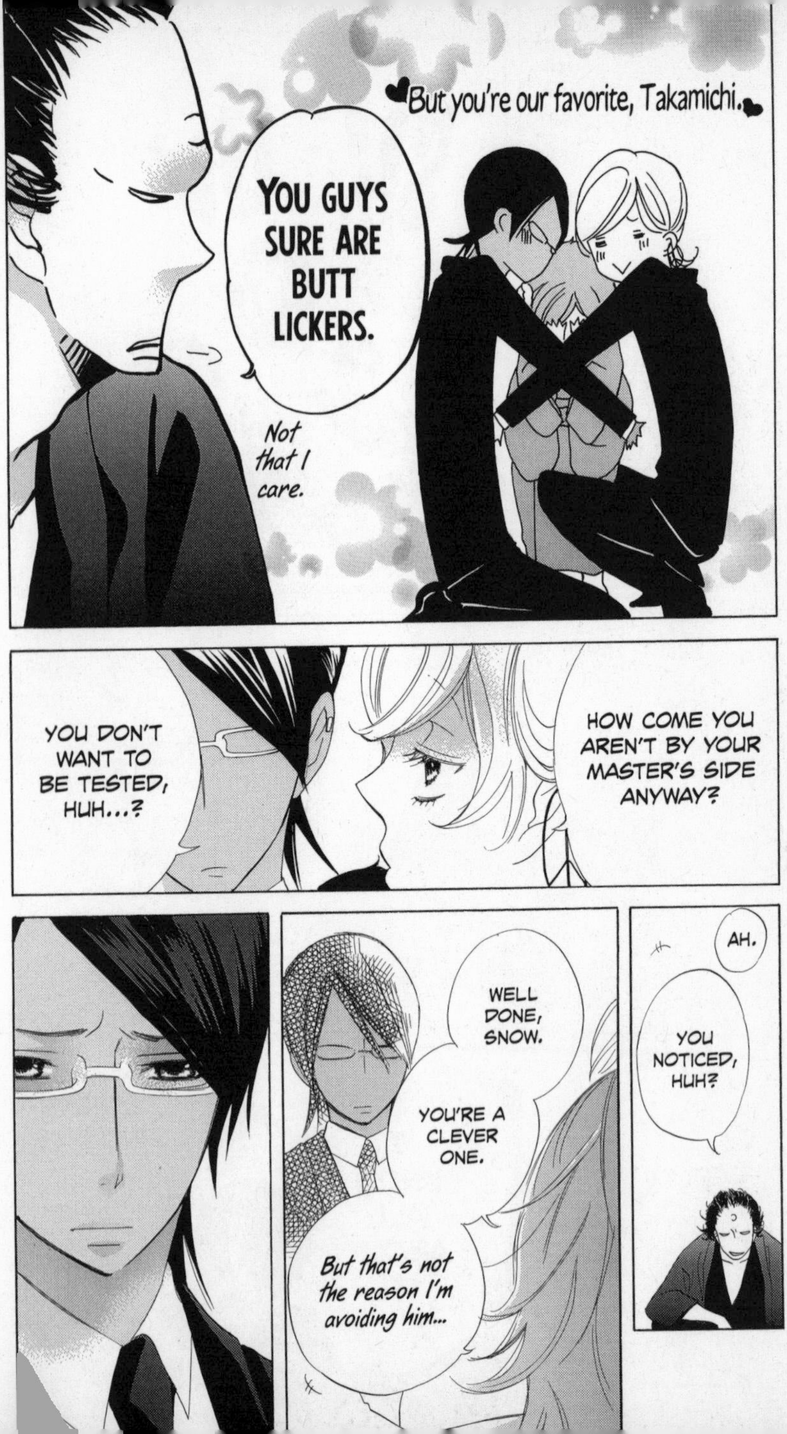
But you're our favorite, Takamichi.
YOU GUYS SURE ARE BUTT LICKERS.
Not that I care.
HOW COME YOU AREN'T BY YOUR MASTER'S SIDE ANYWAY?
YOU DON'T WANT TO BE TESTED, HUH...?
AH.
YOU NOTICED, HUH?
WELL DONE, SNOW.
YOU'RE A CLEVER ONE.
But that's not the reason I'm avoiding him...

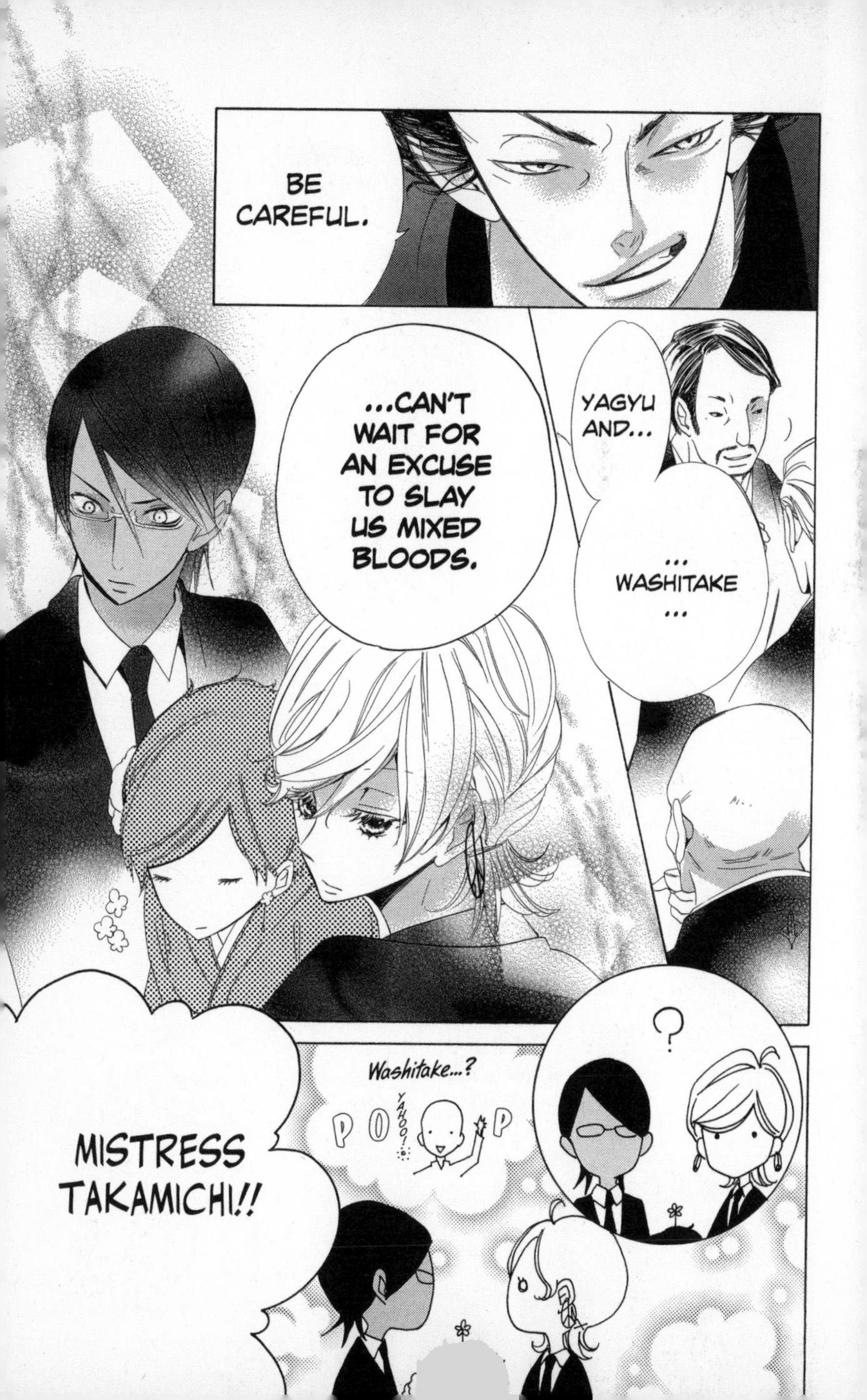
BE CAREFUL.
YAGYU AND...
... WASHITAKE ...
...CAN'T WAIT FOR AN EXCUSE TO SLAY US MIXED BLOODS.
M...
?
Washitake...?
P O YAHOO! P
MISTRESS TAKAMICHI!!

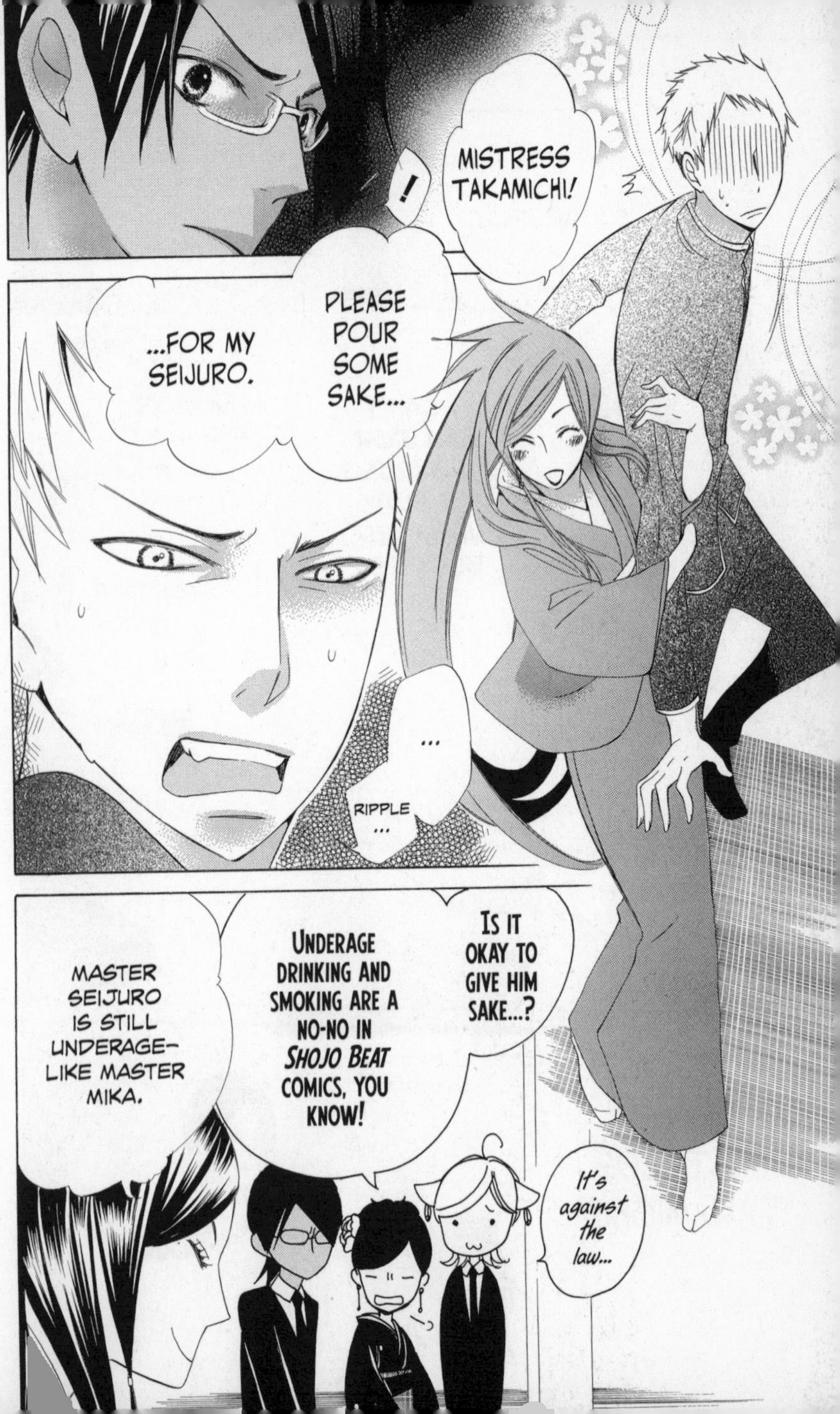
MISTRESS TAKAMICHI!
!
PLEASE POUR SOME SAKE...
...FOR MY SEIJURO.
...
RIPPLE ...
IS IT OKAY TO GIVE HIM SAKE...?
UNDERAGE DRINKING AND SMOKING ARE A NO-NO IN *SHOJO BEAT* COMICS, YOU KNOW!
MASTER SEIJURO IS STILL UNDERAGE— LIKE MASTER MIKA.
It's against the law...

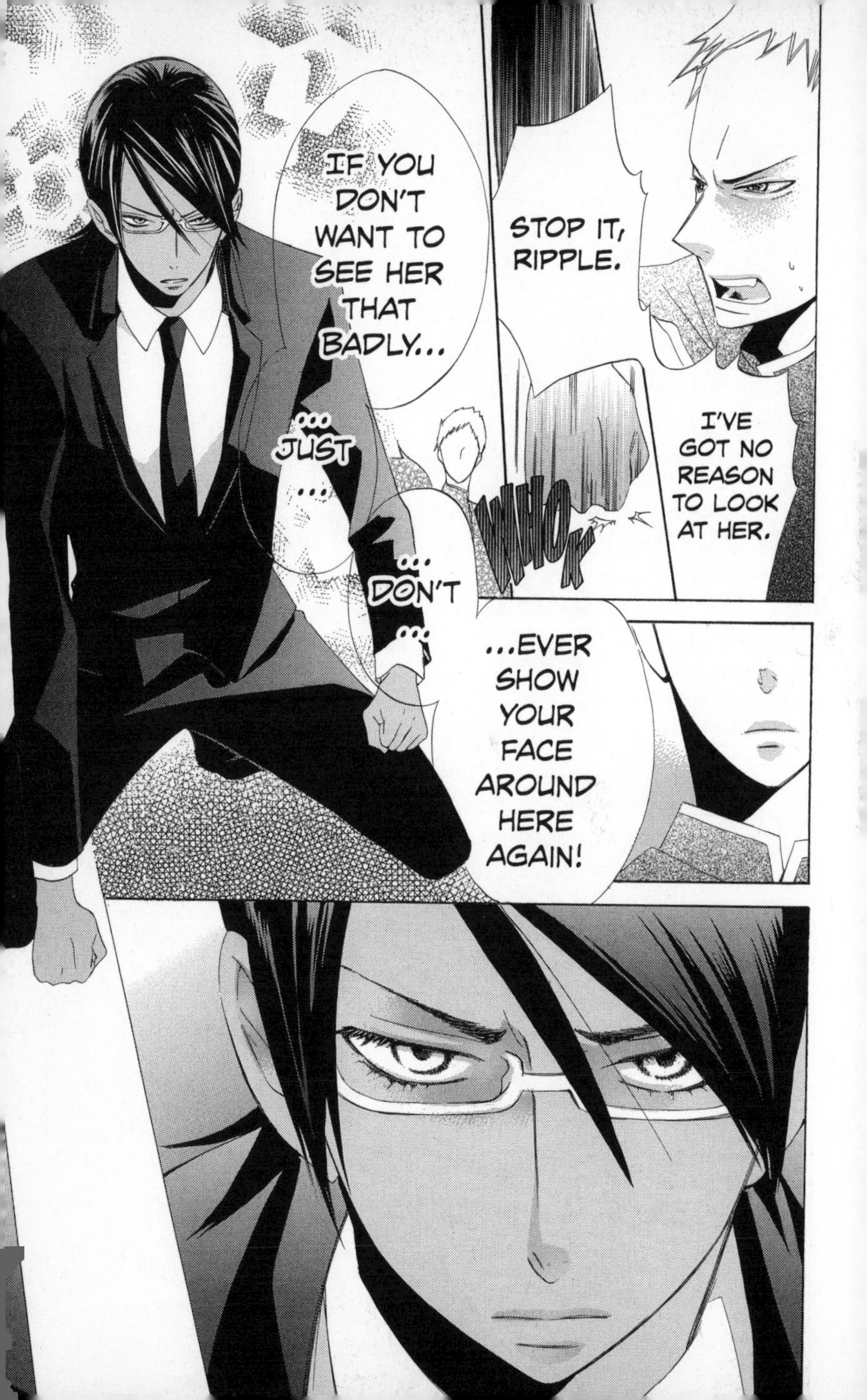
STOP IT, RIPPLE.
I'VE GOT NO REASON TO LOOK AT HER.
WHOK
IF YOU DON'T WANT TO SEE HER THAT BADLY...
...JUST...
...DON'T...
...EVER SHOW YOUR FACE AROUND HERE AGAIN!

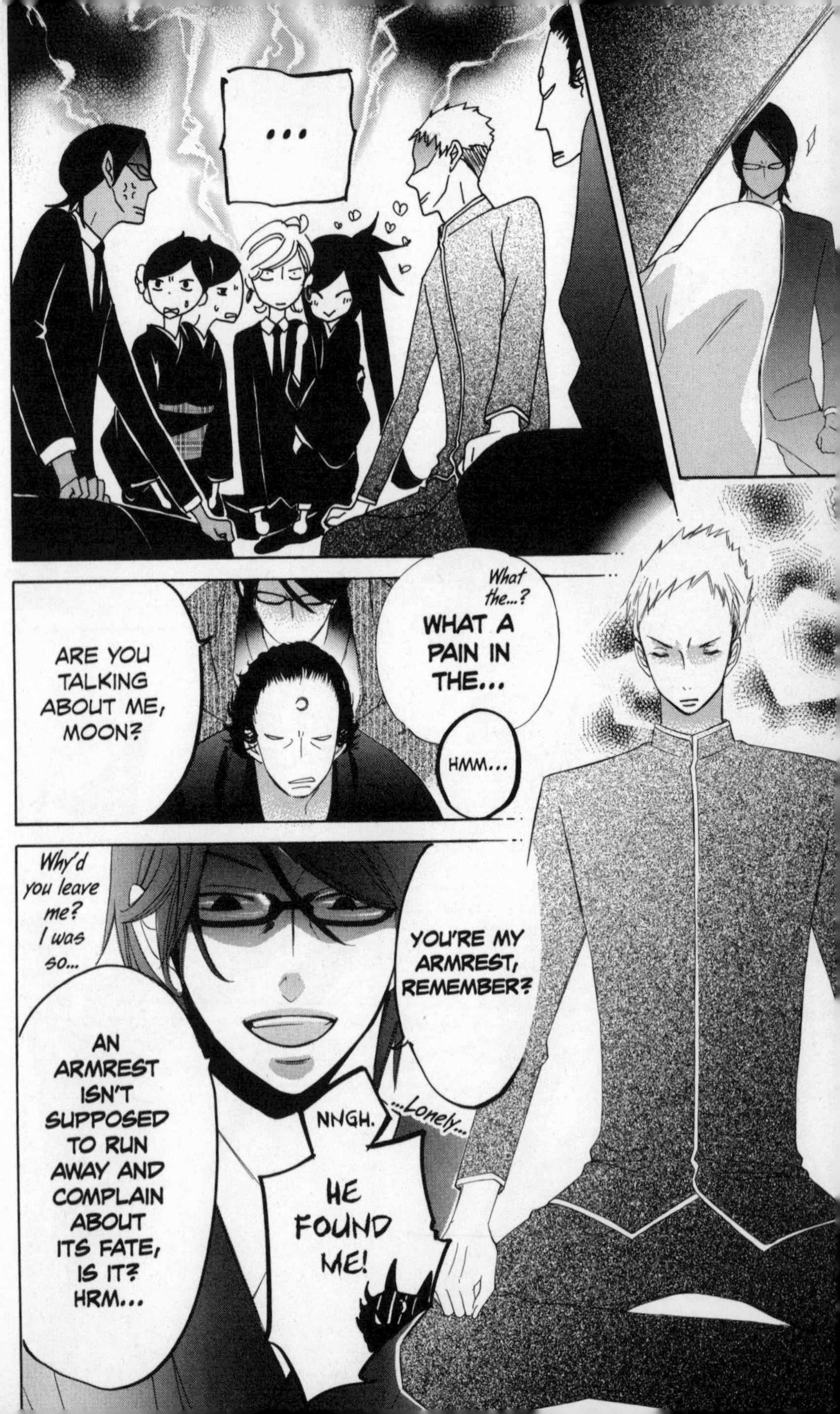
...
What the...?
WHAT A PAIN IN THE...
HMM...
ARE YOU TALKING ABOUT ME, MOON?
YOU'RE MY ARMREST, REMEMBER?
Why'd you leave me? I was so...
...Lonely...
NNGH.
AN ARMREST ISN'T SUPPOSED TO RUN AWAY AND COMPLAIN ABOUT ITS FATE, IS IT? HRM...
HE FOUND ME!

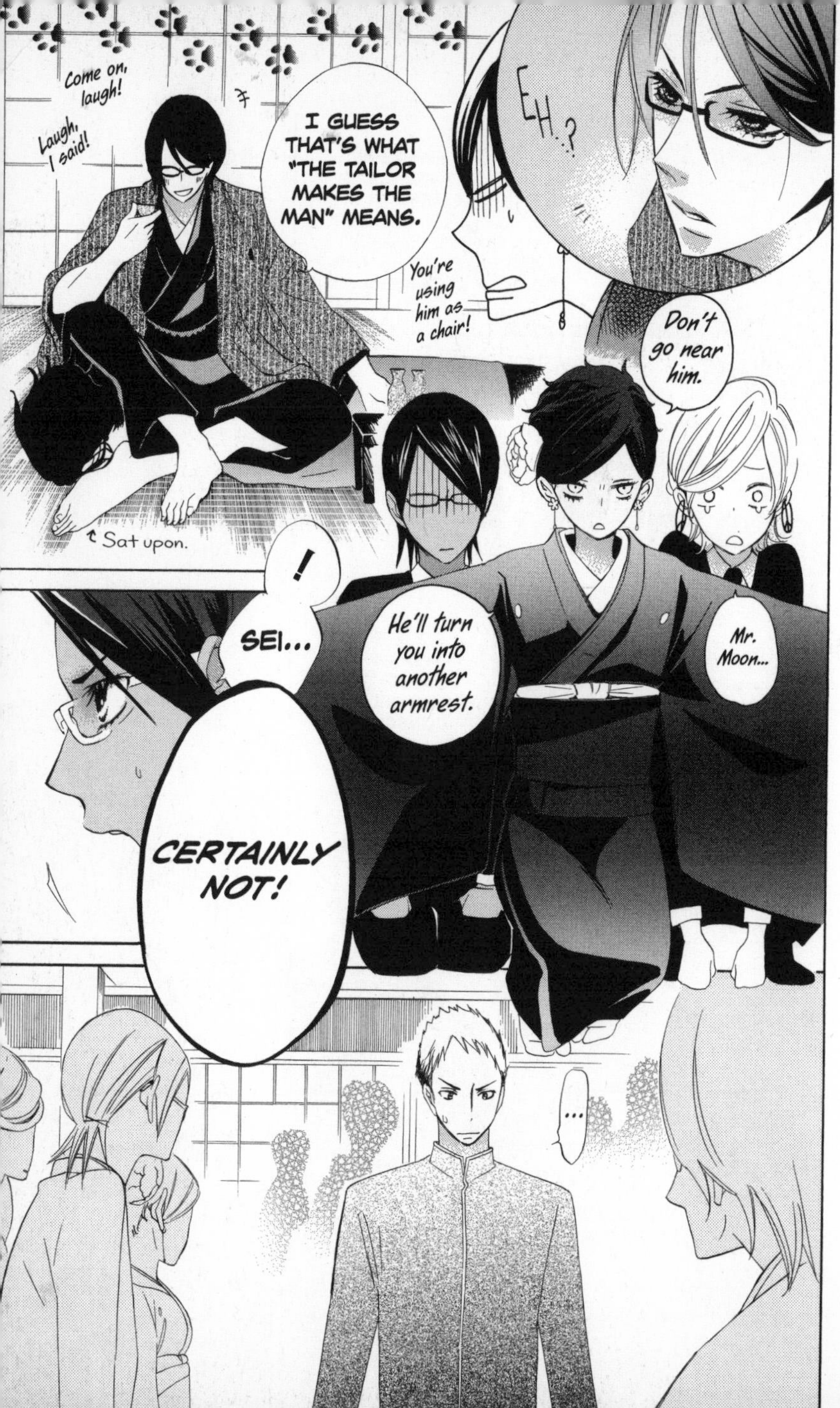
EH...?
You're using him as a chair!
Come on, laugh!
Laugh, I said!
チ
I GUESS THAT'S WHAT "THE TAILOR MAKES THE MAN" MEANS.
Sat upon.
Don't go near him.
He'll turn you into another armrest.
Mr. Moon...
!
SEI...
CERTAINLY NOT!
...

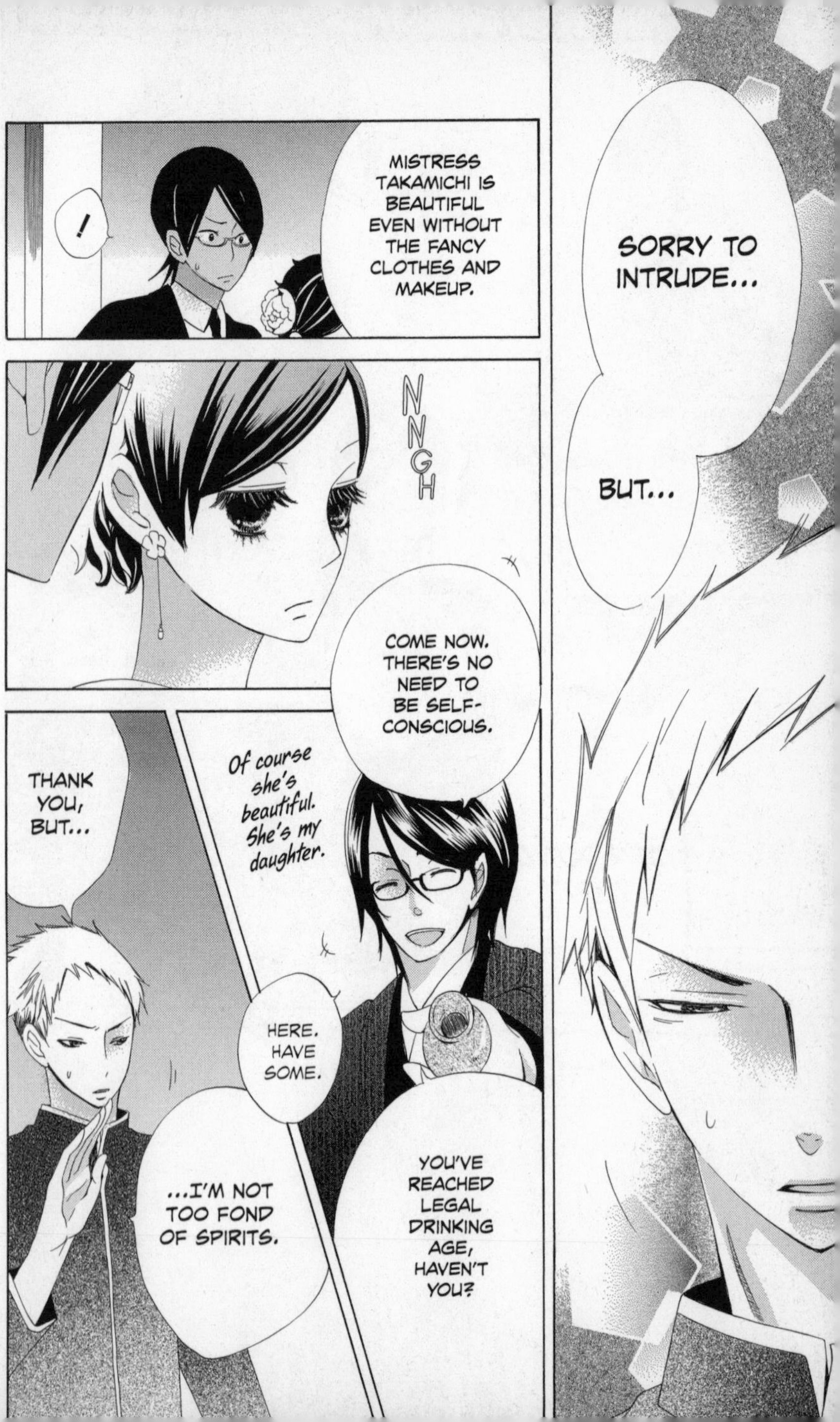
SORRY TO INTRUDE...
BUT...
MISTRESS TAKAMICHI IS BEAUTIFUL EVEN WITHOUT THE FANCY CLOTHES AND MAKEUP.
!
NNGH
COME NOW. THERE'S NO NEED TO BE SELF-CONSCIOUS.
Of course she's beautiful. She's my daughter.
HERE. HAVE SOME.
YOU'VE REACHED LEGAL DRINKING AGE, HAVEN'T YOU?
THANK YOU, BUT...
...I'M NOT TOO FOND OF SPIRITS.

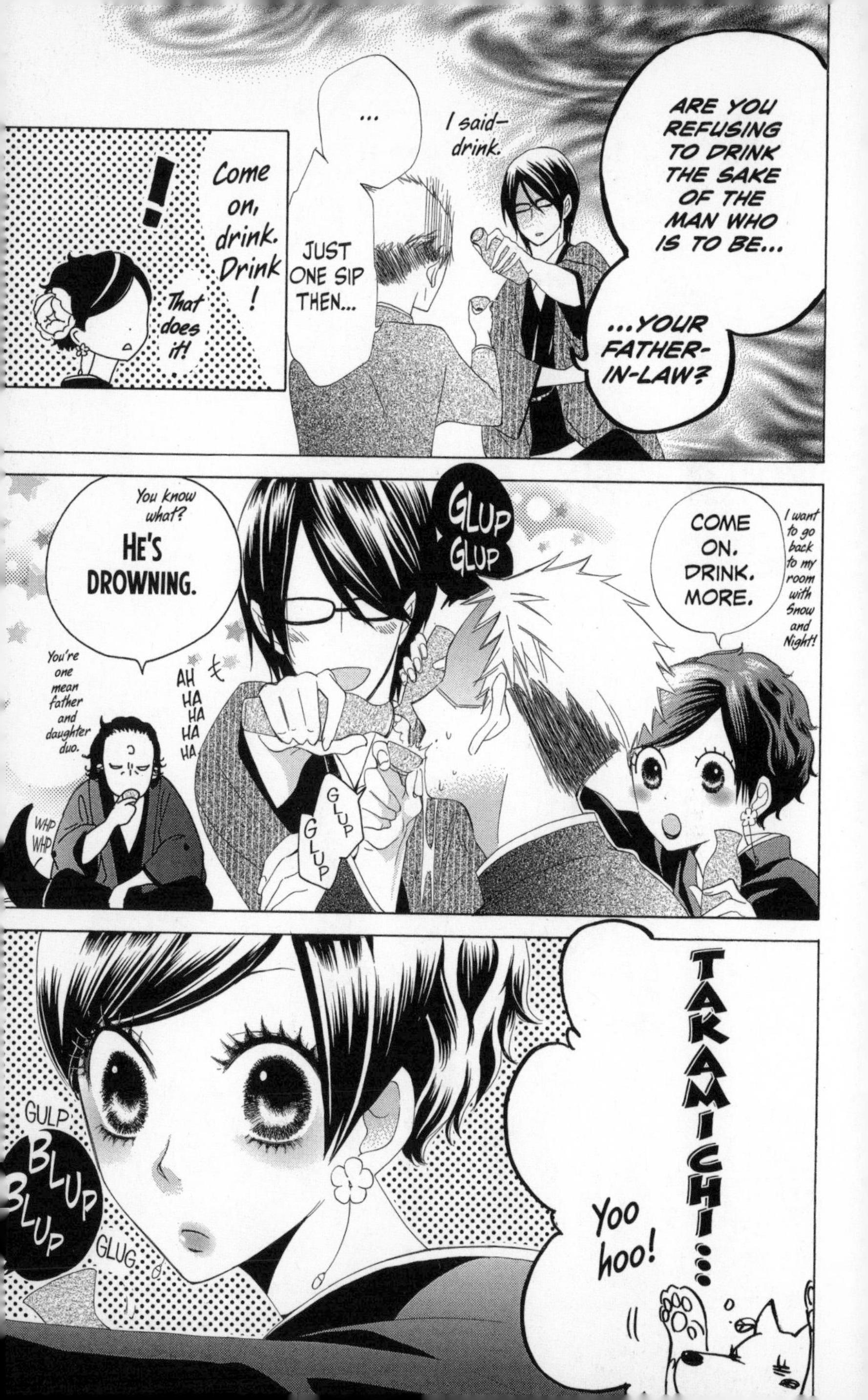

ARE YOU REFUSING TO DRINK THE SAKE OF THE MAN WHO IS TO BE...
...YOUR FATHER-IN-LAW?
I said—drink.
...
JUST ONE SIP THEN...
!
Come on, drink. Drink!
That does it!
I want to go back to my room with Snow and Night!
COME ON. DRINK. MORE.
GLUP GLUP
You know what? HE'S DROWNING.
AH HA HA HA HA
GLUP GLUP
You're one mean father and daughter duo.
WHP WHP
TAKAMICHI...
Yoo hoo!
GULP
BLUP BLUP
GLUG

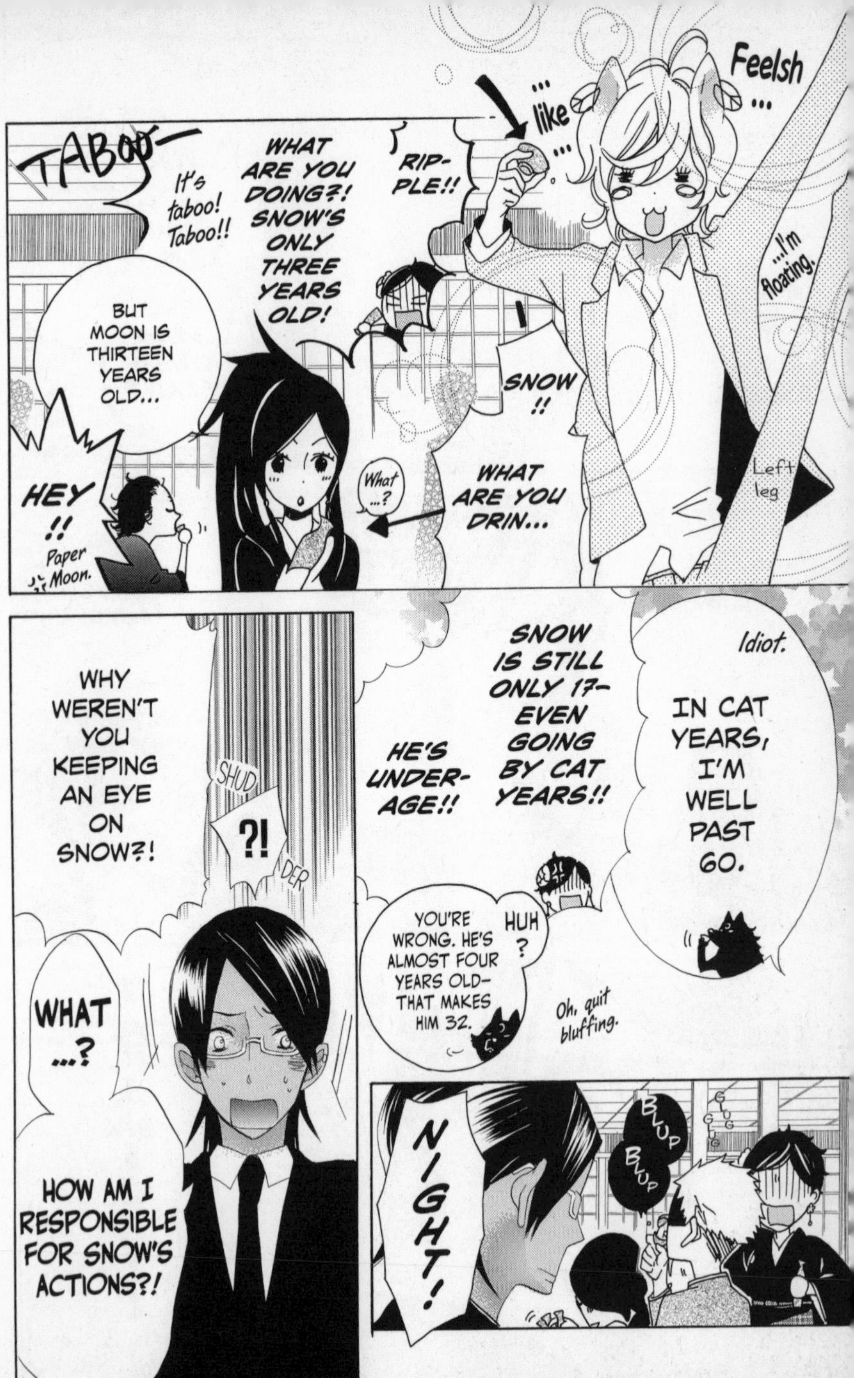
Feelsh ...
... like ...
...I'm floating.
Left leg
RIP-PLE!!
WHAT ARE YOU DOING?! SNOW'S ONLY THREE YEARS OLD!
It's taboo! Taboo!!
TABOO—
SNOW !!
WHAT ARE YOU DRIN...
What ...?
BUT MOON IS THIRTEEN YEARS OLD...
HEY !!
Paper Moon.
Idiot.
IN CAT YEARS, I'M WELL PAST 60.
SNOW IS STILL ONLY 17— EVEN GOING BY CAT YEARS!!
HE'S UNDER-AGE!!
HUH ?
YOU'RE WRONG. HE'S ALMOST FOUR YEARS OLD— THAT MAKES HIM 32.
Oh, quit bluffing.
BLUP
BLUP
GLUG GLUG GLUG
NIGHT!
WHY WEREN'T YOU KEEPING AN EYE ON SNOW?!
SHUD
?!
DER
WHAT ...?
HOW AM I RESPONSIBLE FOR SNOW'S ACTIONS?!

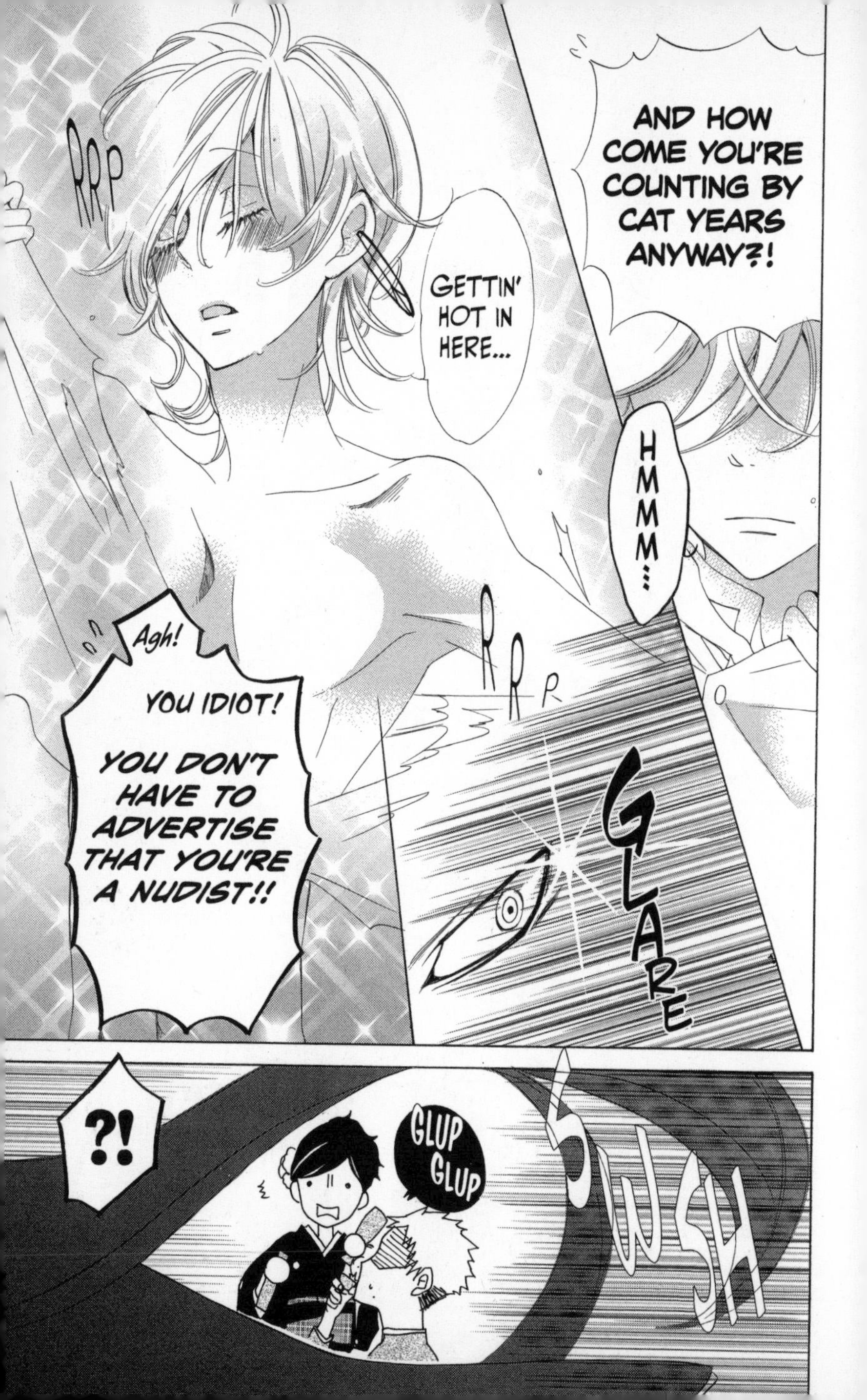
AND HOW COME YOU'RE COUNTING BY CAT YEARS ANYWAY?!
HMMM...
GLARE
GETTIN' HOT IN HERE...
RRP
RRP
Agh!
YOU IDIOT!
YOU DON'T HAVE TO ADVERTISE THAT YOU'RE A NUDIST!!
SWISH
GLUP GLUP
?!

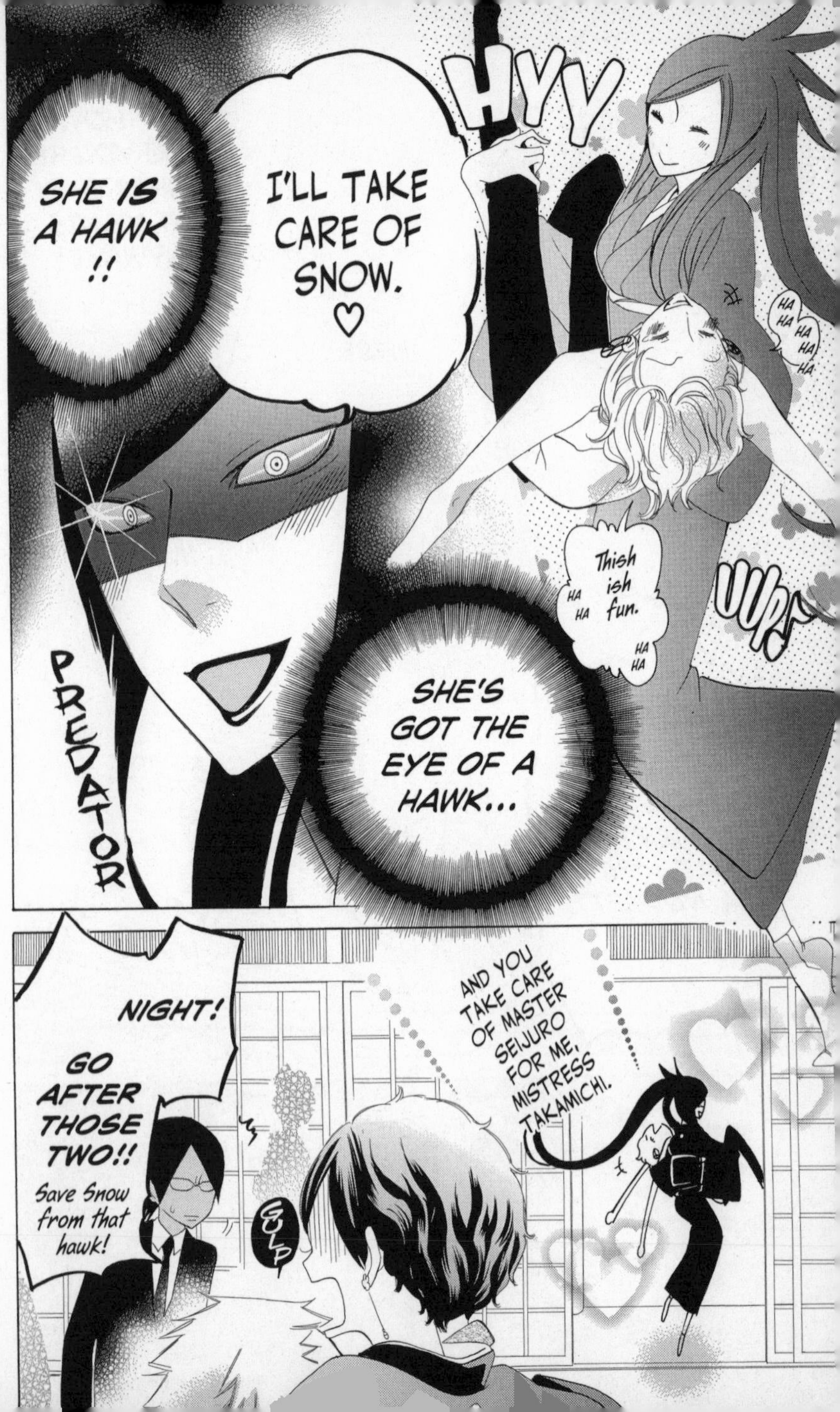
HYY
HA HA HA HA HA
HA HA
Thish ish fun.
HA HA
UUP
I'LL TAKE CARE OF SNOW. ♡
SHE IS A HAWK !!
SHE'S GOT THE EYE OF A HAWK...
PREDATOR
AND YOU TAKE CARE OF MASTER SEIJURO FOR ME, MISTRESS TAKAMICHI.
NIGHT!
GO AFTER THOSE TWO!!
Save Snow from that hawk!
GULP

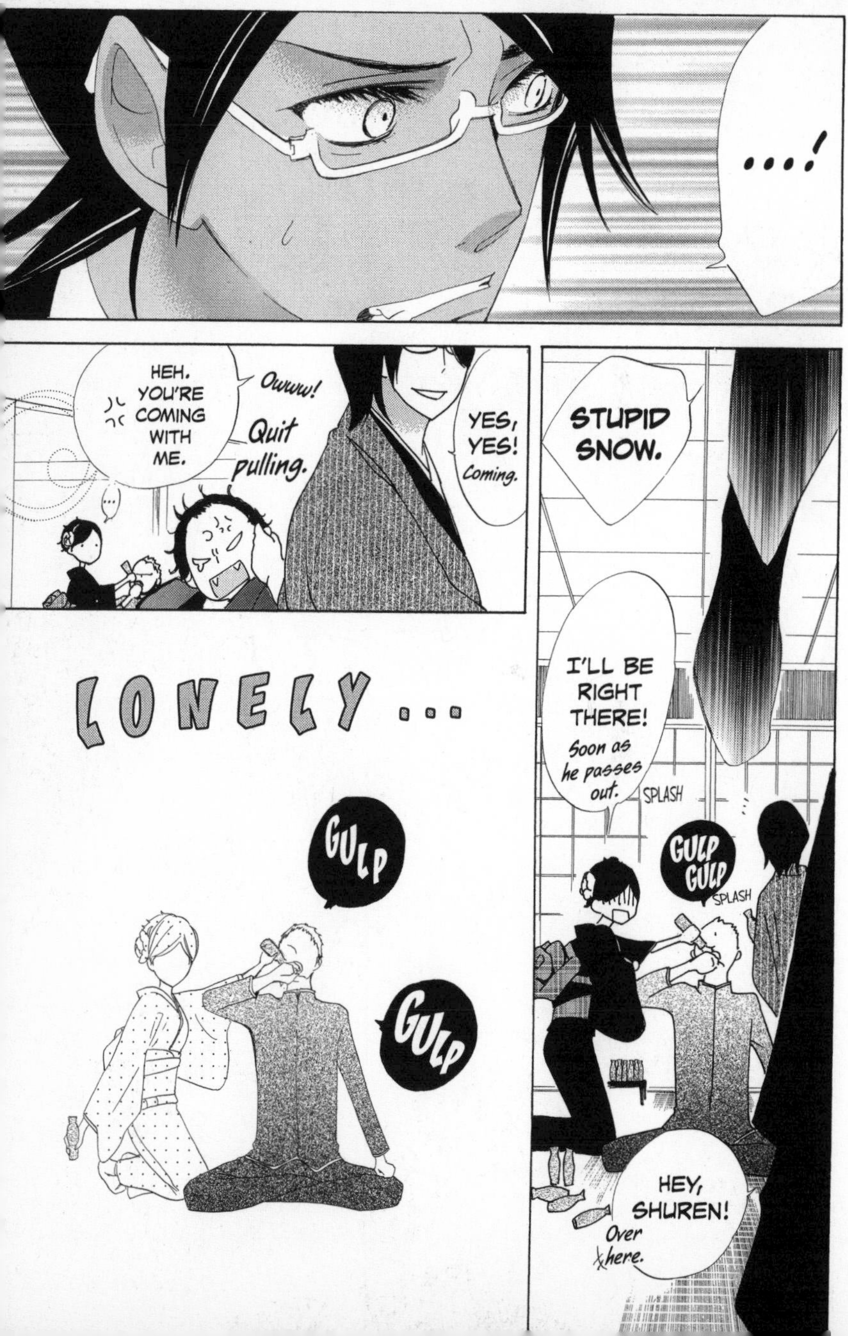
...!
STUPID SNOW.
I'LL BE RIGHT THERE!
Soon as he passes out.
SPLASH
GULP GULP
SPLASH
HEY, SHUREN!
Over here.
YES, YES!
Coming.
HEH. YOU'RE COMING WITH ME.
Owww!
Quit pulling.
...
LONELY...
GULP
GULP

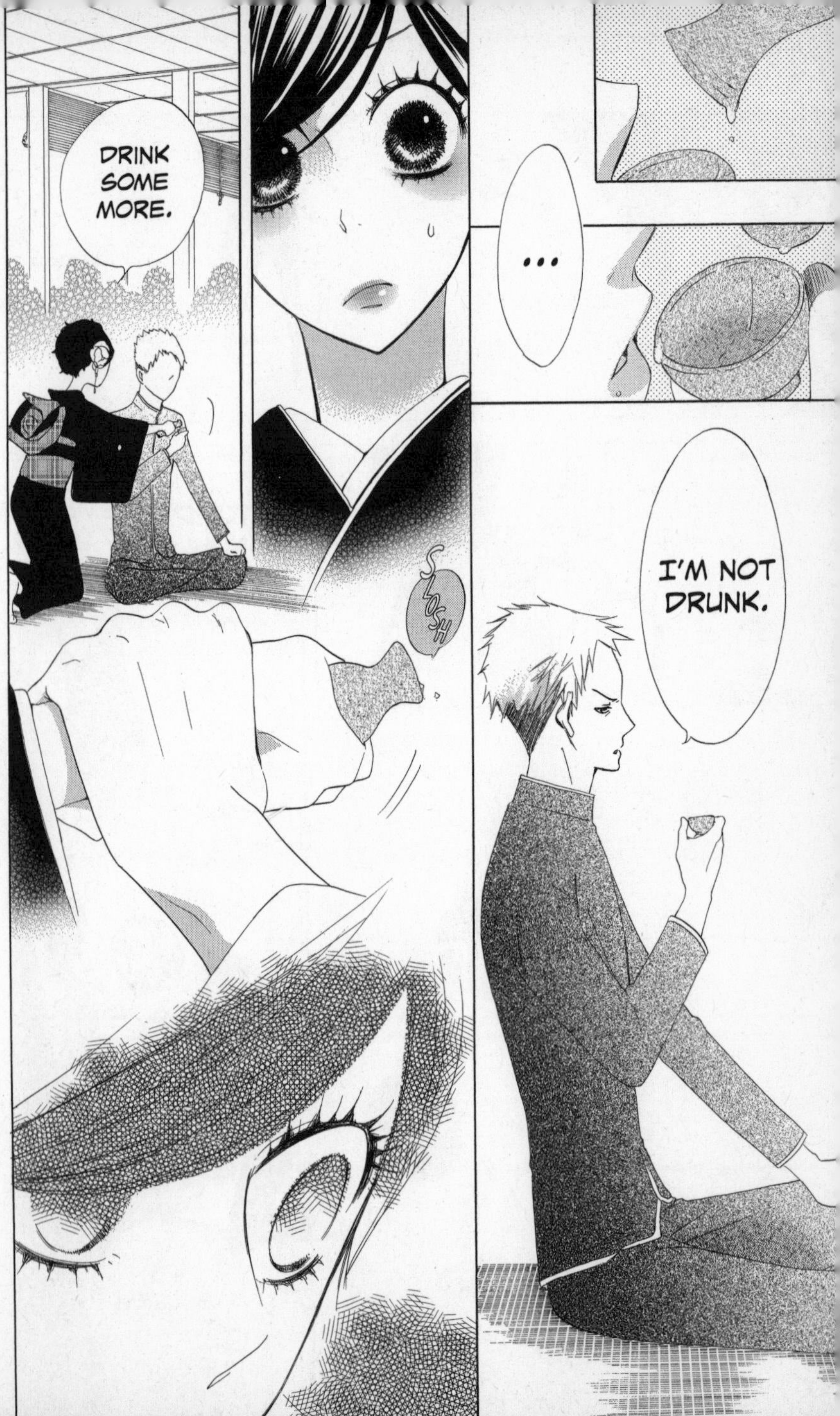
...
I'M NOT DRUNK.
SLOSH
DRINK SOME MORE.

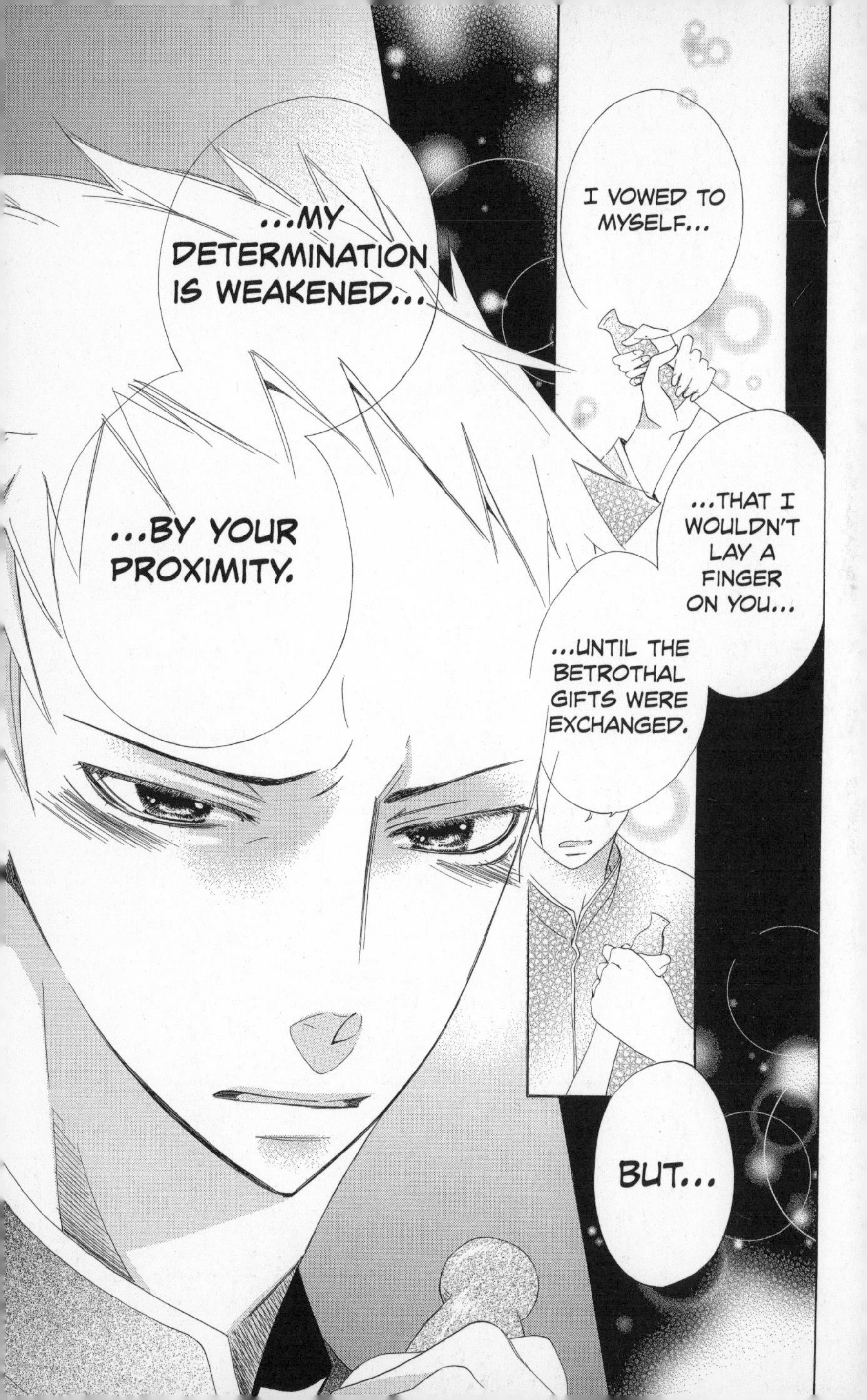
I VOWED TO MYSELF...
...THAT I WOULDN'T LAY A FINGER ON YOU...
...UNTIL THE BETROTHAL GIFTS WERE EXCHANGED.
BUT...
...MY DETERMINATION IS WEAKENED...
...BY YOUR PROXIMITY.

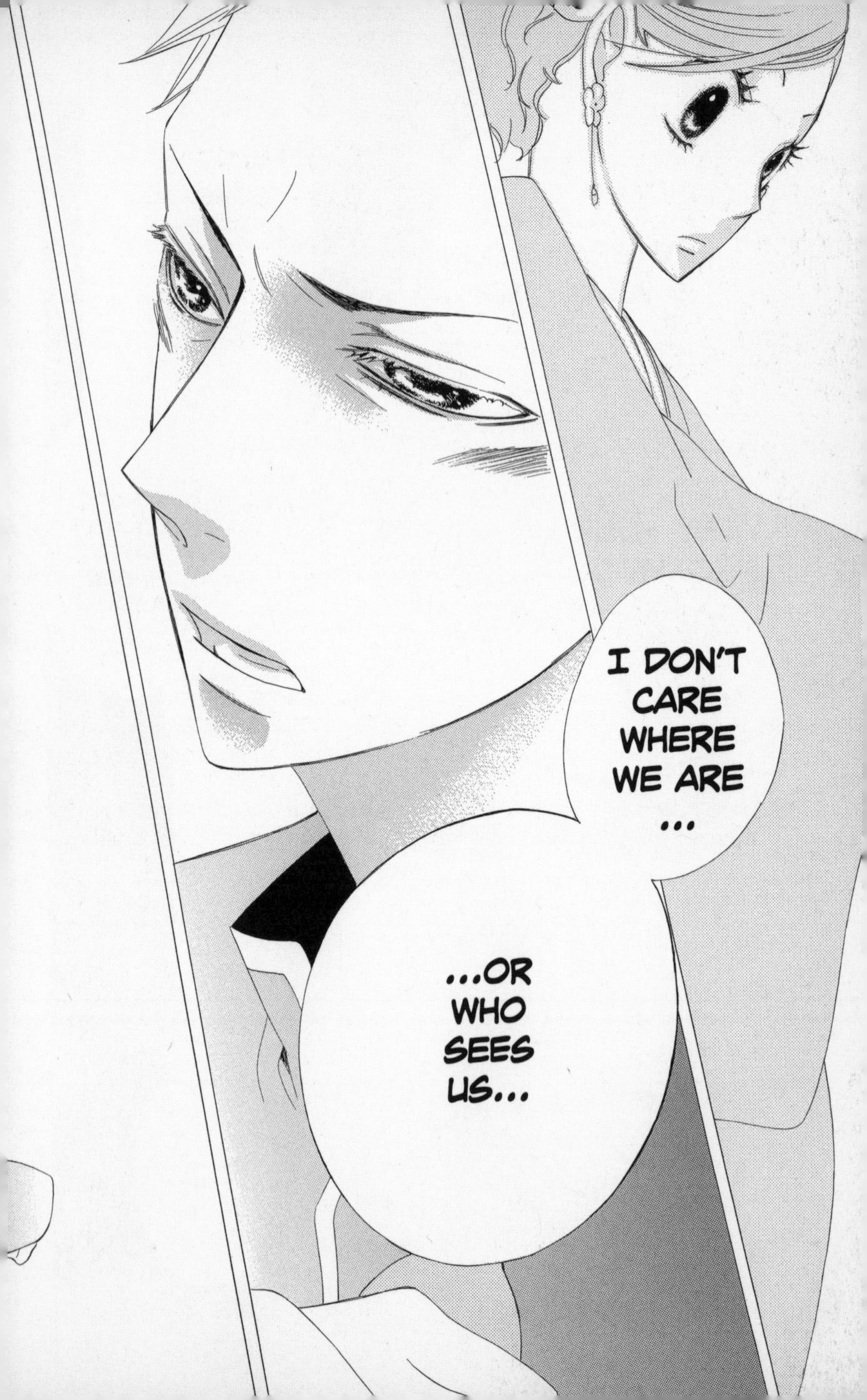
I DON'T CARE WHERE WE ARE ...
...OR WHO SEES US...

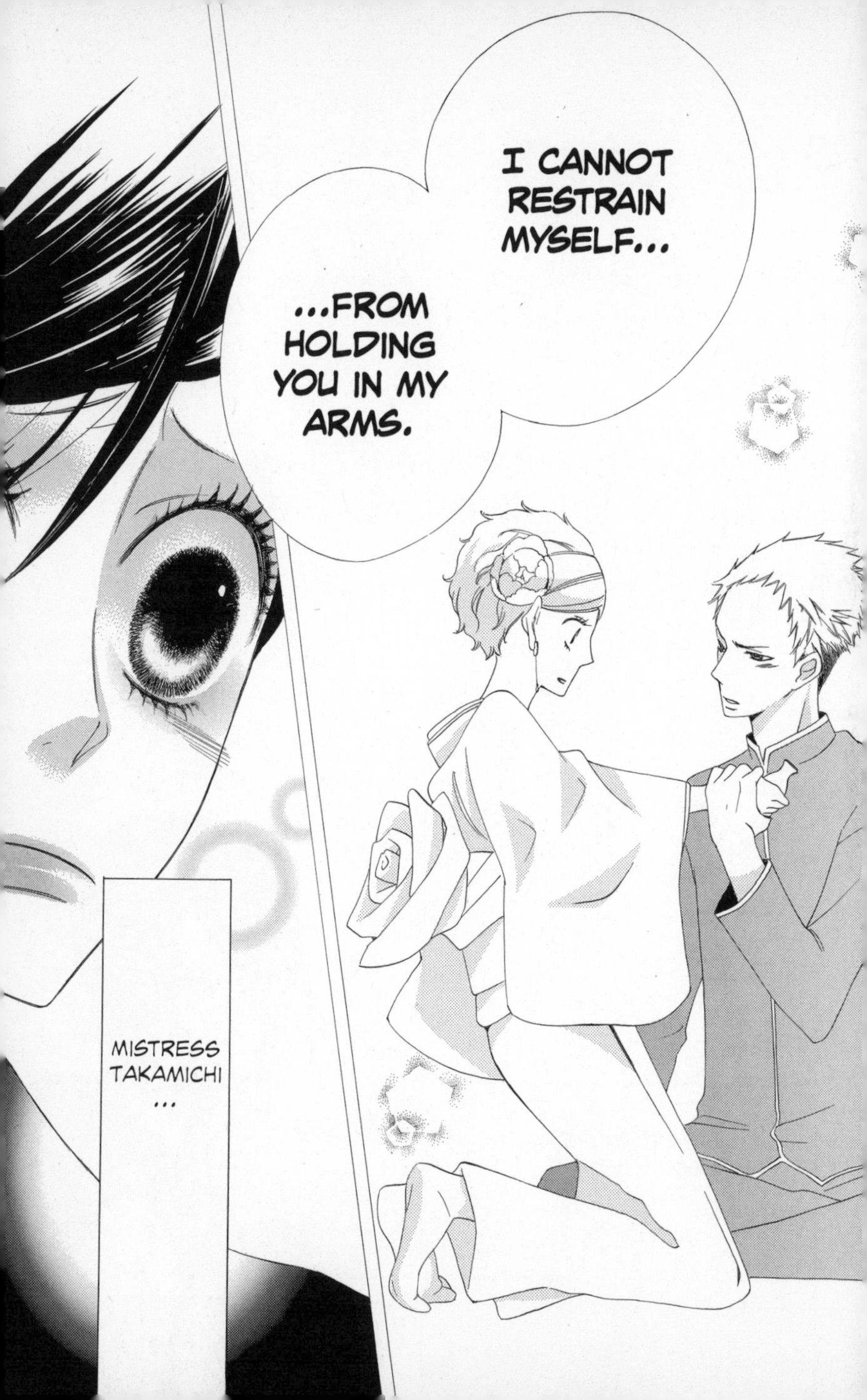
I CANNOT RESTRAIN MYSELF...
...FROM HOLDING YOU IN MY ARMS.
MISTRESS TAKAMICHI ...

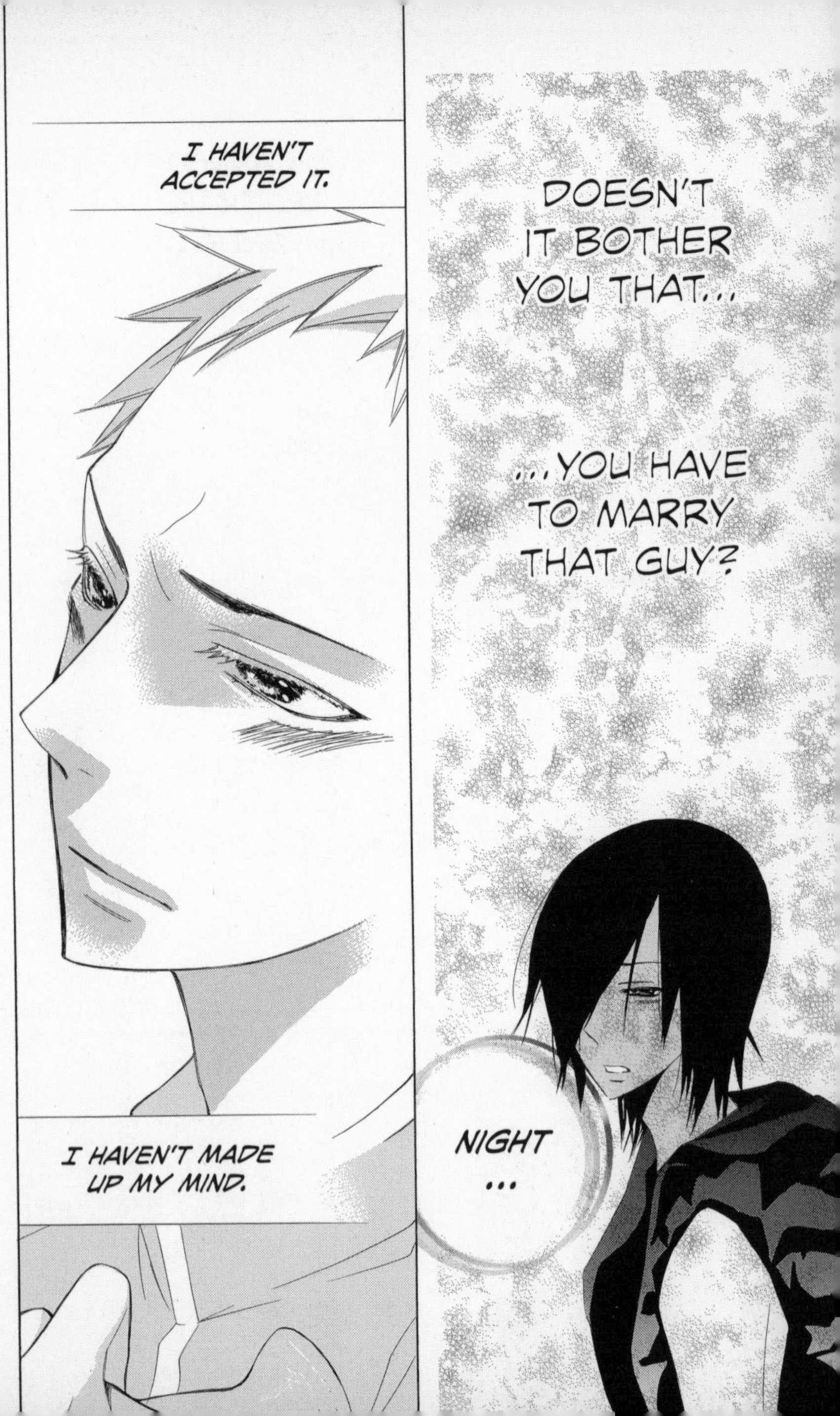
DOESN'T IT BOTHER YOU THAT...
...YOU HAVE TO MARRY THAT GUY?
NIGHT ...
I HAVEN'T ACCEPTED IT.
I HAVEN'T MADE UP MY MIND.

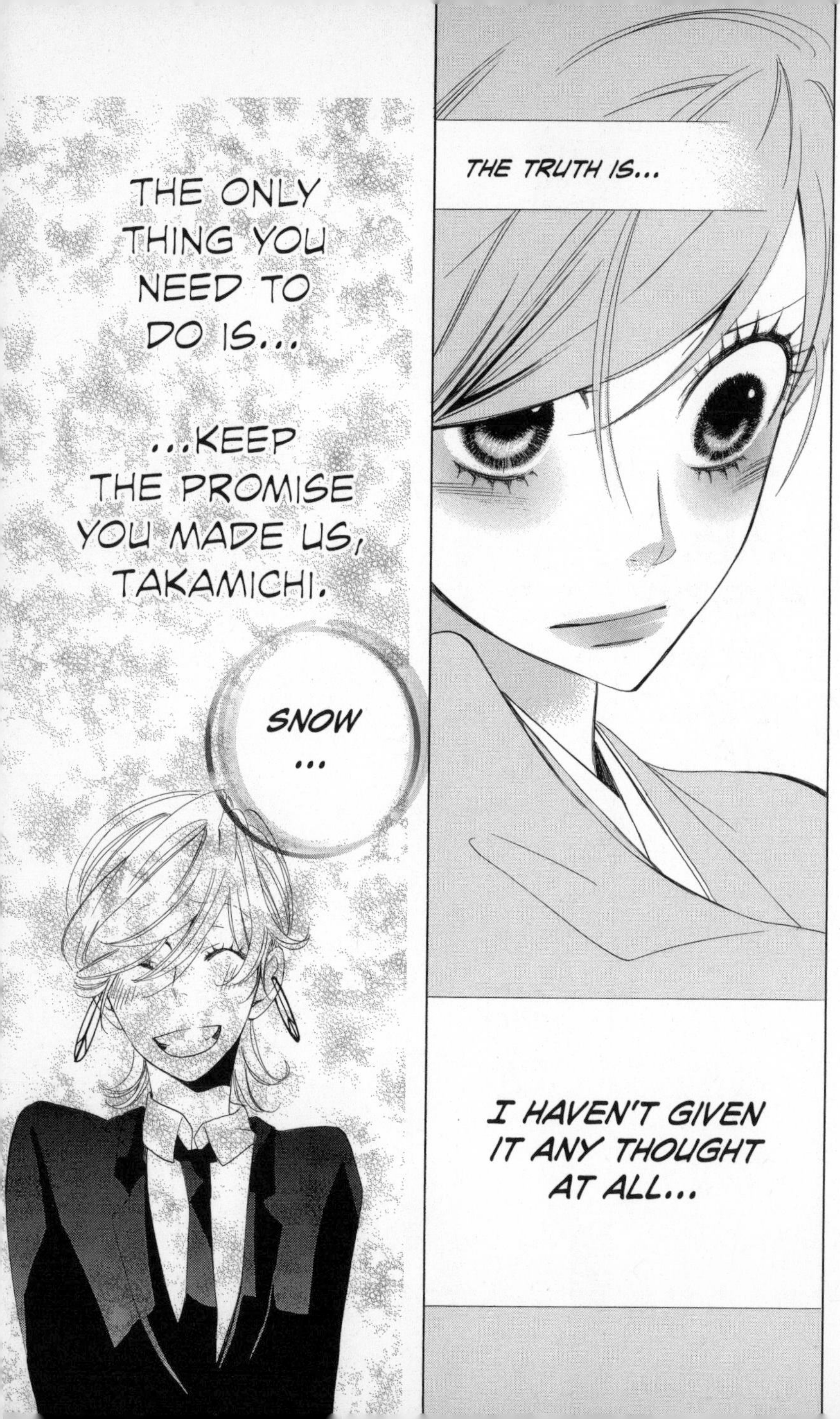
THE TRUTH IS...
I HAVEN'T GIVEN IT ANY THOUGHT AT ALL...
THE ONLY THING YOU NEED TO DO IS...
...KEEP THE PROMISE YOU MADE US, TAKAMICHI.
SNOW ...

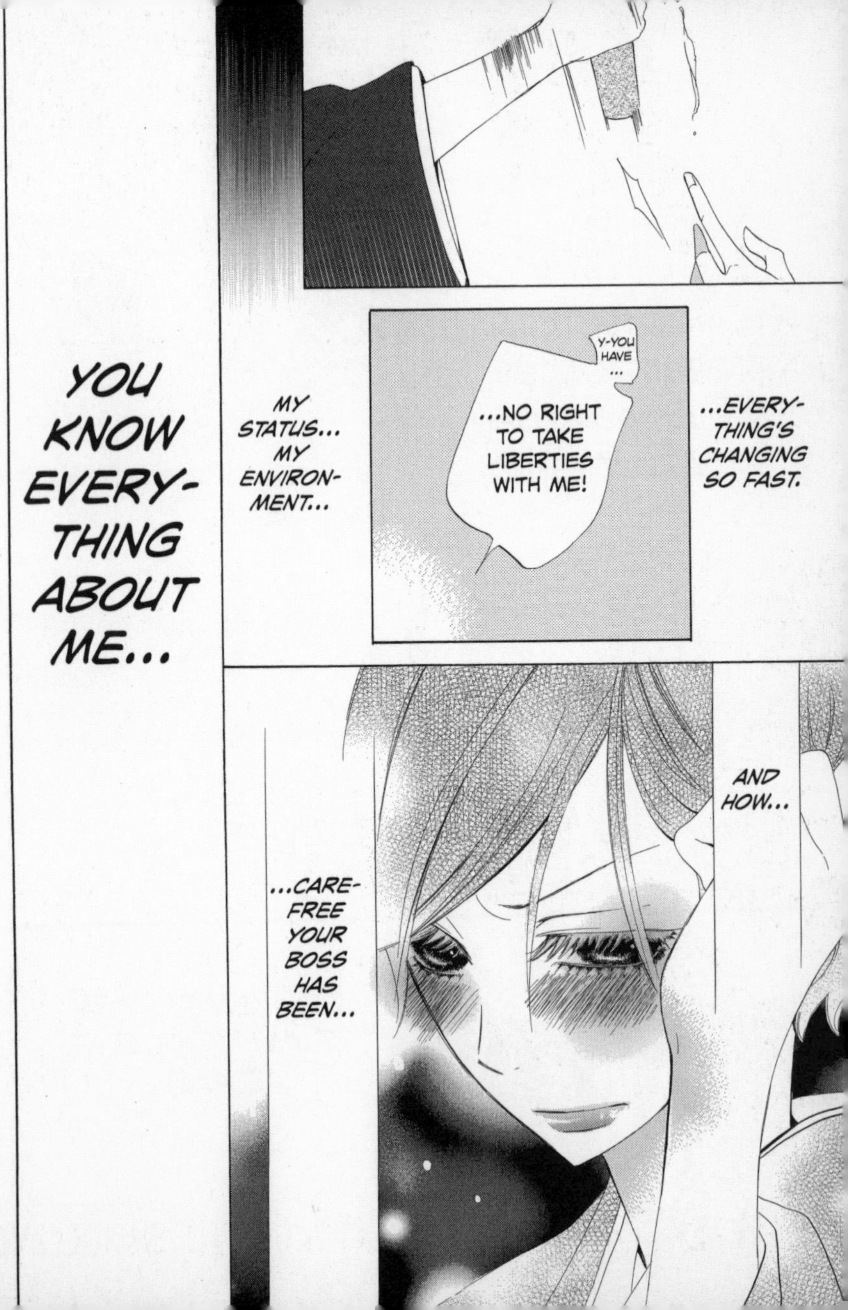
...EVERY-THING'S CHANGING SO FAST.
Y-YOU HAVE...
...NO RIGHT TO TAKE LIBERTIES WITH ME!
MY STATUS... MY ENVIRON-MENT...
AND HOW...
...CARE-FREE YOUR BOSS HAS BEEN...
YOU KNOW EVERY-THING ABOUT ME...

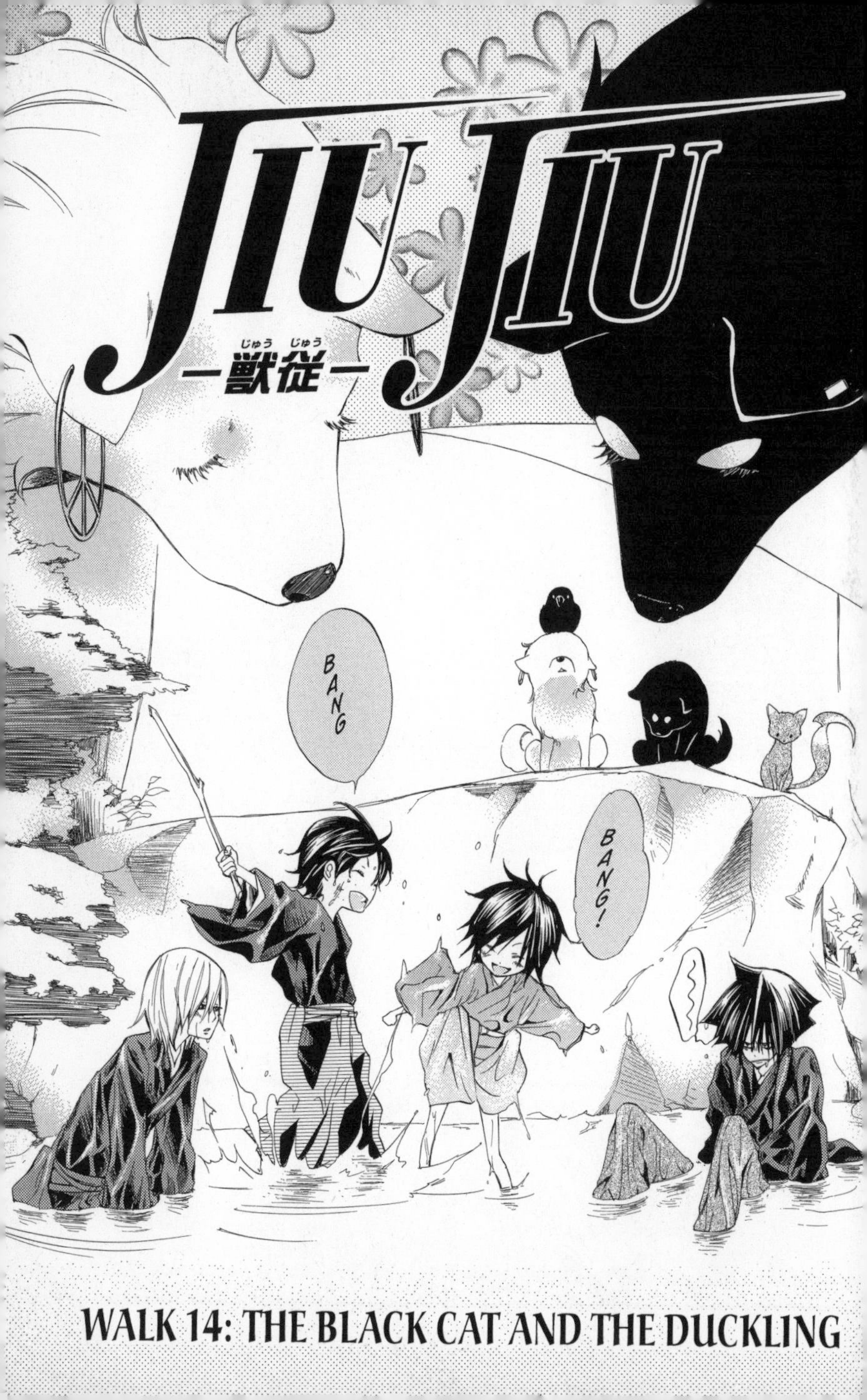
JIU JIU
じゅう じゅう
—獣従—
BANG
BANG!
WALK 14: THE BLACK CAT AND THE DUCKLING

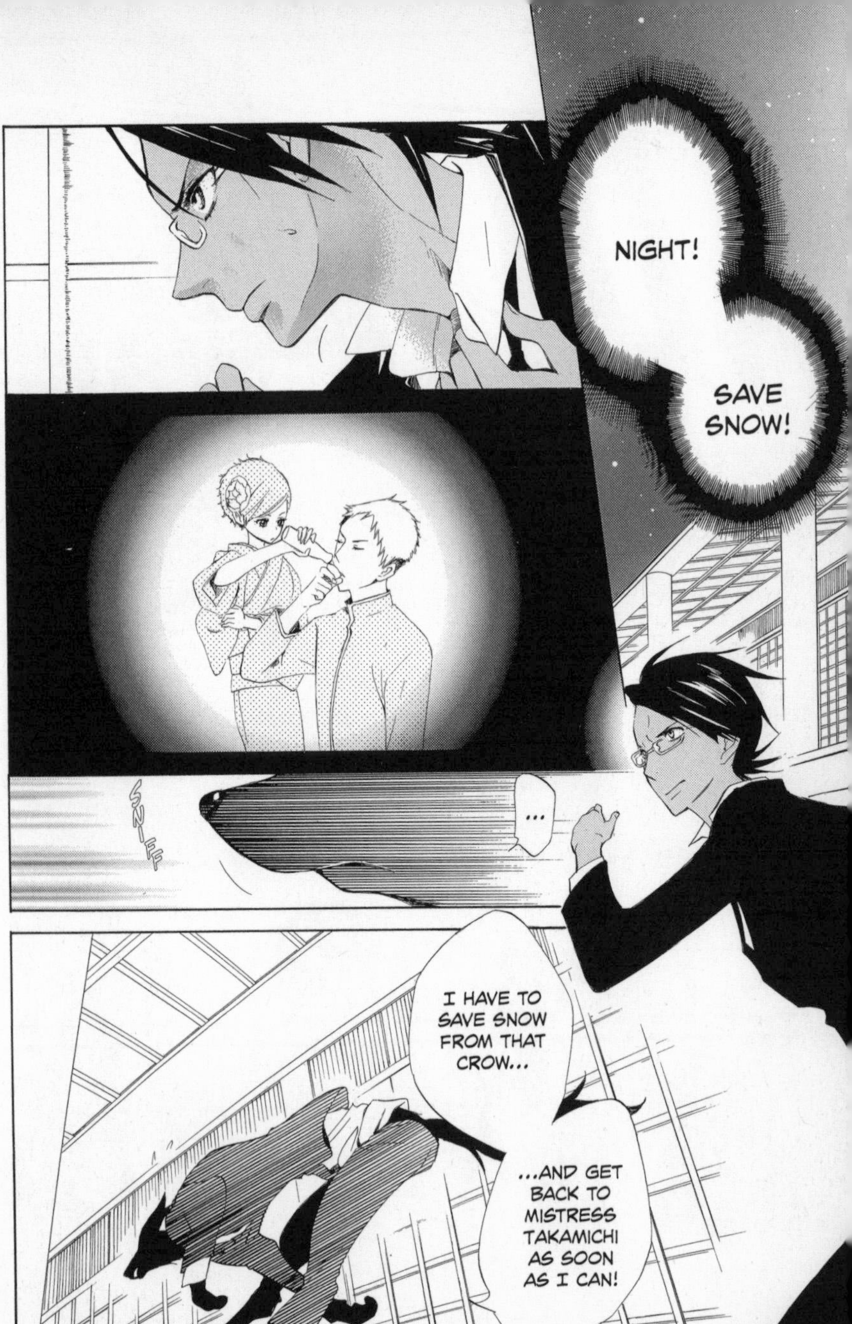
NIGHT!
SAVE SNOW!
...
SNIFF
I HAVE TO SAVE SNOW FROM THAT CROW...
...AND GET BACK TO MISTRESS TAKAMICHI AS SOON AS I CAN!

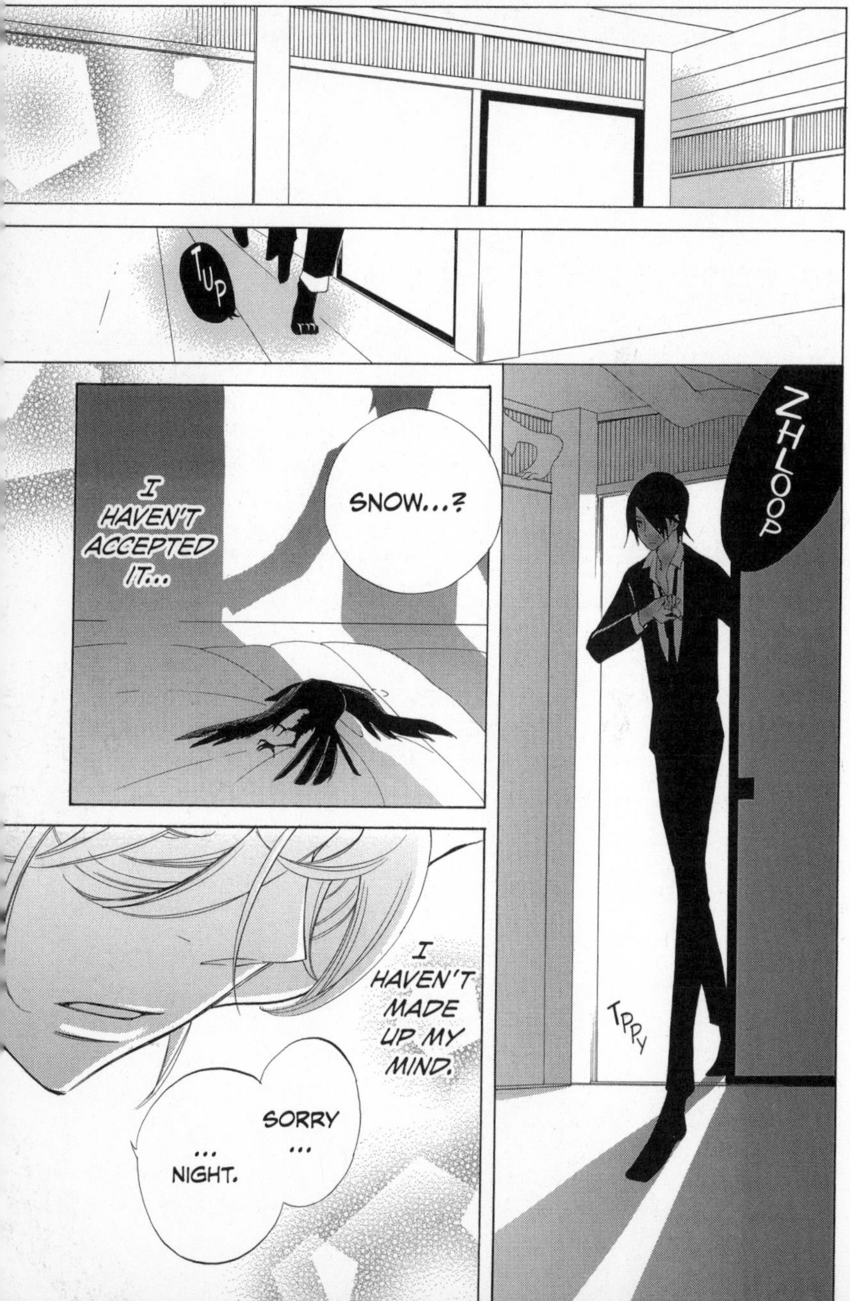
TUP
ZHLOOP
TPPY
SNOW...?
I HAVEN'T ACCEPTED IT...
I HAVEN'T MADE UP MY MIND.
SORRY... ...NIGHT.

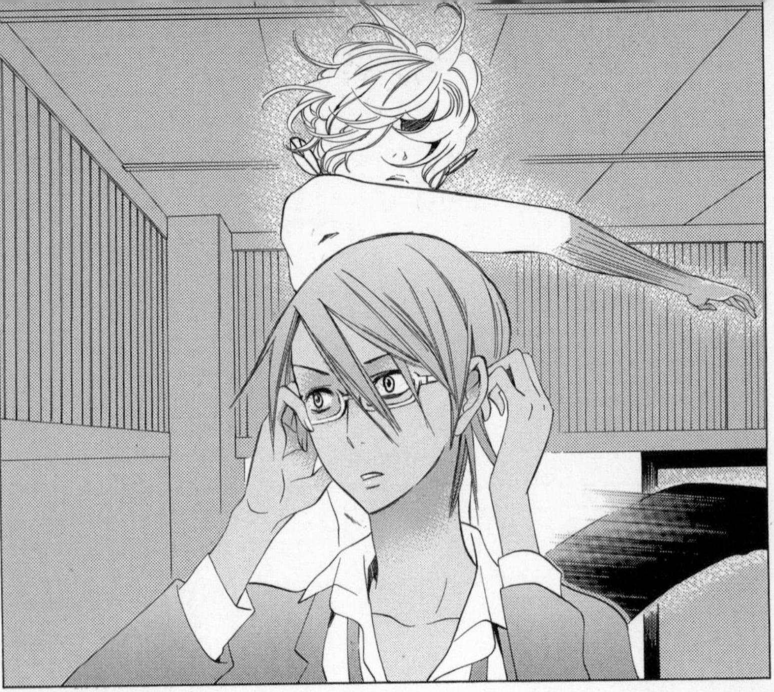

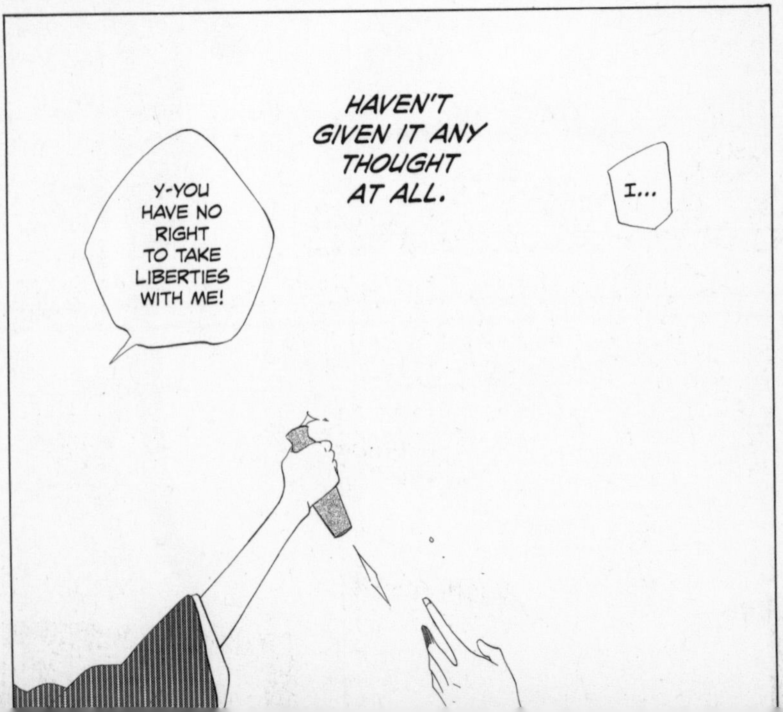
I...
HAVEN'T GIVEN IT ANY THOUGHT AT ALL.
Y-YOU HAVE NO RIGHT TO TAKE LIBERTIES WITH ME!

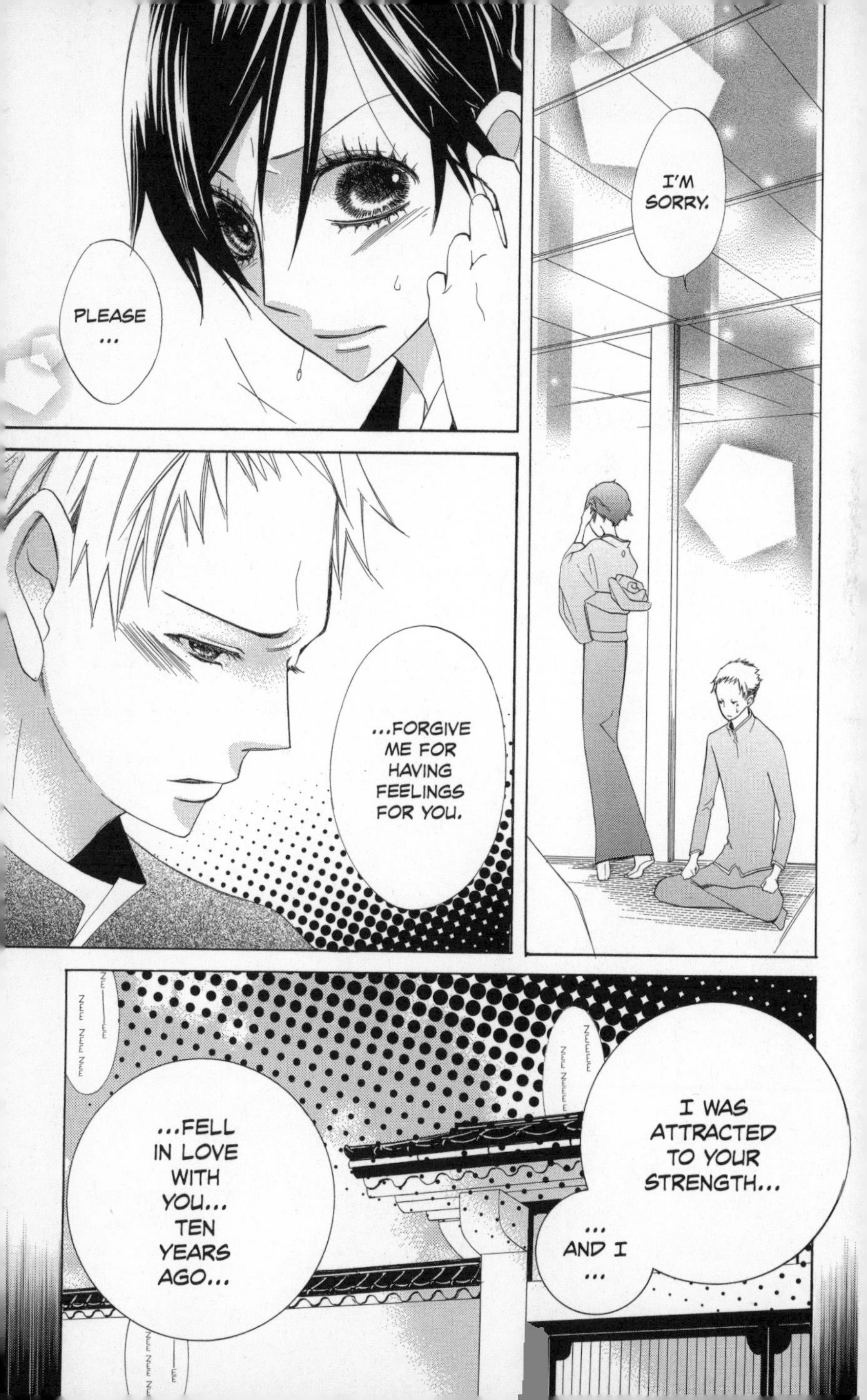
I'M SORRY.
PLEASE ...
...FORGIVE ME FOR HAVING FEELINGS FOR YOU.
I WAS ATTRACTED TO YOUR STRENGTH...
... AND I ...
...FELL IN LOVE WITH YOU... TEN YEARS AGO...

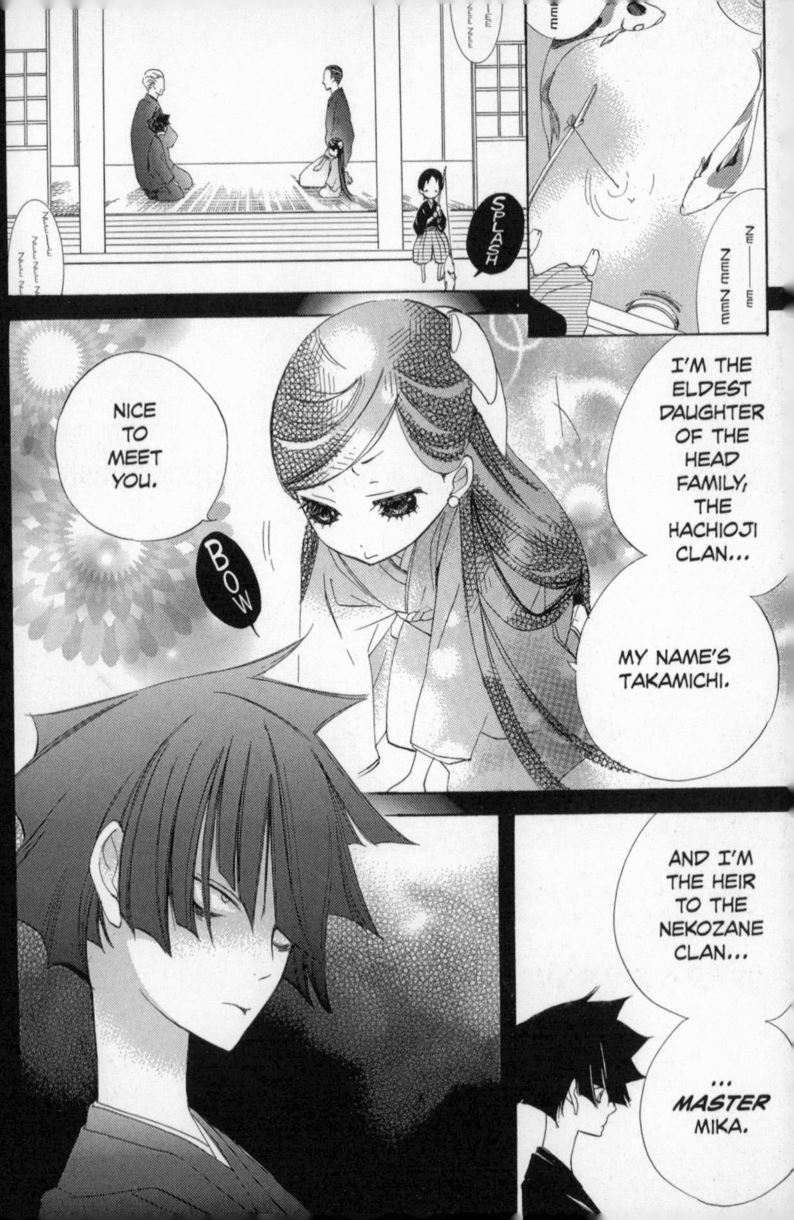
ZE——EE ZEE ZEE
SPLASH
I'M THE ELDEST DAUGHTER OF THE HEAD FAMILY, THE HACHIOJI CLAN...
MY NAME'S TAKAMICHI.
NICE TO MEET YOU.
BOW
AND I'M THE HEIR TO THE NEKOZANE CLAN...
... *MASTER* MIKA.

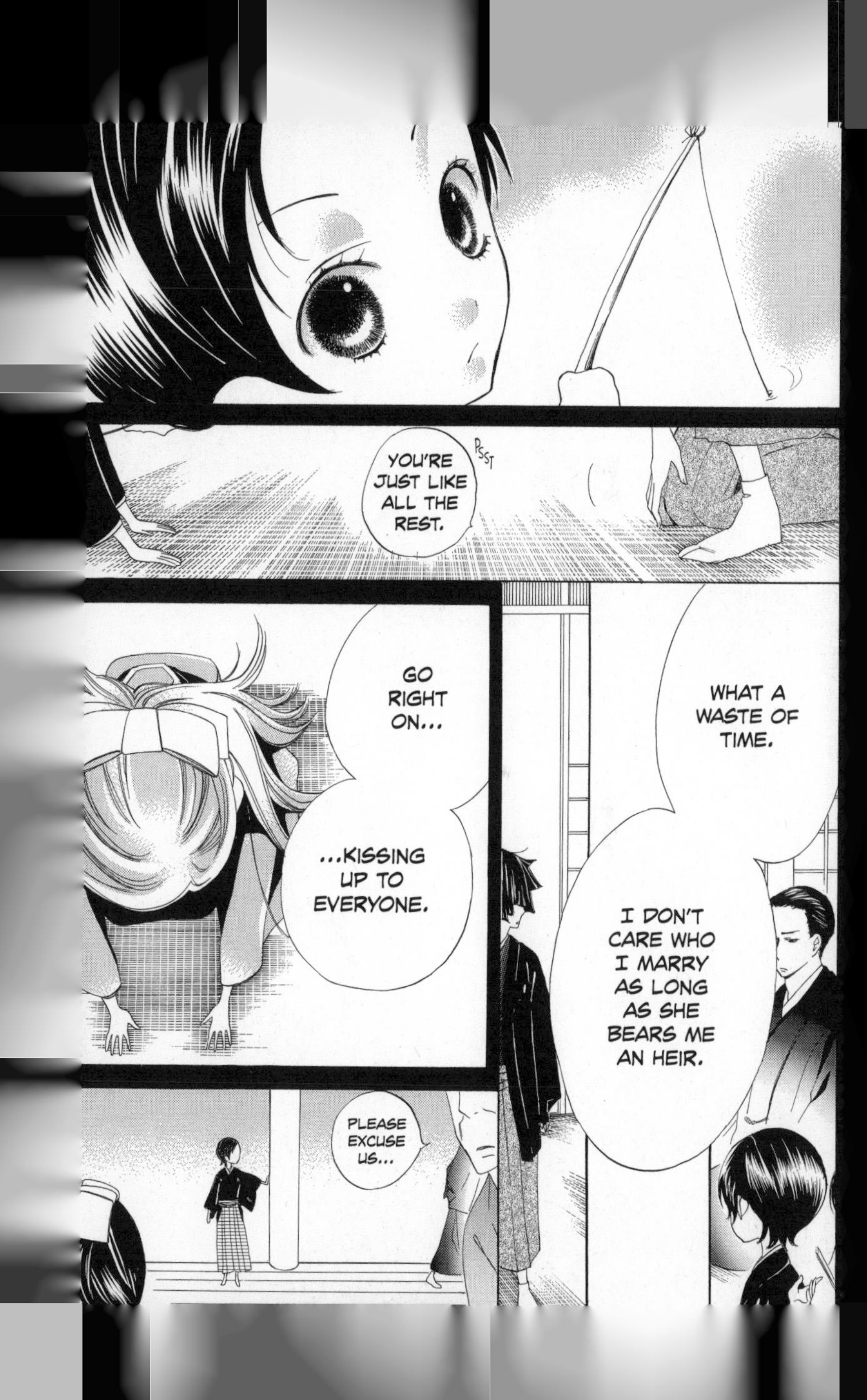
PSSST
YOU'RE JUST LIKE ALL THE REST.
WHAT A WASTE OF TIME.
I DON'T CARE WHO I MARRY AS LONG AS SHE BEARS ME AN HEIR.
GO RIGHT ON...
...KISSING UP TO EVERYONE.
PLEASE EXCUSE US...

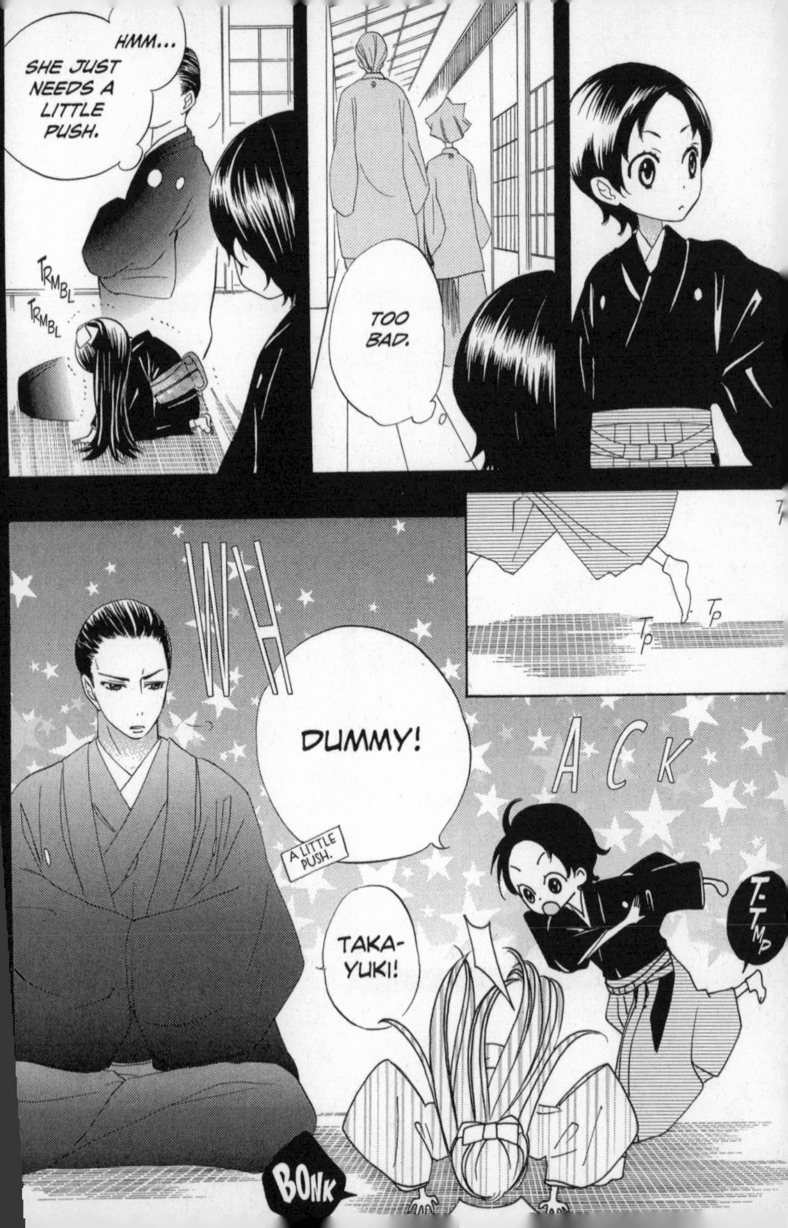
TOO BAD.
HMM... SHE JUST NEEDS A LITTLE PUSH.
TRMBL TRMBL
TP TP
WHA
ACK
DUMMY!
A LITTLE PUSH.
T-TMP
TAKA-YUKI!
BONK

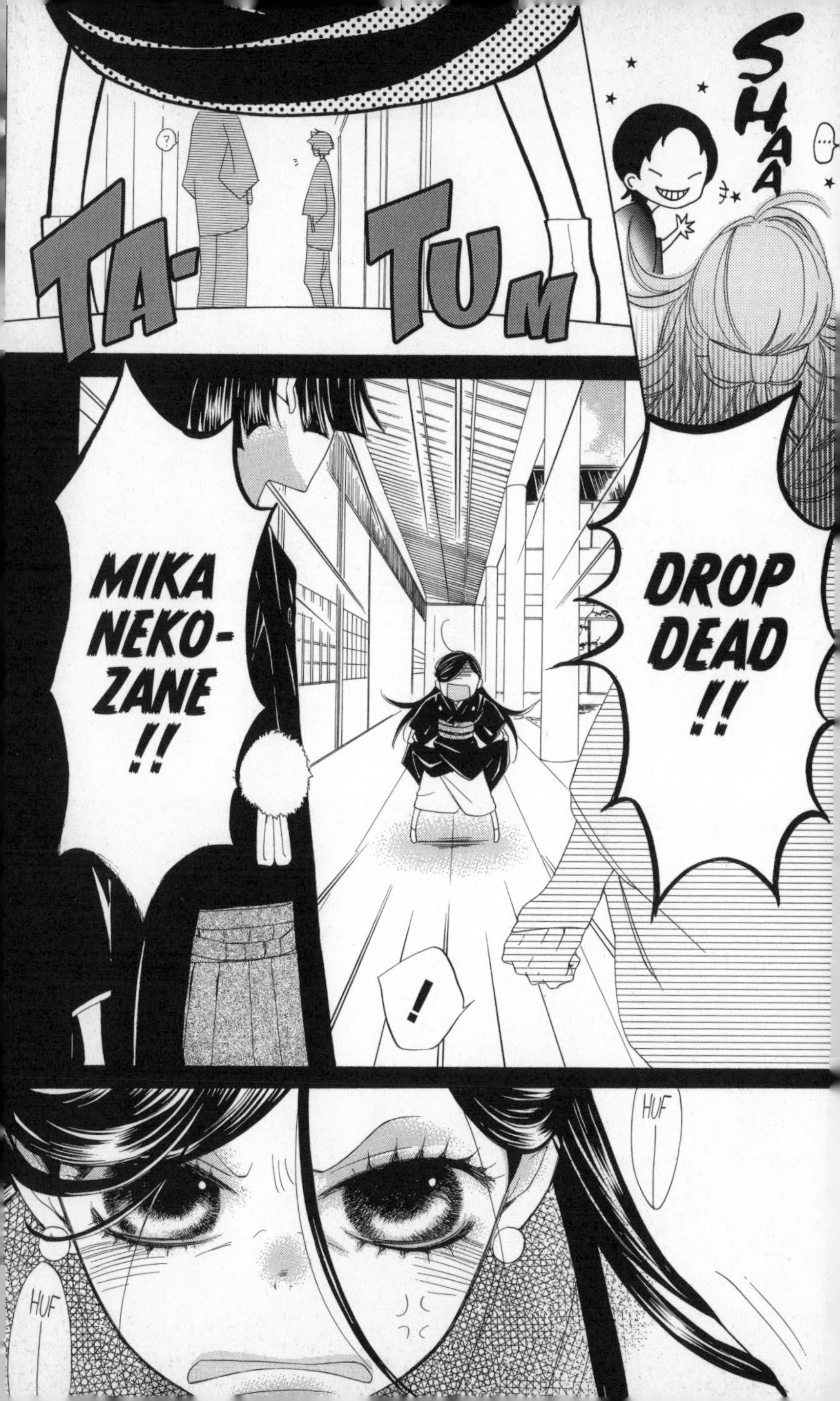
SHAA
…
?
TA-TUM
DROP DEAD!!
MIKA NEKO-ZANE!!
!
HUF
HUF

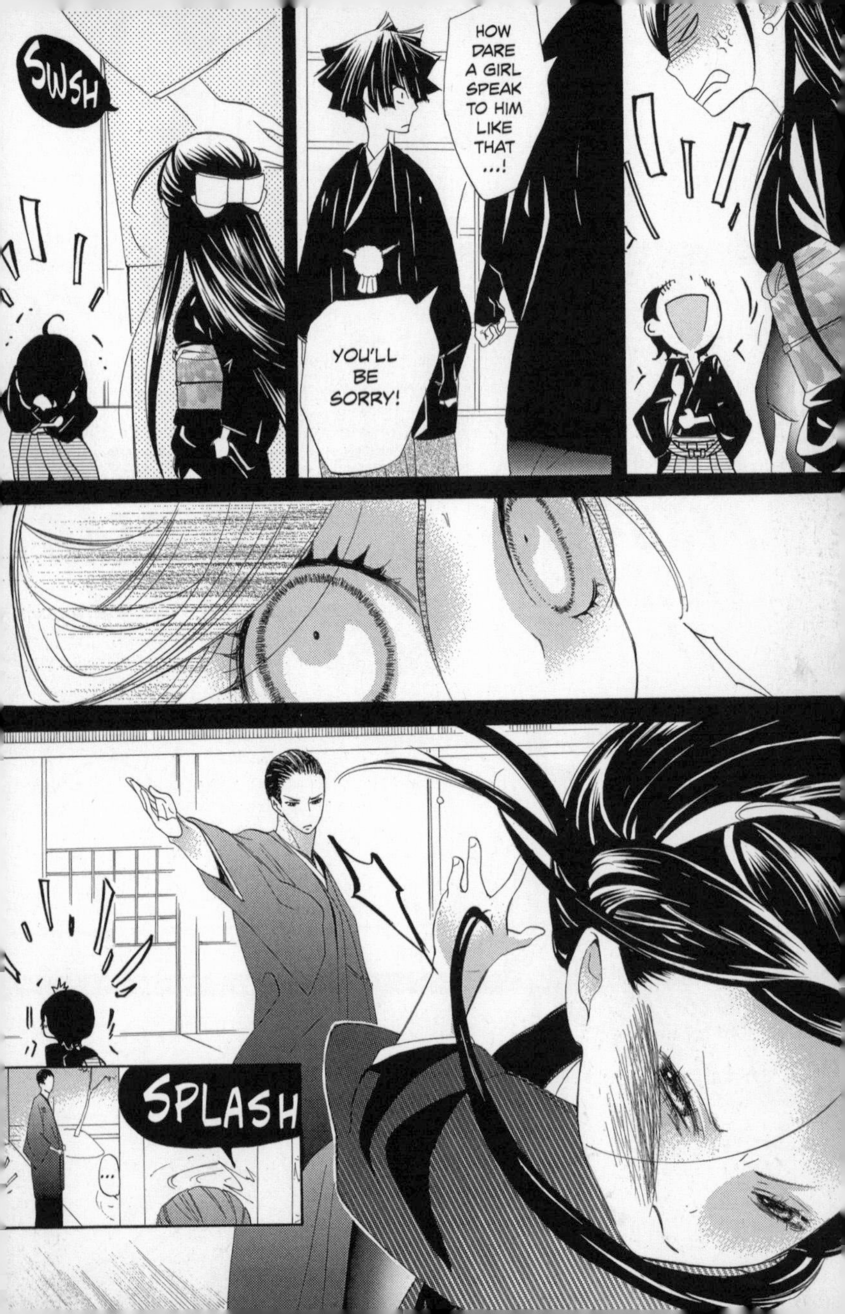
HOW DARE A GIRL SPEAK TO HIM LIKE THAT ...!
YOU'LL BE SORRY!
SWSH
SPLASH
...

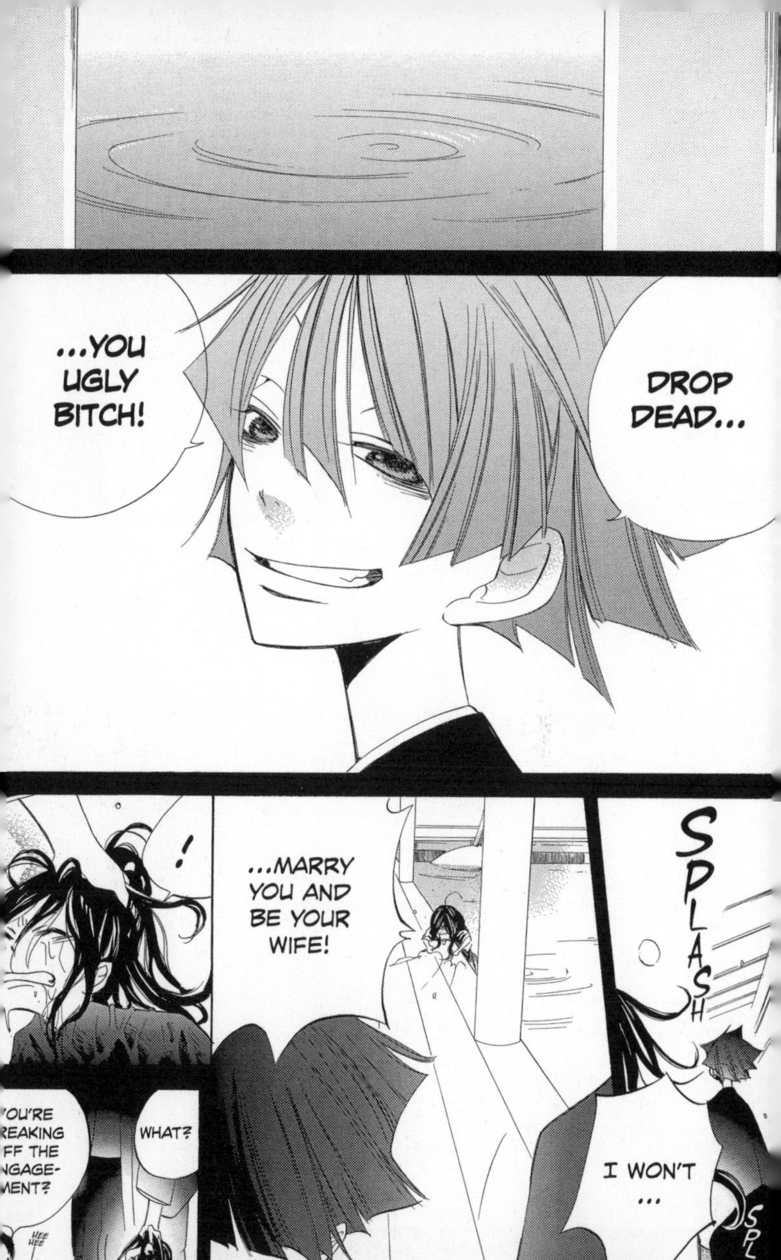
DROP DEAD...
...YOU UGLY BITCH!
SPLASH
I WON'T ...
SPLISH
...MARRY YOU AND BE YOUR WIFE!
!
WHAT?
OU'RE REAKING FF THE NGAGE-MENT?
HEE HEE

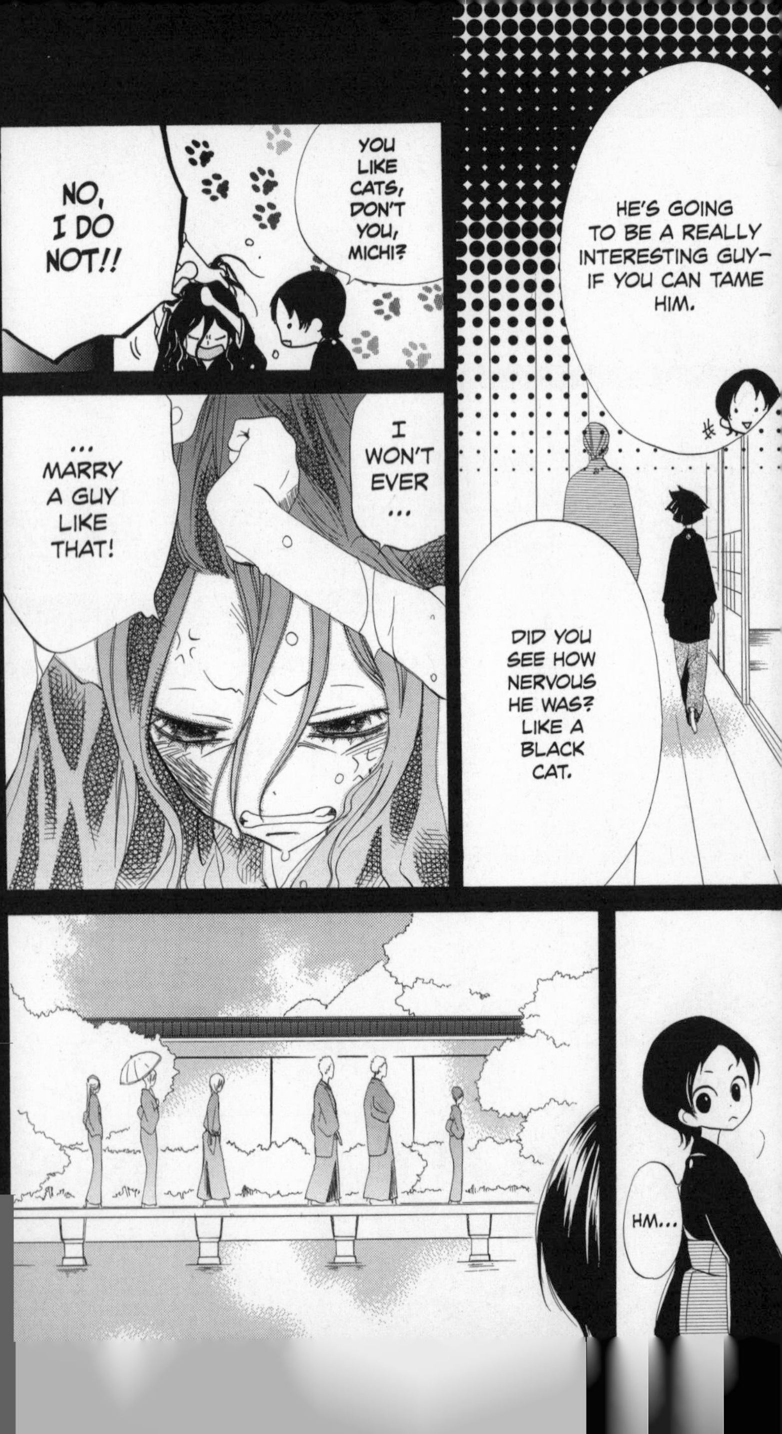
HE'S GOING TO BE A REALLY INTERESTING GUY— IF YOU CAN TAME HIM.
YOU LIKE CATS, DON'T YOU, MICHI?
NO, I DO NOT!!
DID YOU SEE HOW NERVOUS HE WAS? LIKE A BLACK CAT.
I WON'T EVER ...
... MARRY A GUY LIKE THAT!
HM...

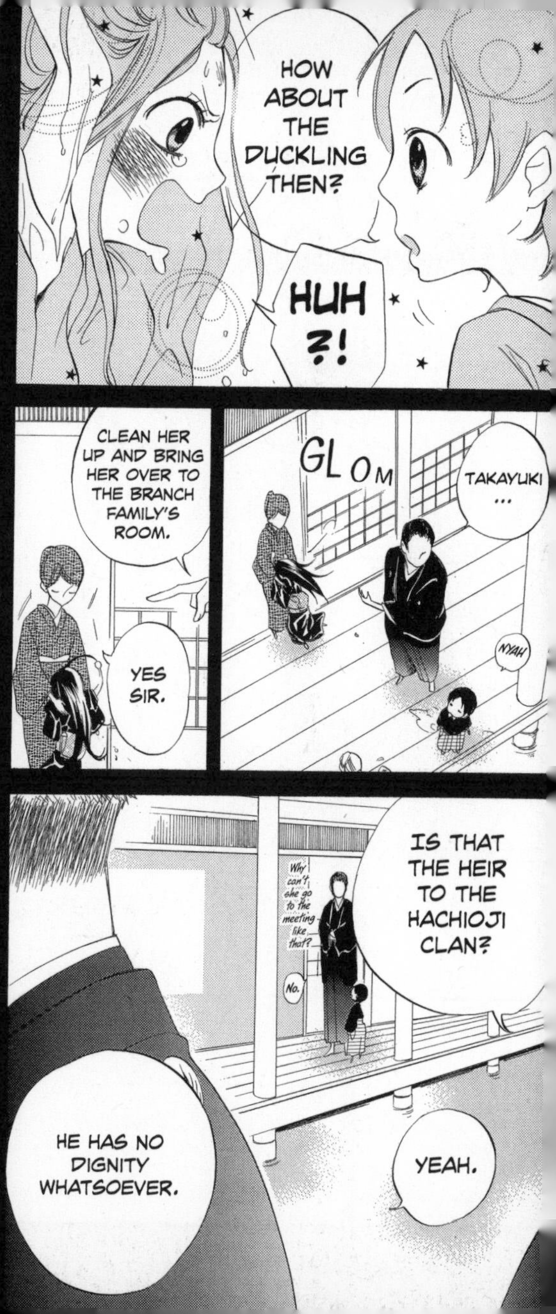
HOW ABOUT THE DUCKLING THEN?
HUH ?!
GLOM
TAKAYUKI ...
NYAH
CLEAN HER UP AND BRING HER OVER TO THE BRANCH FAMILY'S ROOM.
YES SIR.
IS THAT THE HEIR TO THE HACHIOJI CLAN?
Why can't she go to the meeting like that?
No.
HE HAS NO DIGNITY WHATSOEVER.
YEAH.

I drew the hakama totally wrong.

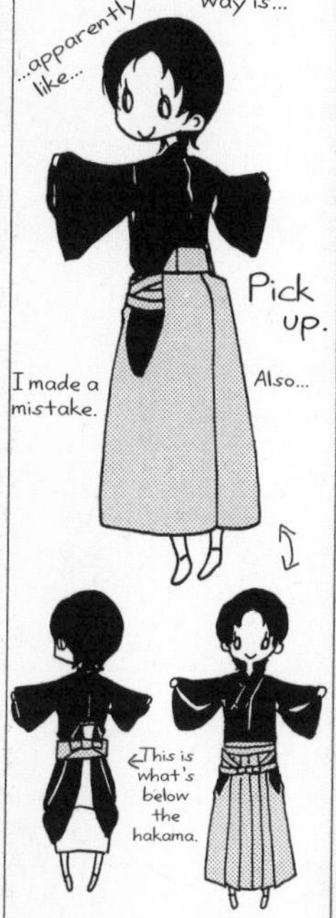
The correct way is...
...apparently like...
Pick up.
I made a mistake.
Also...
This is what's below the hakama.

I actually drew the three of them wearing kimono for the cover illustration, but something didn't look right. When I checked, I realized I'd drawn the hakama wrong again. So I gave up.

The illustration I ended up not using.

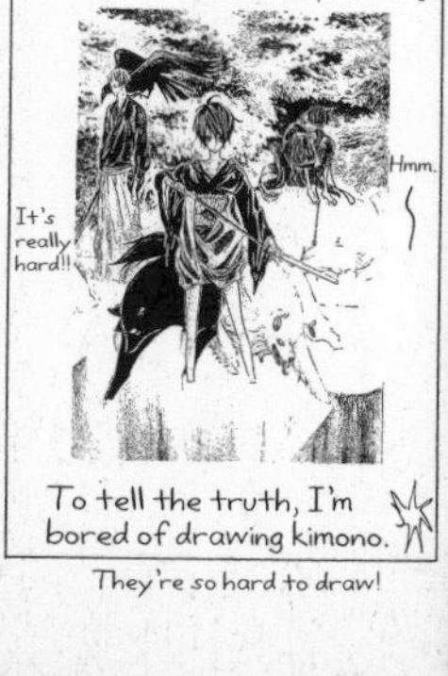
It's really hard!!
Hmm.

To tell the truth, I'm bored of drawing kimono.

They're so hard to draw!

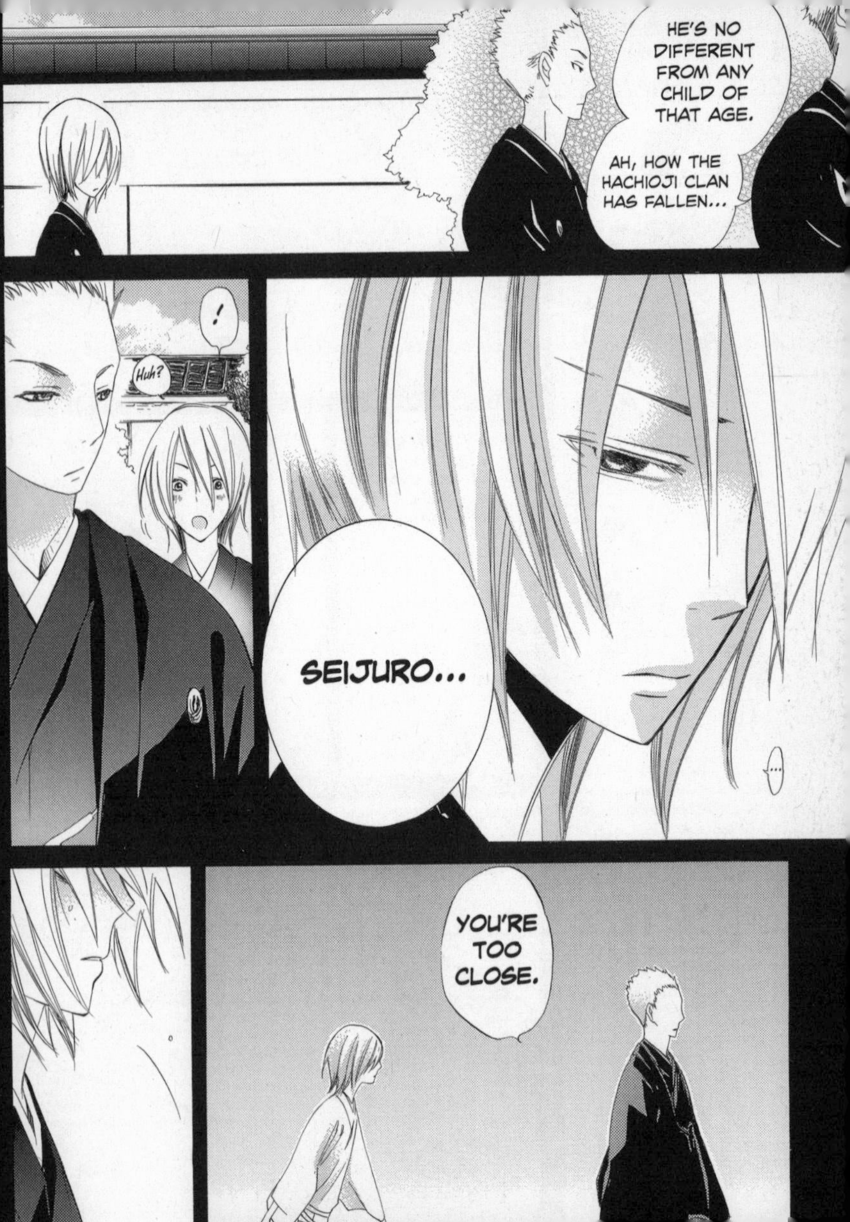
HE'S NO DIFFERENT FROM ANY CHILD OF THAT AGE.
AH, HOW THE HACHIOJI CLAN HAS FALLEN...
...
SEIJURO...
!
Huh?
YOU'RE TOO CLOSE.

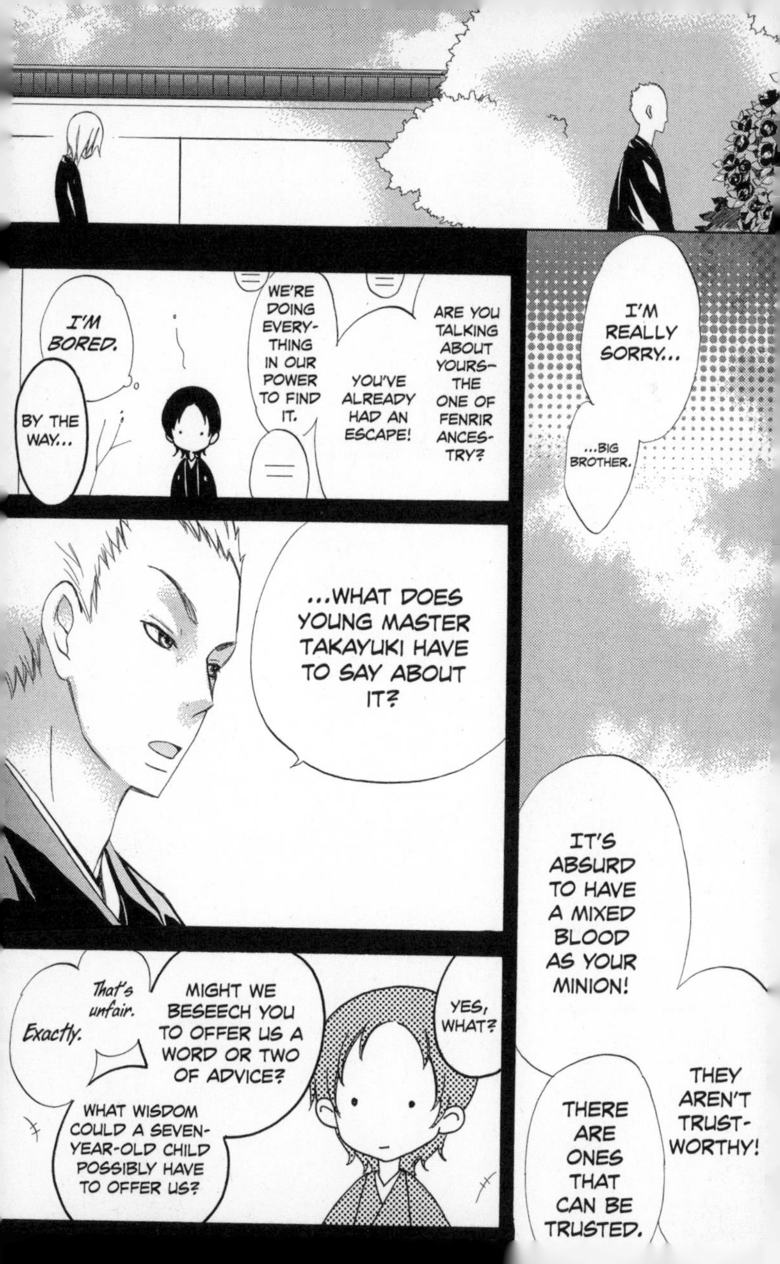
I'M REALLY SORRY...
...BIG BROTHER.
IT'S ABSURD TO HAVE A MIXED BLOOD AS YOUR MINION!
THEY AREN'T TRUST-WORTHY!
THERE ARE ONES THAT CAN BE TRUSTED.
ARE YOU TALKING ABOUT YOURS— THE ONE OF FENRIR ANCES-TRY?
YOU'VE ALREADY HAD AN ESCAPE!
WE'RE DOING EVERY-THING IN OUR POWER TO FIND IT.
I'M BORED.
BY THE WAY...
...WHAT DOES YOUNG MASTER TAKAYUKI HAVE TO SAY ABOUT IT?
YES, WHAT?
MIGHT WE BESEECH YOU TO OFFER US A WORD OR TWO OF ADVICE?
That's unfair.
Exactly.
WHAT WISDOM COULD A SEVEN-YEAR-OLD CHILD POSSIBLY HAVE TO OFFER US?

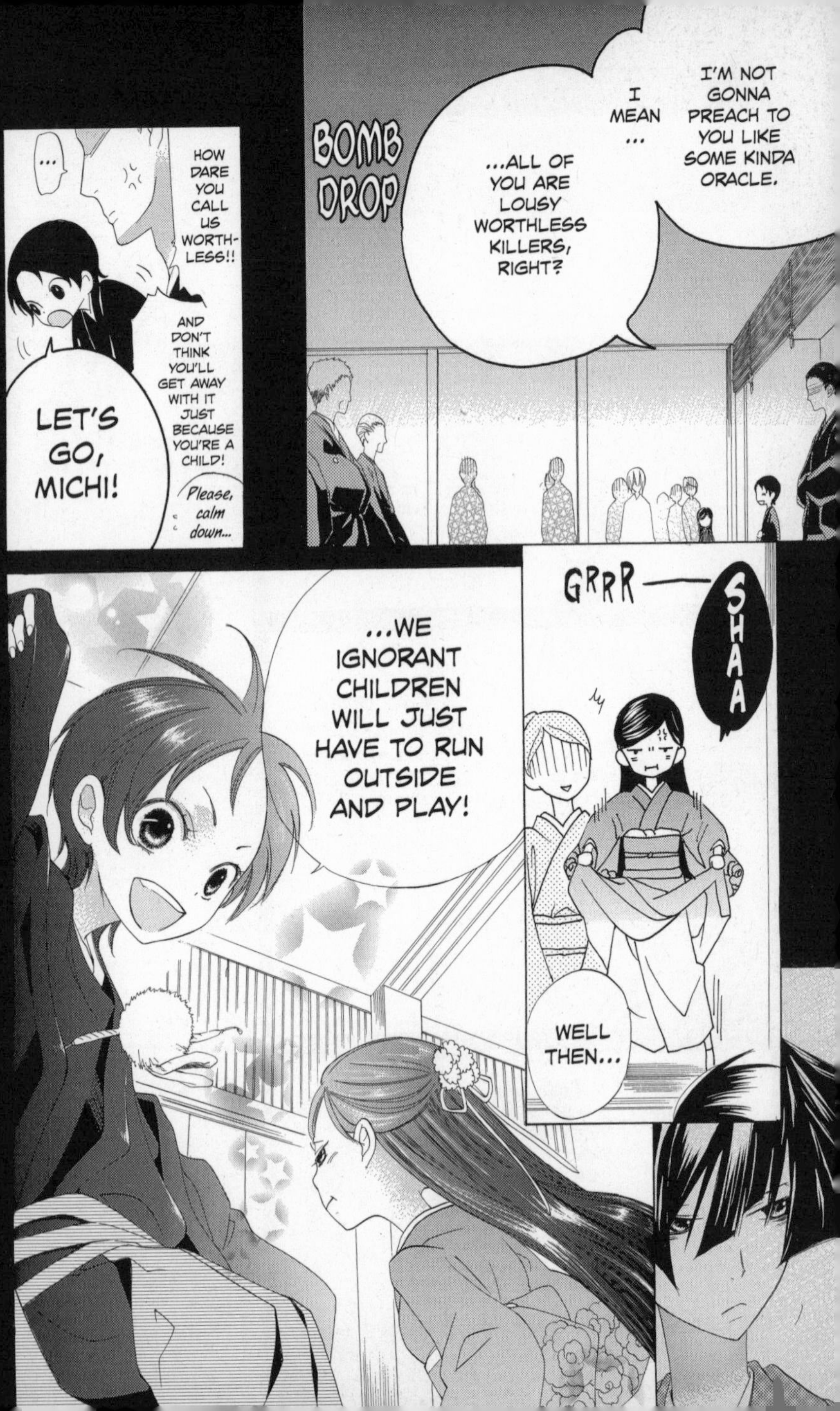
I'M NOT GONNA PREACH TO YOU LIKE SOME KINDA ORACLE.
I MEAN ...
...ALL OF YOU ARE LOUSY WORTHLESS KILLERS, RIGHT?
BOMB DROP
...
HOW DARE YOU CALL US WORTH-LESS!!
AND DON'T THINK YOU'LL GET AWAY WITH IT JUST BECAUSE YOU'RE A CHILD!
Please, calm down...
LET'S GO, MICHI!
GRRR——
SHAA
WELL THEN...
...WE IGNORANT CHILDREN WILL JUST HAVE TO RUN OUTSIDE AND PLAY!

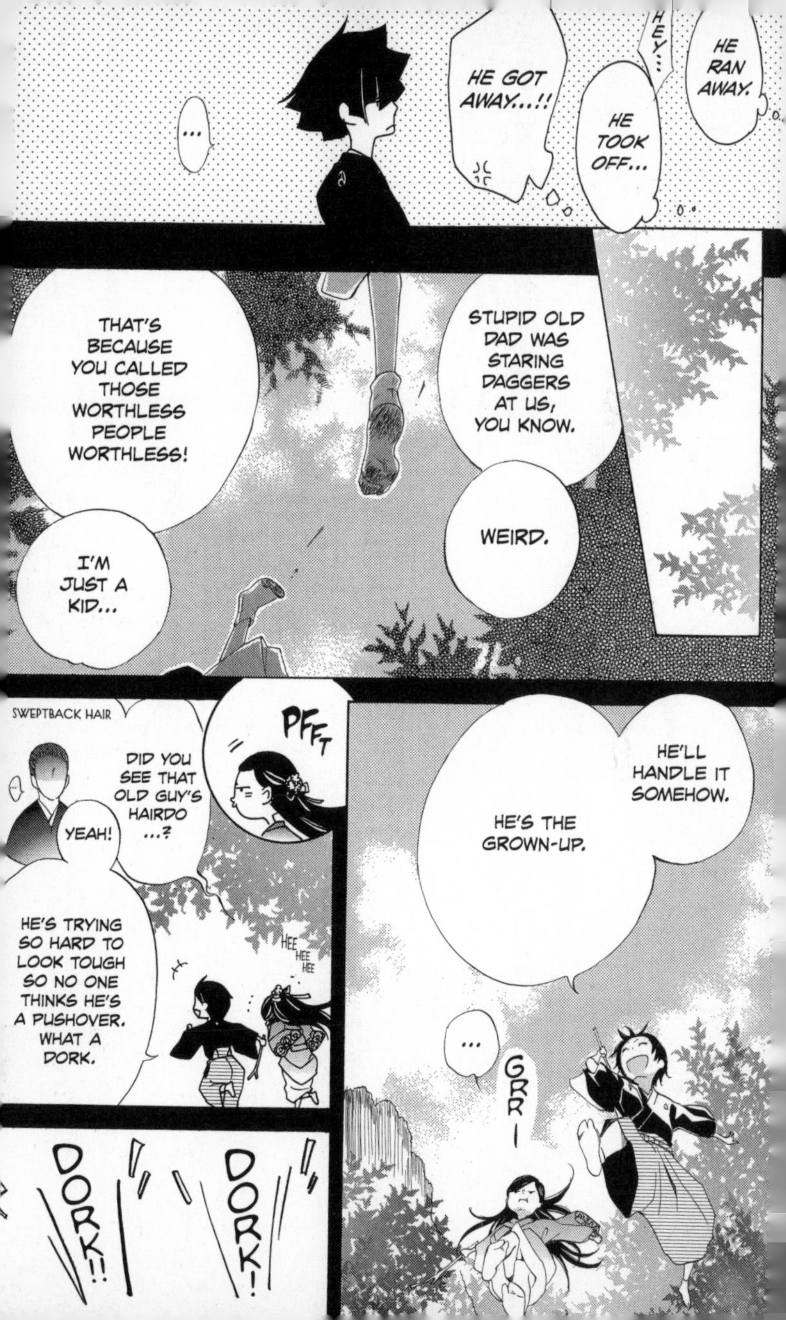
HE RAN AWAY.
HEY...
HE TOOK OFF...
HE GOT AWAY...!!
...
STUPID OLD DAD WAS STARING DAGGERS AT US, YOU KNOW.
THAT'S BECAUSE YOU CALLED THOSE WORTHLESS PEOPLE WORTHLESS!
WEIRD.
I'M JUST A KID...
HE'LL HANDLE IT SOMEHOW.
HE'S THE GROWN-UP.
...
GRR
PFFT
DID YOU SEE THAT OLD GUY'S HAIRDO ...?
SWEPTBACK HAIR
...
YEAH!
HE'S TRYING SO HARD TO LOOK TOUGH SO NO ONE THINKS HE'S A PUSHOVER. WHAT A DORK.
HEE HEE HEE
DORK!
DORK!!

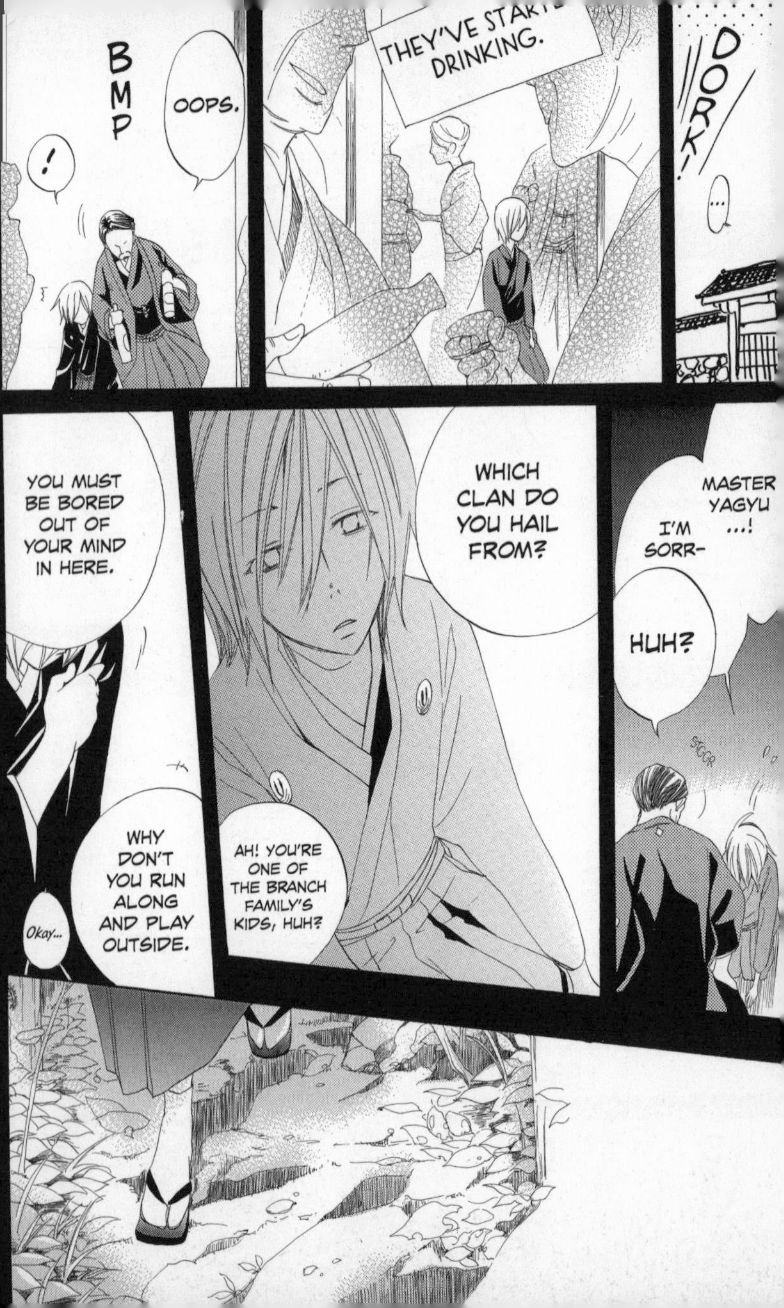
DORK!
...
THEY'VE START
DRINKING.
BMP
OOPS.
!
MASTER YAGYU...!
I'M SORR-
HUH?
STGGR
WHICH CLAN DO YOU HAIL FROM?
AH! YOU'RE ONE OF THE BRANCH FAMILY'S KIDS, HUH?
YOU MUST BE BORED OUT OF YOUR MIND IN HERE.
WHY DON'T YOU RUN ALONG AND PLAY OUTSIDE.
Okay...

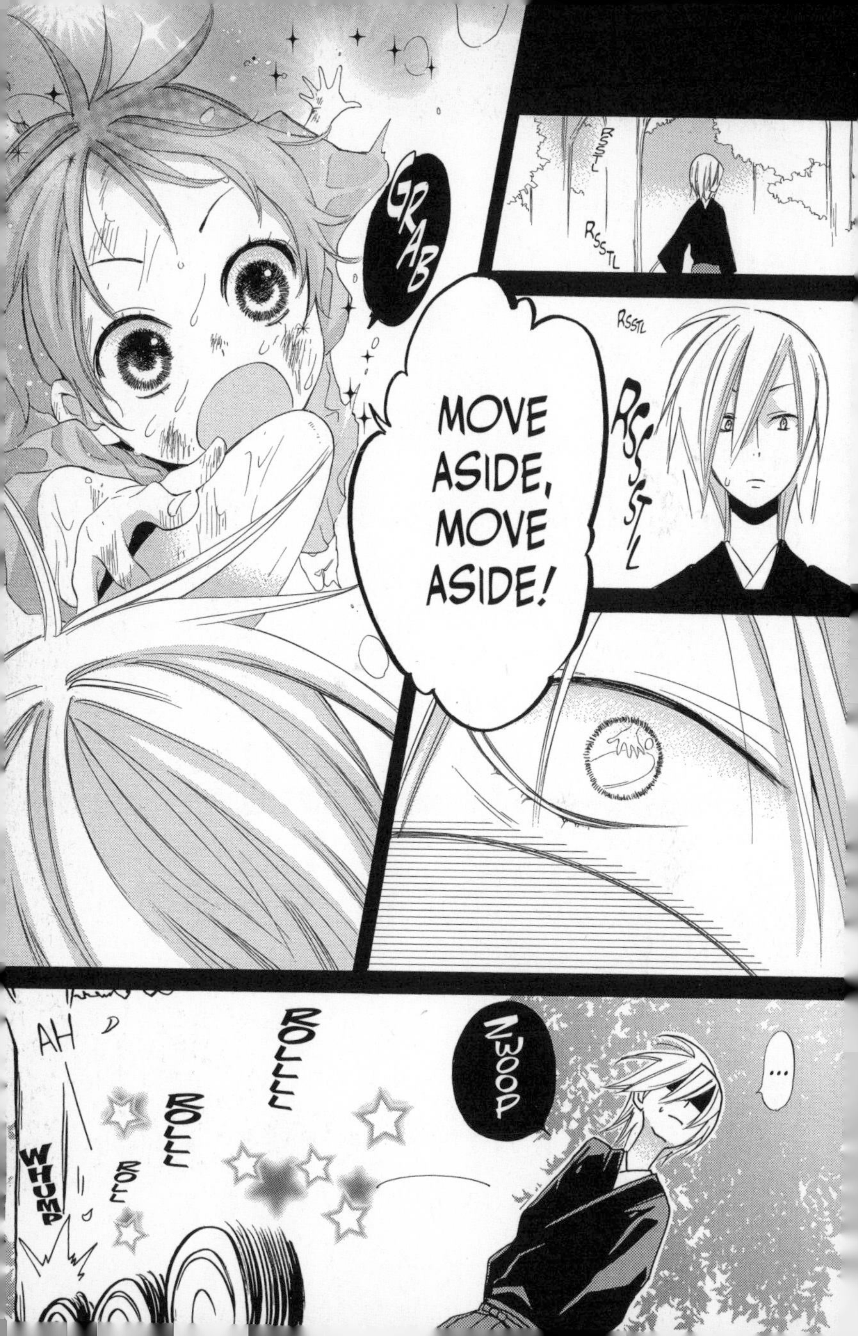
RSSTL
RSSTL
RSSTL
RSSSTL
GRAB
MOVE ASIDE, MOVE ASIDE!
...
ZWOOP
ROLLL
ROLLL
ROLL
AH
WHUMP

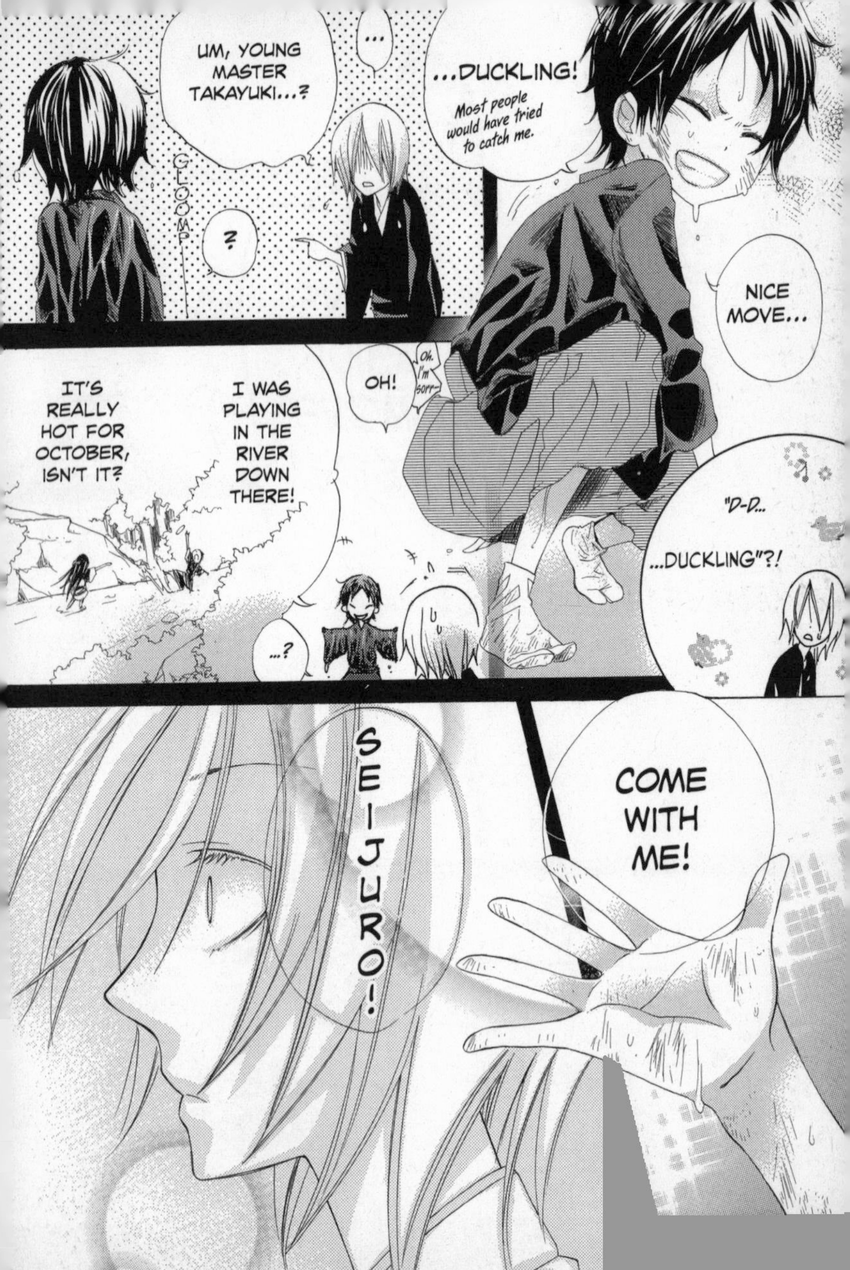
...DUCKLING!
Most people would have tried to catch me.
NICE MOVE...
...
UM, YOUNG MASTER TAKAYUKI...?
GLOOMP
?
"D-D... ...DUCKLING"?!
Oh. I'm sorr--
OH!
I WAS PLAYING IN THE RIVER DOWN THERE!
IT'S REALLY HOT FOR OCTOBER, ISN'T IT?
...?
COME WITH ME!
SEIJURO!

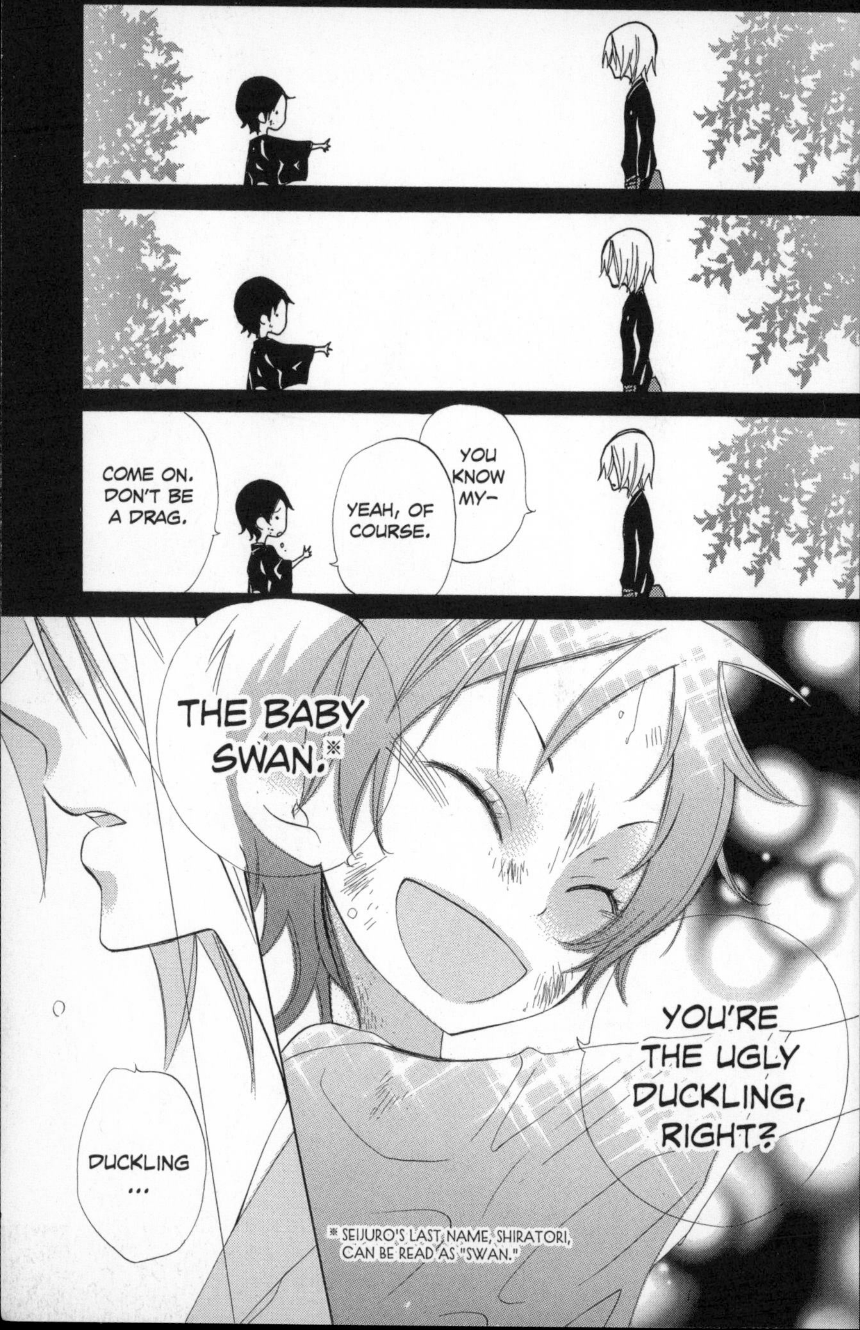
YOU KNOW MY—
YEAH, OF COURSE.
COME ON. DON'T BE A DRAG.
YOU'RE THE UGLY DUCKLING, RIGHT?
THE BABY SWAN.※
DUCKLING ...

※ SEIJURO'S LAST NAME, SHIRATORI, CAN BE READ AS "SWAN."

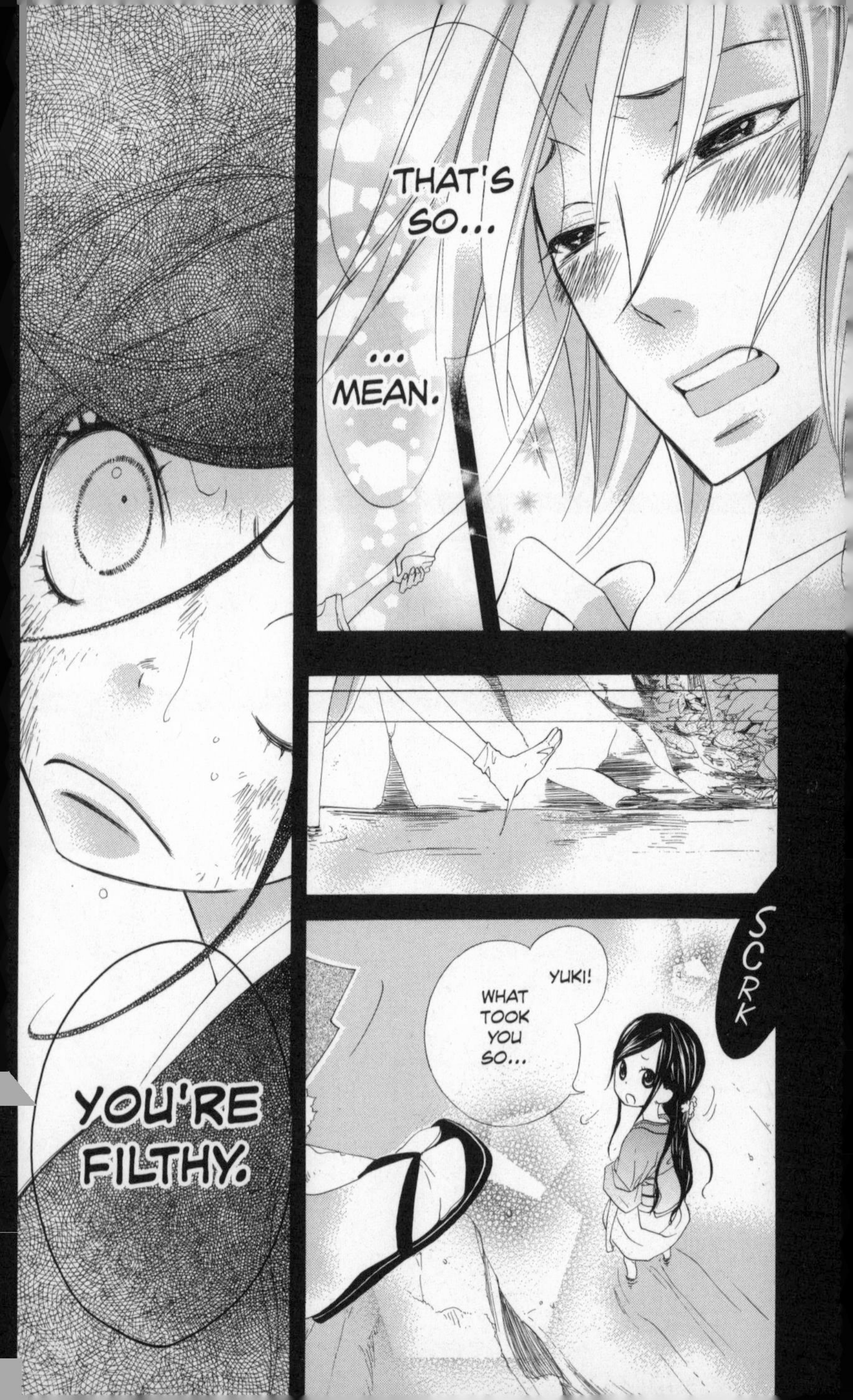
THAT'S SO...
...MEAN.
SCRK
YUKI! WHAT TOOK YOU SO...
YOU'RE FILTHY.

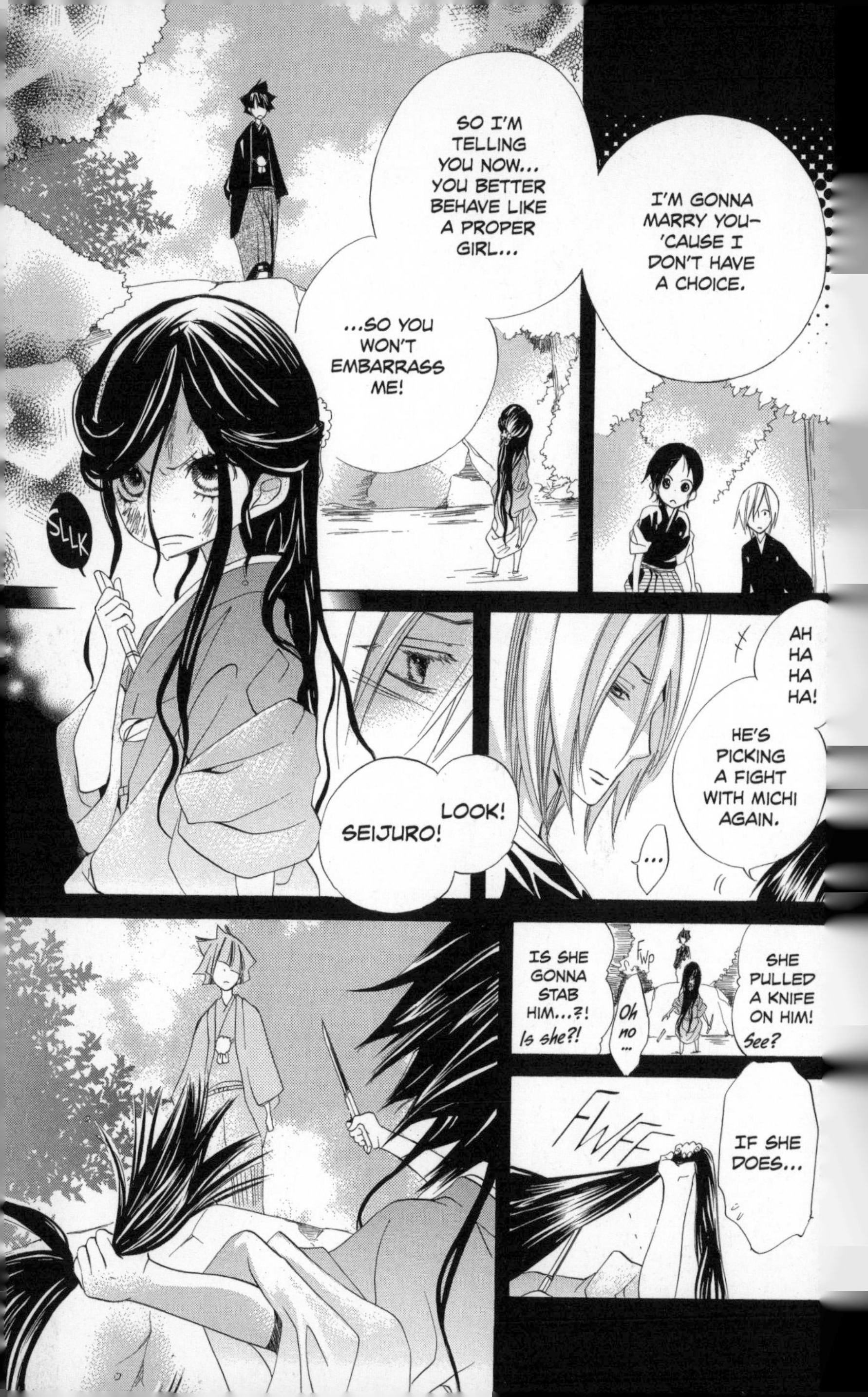
I'M GONNA MARRY YOU—'CAUSE I DON'T HAVE A CHOICE.
SO I'M TELLING YOU NOW... YOU BETTER BEHAVE LIKE A PROPER GIRL...
...SO YOU WON'T EMBARRASS ME!
SLLK
AH HA HA HA!
HE'S PICKING A FIGHT WITH MICHI AGAIN.
...
LOOK! SEIJURO!
SHE PULLED A KNIFE ON HIM!
See?
Oh no...
FWP
IS SHE GONNA STAB HIM...?!
Is she?!
FWFF
IF SHE DOES...

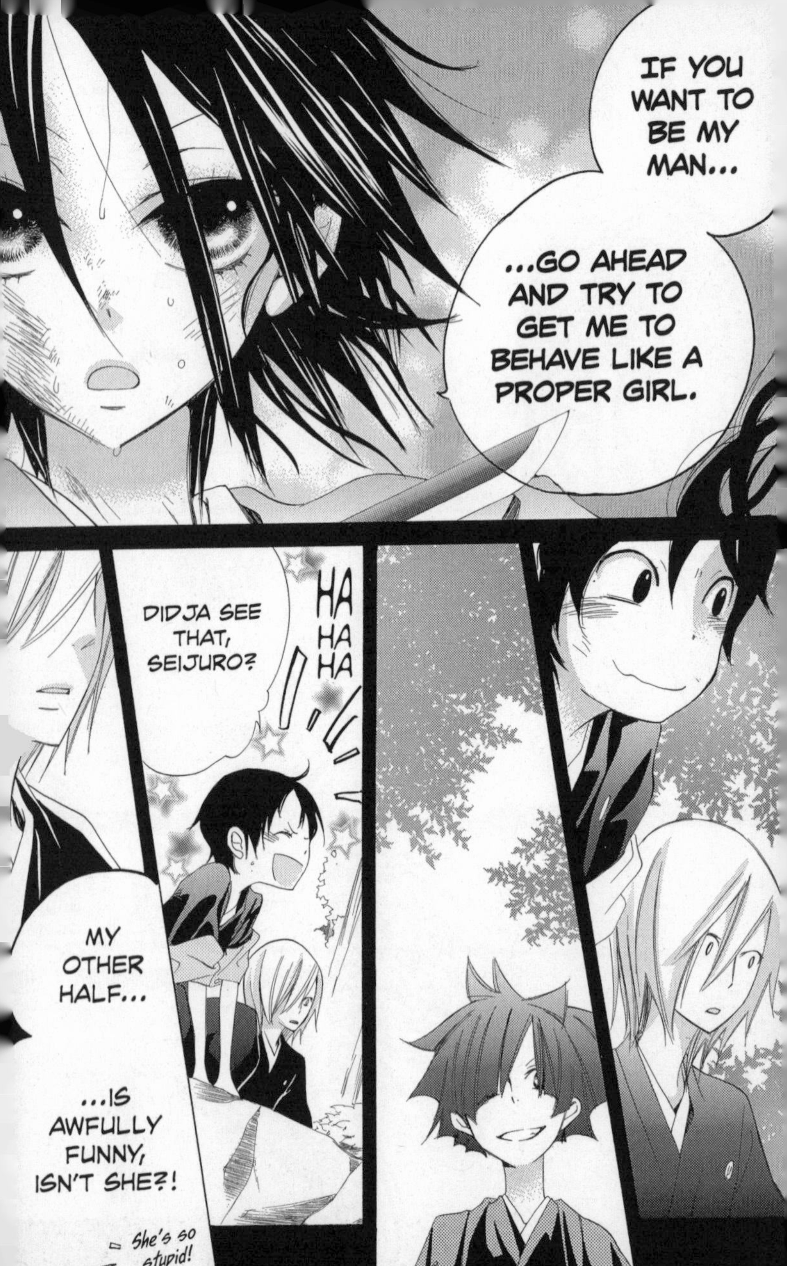
IF YOU WANT TO BE MY MAN...
...GO AHEAD AND TRY TO GET ME TO BEHAVE LIKE A PROPER GIRL.
DIDJA SEE THAT, SEIJURO?
HA HA HA
MY OTHER HALF...
...IS AWFULLY FUNNY, ISN'T SHE?!
She's so stupid!

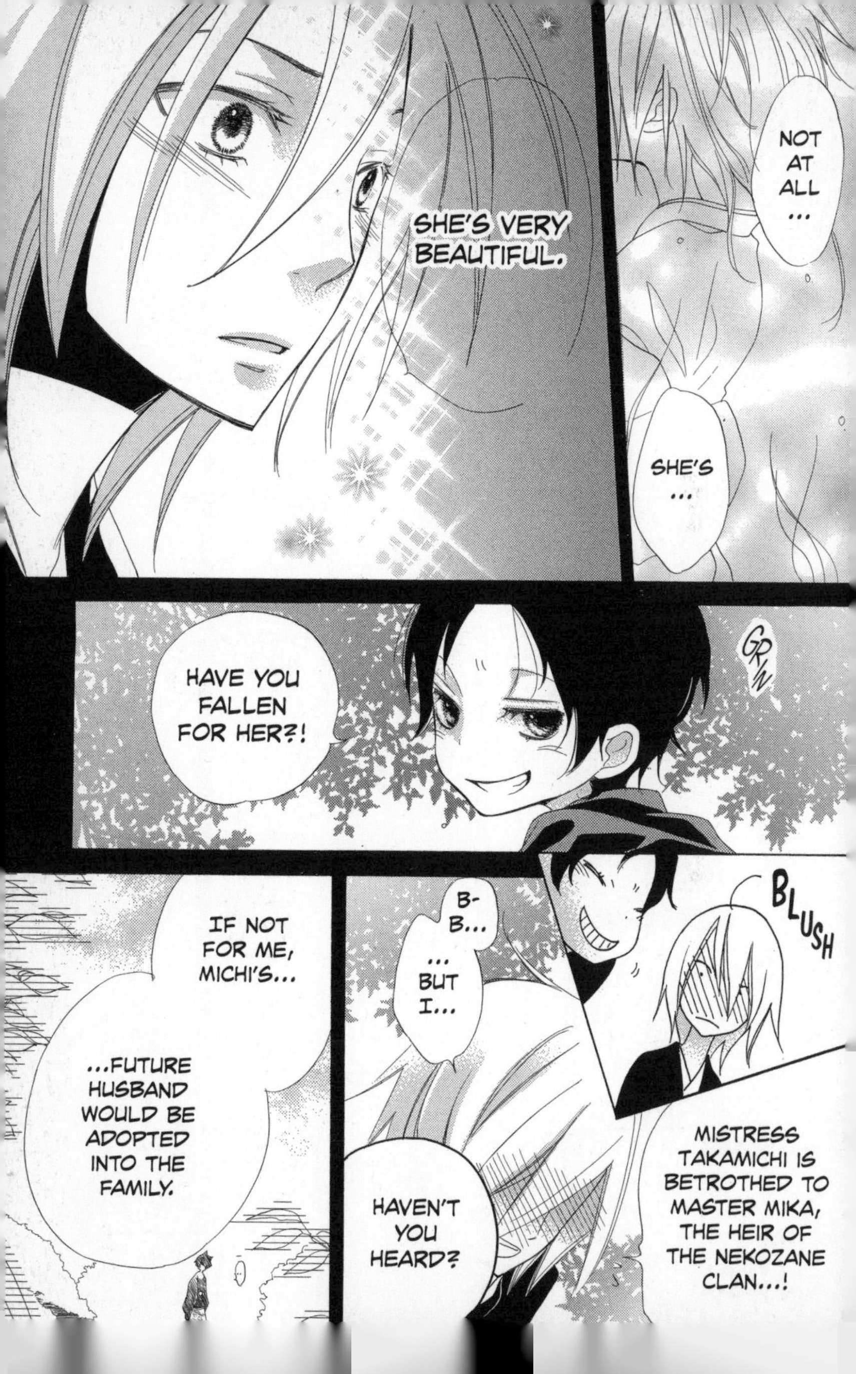
NOT AT ALL...
SHE'S...
SHE'S VERY BEAUTIFUL.
GRIN
HAVE YOU FALLEN FOR HER?!
BLUSH
B-B...
...BUT I...
MISTRESS TAKAMICHI IS BETROTHED TO MASTER MIKA, THE HEIR OF THE NEKOZANE CLAN...!
HAVEN'T YOU HEARD?
IF NOT FOR ME, MICHI'S...
...FUTURE HUSBAND WOULD BE ADOPTED INTO THE FAMILY.

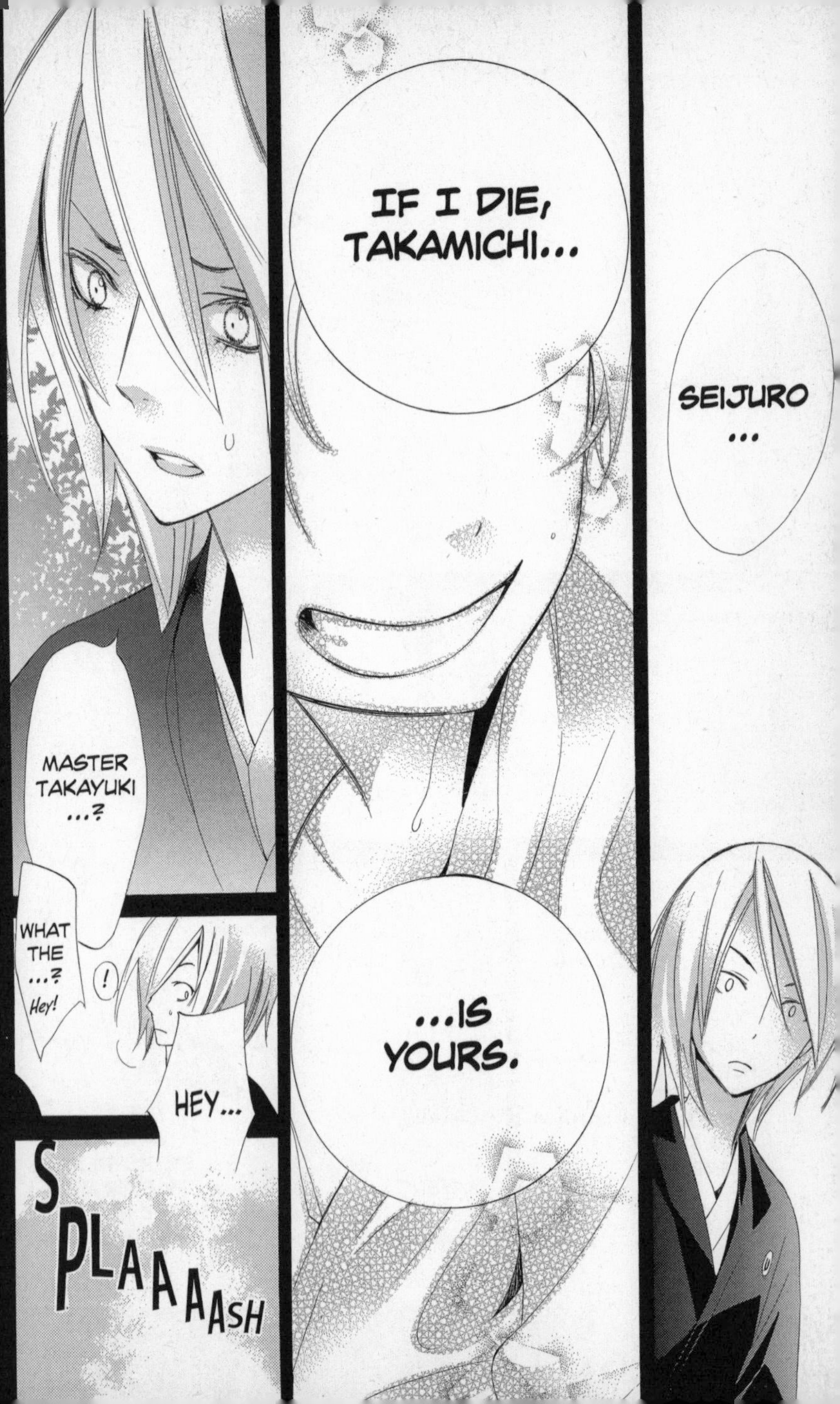
SEIJURO ...
IF I DIE, TAKAMICHI...
...IS YOURS.
MASTER TAKAYUKI ...?
WHAT THE ...? Hey!
!
HEY...
SPLAAAASH

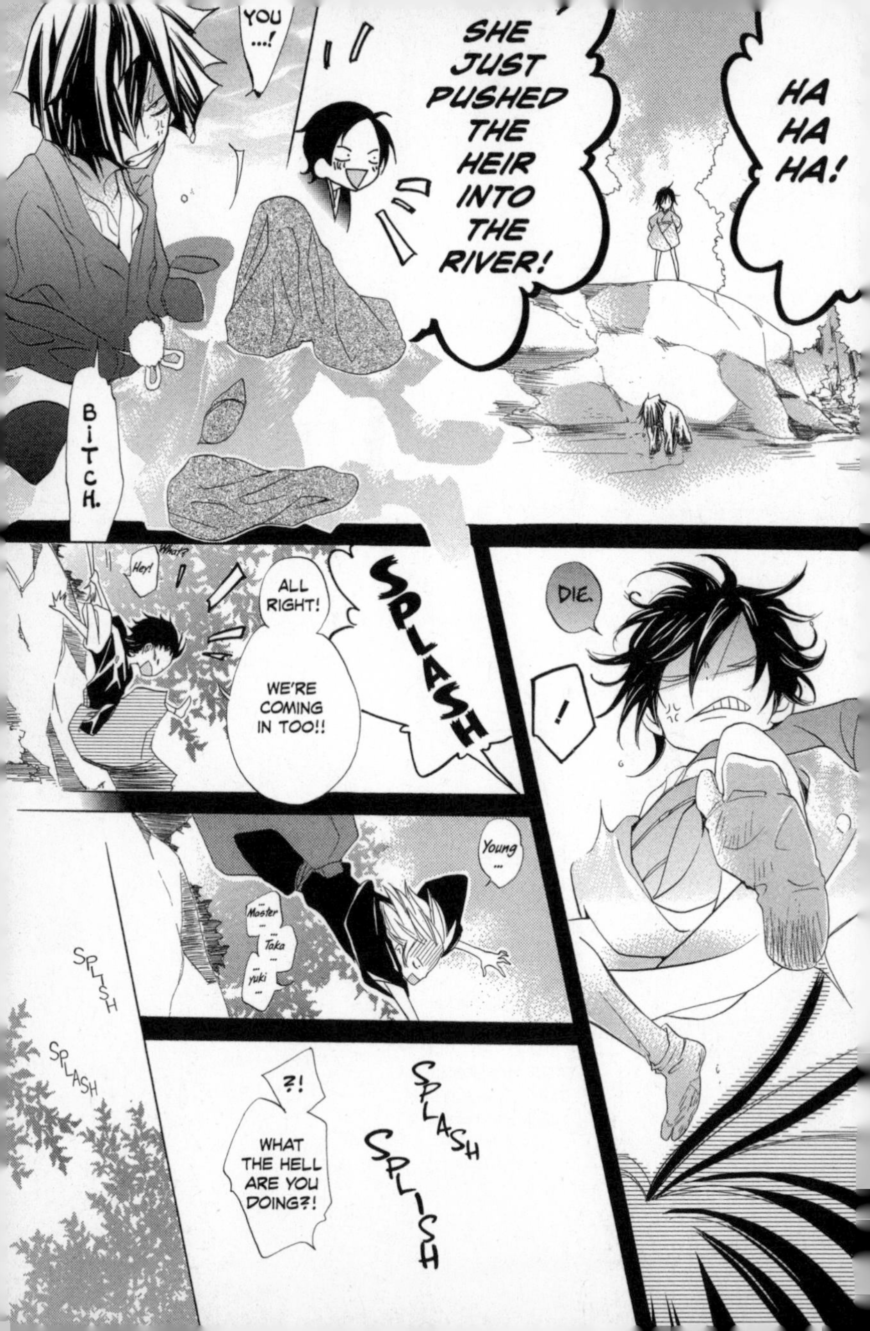
HA HA HA!
SHE JUST PUSHED THE HEIR INTO THE RIVER!
YOU ...!
BITCH.
DIE.
!
SPLASH
ALL RIGHT! WE'RE COMING IN TOO!!
What?
Hey!
Young ...
... Master ... Taka ... yuki ...
SPLASH
SPLASH
SPLISH
?! WHAT THE HELL ARE YOU DOING?!
SPLASH
SPLASH

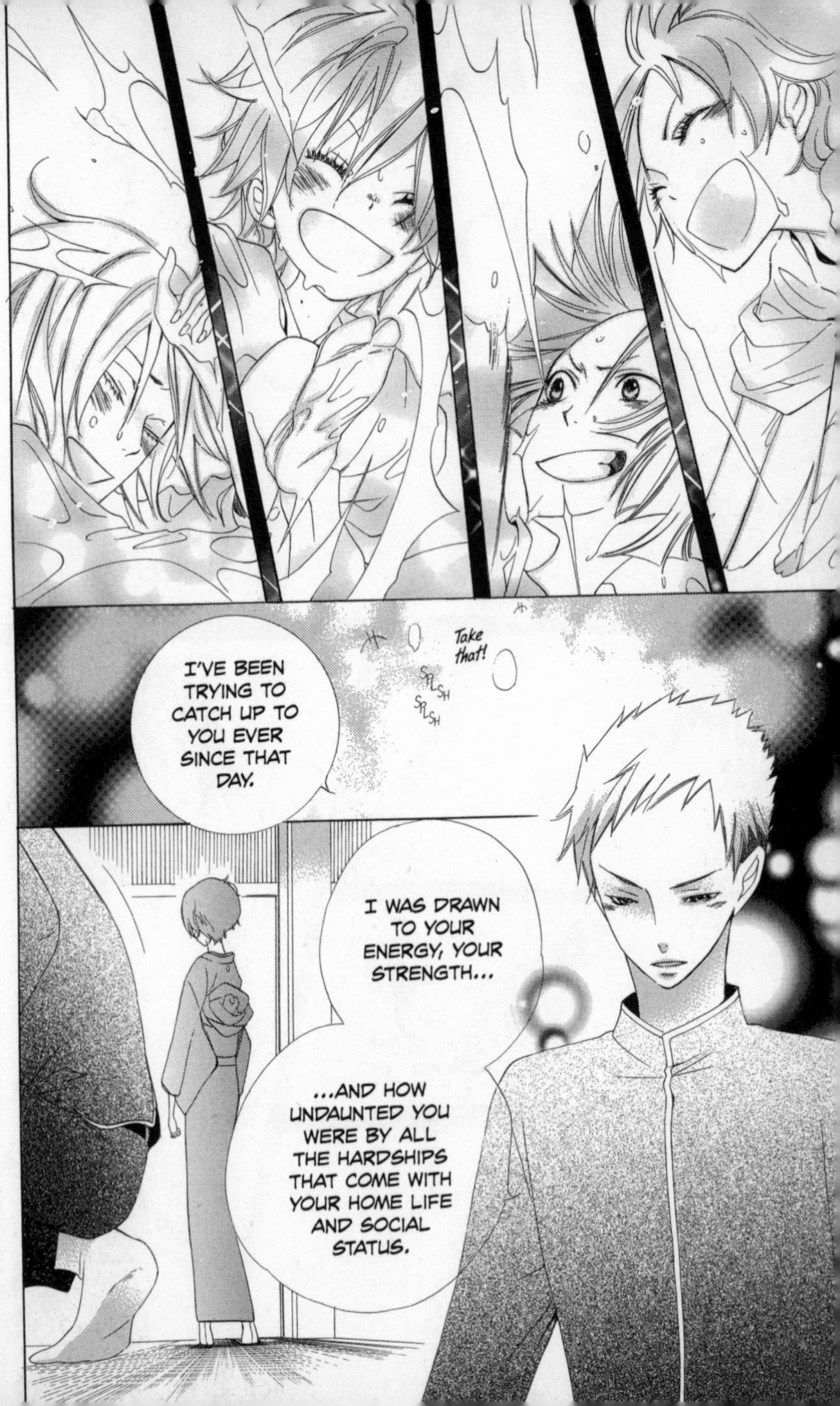
Take that!
SPLSH
SPLSH
I'VE BEEN TRYING TO CATCH UP TO YOU EVER SINCE THAT DAY.
I WAS DRAWN TO YOUR ENERGY, YOUR STRENGTH...
...AND HOW UNDAUNTED YOU WERE BY ALL THE HARDSHIPS THAT COME WITH YOUR HOME LIFE AND SOCIAL STATUS.

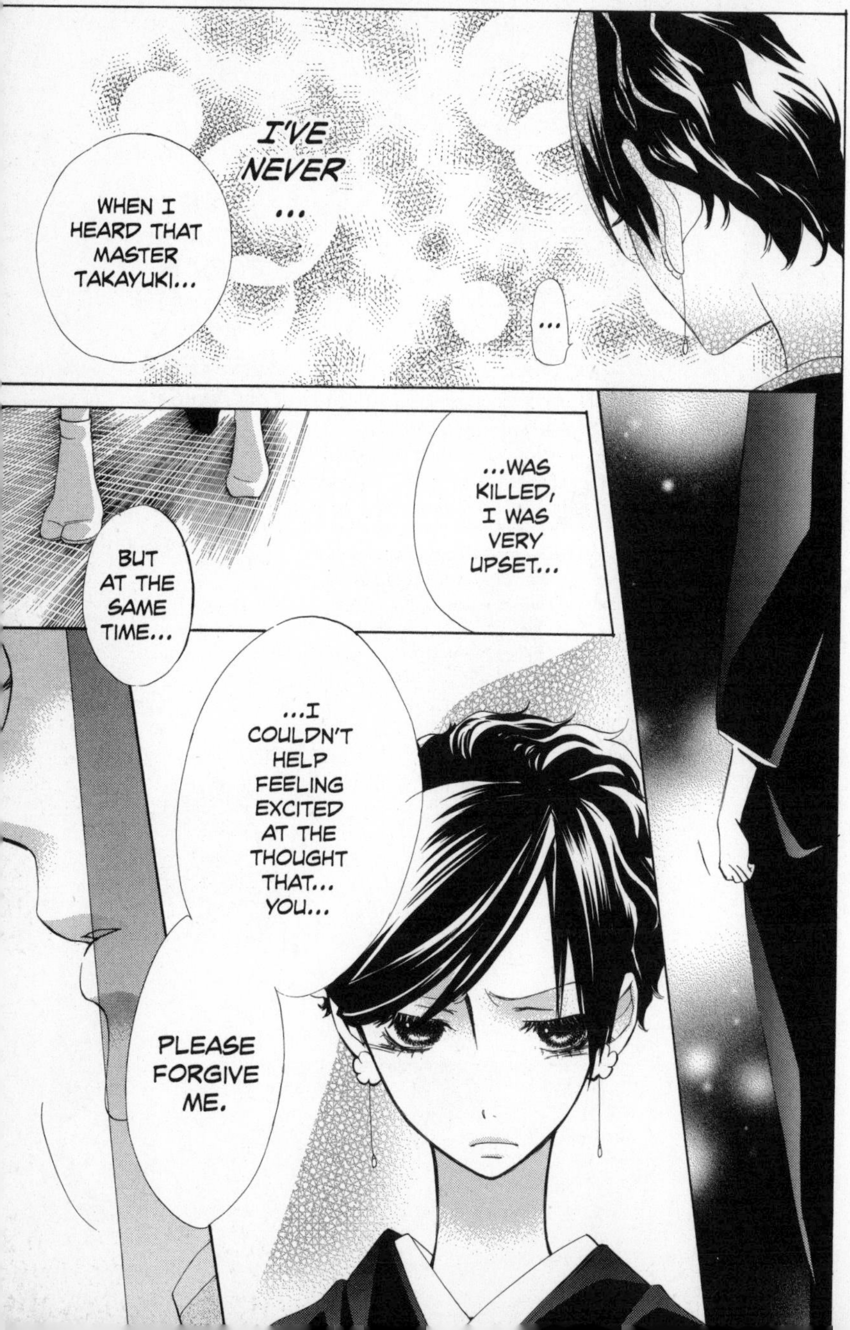
...
I'VE NEVER ...
WHEN I HEARD THAT MASTER TAKAYUKI...
...WAS KILLED, I WAS VERY UPSET...
BUT AT THE SAME TIME...
...I COULDN'T HELP FEELING EXCITED AT THE THOUGHT THAT... YOU...
PLEASE FORGIVE ME.

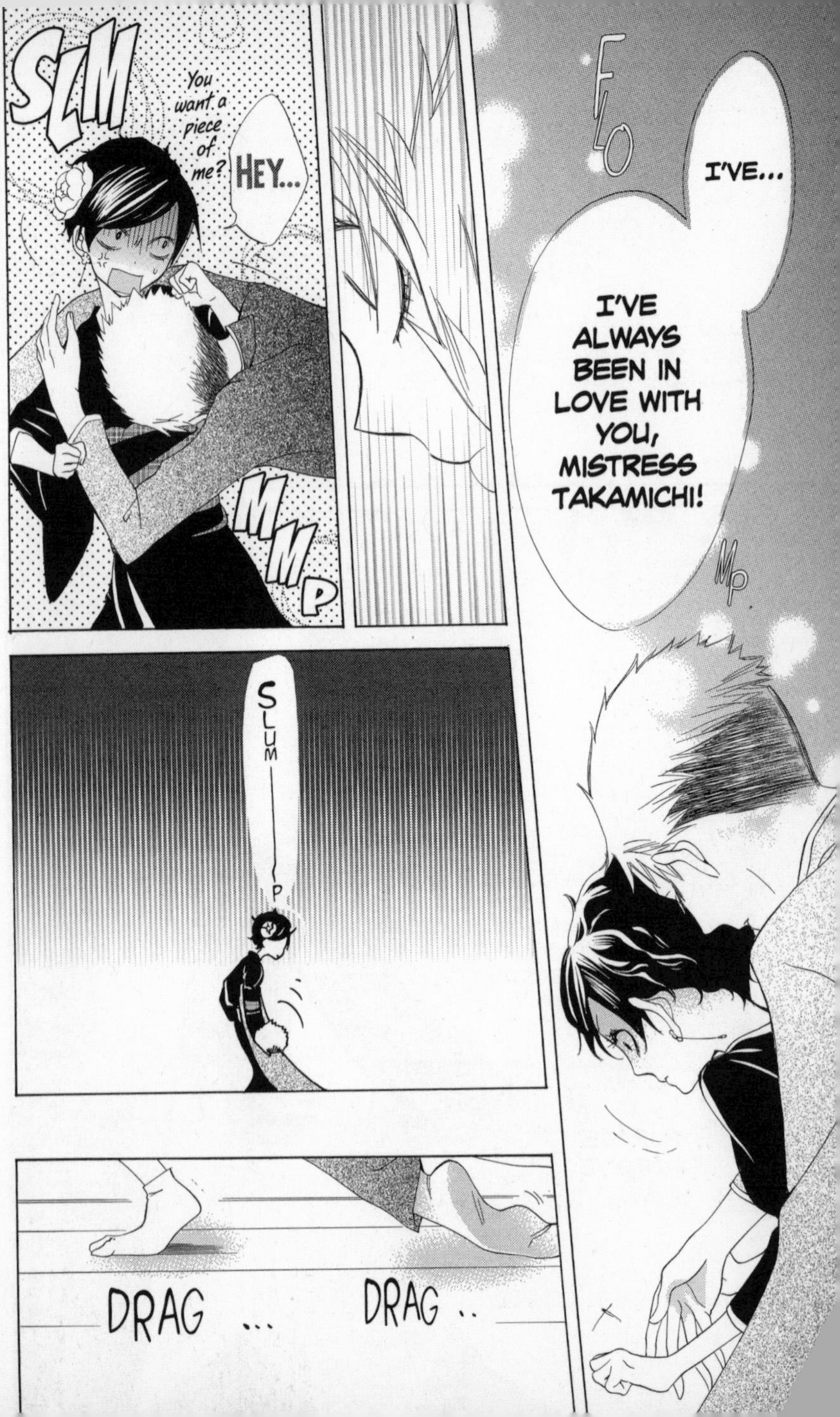
FLO
I'VE...
I'VE ALWAYS BEEN IN LOVE WITH YOU, MISTRESS TAKAMICHI!
MP
HEY...
You want a piece of me?
SLM
MMMP
SLUMP
DRAG ...
DRAG ..

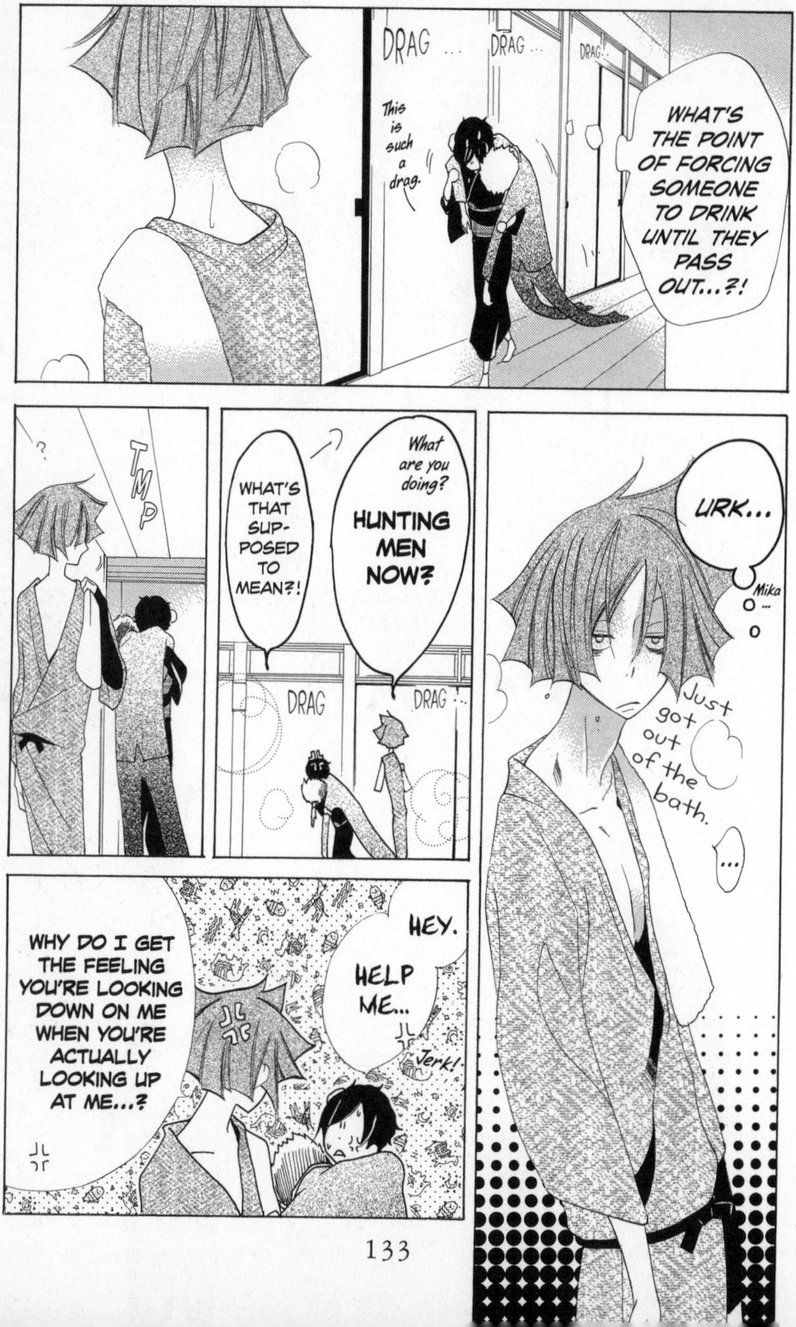
WHAT'S THE POINT OF FORCING SOMEONE TO DRINK UNTIL THEY PASS OUT...?!
DRAG...
DRAG...
DRAG...
This is such a drag.
URK...
Mika...
Just got out of the bath.
...
What are you doing?
HUNTING MEN NOW?
WHAT'S THAT SUP-POSED TO MEAN?!
DRAG...
DRAG
?
TMP
HEY.
HELP ME...
Jerk!
WHY DO I GET THE FEELING YOU'RE LOOKING DOWN ON ME WHEN YOU'RE ACTUALLY LOOKING UP AT ME...?

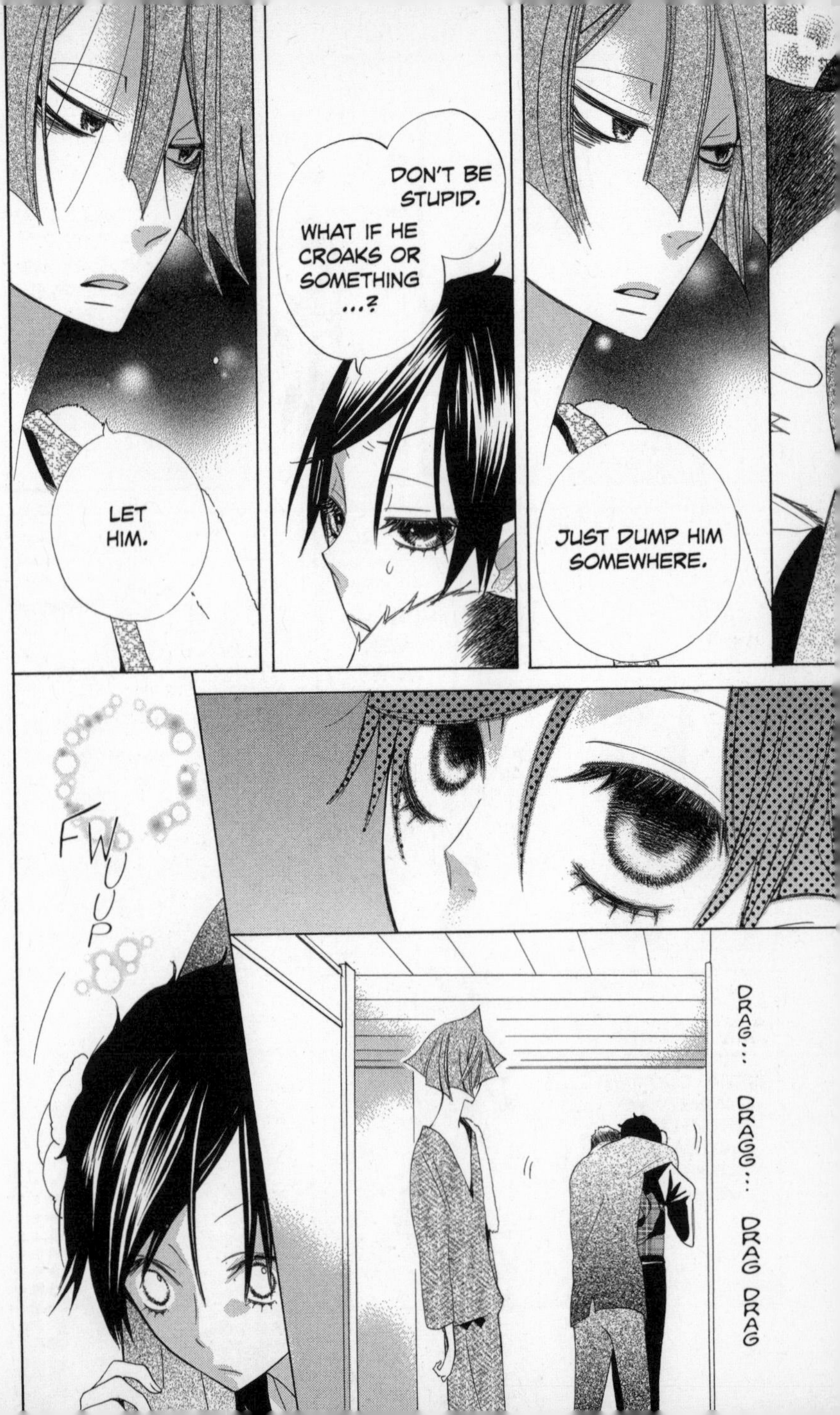
JUST DUMP HIM SOMEWHERE.
DON'T BE STUPID.
WHAT IF HE CROAKS OR SOMETHING ...?
LET HIM.
DRAG... DRAGG... DRAG DRAG
FWUUUP

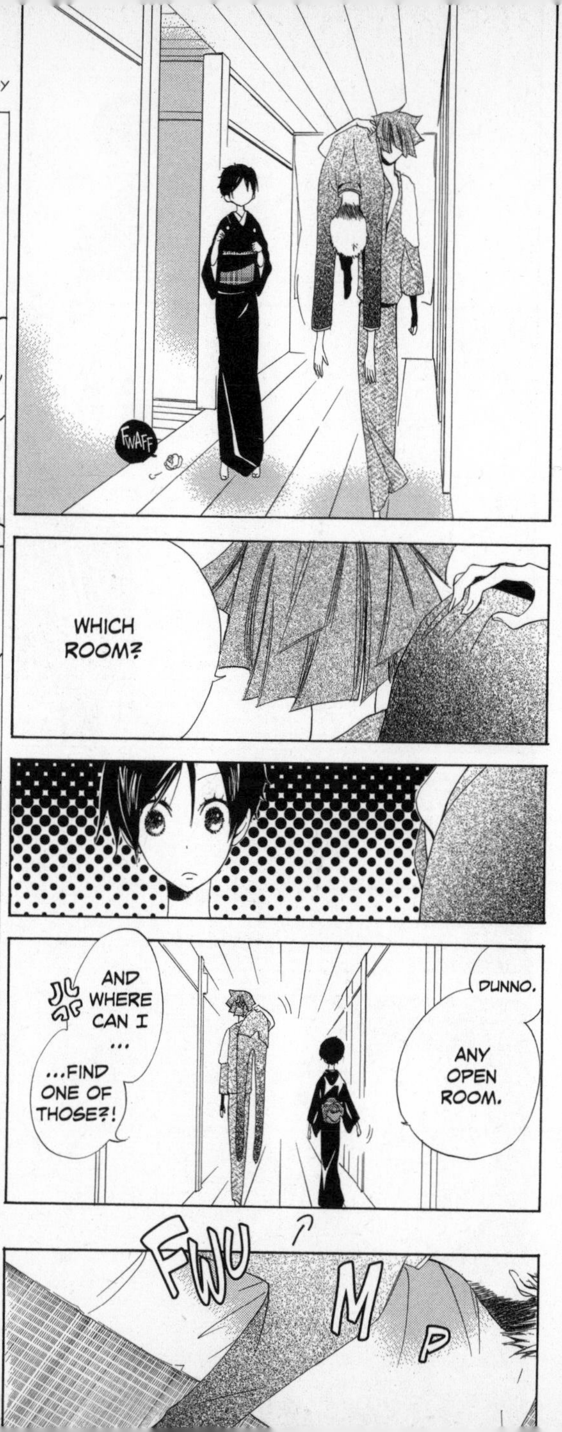
FWAFF
WHICH ROOM?
DUNNO.
ANY OPEN ROOM.
AND WHERE CAN I ...
...FIND ONE OF THOSE?!
FWUMP

I know I'm giving away the story, but...

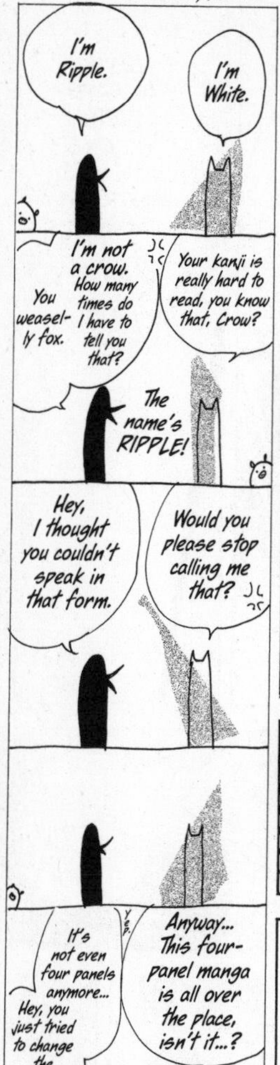
I'm White.
I'm Ripple.
Your kanji is really hard to read, you know that, Crow?
I'm not a crow. How many times do I have to tell you that?
You weasel-ly fox.
The name's RIPPLE!
Would you please stop calling me that?
Hey, I thought you couldn't speak in that form.
Anyway... This four-panel manga is all over the place, isn't it...?
Yep.
It's not even four panels anymore...
Hey, you just tried to change the subject, didn't you?
Didn't you?!
Jiu Jiu vol. 4 coming soon!
My dog.
Did not.
Look for it!

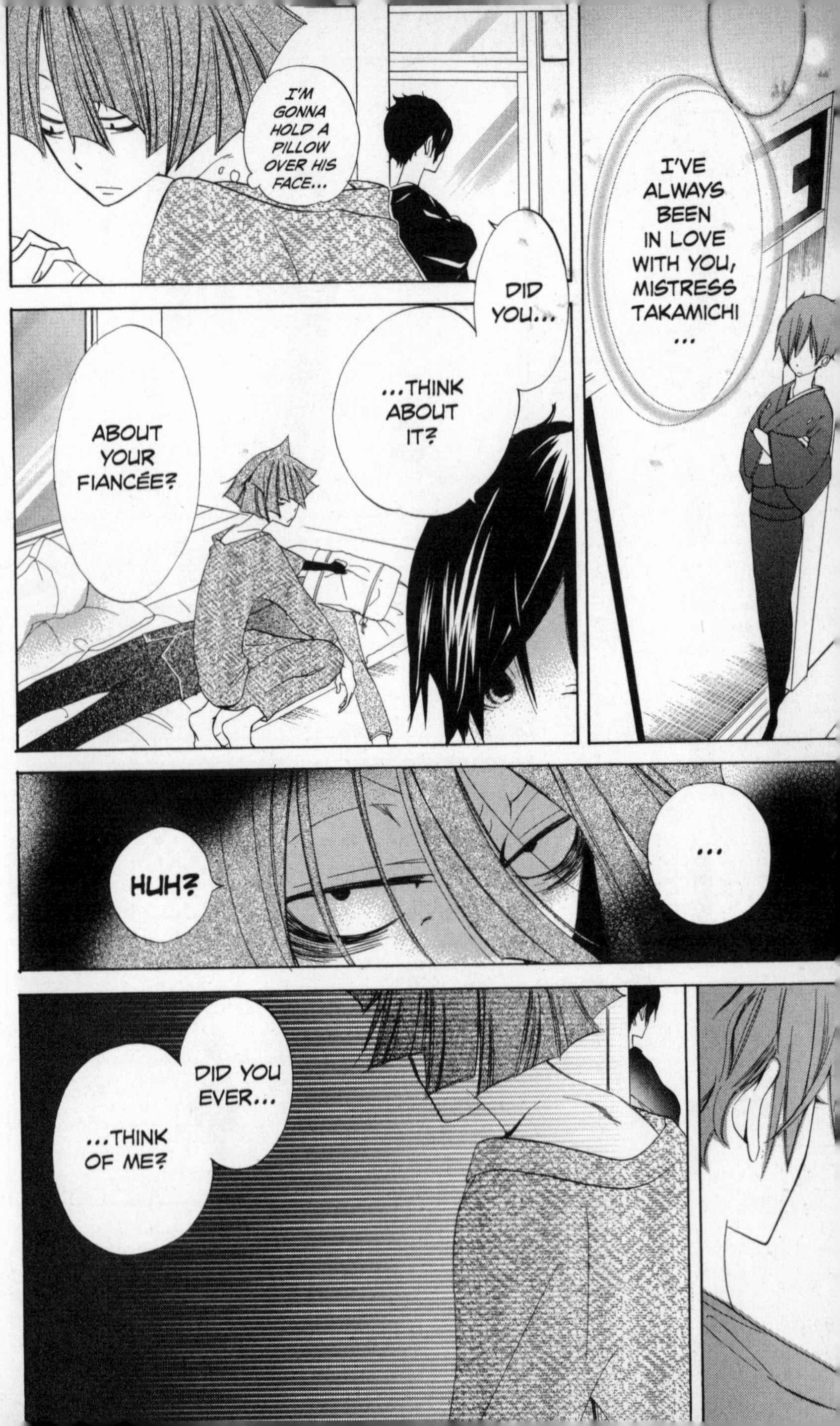
I'VE ALWAYS BEEN IN LOVE WITH YOU, MISTRESS TAKAMICHI...
I'M GONNA HOLD A PILLOW OVER HIS FACE...
DID YOU...
...THINK ABOUT IT?
ABOUT YOUR FIANCÉE?
...
HUH?
DID YOU EVER...
...THINK OF ME?

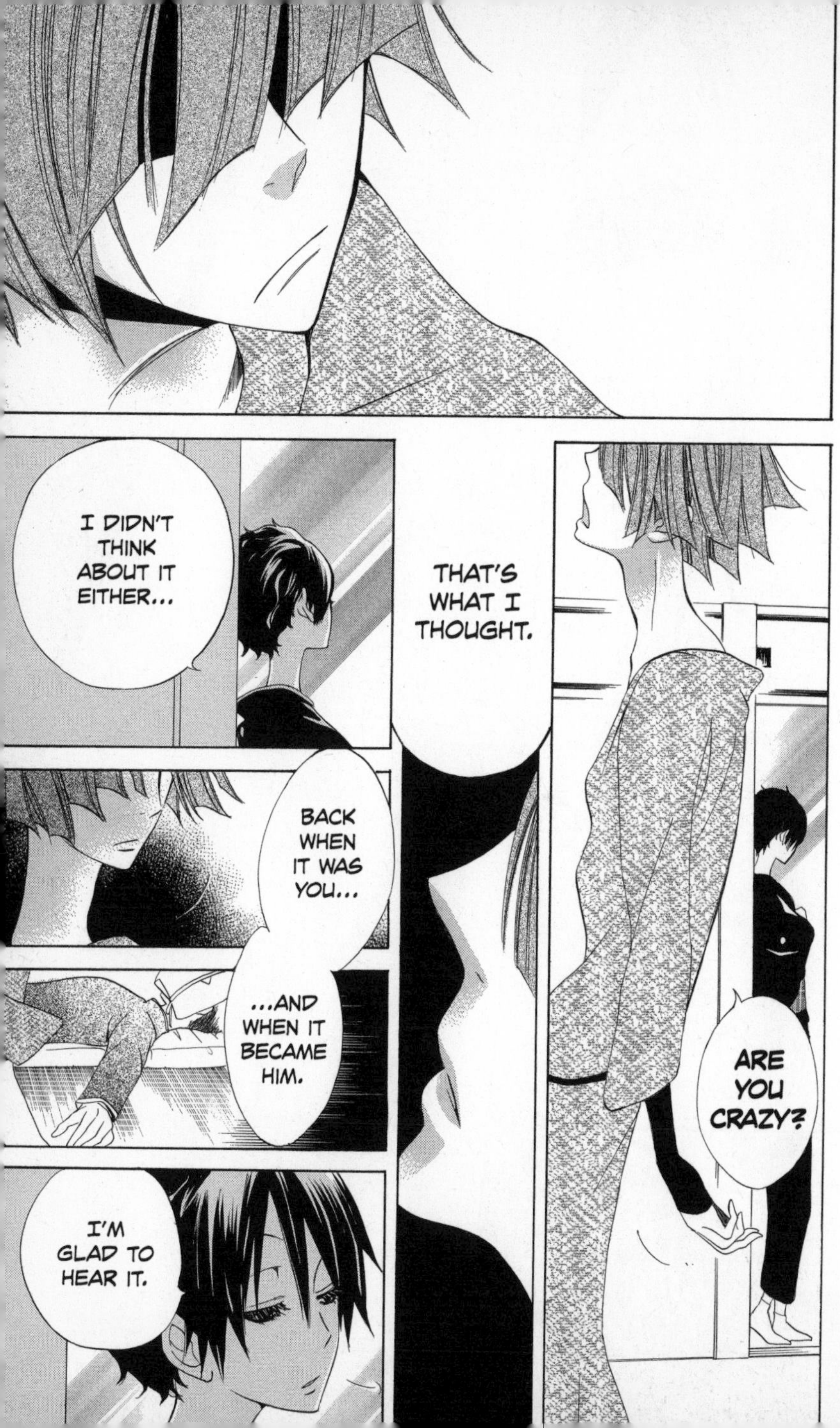
THAT'S WHAT I THOUGHT.
ARE YOU CRAZY?
I DIDN'T THINK ABOUT IT EITHER...
BACK WHEN IT WAS YOU...
...AND WHEN IT BECAME HIM.
I'M GLAD TO HEAR IT.

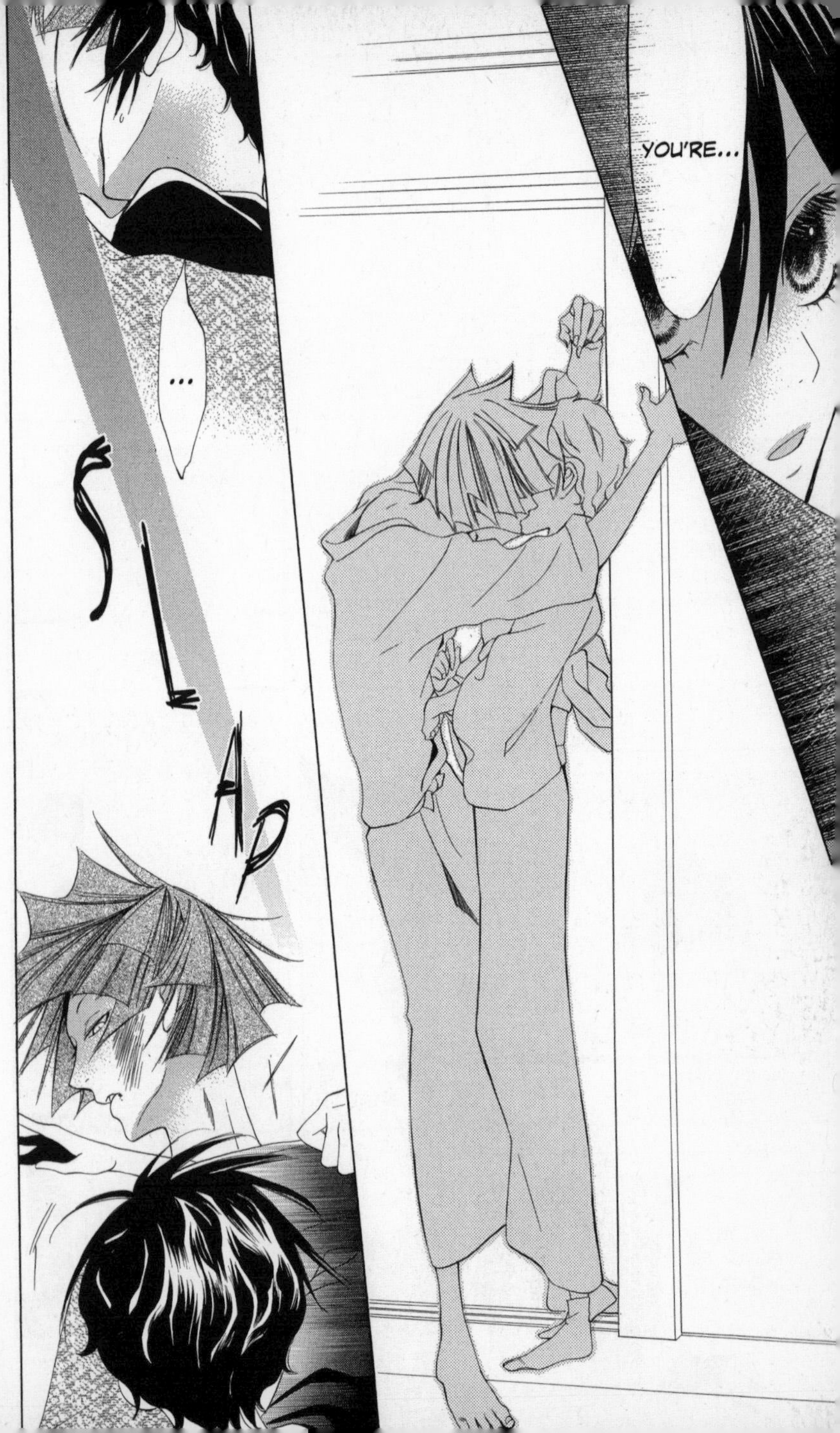
YOU'RE...
...
SLAP

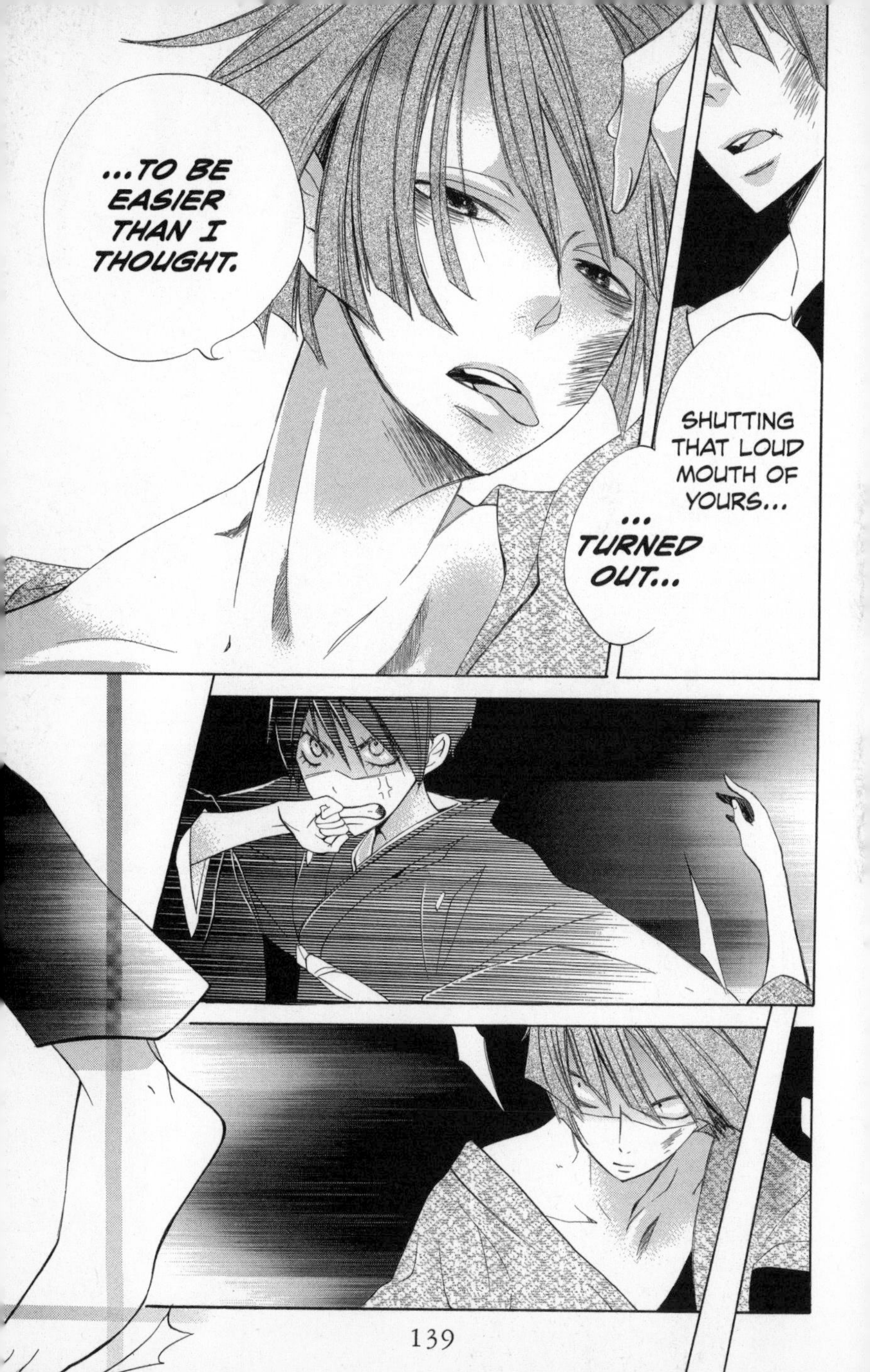
SHUTTING THAT LOUD MOUTH OF YOURS...
...TURNED OUT...
...TO BE EASIER THAN I THOUGHT.

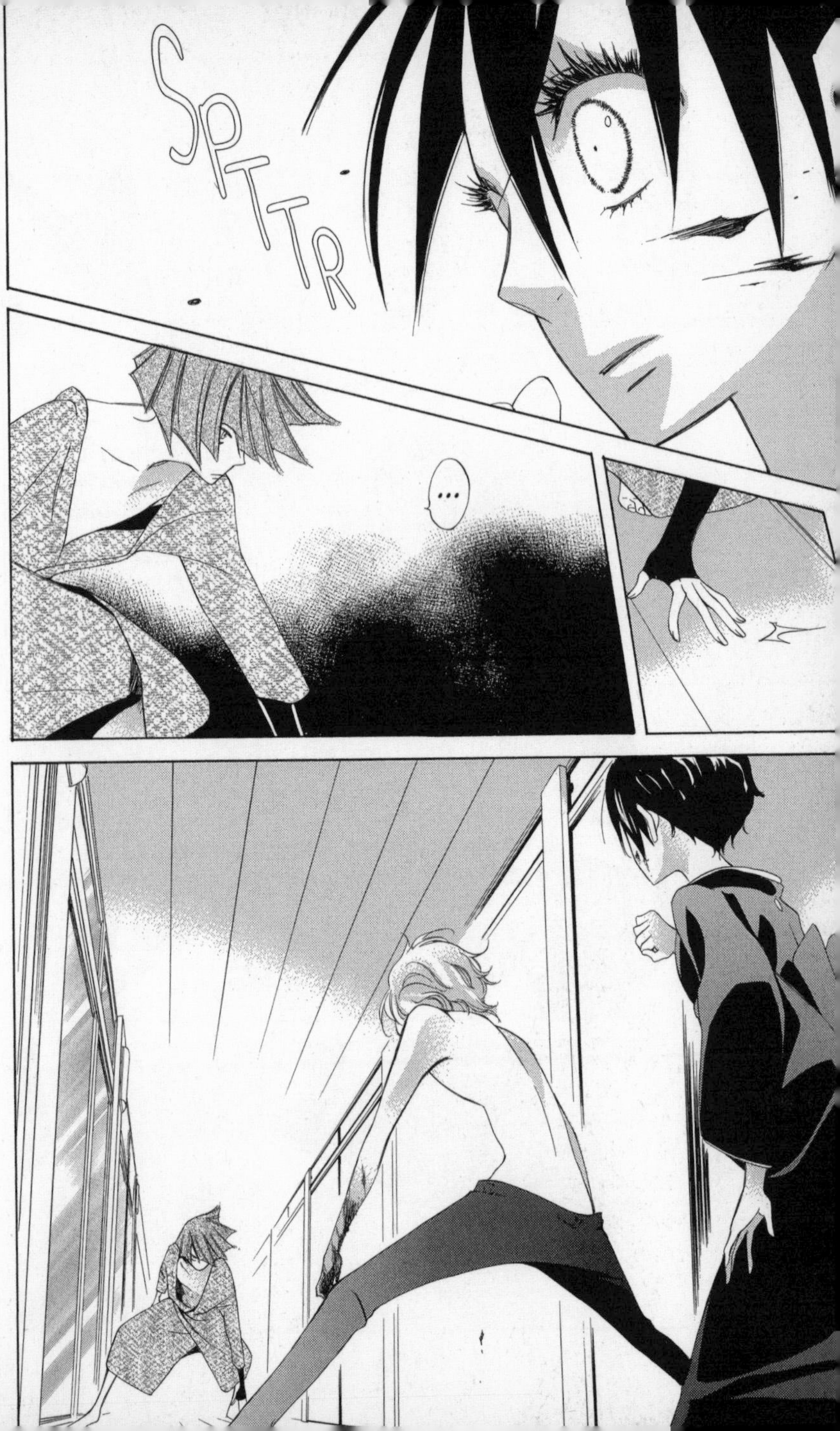
SPTTTR
...

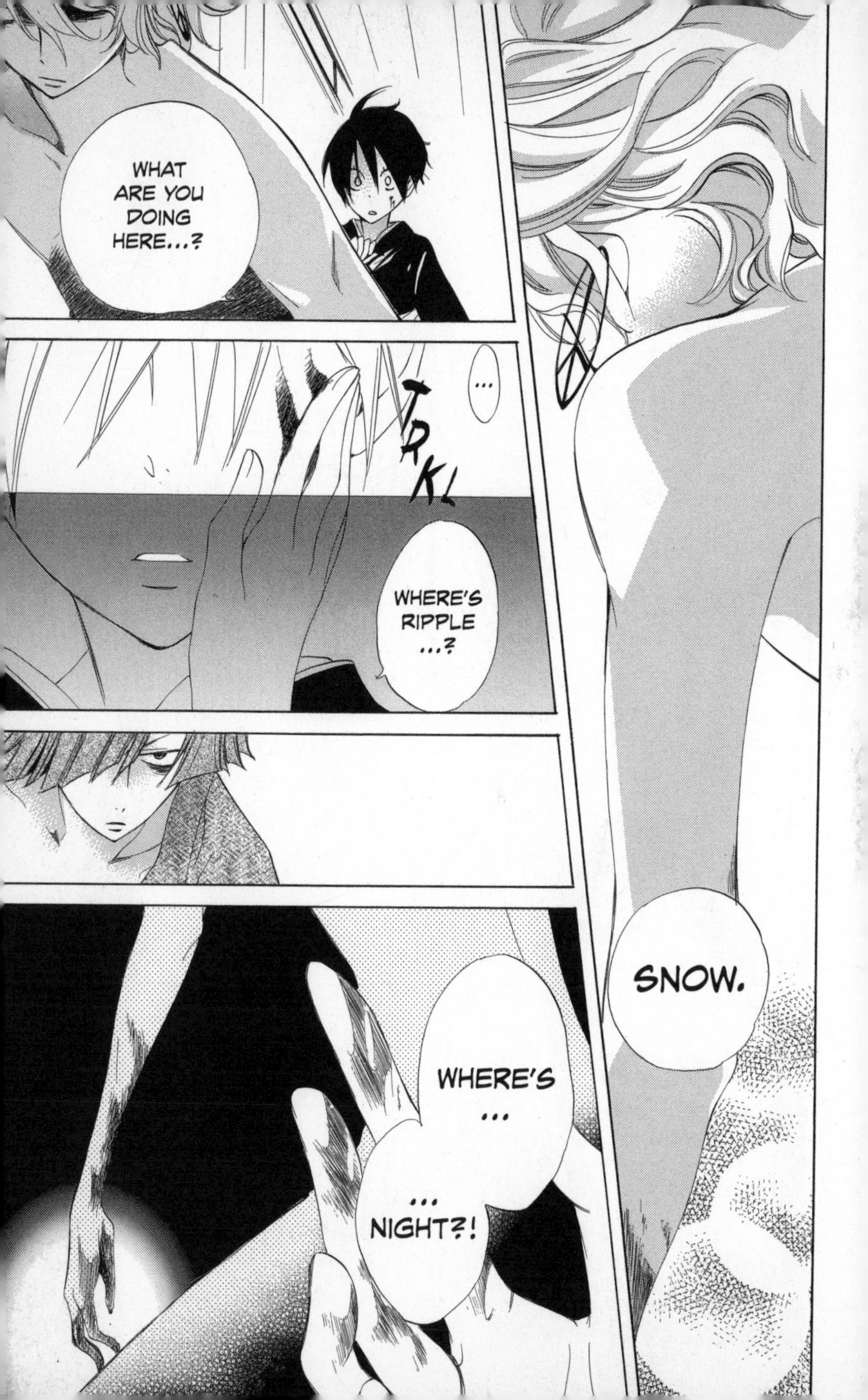
SNOW.
WHAT ARE YOU DOING HERE...?
...
TRKL
WHERE'S RIPPLE ...?
WHERE'S ...
... NIGHT?!

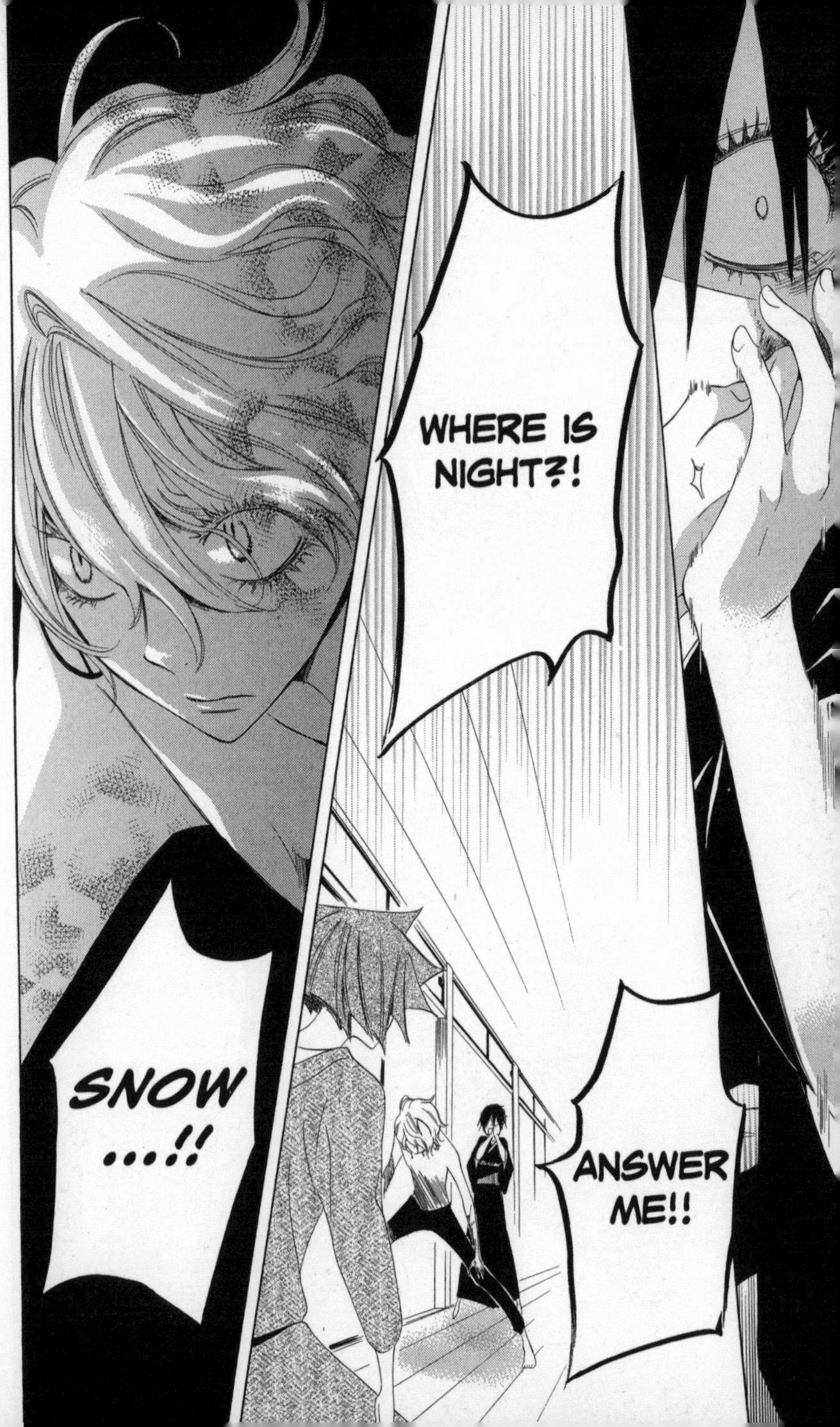
WHERE IS NIGHT?!
ANSWER ME!!
SNOW ...!!

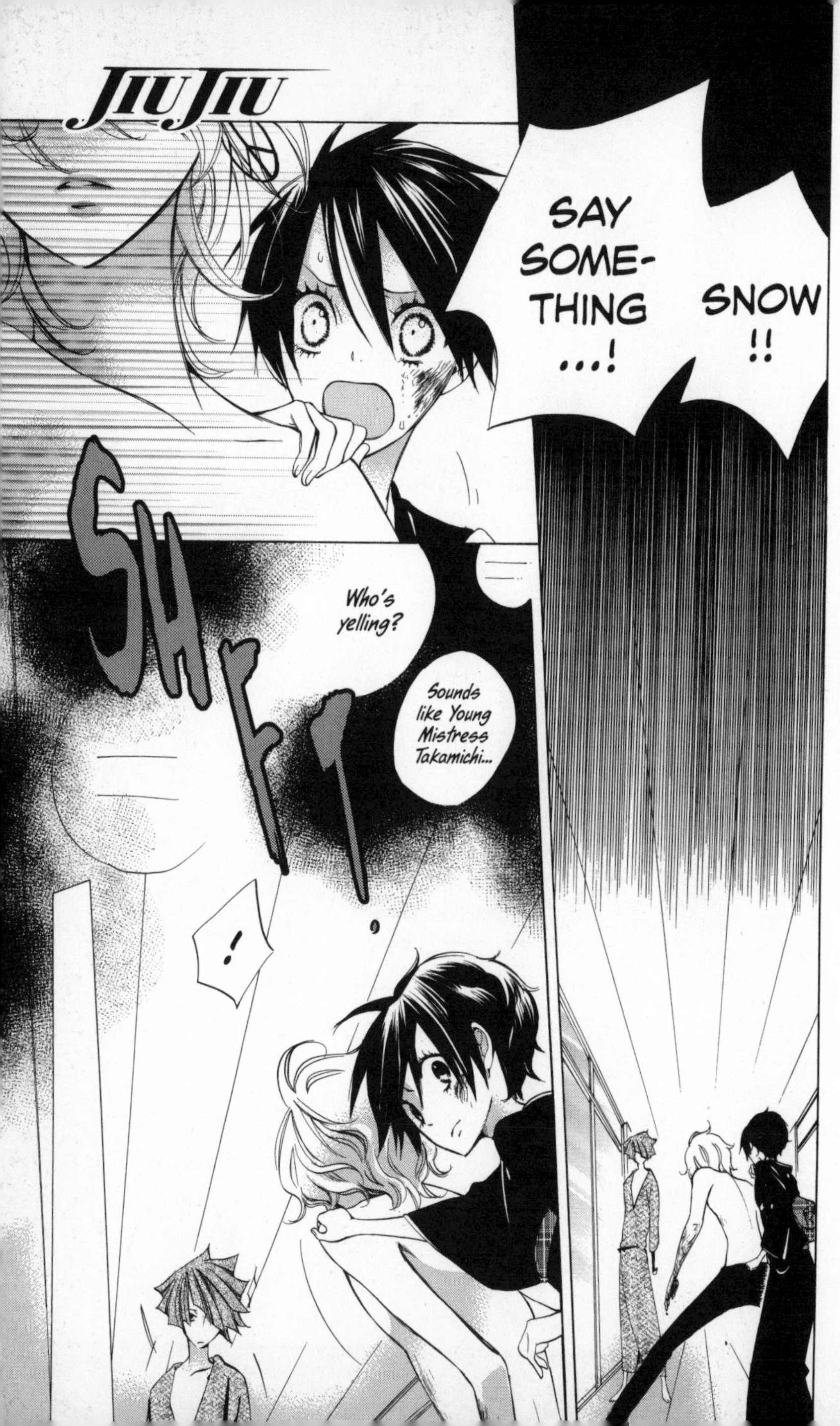
SAY SOME-THING...!
SNOW!!
SHFF
Who's yelling?
Sounds like Young Mistress Takamichi...
!

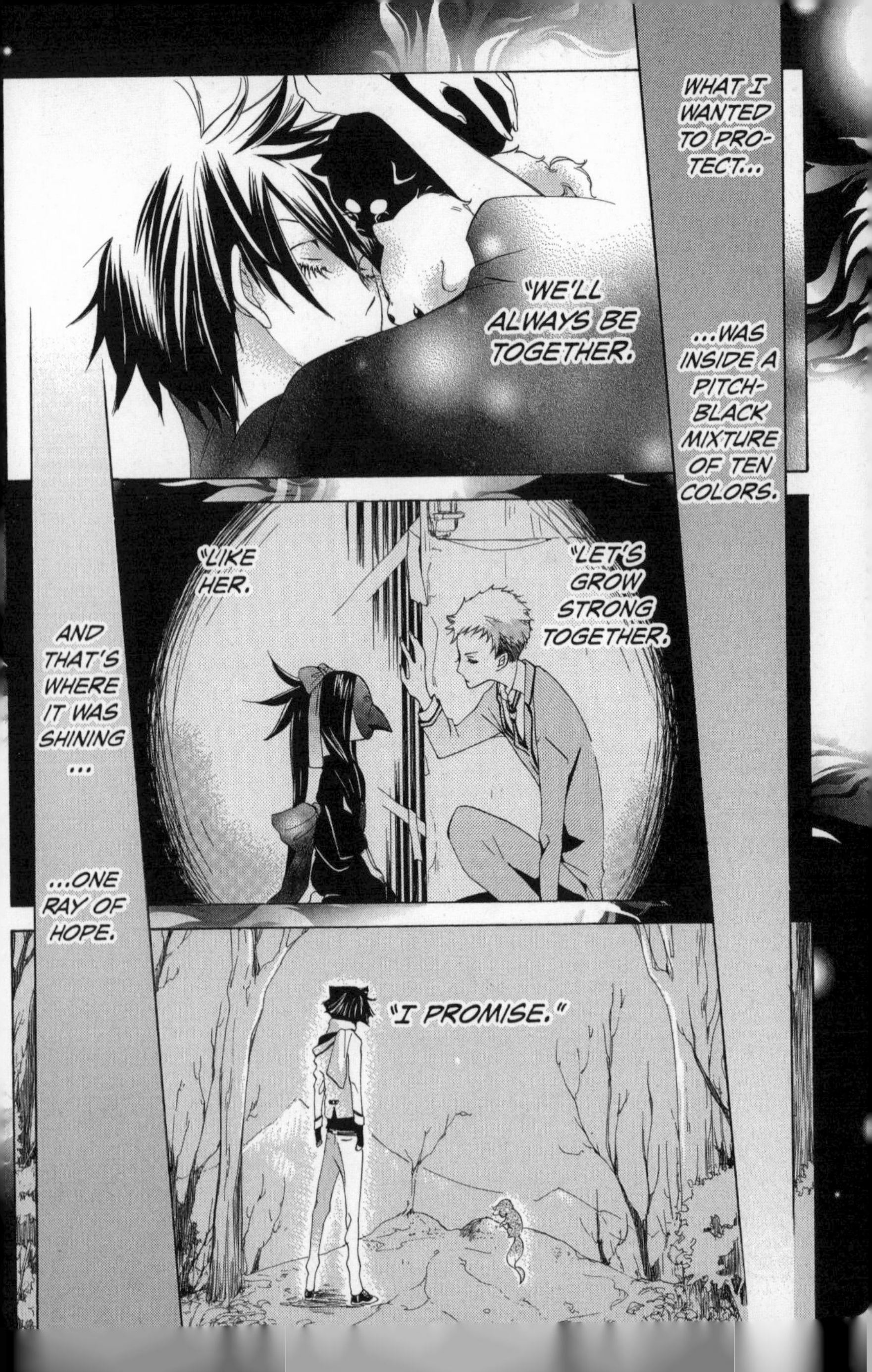
WHAT I WANTED TO PRO-TECT...
"WE'LL ALWAYS BE TOGETHER.
...WAS INSIDE A PITCH-BLACK MIXTURE OF TEN COLORS.
"LET'S GROW STRONG TOGETHER.
"LIKE HER.
AND THAT'S WHERE IT WAS SHINING...
...ONE RAY OF HOPE.
"I PROMISE."

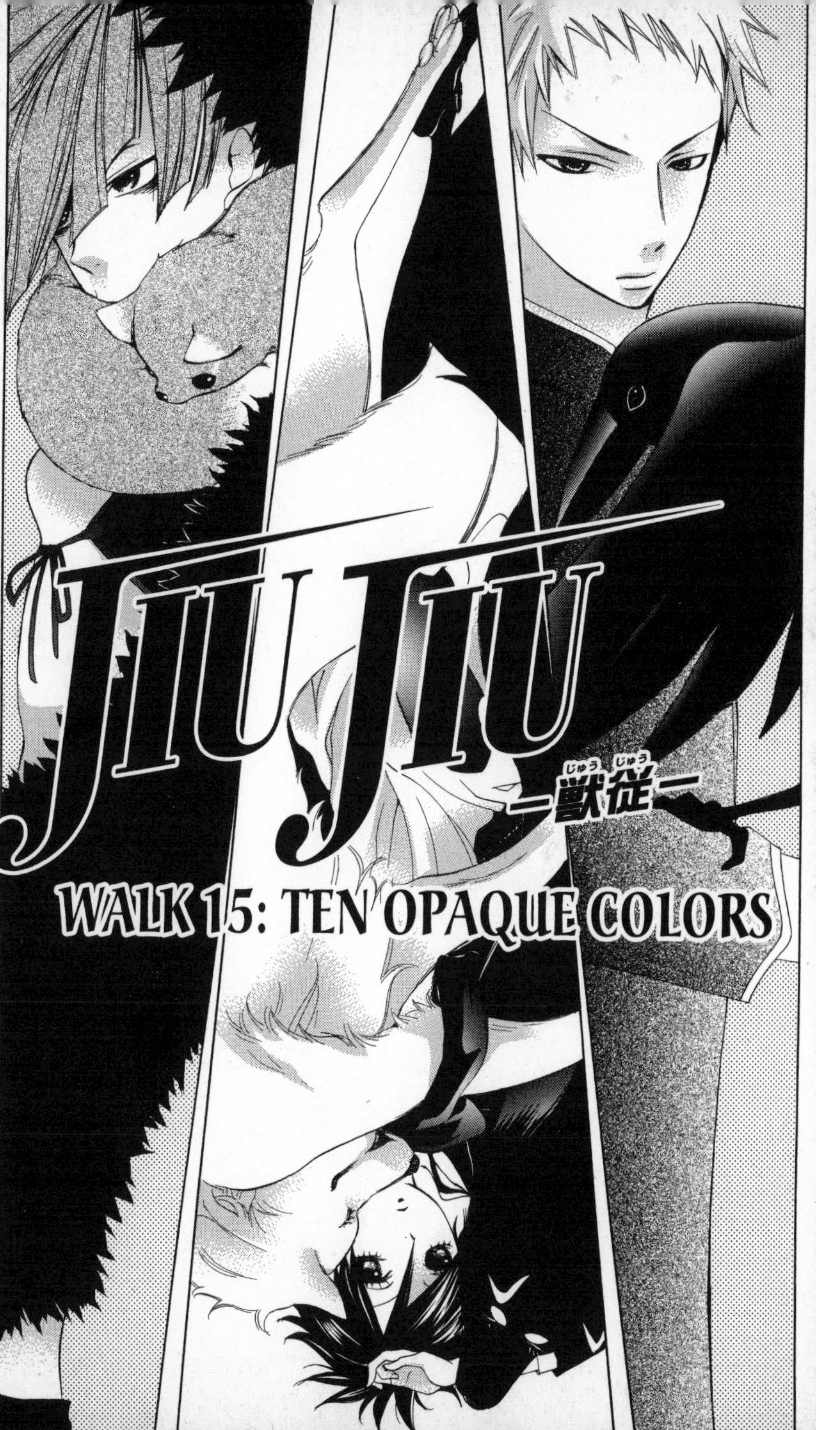
JIU JIU
じゅう じゅう
—獣従—
WALK 15: TEN OPAQUE COLORS

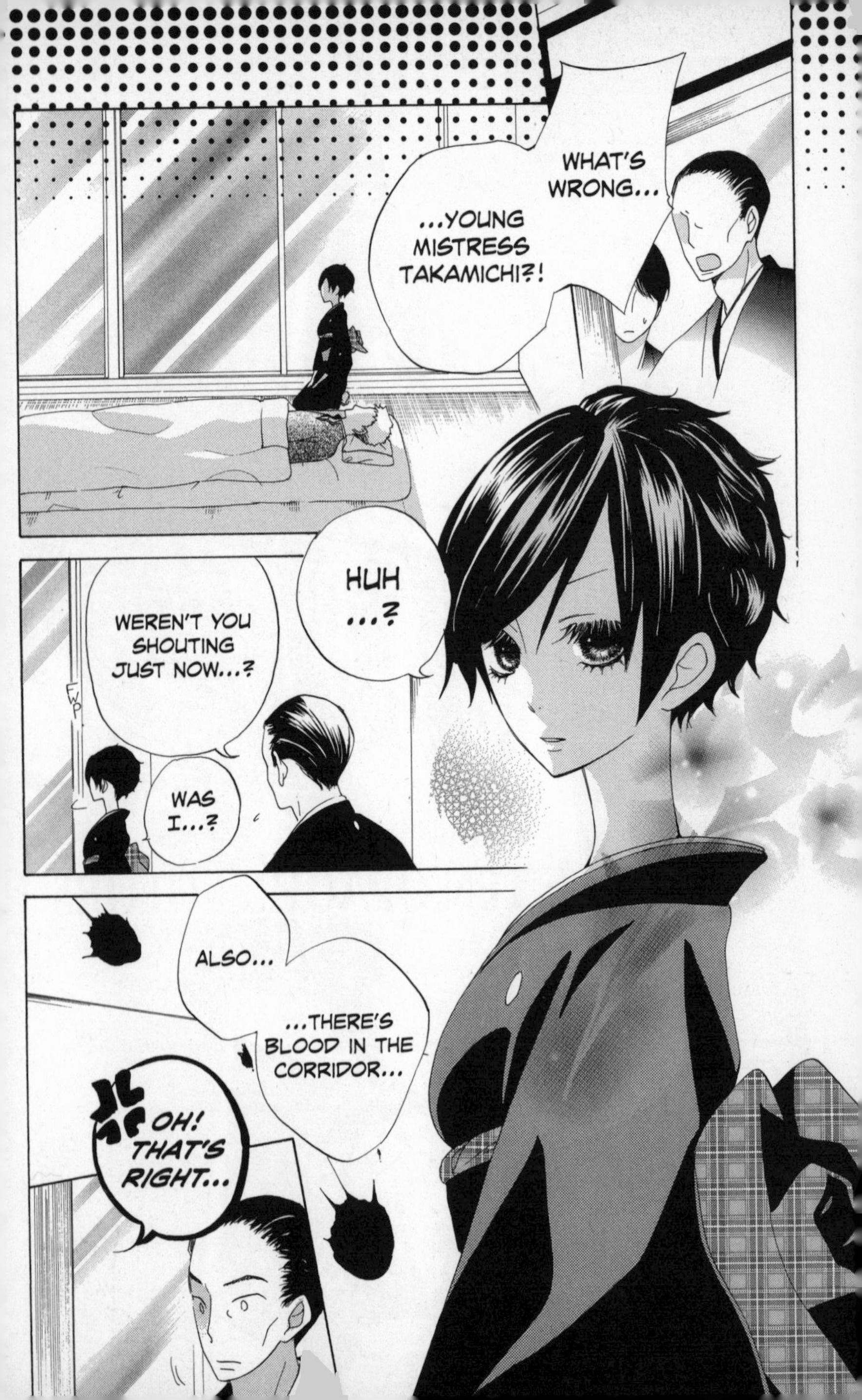
WHAT'S WRONG...
...YOUNG MISTRESS TAKAMICHI?!
HUH ...?
WEREN'T YOU SHOUTING JUST NOW...?
FWP
WAS I...?
ALSO...
...THERE'S BLOOD IN THE CORRIDOR...
OH! THAT'S RIGHT...

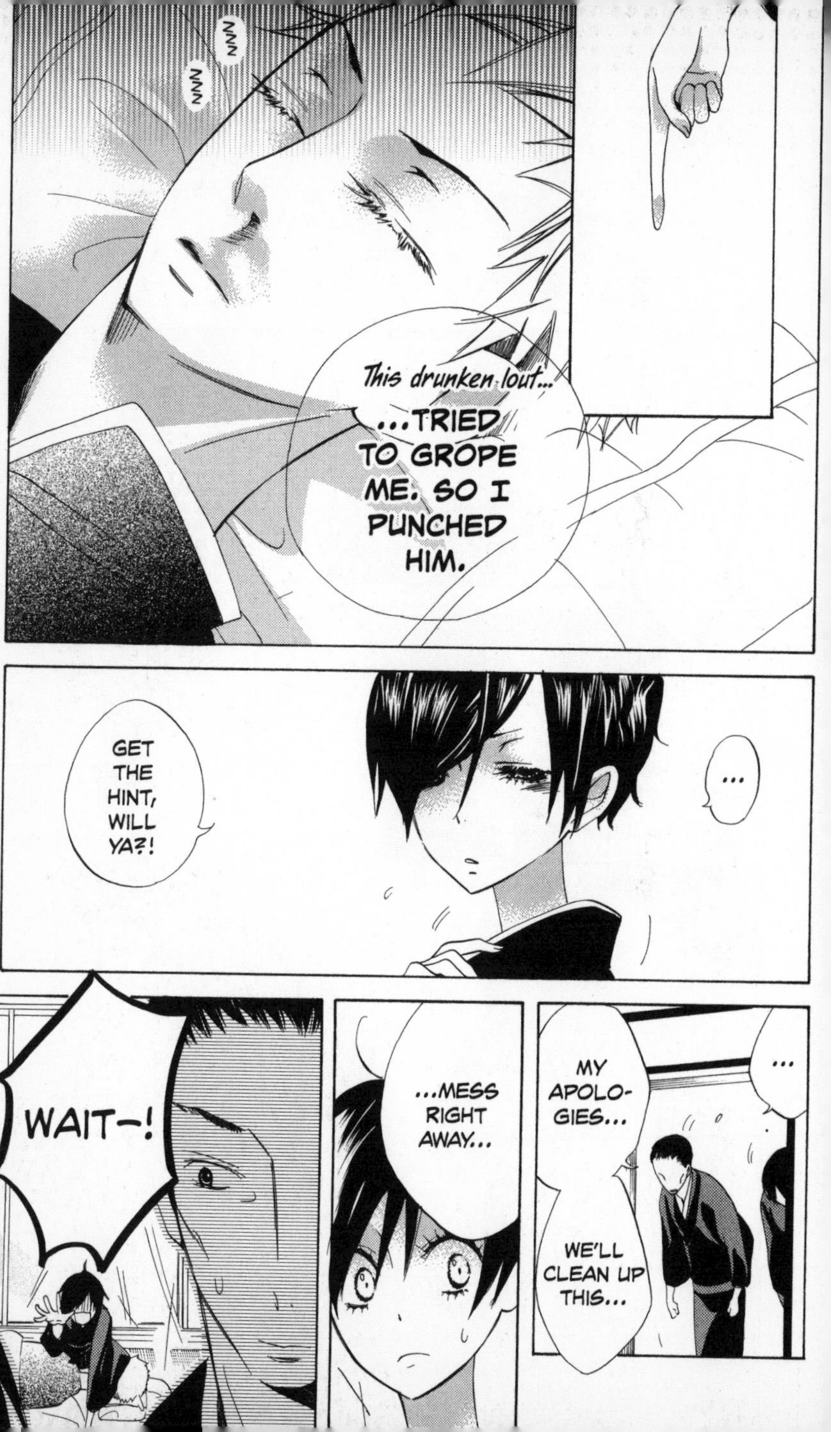
NNN
NNN
This drunken lout...
...TRIED TO GROPE ME. SO I PUNCHED HIM.
...
GET THE HINT, WILL YA?!
...
MY APOLOGIES...
WE'LL CLEAN UP THIS...
...MESS RIGHT AWAY...
WAIT-!

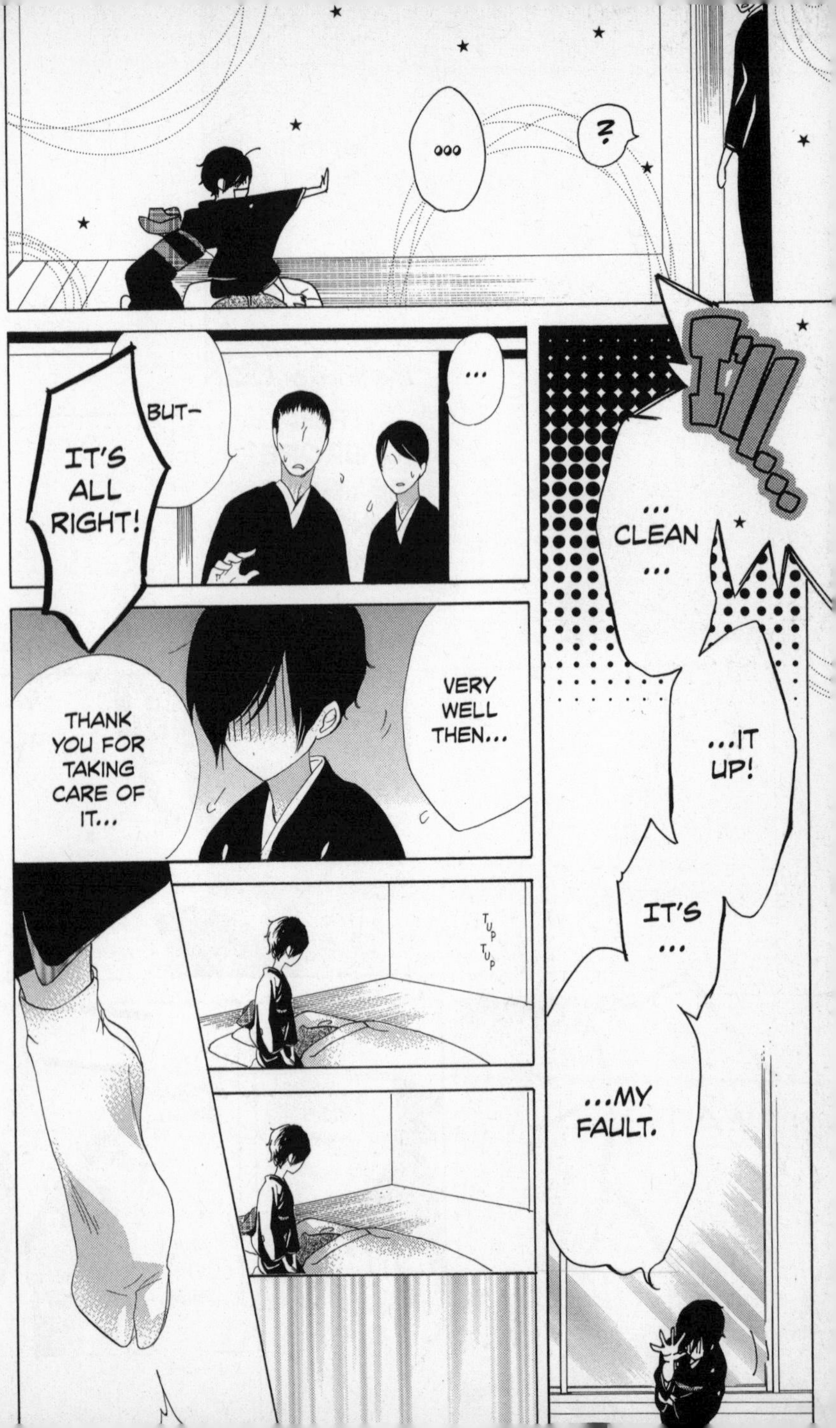
?
...
I'LL...
...CLEAN...
...IT UP!
IT'S...
...MY FAULT.
...
BUT-
IT'S ALL RIGHT!
VERY WELL THEN...
THANK YOU FOR TAKING CARE OF IT...
TUP TUP

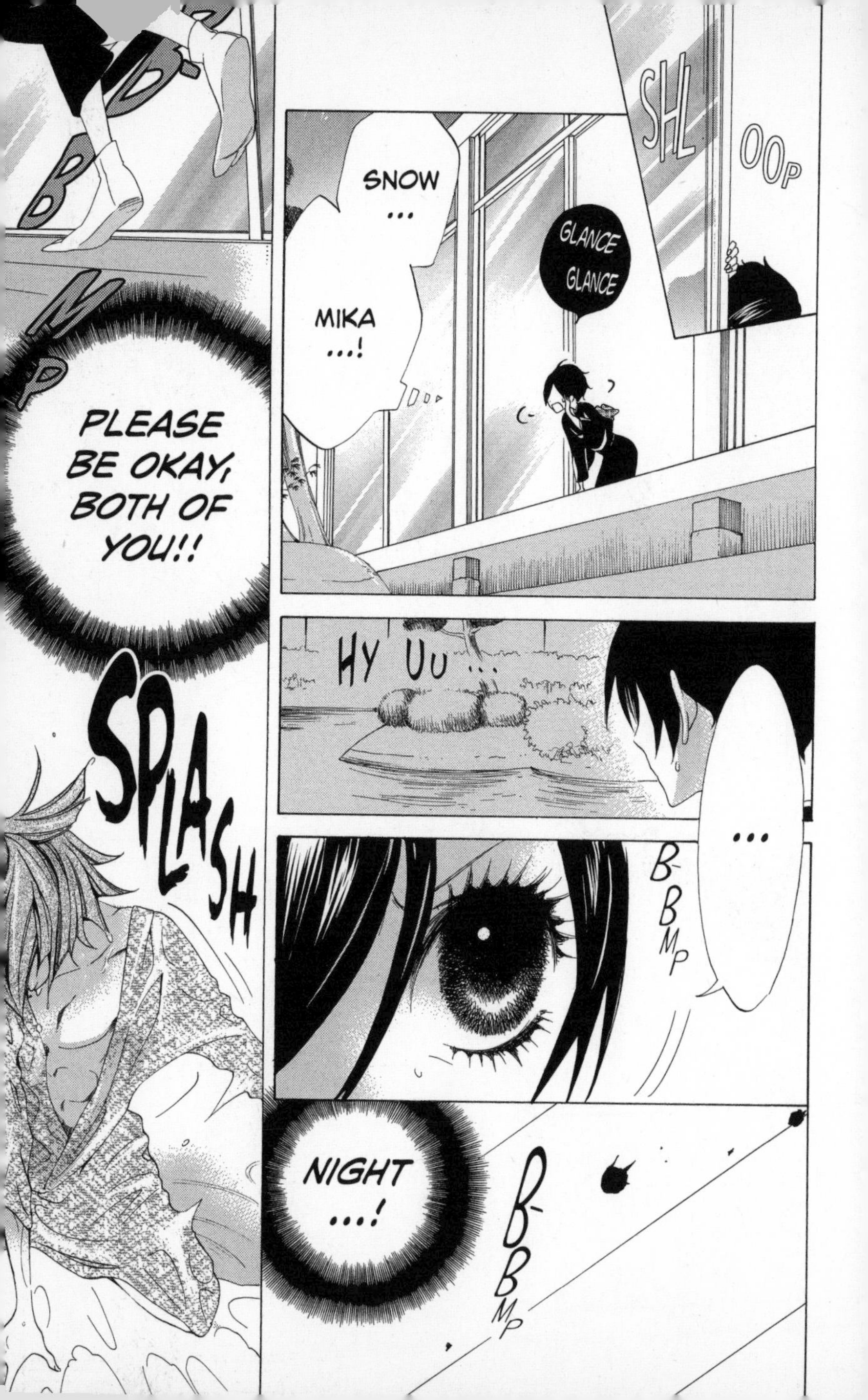
SHLOOP
SNOW ...
MIKA ...!
GLANCE GLANCE
HYUU...
...
B-BMP
NIGHT ...!
B-BMP
PLEASE BE OKAY, BOTH OF YOU!!
SPLASH

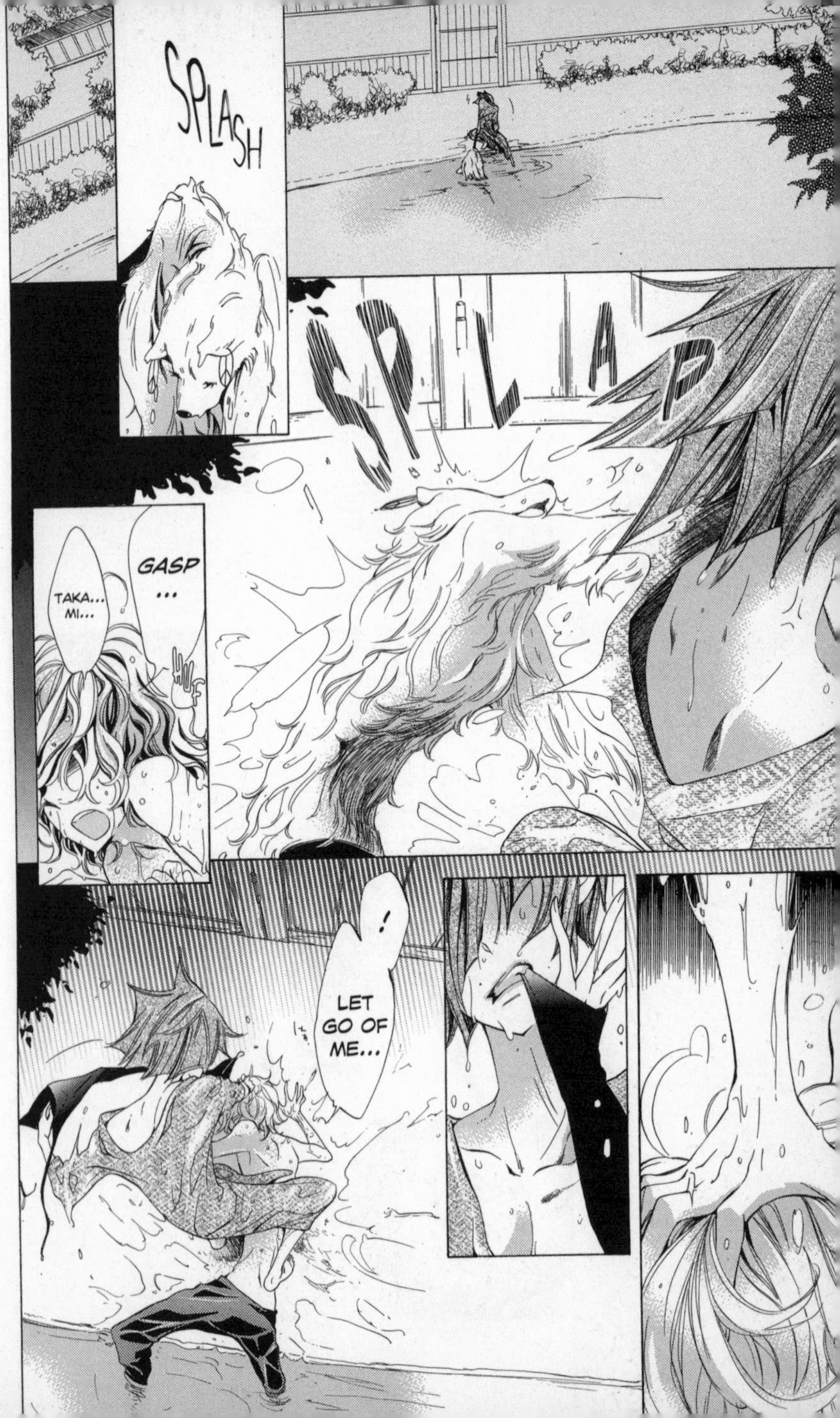
SPLASH
SPLAP
GASP ...
HUFF
TAKA... MI...
!
LET GO OF ME...

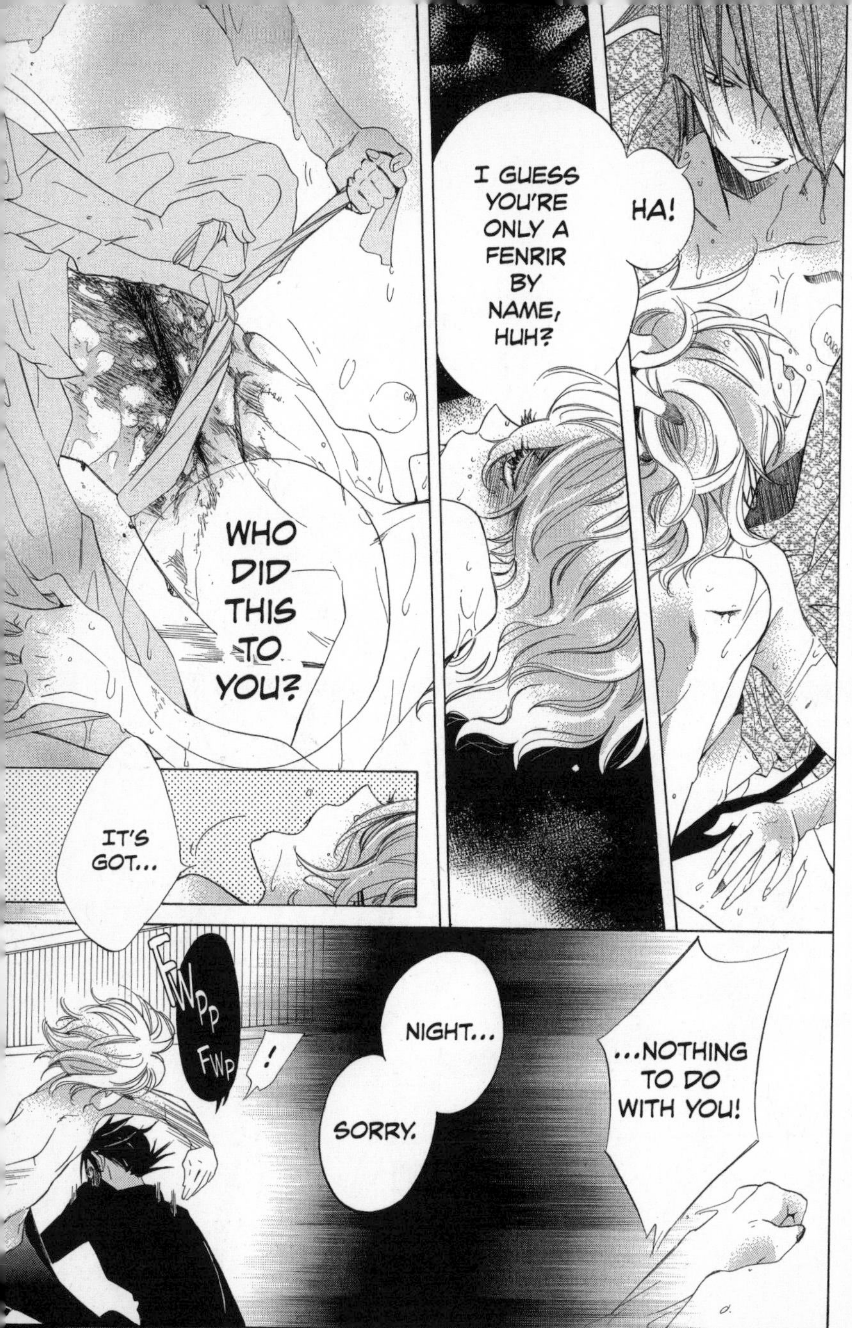
HA!
I GUESS YOU'RE ONLY A FENRIR BY NAME, HUH?
WHO DID THIS TO YOU?
IT'S GOT...
...NOTHING TO DO WITH YOU!
NIGHT...
SORRY.
!
FWPP FWP

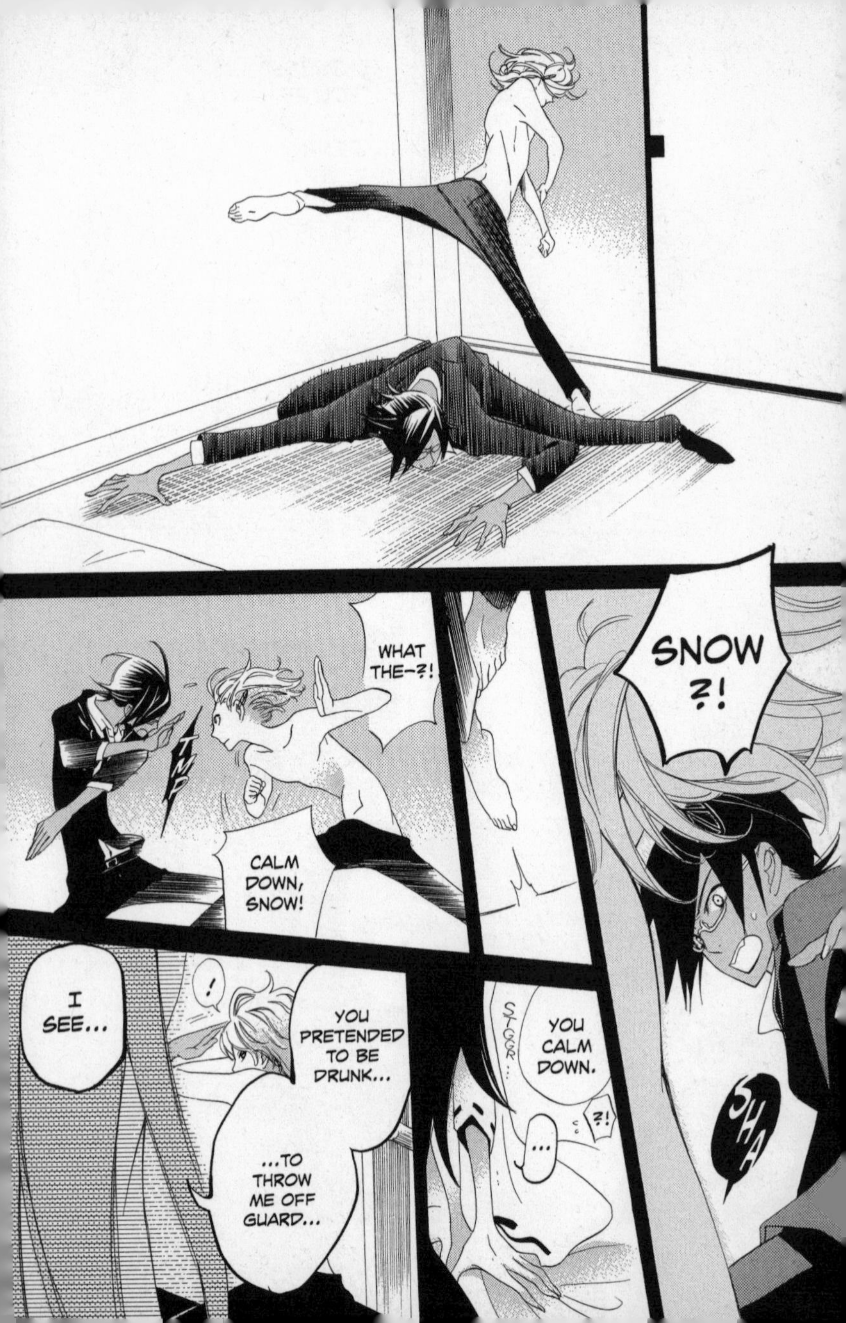

SNOW ?!
SHA
WHAT THE-?!
TMP
CALM DOWN, SNOW!
YOU CALM DOWN.
STGGR...
?!
...
!
I SEE...
YOU PRETENDED TO BE DRUNK...
...TO THROW ME OFF GUARD...

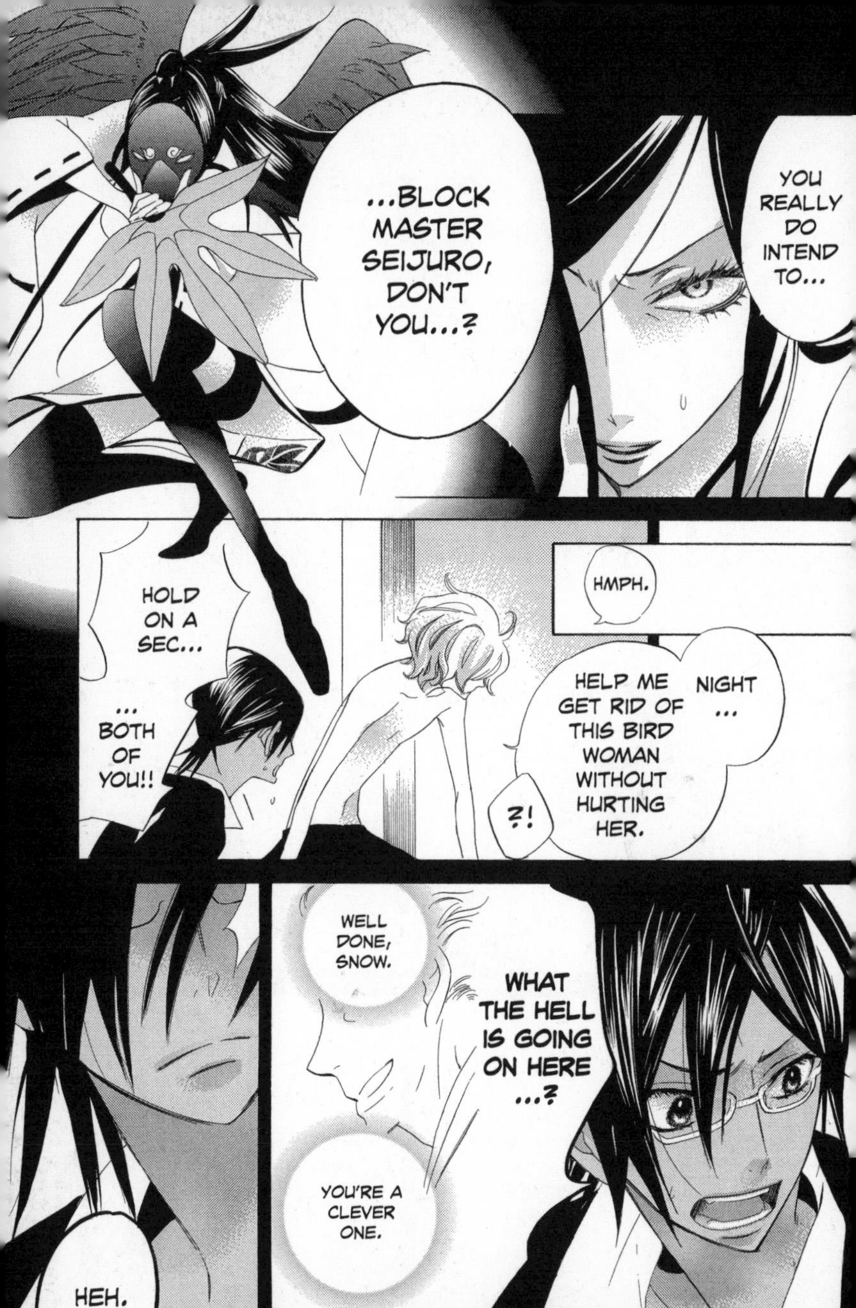
YOU REALLY DO INTEND TO...
...BLOCK MASTER SEIJURO, DON'T YOU...?
HMPH.
NIGHT...
HELP ME GET RID OF THIS BIRD WOMAN WITHOUT HURTING HER.
?!
HOLD ON A SEC...
...BOTH OF YOU!!
WHAT THE HELL IS GOING ON HERE...?
WELL DONE, SNOW.
YOU'RE A CLEVER ONE.
HEH.

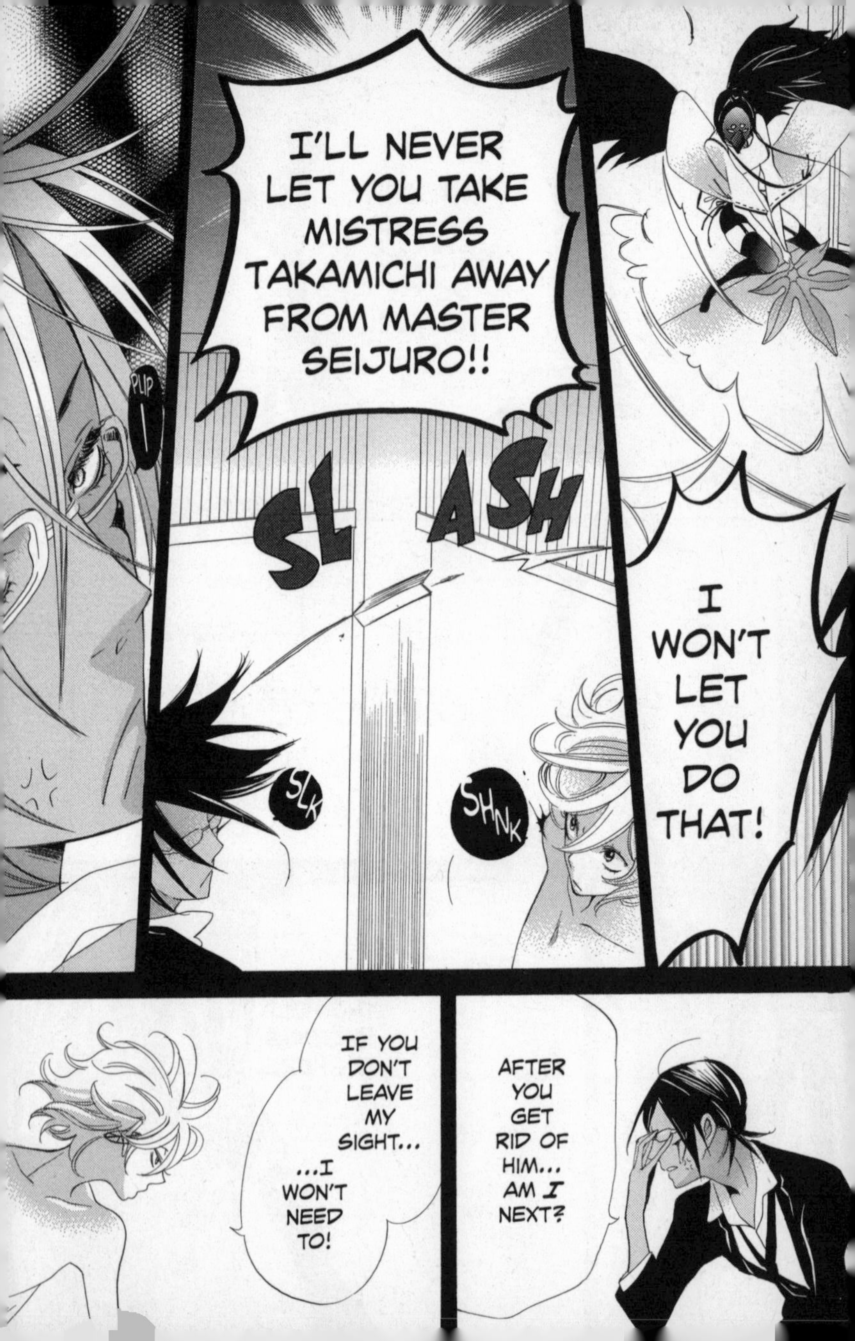
I WON'T LET YOU DO THAT!
I'LL NEVER LET YOU TAKE MISTRESS TAKAMICHI AWAY FROM MASTER SEIJURO!!
SLASH
SHNK
SLK
PLIP
AFTER YOU GET RID OF HIM... AM I NEXT?
IF YOU DON'T LEAVE MY SIGHT...
...I WON'T NEED TO!

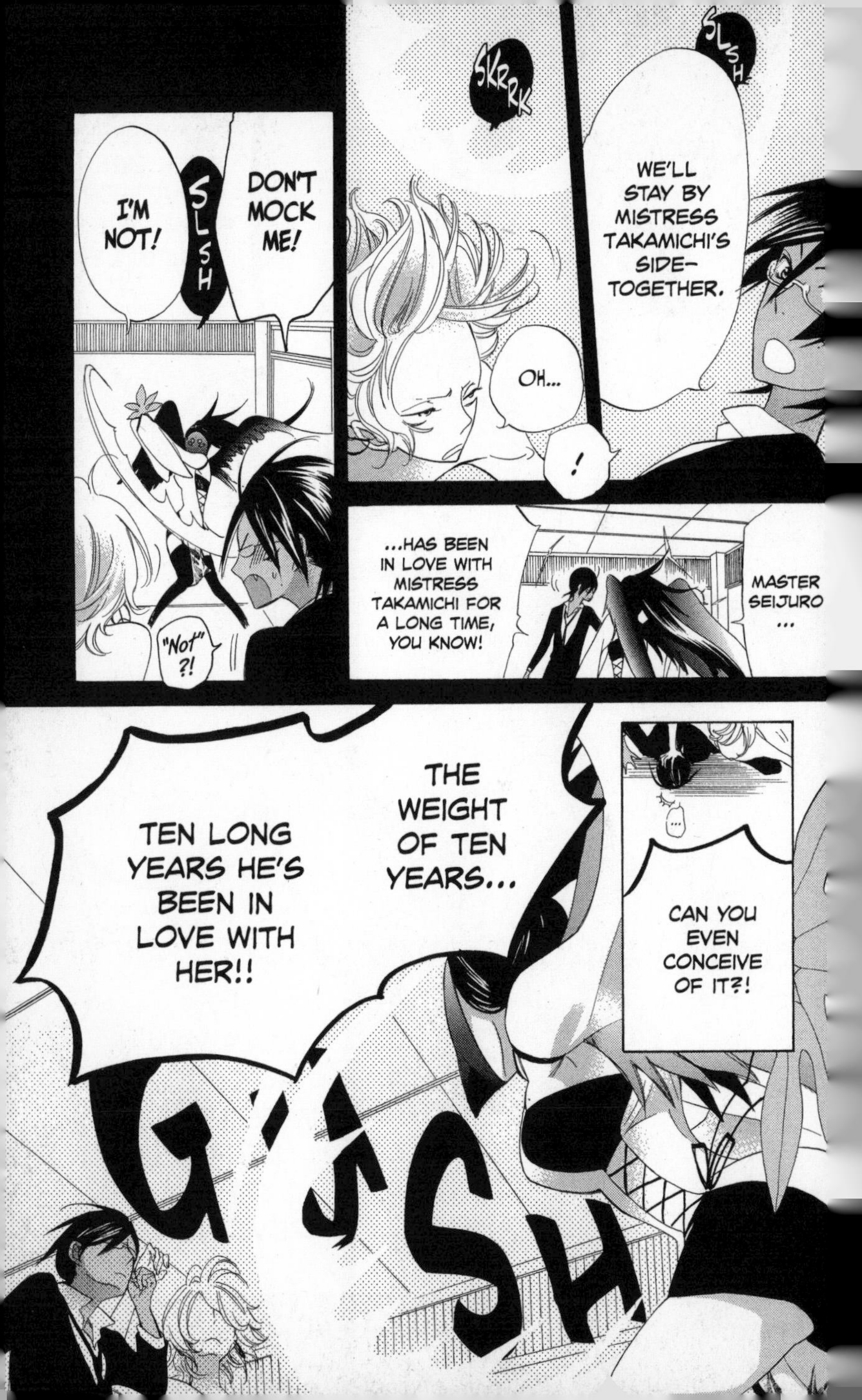
SLSH
WE'LL STAY BY MISTRESS TAKAMICHI'S SIDE— TOGETHER.
!
SKRRK
OH...
MASTER SEIJURO ...
...HAS BEEN IN LOVE WITH MISTRESS TAKAMICHI FOR A LONG TIME, YOU KNOW!
DON'T MOCK ME!
SLSH
I'M NOT!
"Not" ?!
...
CAN YOU EVEN CONCEIVE OF IT?!
THE WEIGHT OF TEN YEARS...
TEN LONG YEARS HE'S BEEN IN LOVE WITH HER!!
GASH

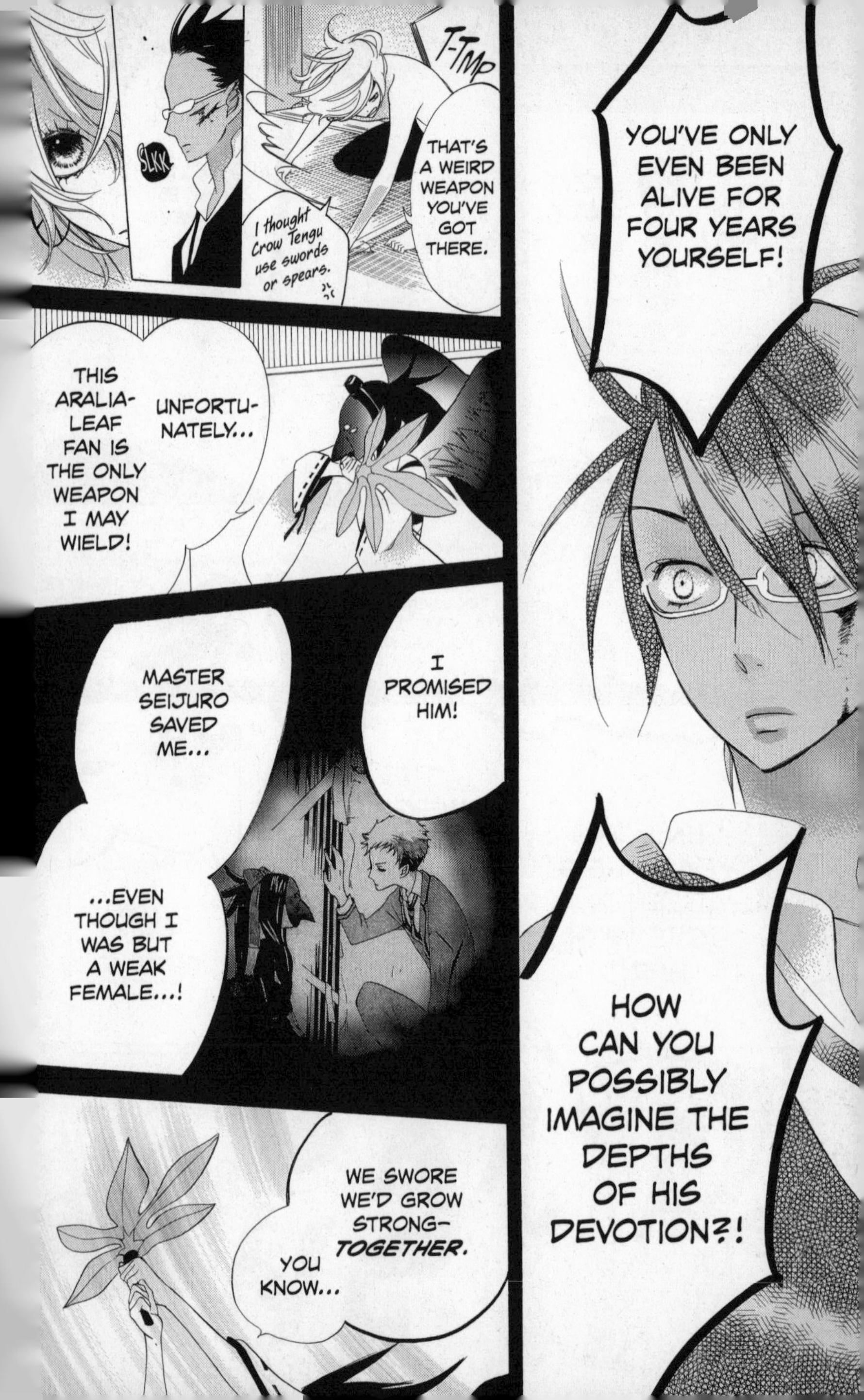
YOU'VE ONLY EVEN BEEN ALIVE FOR FOUR YEARS YOURSELF!
HOW CAN YOU POSSIBLY IMAGINE THE DEPTHS OF HIS DEVOTION?!
T-TMP
THAT'S A WEIRD WEAPON YOU'VE GOT THERE.
I thought Crow Tengu use swords or spears.
SLKK
UNFORTUNATELY...
THIS ARALIA-LEAF FAN IS THE ONLY WEAPON I MAY WIELD!
I PROMISED HIM!
MASTER SEIJURO SAVED ME...
...EVEN THOUGH I WAS BUT A WEAK FEMALE...!
WE SWORE WE'D GROW STRONG—*TOGETHER*.
YOU KNOW...

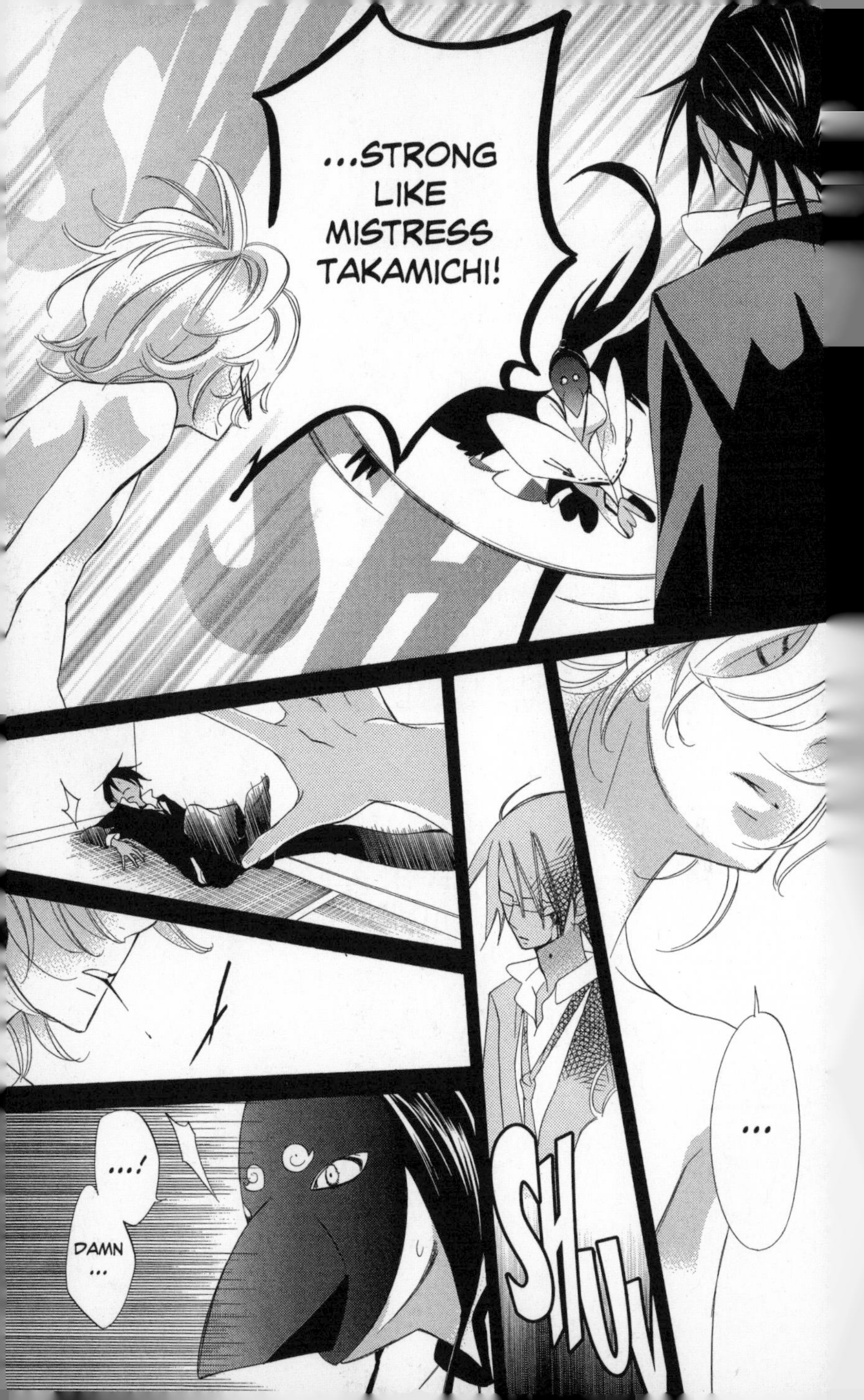
...STRONG LIKE MISTRESS TAKAMICHI!
...
SHU
....!
DAMN ...

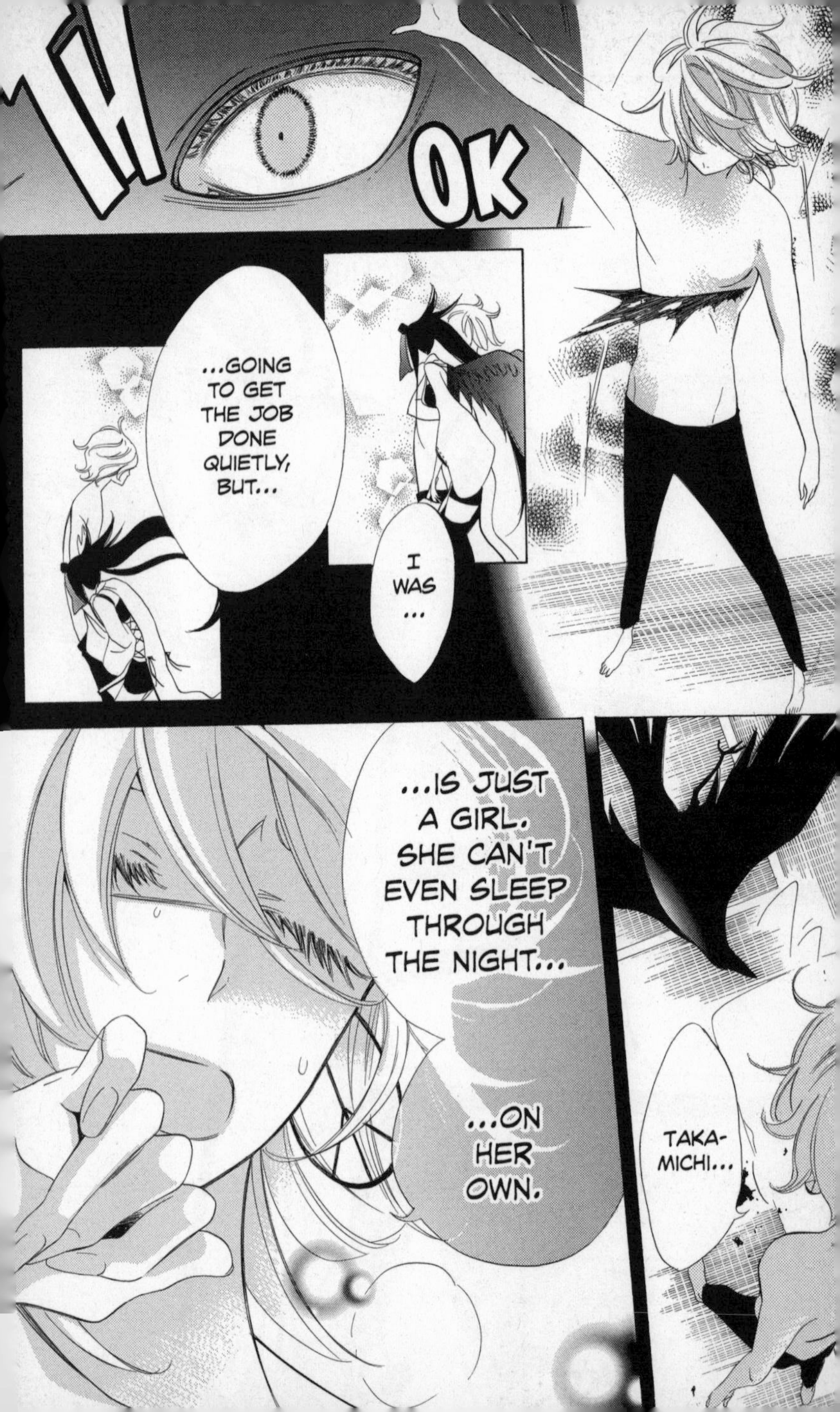
OK
!!
I WAS ...
...GOING TO GET THE JOB DONE QUIETLY, BUT...
TAKA-MICHI...
...IS JUST A GIRL. SHE CAN'T EVEN SLEEP THROUGH THE NIGHT...
...ON HER OWN.

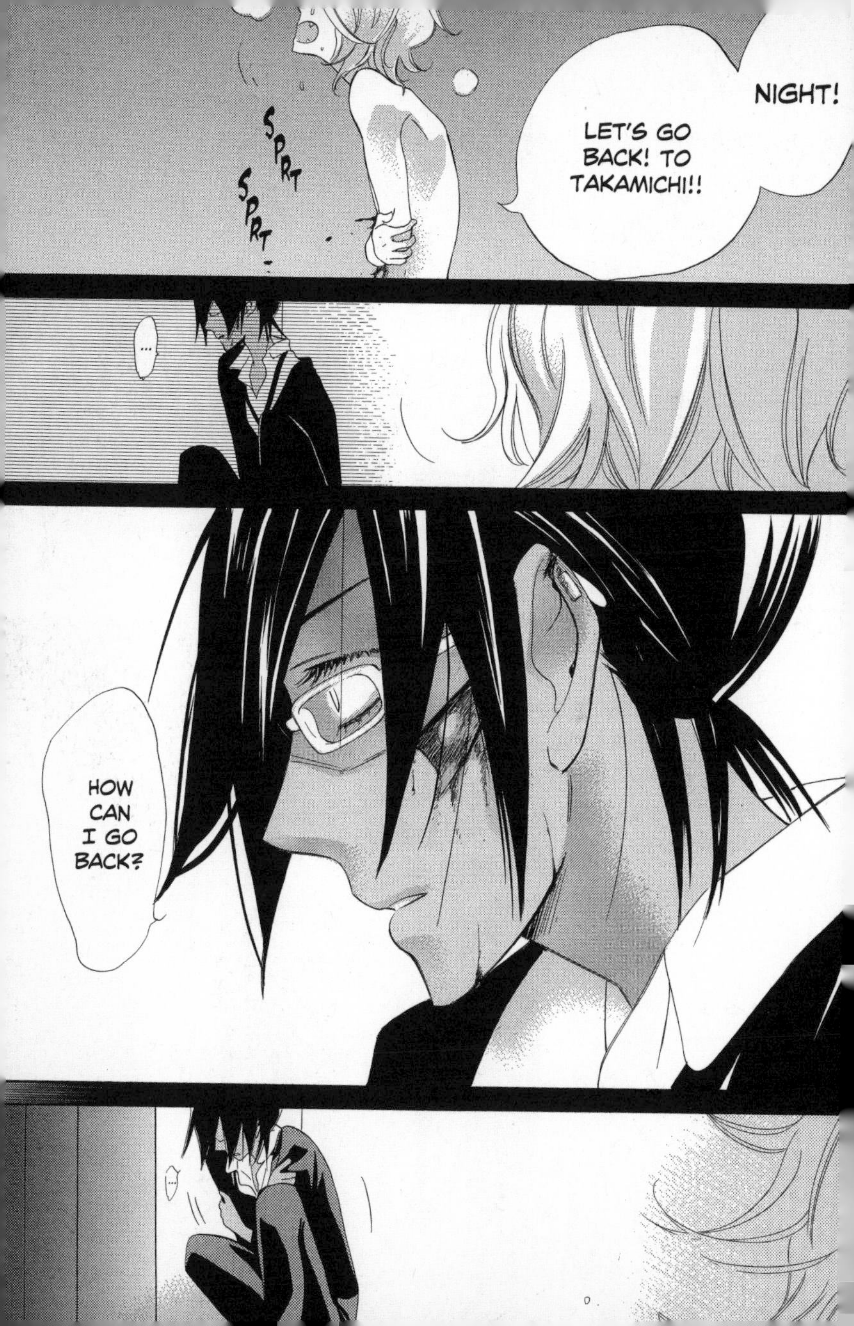
NIGHT! LET'S GO BACK! TO TAKAMICHI!!
SPRT SPRT
...
HOW CAN I GO BACK?
...

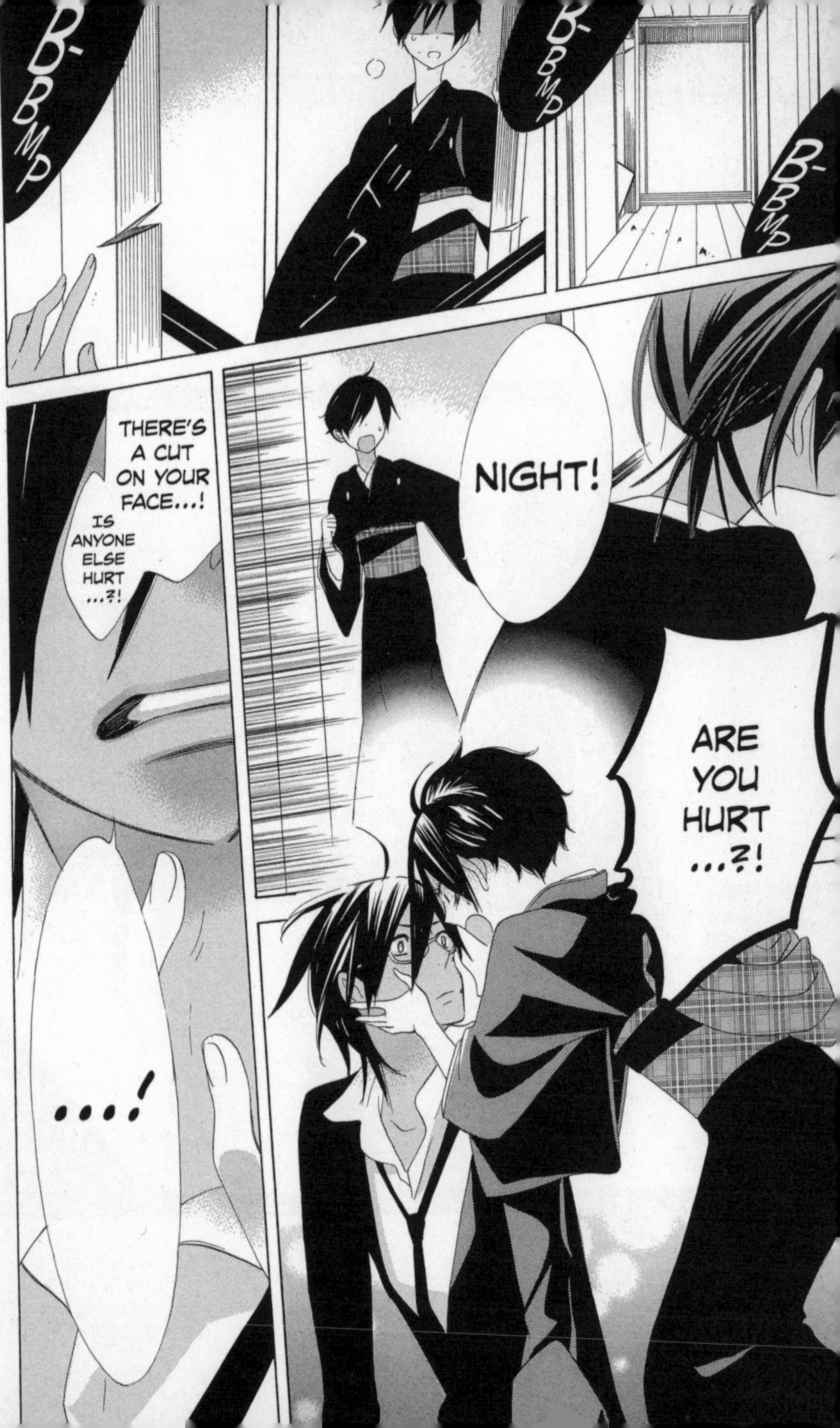
B-BMP
B-BMP
B-BMP
NIGHT!
ARE YOU HURT ...?!
THERE'S A CUT ON YOUR FACE...!
IS ANYONE ELSE HURT ...?!
...!

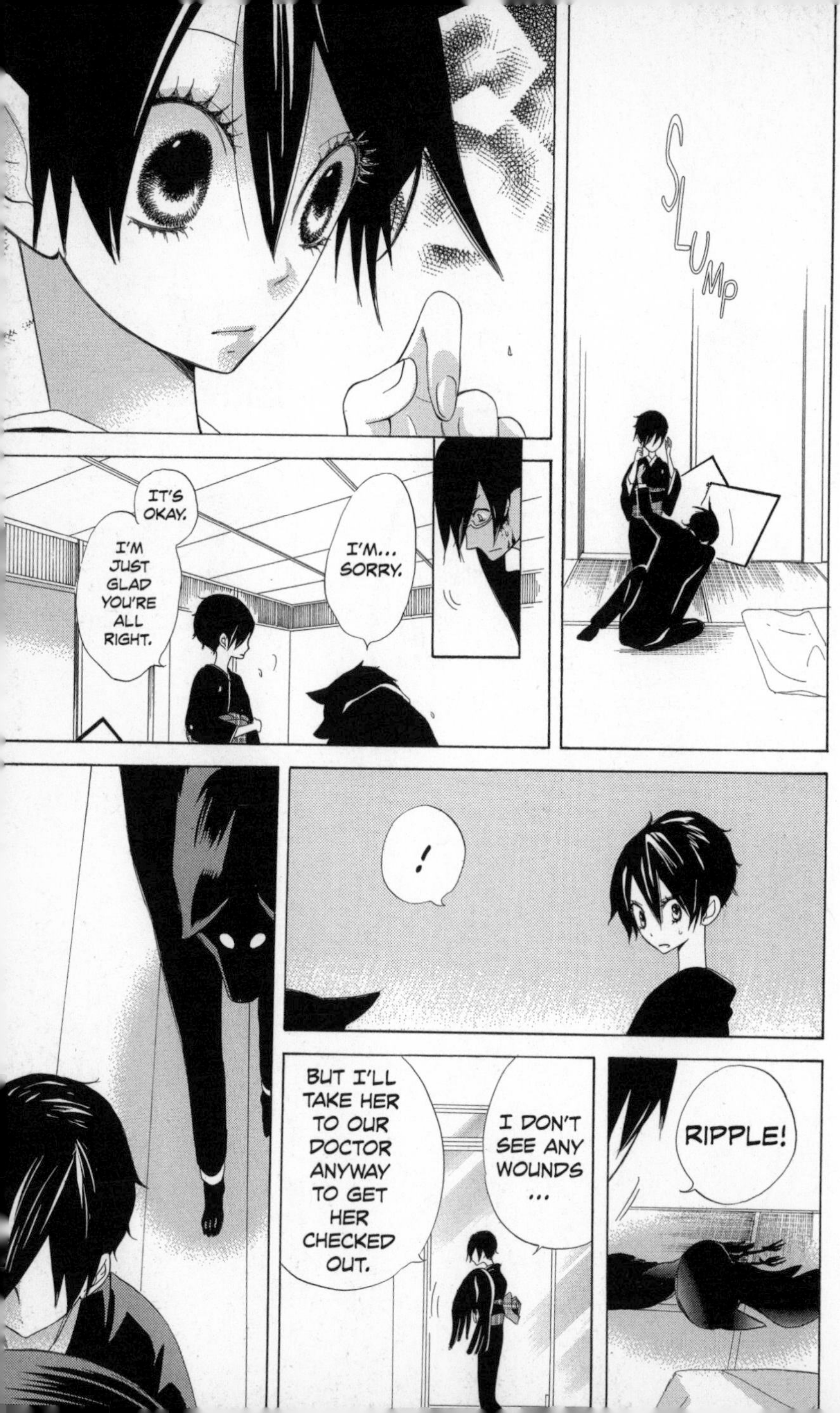
SLUMP
I'M... SORRY.
IT'S OKAY.
I'M JUST GLAD YOU'RE ALL RIGHT.
!
RIPPLE!
I DON'T SEE ANY WOUNDS ...
BUT I'LL TAKE HER TO OUR DOCTOR ANYWAY TO GET HER CHECKED OUT.

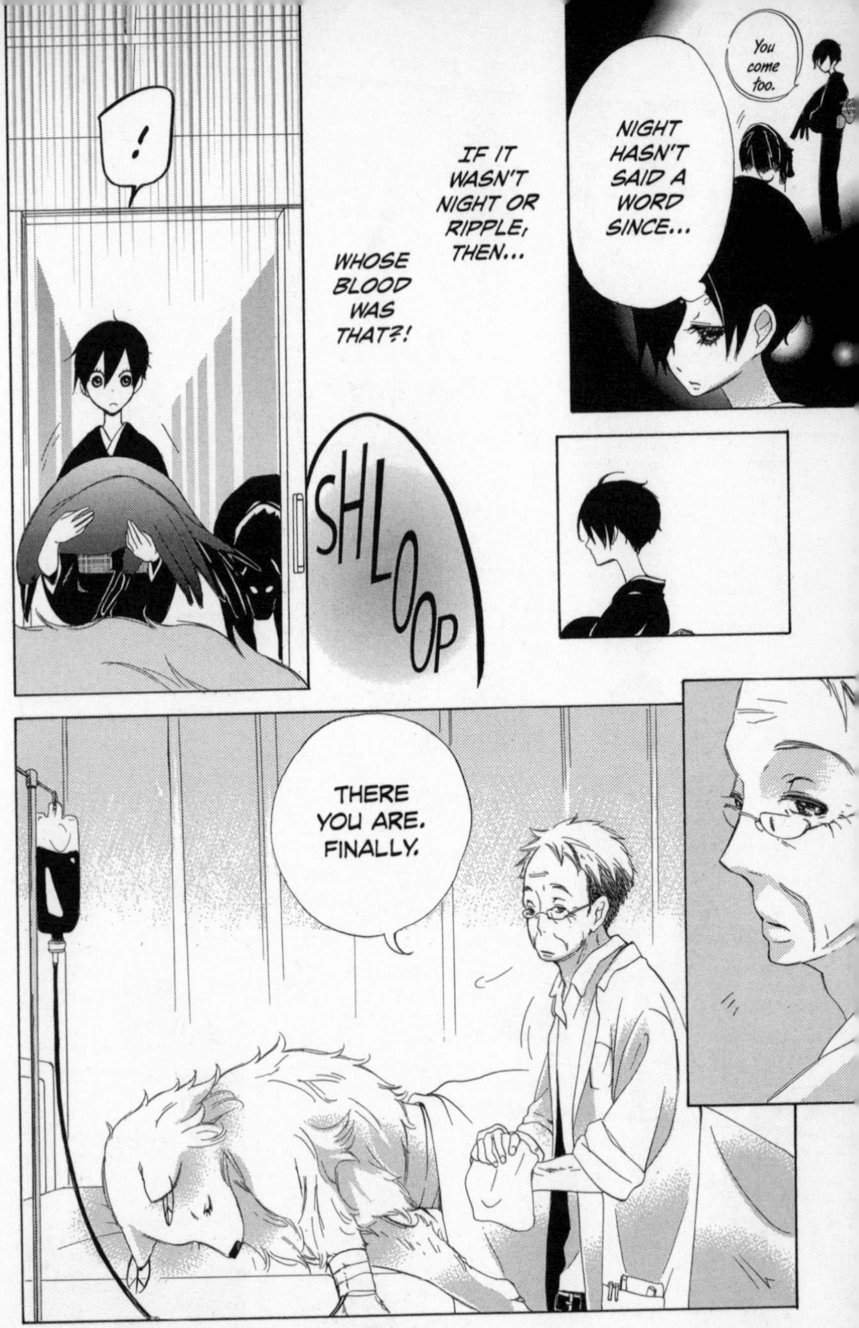
You come too.
NIGHT HASN'T SAID A WORD SINCE...
IF IT WASN'T NIGHT OR RIPPLE, THEN...
WHOSE BLOOD WAS THAT?!
!
SHLOOP
THERE YOU ARE. FINALLY.

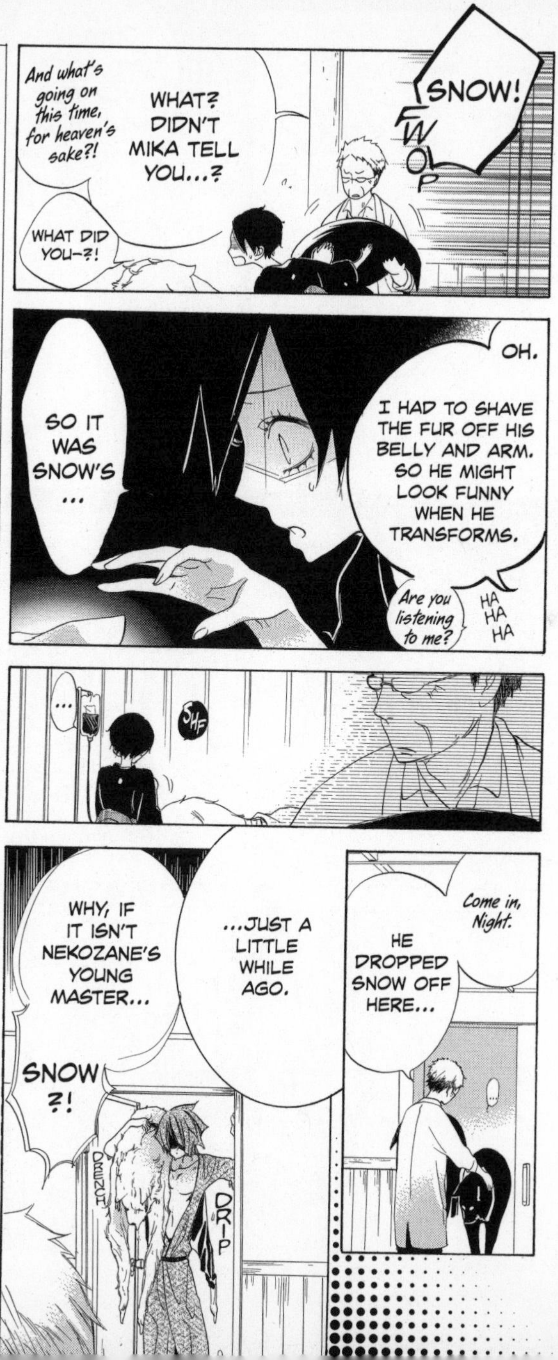
SNOW!
FWOP
WHAT? DIDN'T MIKA TELL YOU...?
And what's going on this time, for heaven's sake?!
WHAT DID YOU-?!
OH.
I HAD TO SHAVE THE FUR OFF HIS BELLY AND ARM. SO HE MIGHT LOOK FUNNY WHEN HE TRANSFORMS.
HA HA HA
Are you listening to me?
SO IT WAS SNOW'S ...
SHF
...
Come in, Night.
HE DROPPED SNOW OFF HERE...
...
...JUST A LITTLE WHILE AGO.
WHY, IF IT ISN'T NEKOZANE'S YOUNG MASTER...
SNOW ?!
DRIP
DRENCH

Question Corner 2

I wasn't sure what to write here. I worried about it for four days. I went shopping, took my dog for a drive, took my dog for a walk... and then I remembered I still had some questions left to answer!! So, here they are...

What kind of drawing materials do you use? If you use Copic markers, please tell me the color numbers.

Fukushima Prefecture: Matsuri Saito

Judging by the second question, I'm assuming you're asking what materials I use for color drawing. For this volume, I used Pilot's security ink to draw the outlines and colored them in using Copic markers and watercolor pencils on illustration board. But usually I just photocopy the outlines and color with Copic markers.

For Mistress Takamichi...

Skin → E0000, E00, E01YR00, R20, R00, and more E0000.

Hair → 110, C8, C4, 100, 110, 0

When I want a purple effect, I add V06 on top.

Snow...

Skin → E0000, R20, R00, YR000

Hair → E40, E43, E41

Night...

Skin → E40, E43, E44, E40

Hair → 100, C10, 0

When I add a blue effect, I use B06 on top.

I've been working with Copic markers for 15 years now, but I still haven't mastered them... I'm pretty bad with them, really.

By the way, when I'm doing the final black-and-white draft, I use IC110 manga paper, draw a rough outline on it with a 0.7mm light-blue mechanical pencil, make a clean copy over that with a 0.5mm black mechanical pencil, then trace that onto IC135 manga paper and ink it with a Nikko mapping pen (Sometimes a Zebra G-pen). I use ART ink pure-black.

↑ I've never seen any other manga artist use this though.

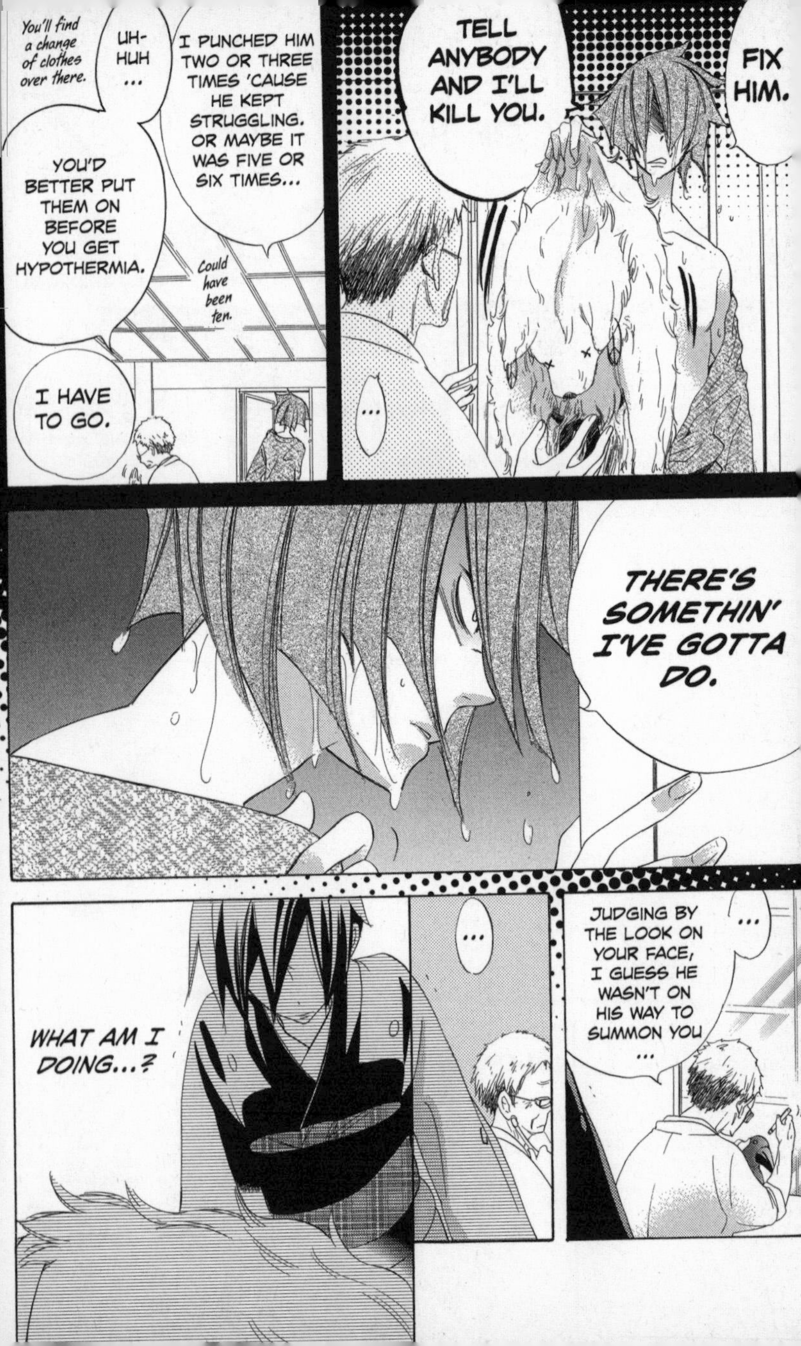
FIX HIM.
TELL ANYBODY AND I'LL KILL YOU.
...
I PUNCHED HIM TWO OR THREE TIMES 'CAUSE HE KEPT STRUGGLING. OR MAYBE IT WAS FIVE OR SIX TIMES...
UH-HUH ...
You'll find a change of clothes over there.
Could have been ten.
YOU'D BETTER PUT THEM ON BEFORE YOU GET HYPOTHERMIA.
I HAVE TO GO.
THERE'S SOMETHIN' I'VE GOTTA DO.
...
JUDGING BY THE LOOK ON YOUR FACE, I GUESS HE WASN'T ON HIS WAY TO SUMMON YOU ...
...
WHAT AM I DOING...?

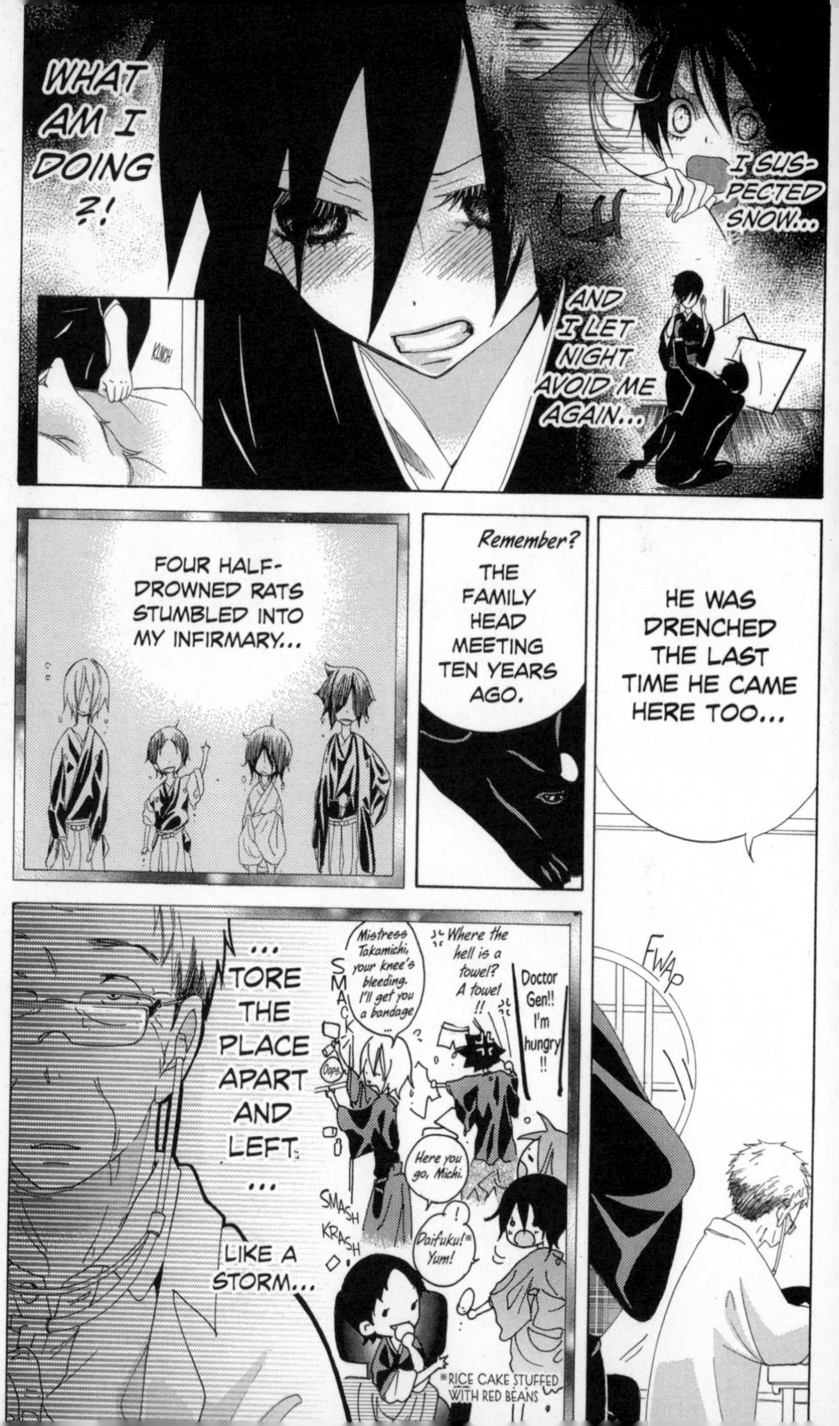

I SUSPECTED SNOW...
AND I LET NIGHT AVOID ME AGAIN...
WHAT AM I DOING?!
KLINCH
HE WAS DRENCHED THE LAST TIME HE CAME HERE TOO...
FWAP
Remember?
THE FAMILY HEAD MEETING TEN YEARS AGO.
FOUR HALF-DROWNED RATS STUMBLED INTO MY INFIRMARY...
Doctor Gen!! I'm hungry!!
Where the hell is a towel? A towel!!
Mistress Takamichi, your knee's bleeding. I'll get you a bandage...
SMACK
Oops.
...TORE THE PLACE APART AND LEFT...
Here you go, Michi.
Daifuku!* Yum!
SMASH
KRASH
LIKE A STORM...
*RICE CAKE STUFFED WITH RED BEANS

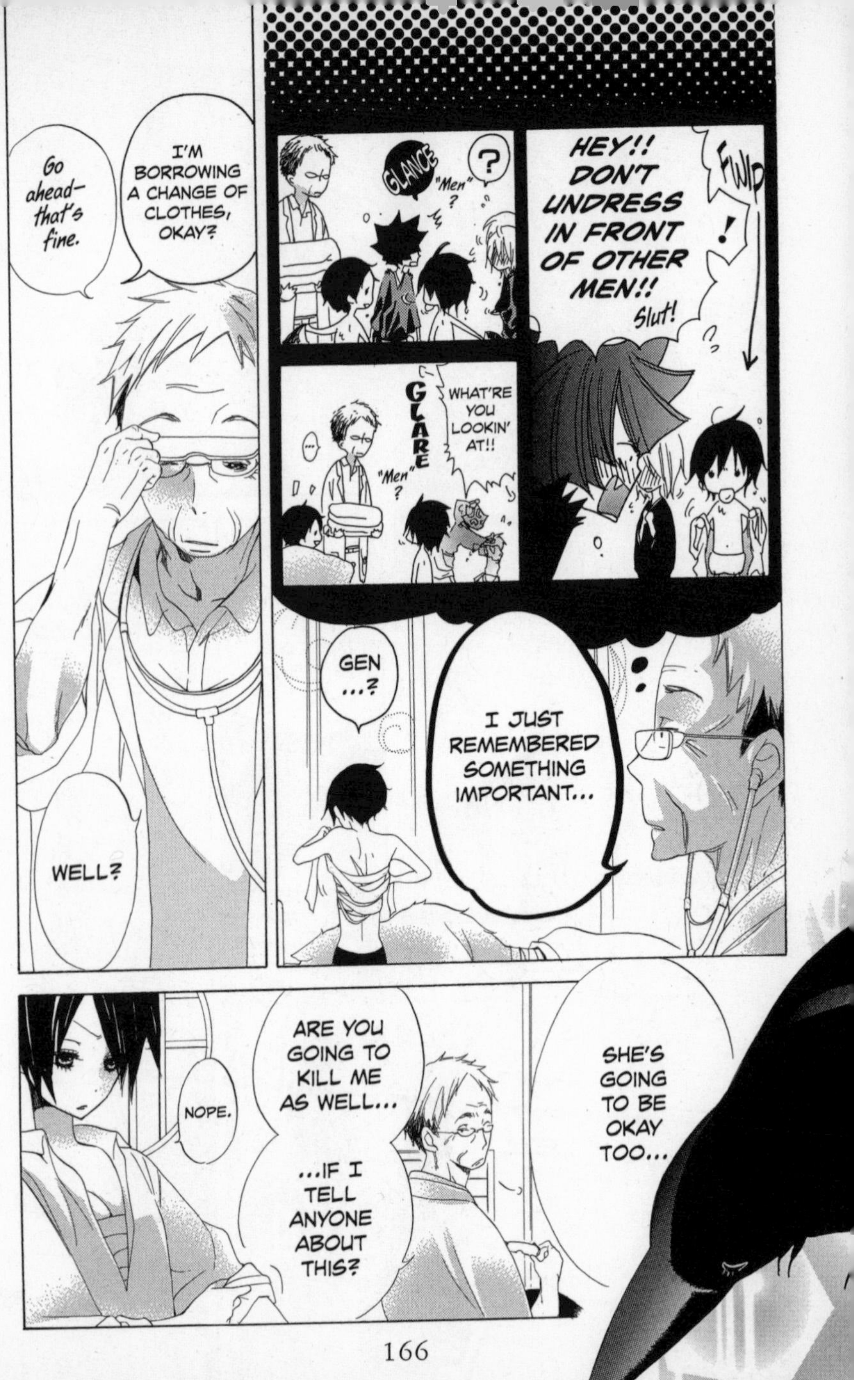
FWIP
!
HEY!! DON'T UNDRESS IN FRONT OF OTHER MEN!!
Slut!
GLANCE
"Men"?
?
GLARE
WHAT'RE YOU LOOKIN' AT!!
"Men"?
I JUST REMEMBERED SOMETHING IMPORTANT...
GEN ...?
I'M BORROWING A CHANGE OF CLOTHES, OKAY?
Go ahead—that's fine.
WELL?
SHE'S GOING TO BE OKAY TOO...
ARE YOU GOING TO KILL ME AS WELL...
...IF I TELL ANYONE ABOUT THIS?
NOPE.

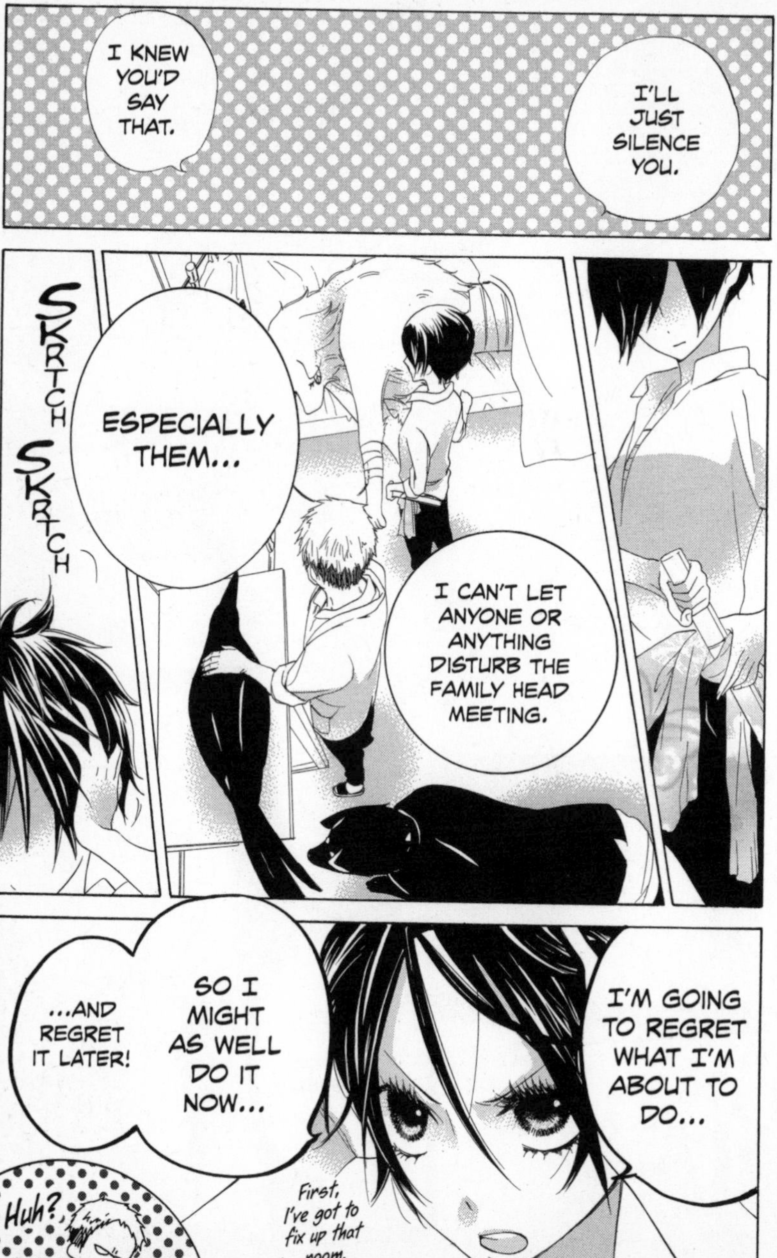
I'LL JUST SILENCE YOU.
I KNEW YOU'D SAY THAT.
I CAN'T LET ANYONE OR ANYTHING DISTURB THE FAMILY HEAD MEETING.
ESPECIALLY THEM...
SKRTCH SKRTCH
I'M GOING TO REGRET WHAT I'M ABOUT TO DO...
SO I MIGHT AS WELL DO IT NOW...
...AND REGRET IT LATER!
First, I've got to fix up that room.
Huh?

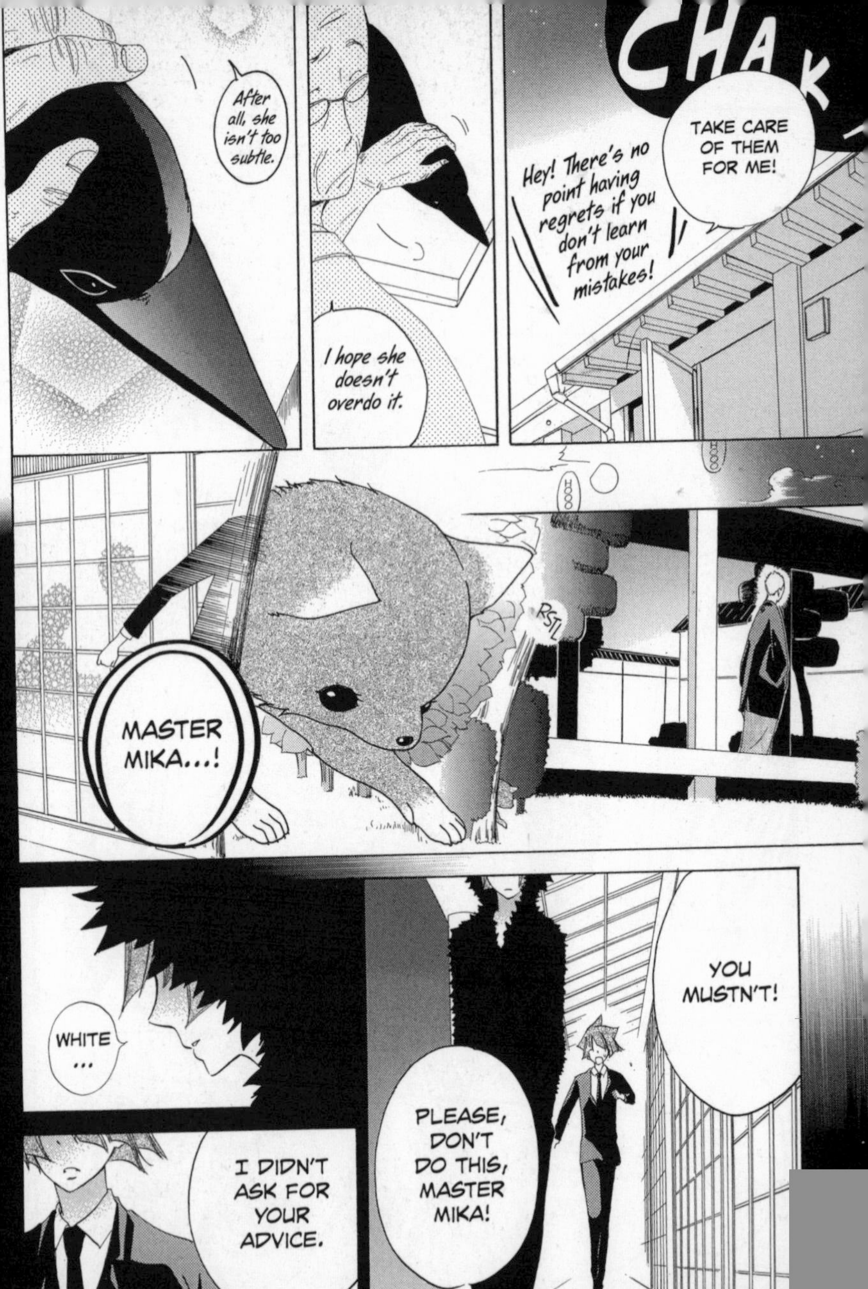
CHAK
TAKE CARE OF THEM FOR ME!
Hey! There's no point having regrets if you don't learn from your mistakes!
I hope she doesn't overdo it.
After all, she isn't too subtle.
HOOO
HOOO
RSTL
MASTER MIKA...!
YOU MUSTN'T!
PLEASE, DON'T DO THIS, MASTER MIKA!
WHITE ...
I DIDN'T ASK FOR YOUR ADVICE.

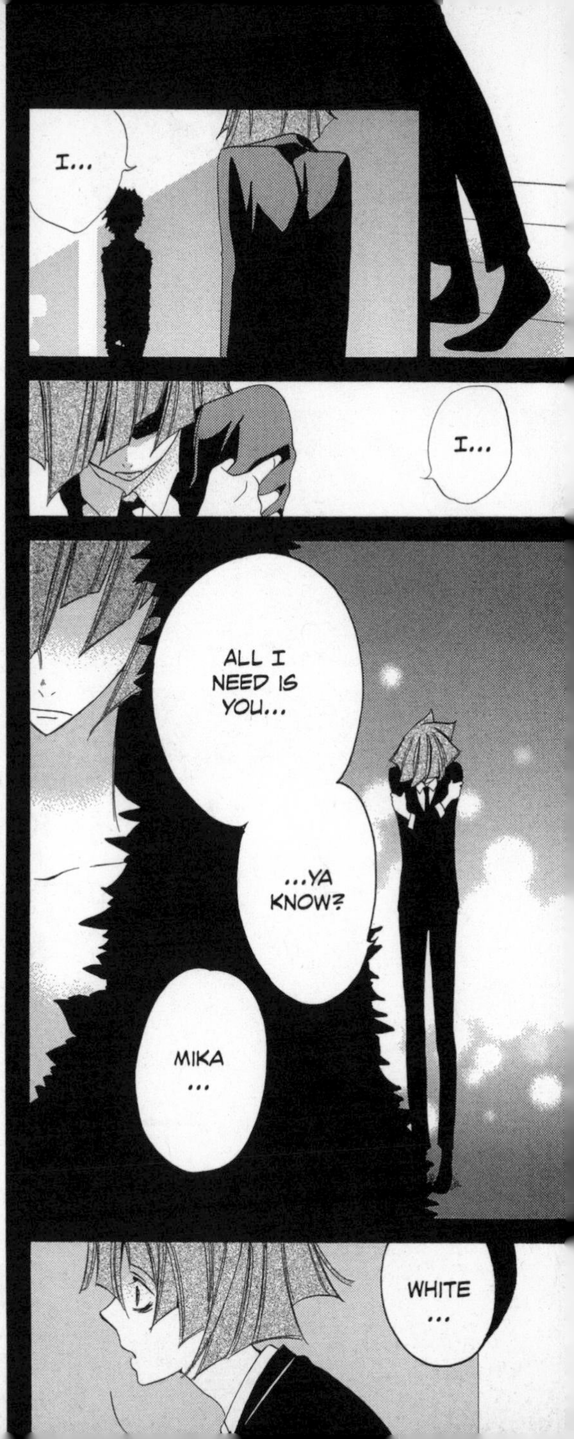
I...
I...
ALL I NEED IS YOU...
...YA KNOW?
MIKA...
WHITE...

Your reading this is a miracle too.

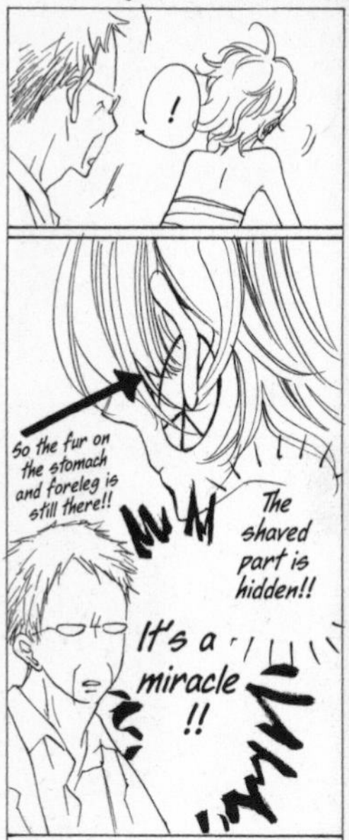
!
So the fur on the stomach and foreleg is still there!!
The shaved part is hidden!!
It's a miracle!!

So go ahead and send me your questions and illustrations.

And if you don't mind them being printed in the graphic novel, please write, "I don't mind" on them. Also, if you want to use a pseudonym, please include it.

Of course, I still eagerly await the arrival of your love letters every single day!!

Please send love letters, questions and illustrations to the address below.

Jiu Jiu/Shojo Beat
c/o Viz Media, LLC
P.O. Box 77010
San Francisco, CA 94107

Till next time!
Don't forget me!

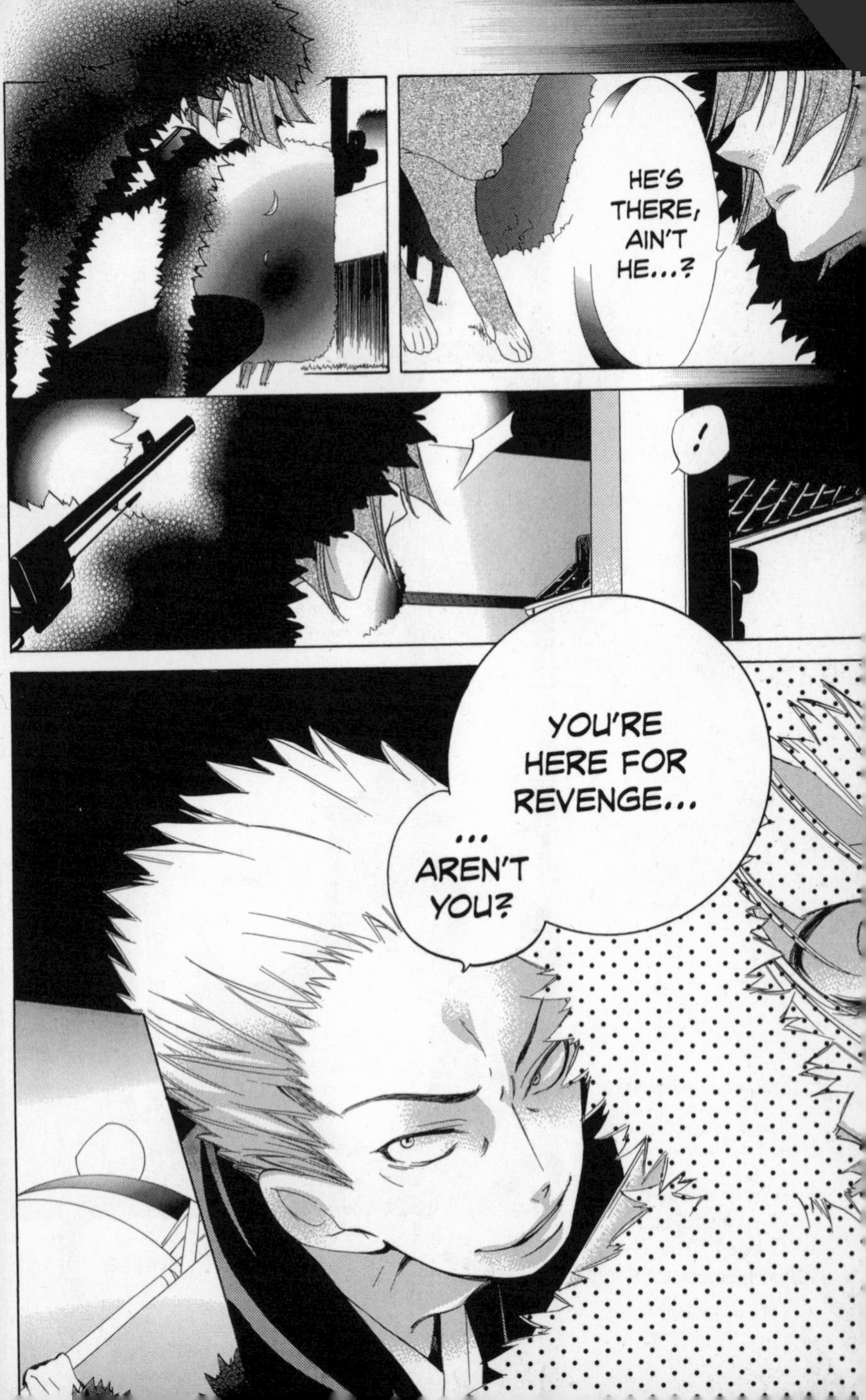
HE'S THERE, AIN'T HE...?
!
YOU'RE HERE FOR REVENGE...
... AREN'T YOU?

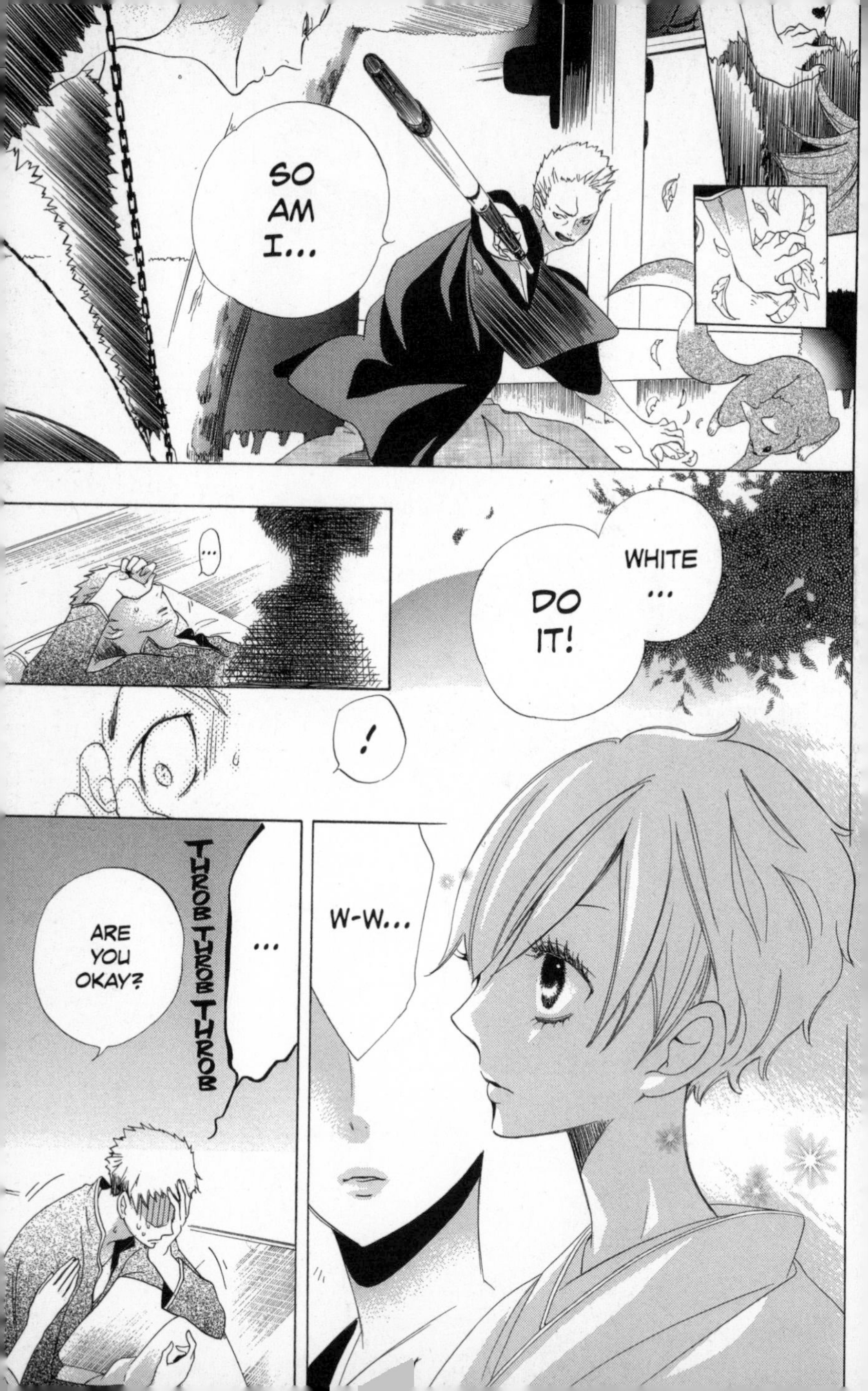
SO AM I...
WHITE... DO IT!
...
!
W-W...
...
THROB THROB THROB
ARE YOU OKAY?

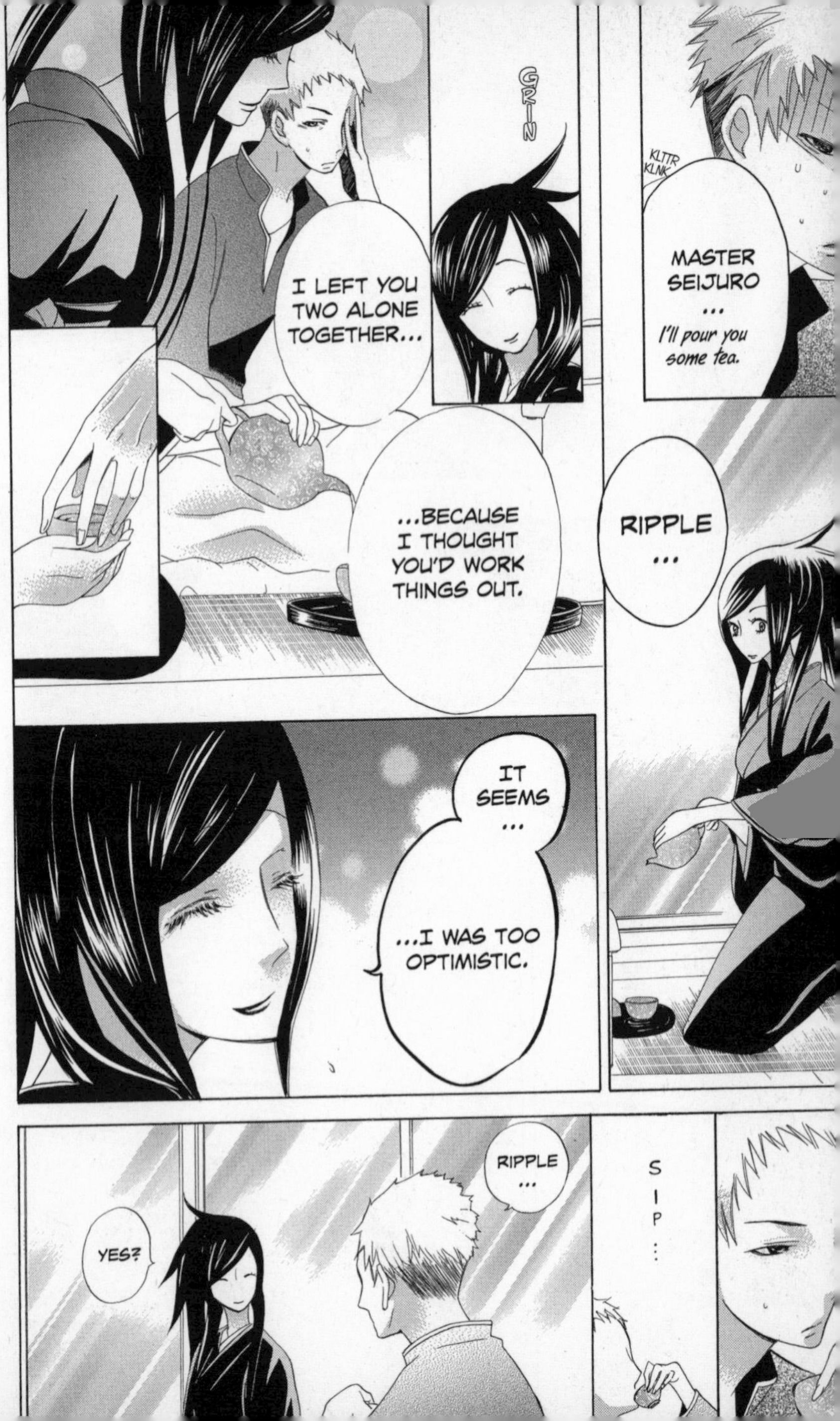
KLTTR KLNK
MASTER SEIJURO ... I'll pour you some tea.
GRIN
I LEFT YOU TWO ALONE TOGETHER...
RIPPLE ...
...BECAUSE I THOUGHT YOU'D WORK THINGS OUT.
IT SEEMS ...
...I WAS TOO OPTIMISTIC.
SIP ...
RIPPLE ...
YES?

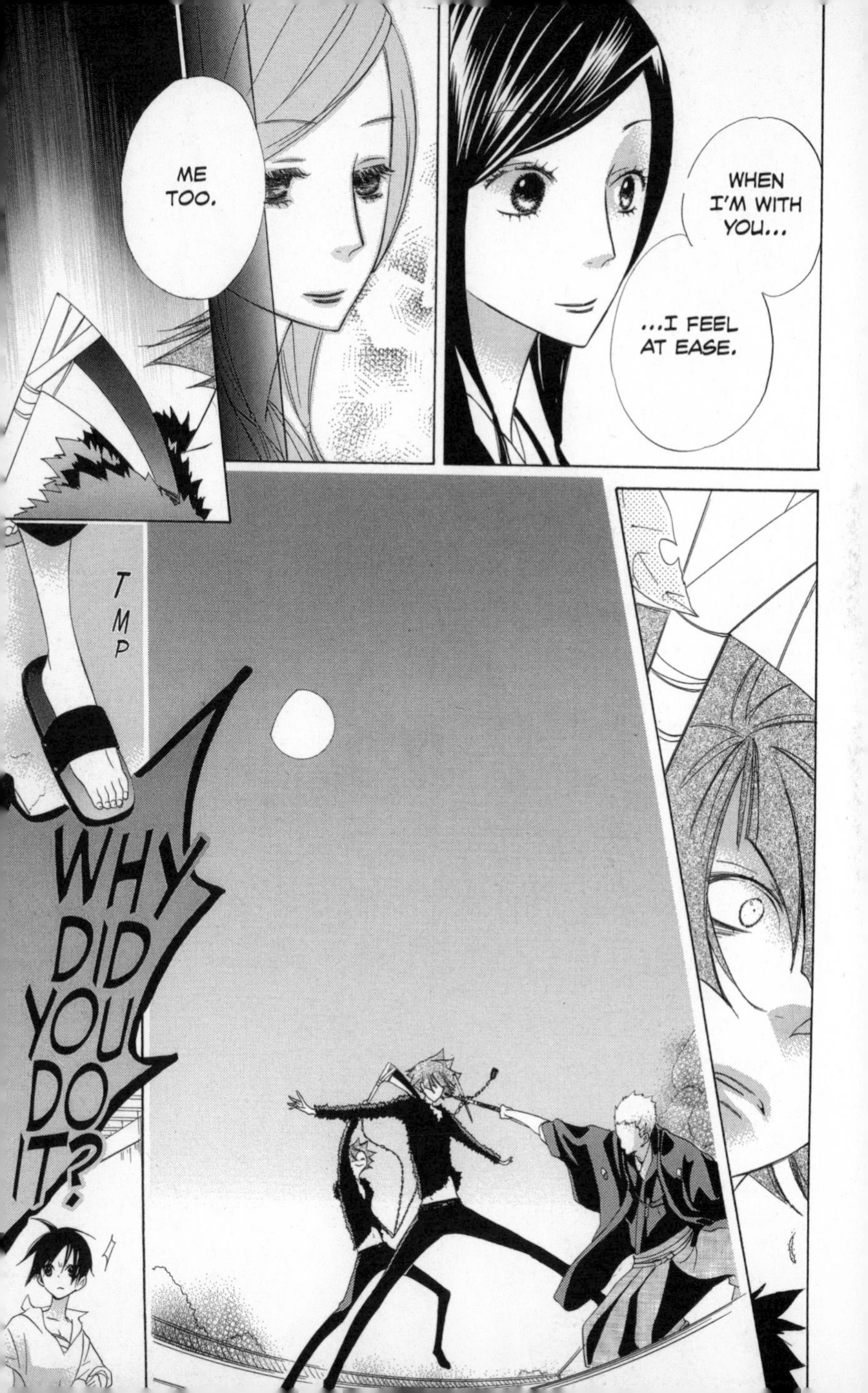
WHEN I'M WITH YOU...
...I FEEL AT EASE.
ME TOO.
TMP
WHY DID YOU DO IT?

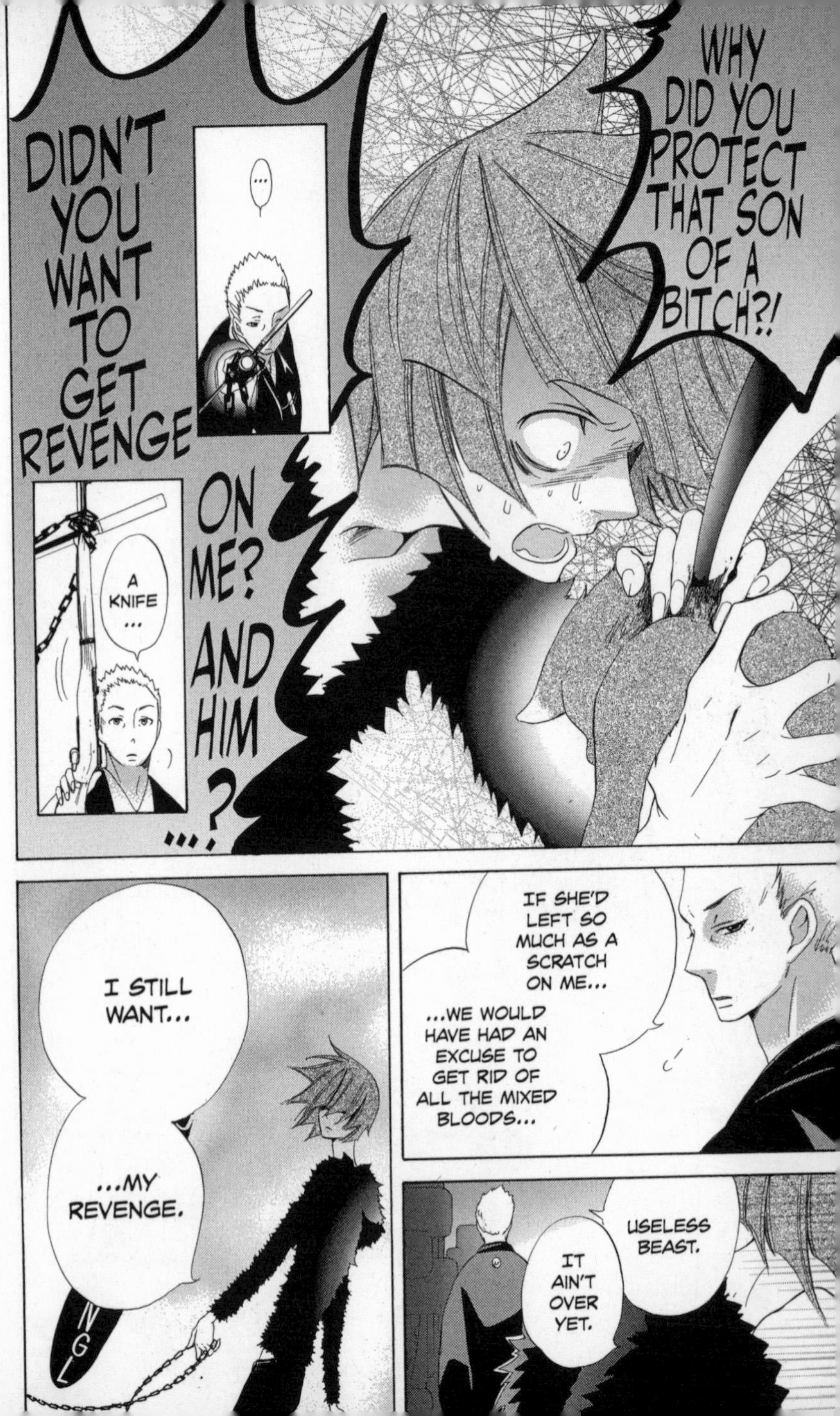
WHY DID YOU PROTECT THAT SON OF A BITCH?!
...
DIDN'T YOU WANT TO GET REVENGE
ON ME?
A KNIFE ...
AND HIM ...?
IF SHE'D LEFT SO MUCH AS A SCRATCH ON ME...
...WE WOULD HAVE HAD AN EXCUSE TO GET RID OF ALL THE MIXED BLOODS...
USELESS BEAST.
IT AIN'T OVER YET.
I STILL WANT...
...MY REVENGE.
NGL

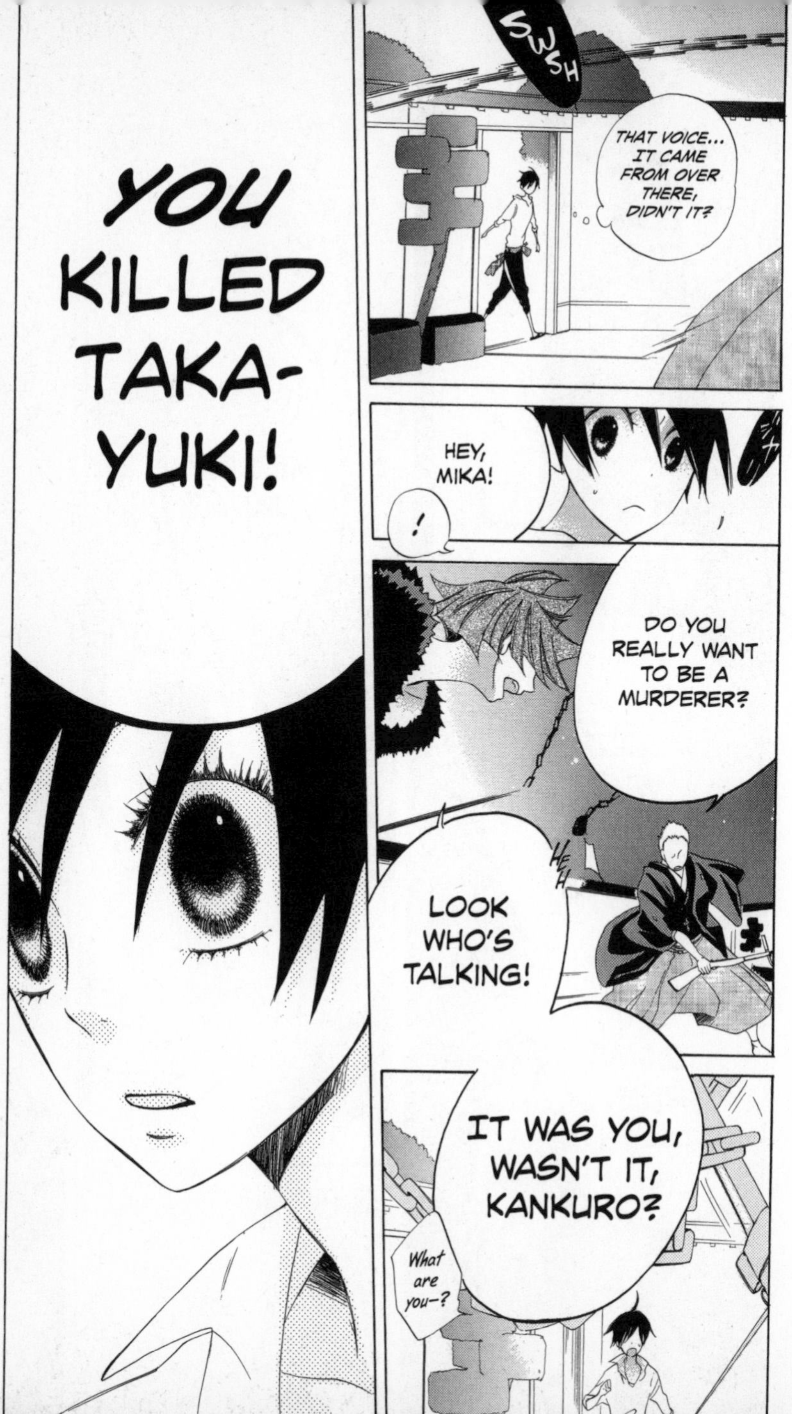
SWSH
THAT VOICE... IT CAME FROM OVER THERE, DIDN'T IT?
HEY, MIKA!
!
DO YOU REALLY WANT TO BE A MURDERER?
HEH
LOOK WHO'S TALKING!
IT WAS YOU, WASN'T IT, KANKURO?
What are you—?
YOU KILLED TAKA-YUKI!

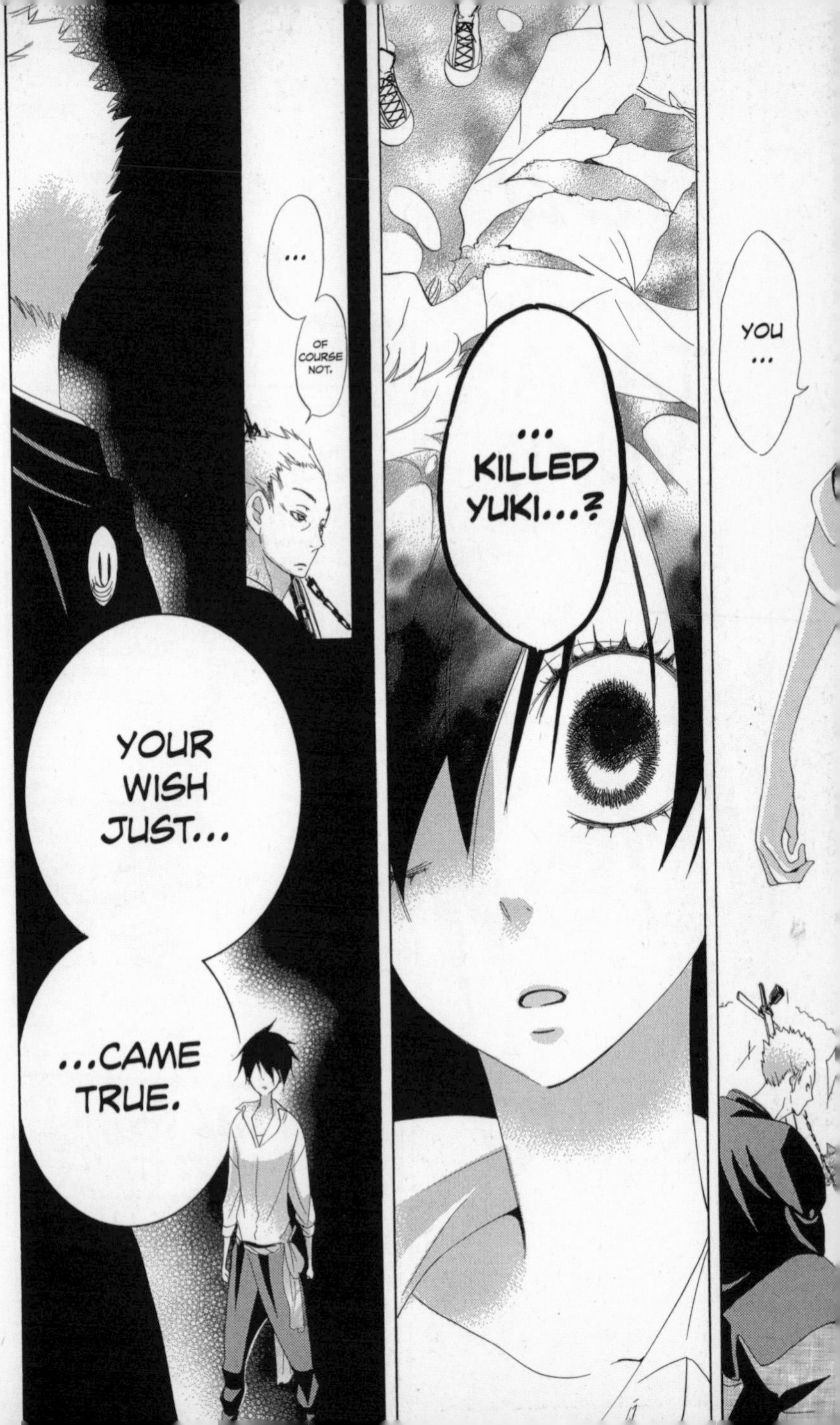
YOU ...
... KILLED YUKI...?
...
OF COURSE NOT.
YOUR WISH JUST...
...CAME TRUE.

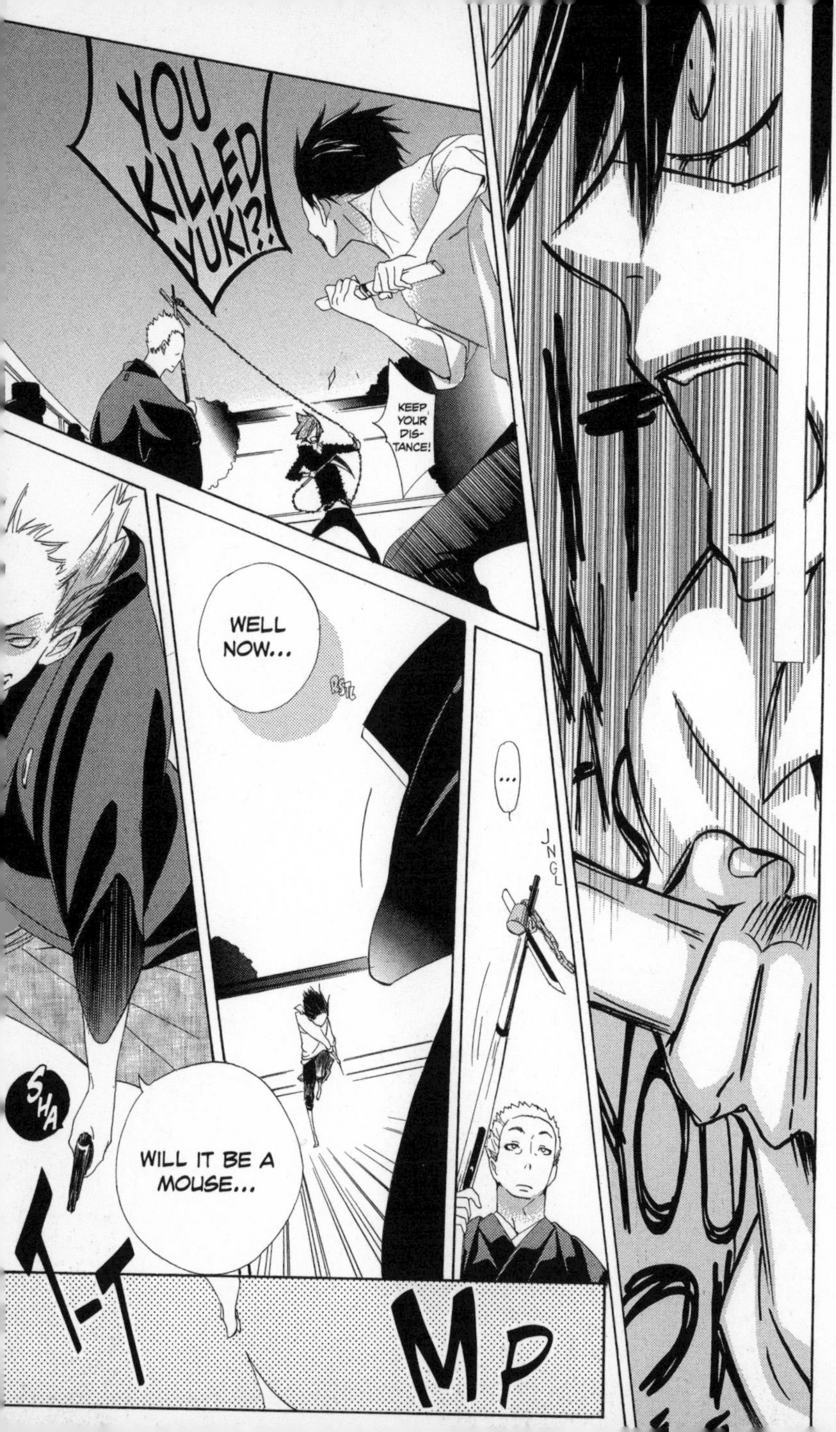
YOU KILLED YUKI?!
KEEP YOUR DIS-TANCE!
...
JNGL
WELL NOW...
RSTL
SHA
WILL IT BE A MOUSE...
T-T
MP

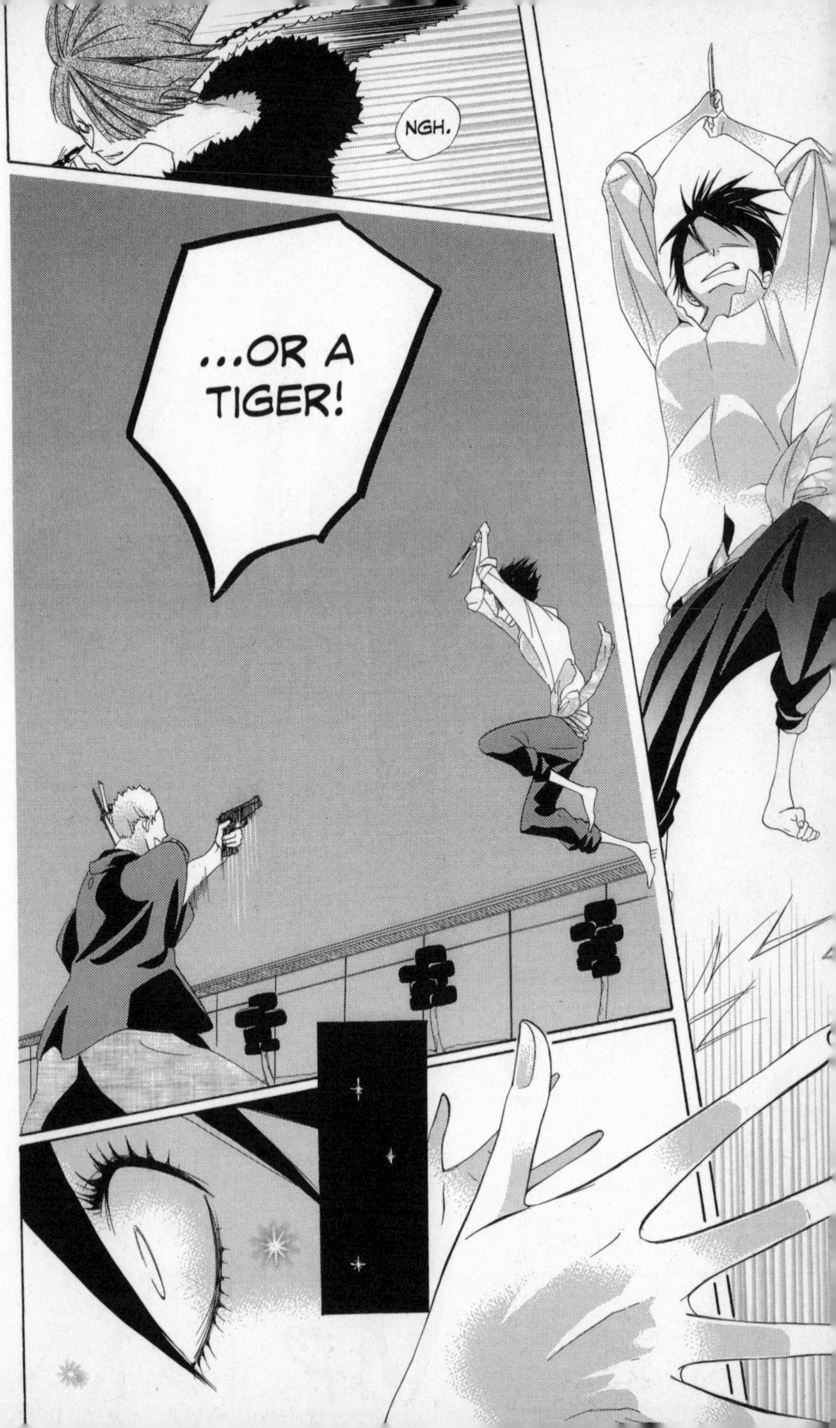
NGH.
...OR A TIGER!

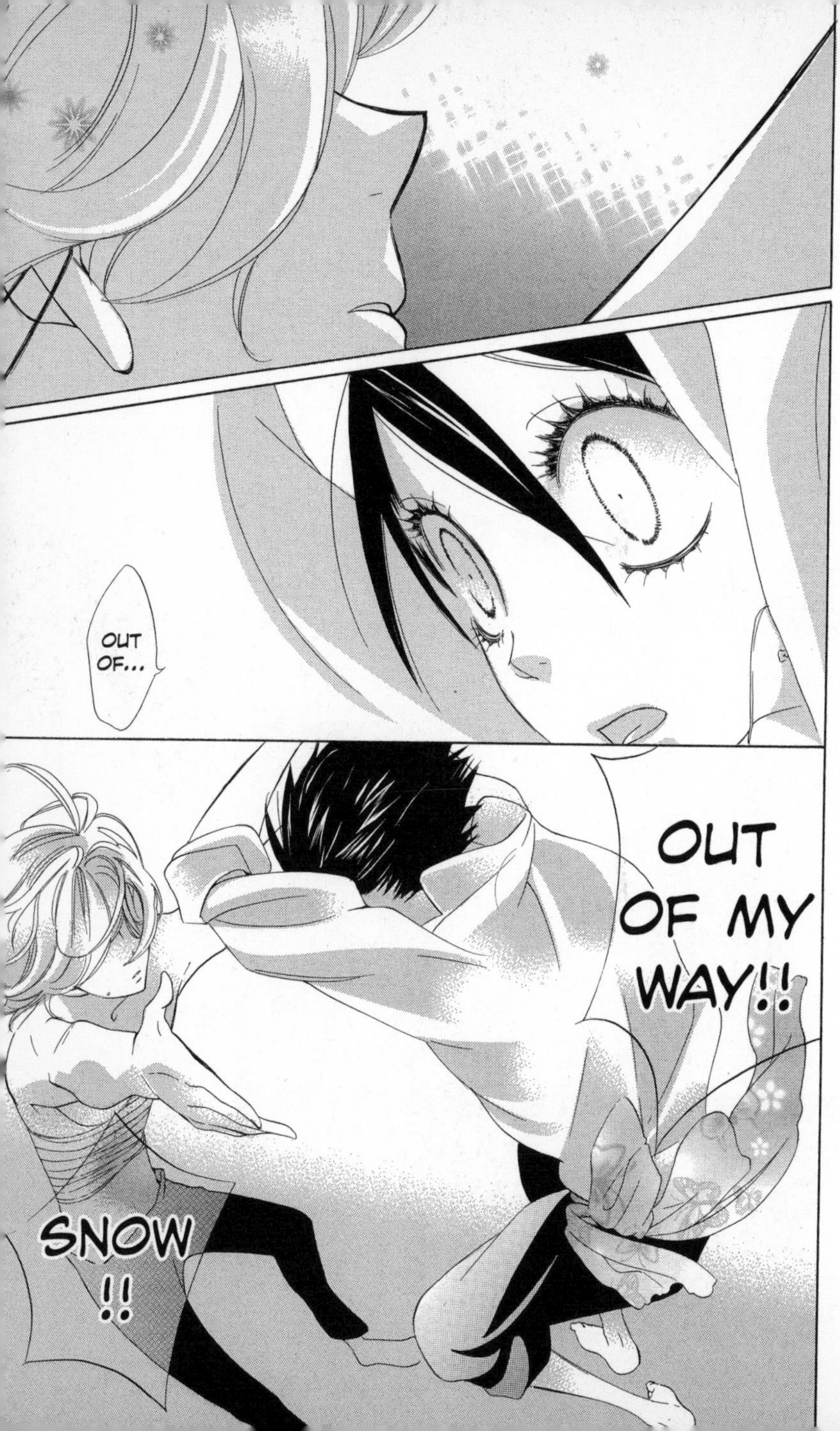
OUT OF...
OUT OF MY WAY!!
SNOW !!

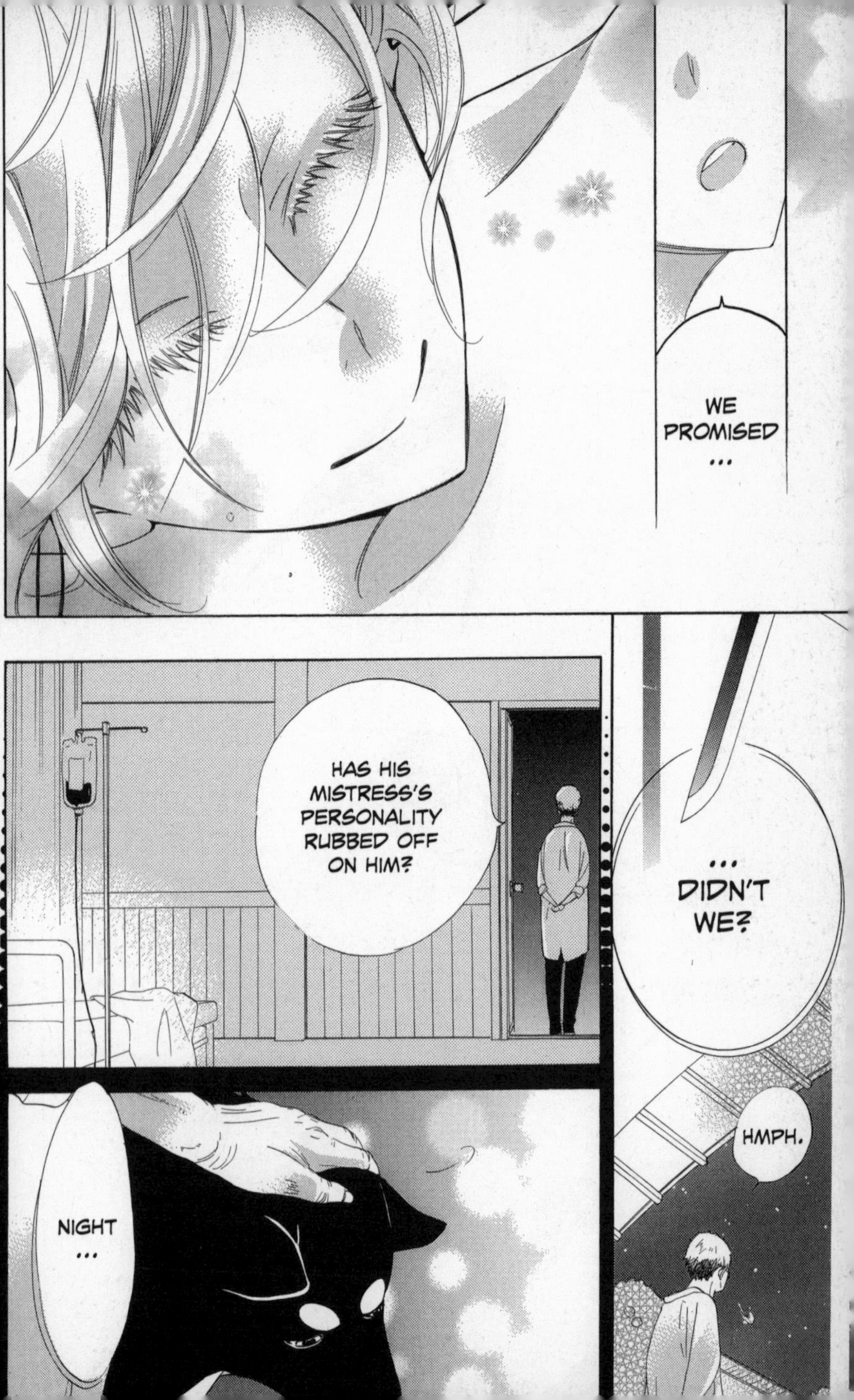
WE PROMISED ...
... DIDN'T WE?
HAS HIS MISTRESS'S PERSONALITY RUBBED OFF ON HIM?
HMPH.
NIGHT ...

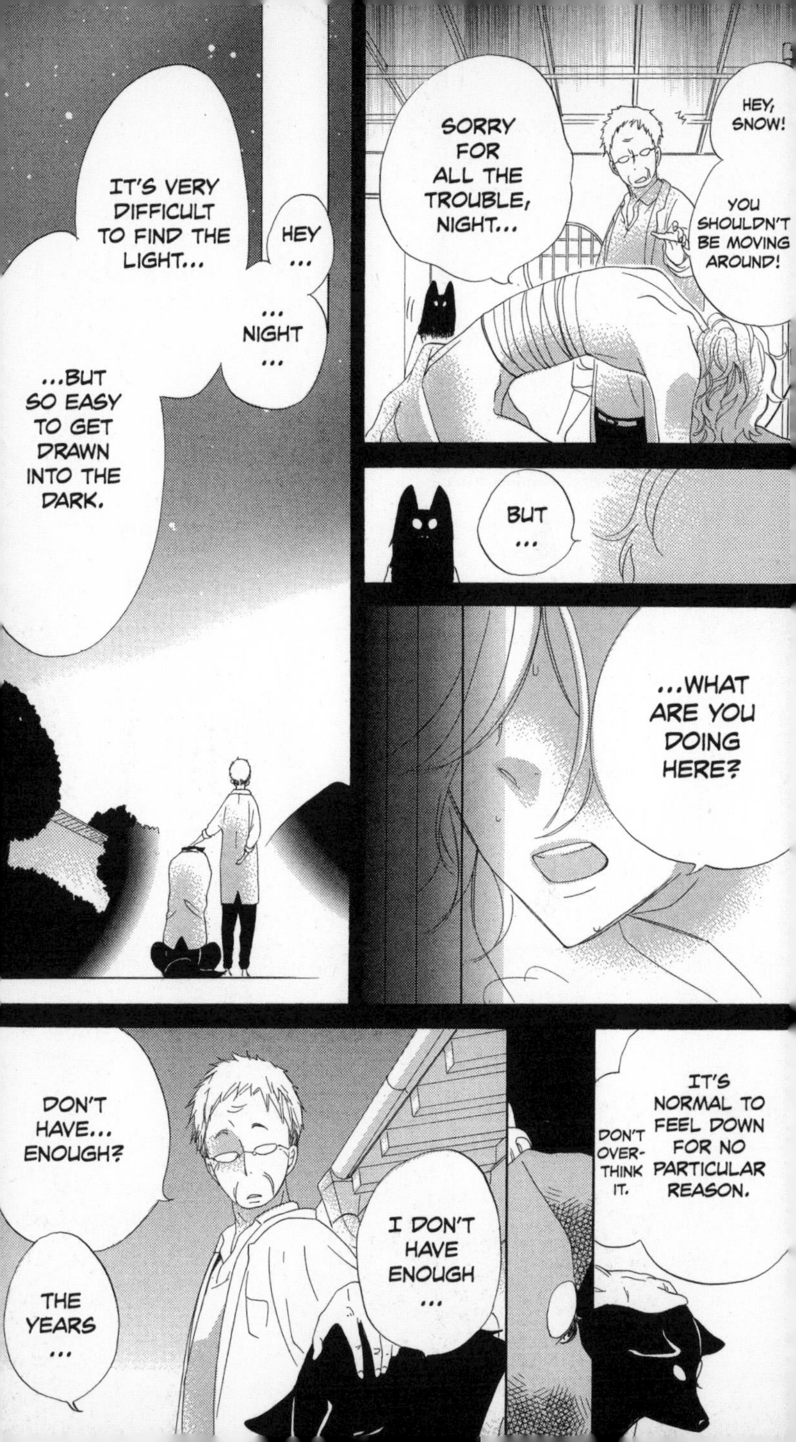
HEY, SNOW!
YOU SHOULDN'T BE MOVING AROUND!
SORRY FOR ALL THE TROUBLE, NIGHT...
BUT ...
...WHAT ARE YOU DOING HERE?
IT'S VERY DIFFICULT TO FIND THE LIGHT...
HEY ...
... NIGHT ...
...BUT SO EASY TO GET DRAWN INTO THE DARK.
IT'S NORMAL TO FEEL DOWN FOR NO PARTICULAR REASON.
DON'T OVER-THINK IT.
I DON'T HAVE ENOUGH ...
DON'T HAVE... ENOUGH?
THE YEARS ...

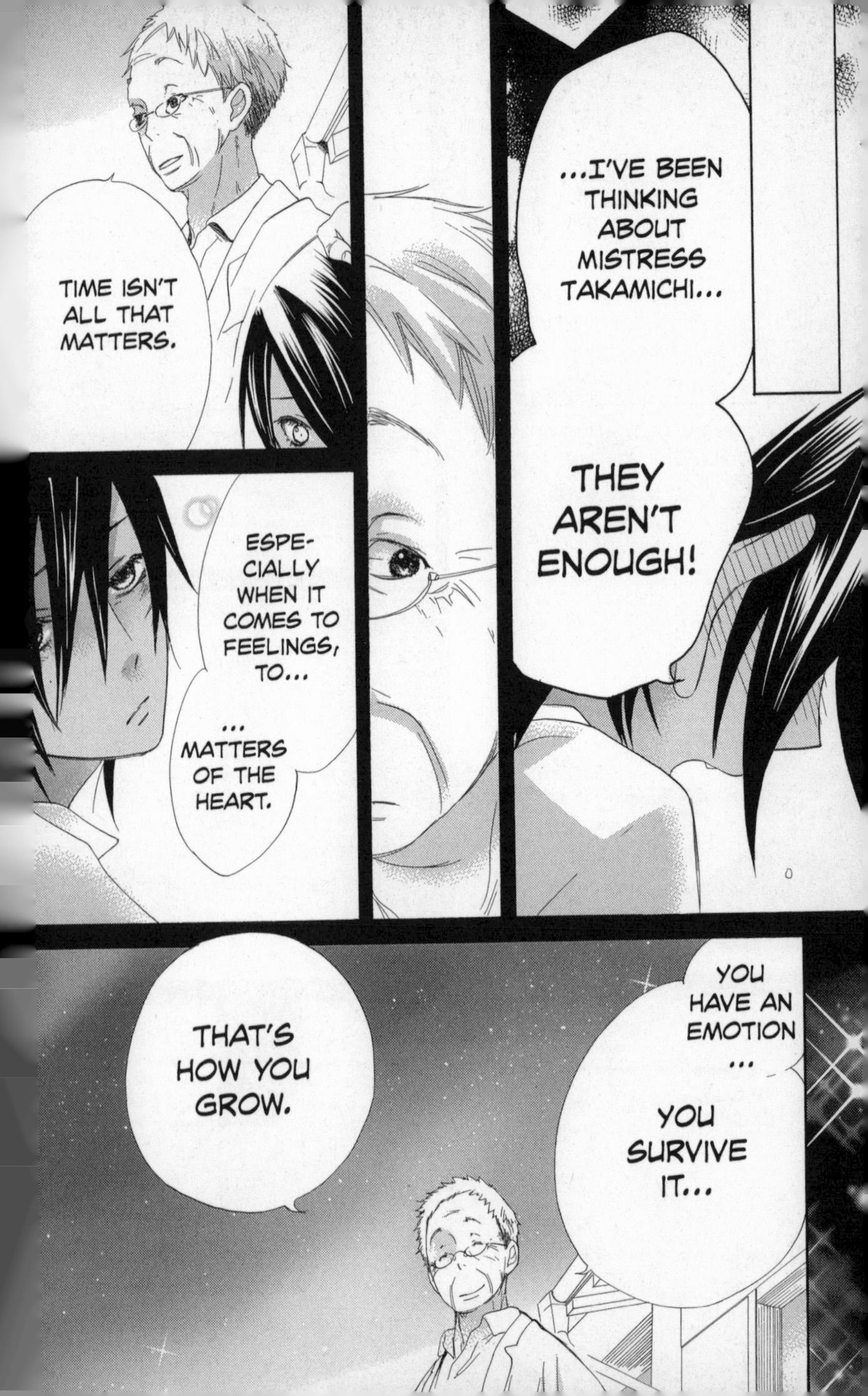
...I'VE BEEN THINKING ABOUT MISTRESS TAKAMICHI...
THEY AREN'T ENOUGH!
TIME ISN'T ALL THAT MATTERS.
ESPE-CIALLY WHEN IT COMES TO FEELINGS, TO...
...MATTERS OF THE HEART.
YOU HAVE AN EMOTION...
YOU SURVIVE IT...
THAT'S HOW YOU GROW.

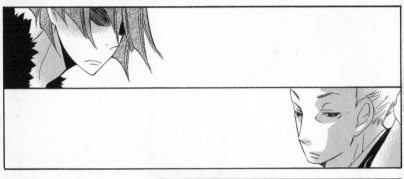

...I'M LATE.

SORRY...

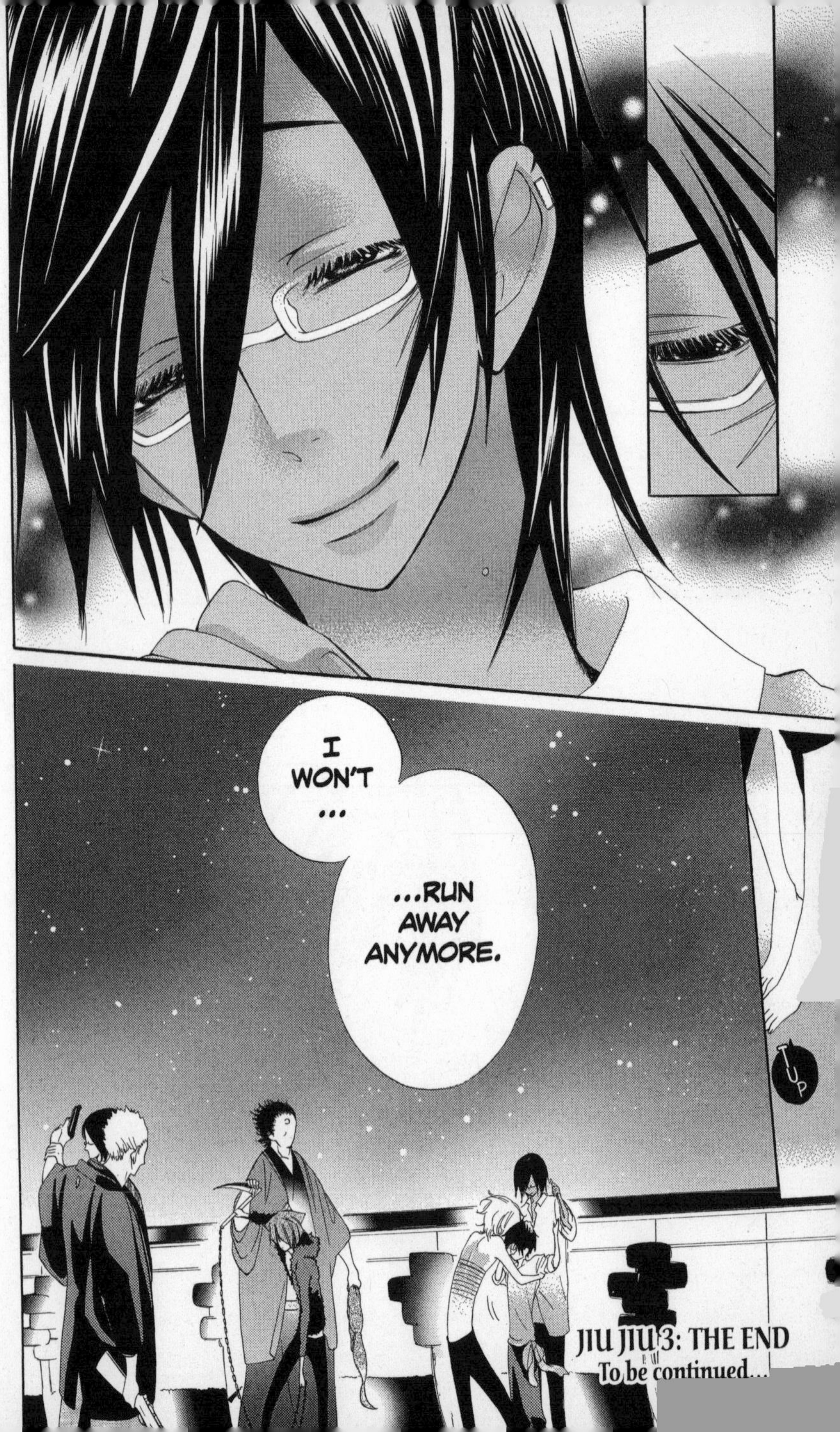
I WON'T ...
...RUN AWAY ANYMORE.
TUP
JIU JIU 3: THE END
To be continued...

SLEEPING ON THE TATAMI.*

*STRAW MAT

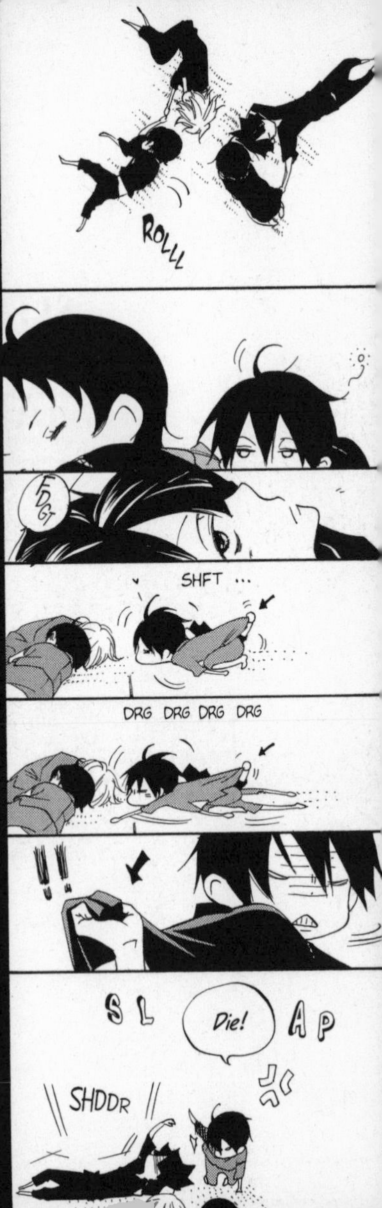
ROLLL
FDGT
SHFT ...
DRG DRG DRG DRG
!!
SL AP
Die!
SHDDR
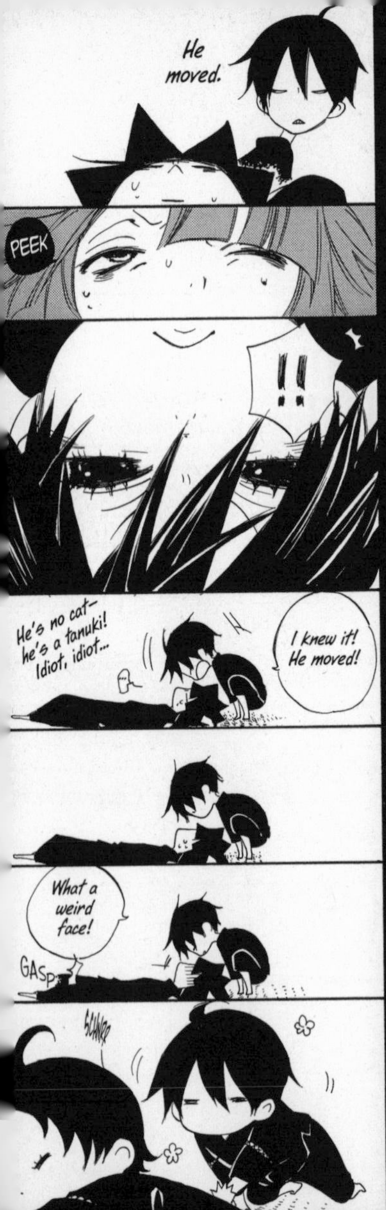
He moved.
PEEK
!!
I knew it! He moved!
He's no cat— he's a tanuki! Idiot, idiot...
What a weird face!
GASP

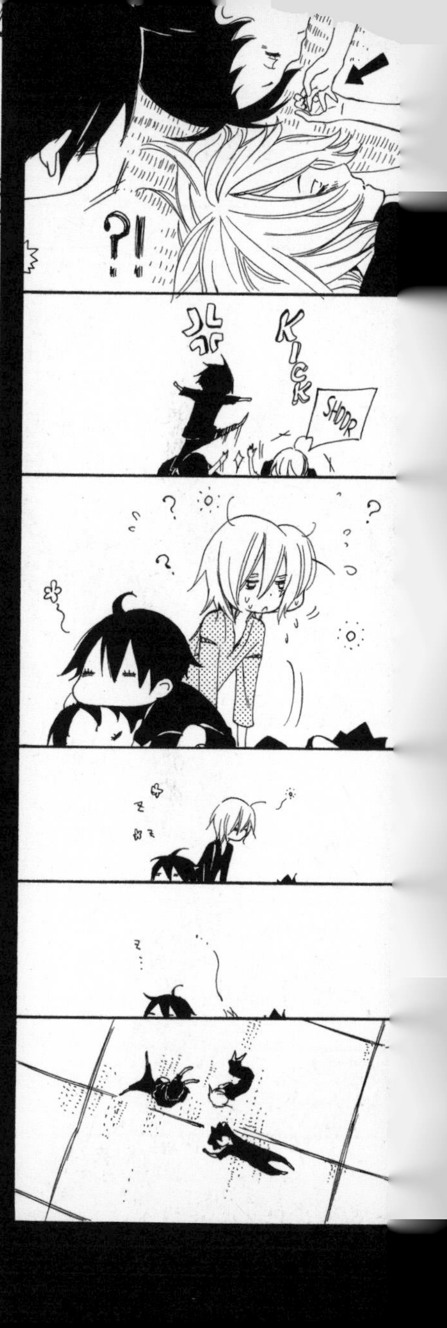
?!
KICK
SHOOR
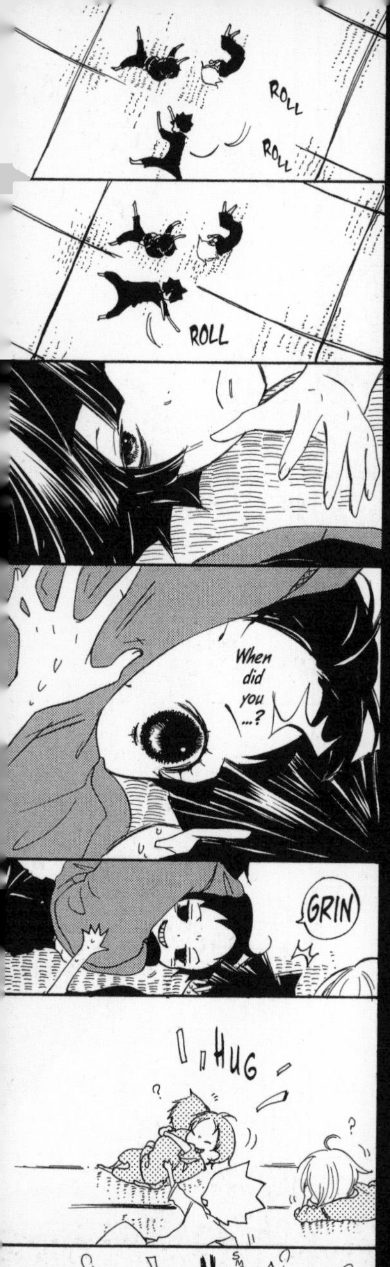
ROLL
ROLL
ROLL
When did you ...?
GRIN
HUG
SMOOCH
!!

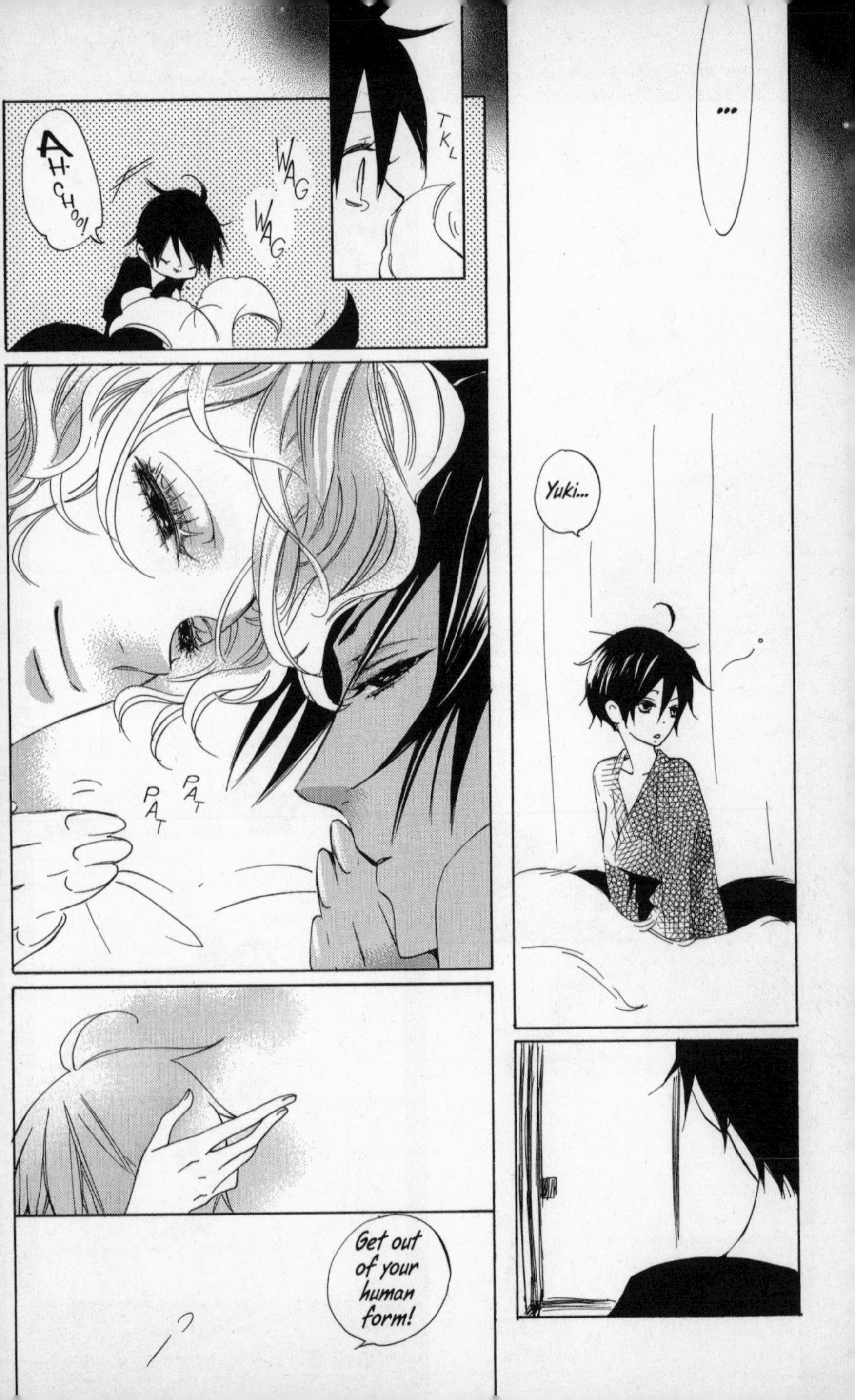
...
Yuki...
TKL
WAG WAG
A-CHOO!
PAT PAT
Get out of your human form!

A parallel world:
An everyday life that seems
to exist but doesn't.

I've got so many characters now...
But there are still several
I haven't introduced yet...!!

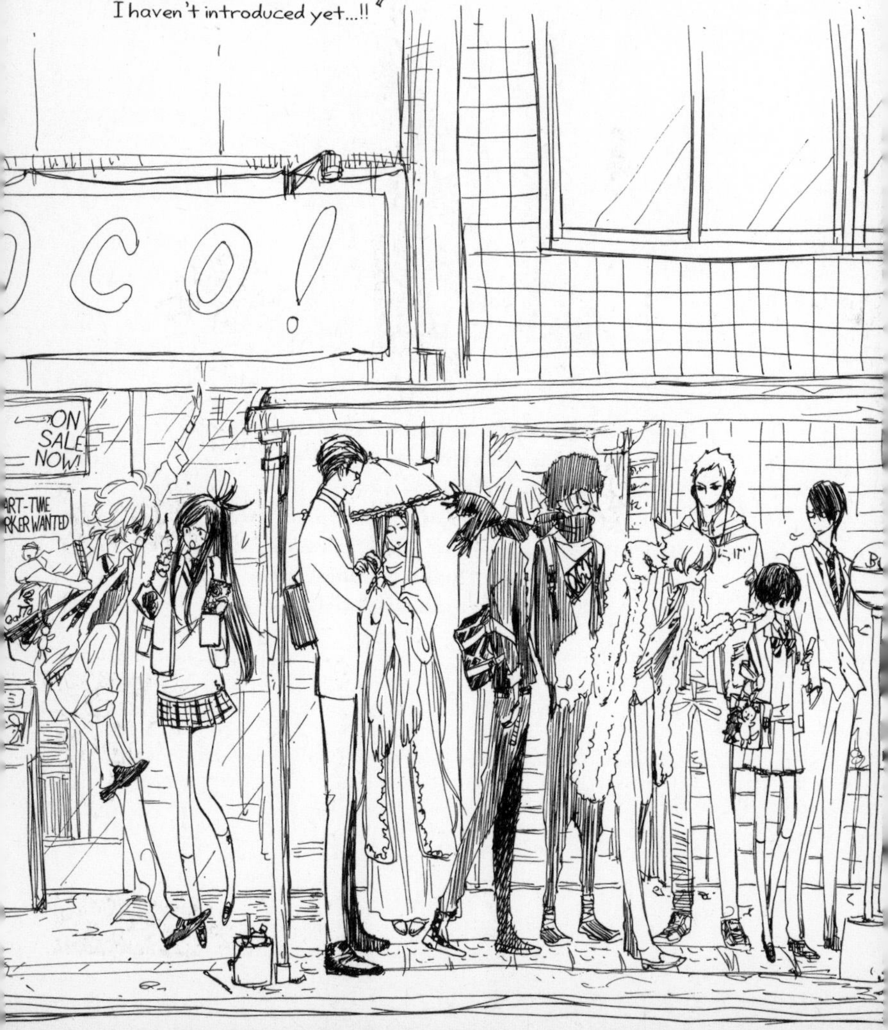
CO!
ON SALE NOW!
ART-TIME
RKER WANTED

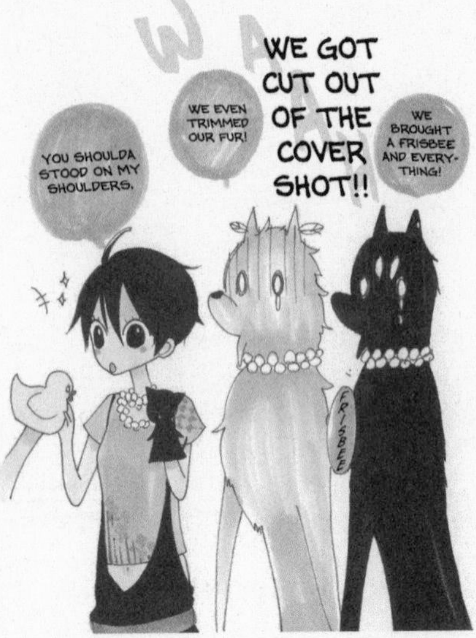
WE GOT CUT OUT OF THE COVER SHOT!!
WE BROUGHT A FRISBEE AND EVERYTHING!
WE EVEN TRIMMED OUR FUR!
YOU SHOULDA STOOD ON MY SHOULDERS.
FRISBEE

Touya Tobina is from Tokyo. Her birthday is May 23 and her blood type is O. In 2005, her series *Keppeki Shonen Kanzen Soubi* (*Clean Freak Fully Equipped*) won the grand prize in the 30th Hakusensha Athena Shinjin Taisho (Hakusensha Athena Newcomers Awards).

JIU JIU
VOL. 3
Shojo Beat Edition

STORY AND ART BY
Touya Tobina

English Translation/Tetsuichiro Miyaki
English Adaptation/Annette Roman
Touch-up Art & Lettering/James Gaubatz
Design/Yukiko Whitley
Editor/Annette Roman

JIUJIU by Touya Tobina
© Touya Tobina 2010
All rights reserved.
First published in Japan in 2010 by HAKUSENSHA, Inc., Tokyo.
English language translation rights arranged with HAKUSENSHA, Inc., Tokyo.

The rights of the author(s) of the work(s) in this publication to be so identified
have been asserted in accordance with the Copyright, Designs and Patents Act
1988. A CIP catalogue record for this book is available from the British Library.

Printed in the U.S.A.

Published by VIZ Media, LLC
P.O. Box 77010
San Francisco, CA 94107

10 9 8 7 6 5 4 3 2 1
First printing, January 2013

www.viz.com   www.shojobeat.com

This is the last page.

In keeping with the original Japanese comic format, this book reads from right to left—so action, sound effects, and word balloons are completely reversed. This preserves the orientation of the original artwork—plus, it's fun! Check out the diagram shown here to get the hang of things, and then turn to the other side of the book to get started!

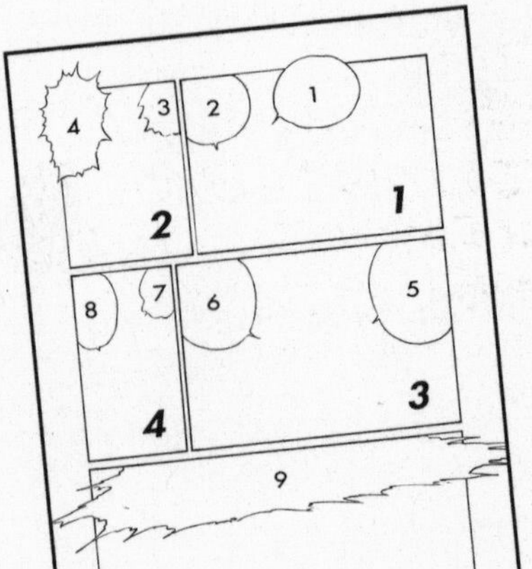
1
2
3
4
1
2
5
6
7
8
3
4
9
5
142

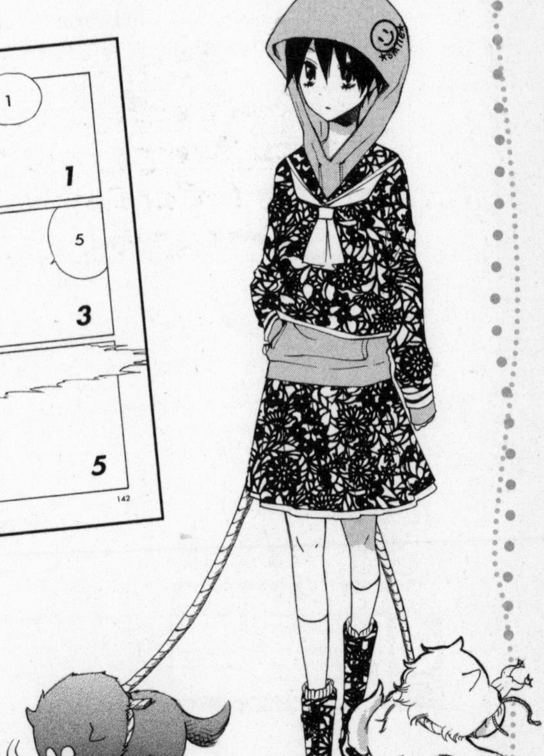
SMILE